W9-AAP-636

LIFE ON THE RIVER

LIFE ON THE RIVER

A PICTORIAL HISTORY OF THE MISSISSIPPI, THE MISSOURI, AND THE WESTERN RIVER SYSTEM

by NORBURY L. WAYMAN

BONANZA BOOKS • NEW YORK

Copyright © MCMLXXI by Norbury L. Wayman
Library of Congress Catalog Card Number: 78-168330
All rights reserved.
This edition is published by Bonanza Books
a division of Crown Publishers, Inc.
by arrangement with Crown Publishers, Inc.
a b c d e f g h

Manufactured in the United States of America

To my wife, Amy,
for her patience and understanding
in the preparation of this book

FOREWORD

The history of the Mississippi Valley and its river system is the story of the development of our nation's vast midwestern heartland.

In the valley's progress from a lush wilderness, inhabited by savage Indian tribes, to the sophisticated civilization of today, the steamboat played a major role. This book illustrates and describes that progress and its multifaceted life, on the boats and along the rivers, in an effort to record this mighty pageant of expansion and attainment.

This colorful mosaic of the valley's history begins with the explorers, fur traders, and settlers who laid its foundation, and continues through the careers of the river men and city builders who were responsible for its growth, to the vast assemblage of rural and urban dwellers of the present who are guiding the valley toward the future. But forever entwined in the annals of the river valley is the dramatic record of the rise and decline of the western river steamboat—with its legendary luxury, romance, adventure, and disasters—the basis for the successful river commerce of today.

ACKNOWLEDGMENTS

I gratefully acknowledge the assistance and advice of the following persons and organizations in the preparation of this book: Association of American Railroads for permission to reproduce the series of maps from their booklet "American Railroads: Their Growth and Development"; Boatmen's National Bank of St. Louis, William Pagenstecher, vice-president, for the generous loan of photographs from their collection of river subjects and for permission to reproduce drawings, prints, and paintings from their fine-arts collection; William Pagenstecher personally for permission to copy drawings from his own collection; August A. Busch, Jr., for permission to reproduce paintings by Oscar E. Berninghaus from the Anheuser-Busch publication "Epoch Marking Events of American History"; City Plan Commission of St. Louis for the use of photographs of the St. Louis riverfront; Gary Crabtree for helpful assistance relating to photographic problems; Ruth Ferris for useful information on various phases of river history; Harbor and Port Commission of the City of Vicksburg, Mississippi, for permission to use the photograph of the towboat *Sprague;* Jefferson National Expansion Memorial of the National Park Service at St. Louis, Clarence H. Schultz, historian, for the generous loan of photographs and the use of materials in their collection of western Americana; Mrs. Martin Kerwin of the Becky Thatcher Gift Shop, St. Louis, for the loan of pictures and reference material; Fred Leyhe for the loan of photographs and information about the Eagle Packet Company; Mercantile Library Association of St. Louis, Elizabeth Kirchner, librarian, and Mary Mewes, reference librarian, for their permission to reproduce prints and maps from rare books in the library's extensive reference collection; Missouri Historical Society, St. Louis, George Brooks, director, and Ruth K. Field, curator of pictorial history, for permission to reproduce graphic material and exhibits from their River Room in the Jefferson Memorial Building in Forest Park, St. Louis; Missouri Pacific Railroad for permission to reproduce paintings of early Missouri railroad scenes; Frank Pierson of the Golden Rod Showboat for the use of photographs and for historical information regarding showboats on the western rivers; St. Louis *Globe-Democrat* for permission to reproduce paintings from their series on the Louisiana Purchase; St. Louis Public Library, Art Room, Martha M. Scharff, librarian, Eleanor Rench, and Maja Bardot for aid in locating river-history pictures and for permission to reproduce many of them, Reference Department, Marie H. Roberts, librarian, for her assistance in locating factual information on river subjects, and Municipal Reference Branch, Charles H. Cornwell, librarian, for help in finding historical data about various river cities; St. Louis Ship Division of Pott Industries, Inc., Joseph D. McMichael, for furnishing photographs and information regarding towboats and barges; State Historical Society of Missouri, Columbia, Missouri, Dorothy Caldwell, for permission to copy prints, maps, and photographs of river subjects from the society's collections; Streckfus Steamers, Inc., St. Louis, Andrew Mungenast, for the loan of photographs relating to the history of excursion boats; Ardell Thompson for his generous permission to reproduce prints and books from his collection of Americana; United States Army Corps of Engineers, Pittsburgh District, Dale K. Williams, for the use of photographs and reference material concerning the Ohio River; United States Army Corps of Engineers, St. Louis District, Kenneth Kruchowski, for his help in locating and permission to use photographs of river improvement construction and equipment; United States Army Corps of Engineers, Little Rock, New Orleans, and Vicksburg districts, for the loan of photographs of river improvements in their respective districts; Water Resources Congress, Clayton, Missouri, Anthony Kucera, for maps and information regarding the inland waterways; *Waterways Journal,* St. Louis, James V. Swift and J. Benton Wilkins, for great assistance in furnishing information on river history and for the use of photographs from their collection of historical river material; Webster Groves Book Shop, Webster Groves, Missouri, Natalie Sheetz and Julie Robinson, for the use of river material from their collection and special thanks for their encouragement during the inception and writing of this book; tourism, publicity, and conservation departments of the states of Arkansas, Illinois, Indiana, Iowa, Kentucky, Louisiana, Minnesota, Mississippi, Missouri, Nebraska, Ohio, Tennessee, Wisconsin, and West Virginia for providing photographs of points of interest along the rivers in their respective states; Chambers of Commerce in the cities of Cincinnati, Little Rock, Paducah, Pittsburgh, Shreveport, Tulsa, and St. Louis for historical information and pictures.

The jacket illustration is of Dean Cornwell's painting of the race between the *Robert E. Lee* and the *Natchez* and is from the Collection of the Boatmen's National Bank of St. Louis.

Norbury L. Wayman
Saint Louis, Missouri

Contents

LIFE ON THE RIVER

I
Before the Steamboat

HOW NATURE FORMED THE MISSISSIPPI VALLEY

The origin of the Mississippi Valley dates from the creation of the planet, during the time when the earth was cooling from its molten state. As the cooling progressed, the planet solidified and contracted, causing vast disruptions in the earth's surface, resulting in the formation of continents and oceans. The story of how the earth's surface crust was formed is told in its rock formations. These are divided into four classes, or periods: Azoic, Paleozoic, Mesozoic, and Cenozoic, which are further characterized by ages. Strata from the Azoic period are devoid of any form of life; in the three succeeding rock layers, evidence of various life forms has been found.

During the long span of time between the first appearance of life forms in the early Paleozoic period and the mid-Cenozoic period, which is known as the Glacial Epoch, or Ice Age, the earth's surface underwent a great series of convulsions and disturbances. These surface disruptions caused the already existing continental land levels to rise above the surrounding sea, thus creating mountains and inland seas. It was not until the end of the Ice Age, after millions of years of transition, that the Mississippi Valley assumed its present shape and configuration, along with its vast deposits of minerals and coal. Following the Ice Age, melting glaciers created a vast inland sea, and the present system of riv-

Ohio River fossil beds containing evidences of early life forms. They are at the falls opposite Louisville, Kentucky, adjacent to Clarksville, Indiana. *Photo by Ken Williams. Courtesy Department of Natural Resources, State of Indiana*

1

Vertical outcroppings of limestone forming bluffs at Mississippi Palisades State Park in northwestern Illinois. These spectacular formations are evidence of tremendous upheavals in the earth's crust during the forming of the river valley. *Courtesy State of Illinois, Department of Conservation*

ers that drain the Mississippi Valley basin were formed. Drift deposits, created during the runoff of these waters, made a scouring action, causing rolling prairies, and level plains resulted where shallow lakes and marshes had formerly existed. The plains that gradually rise from the Missouri River at the western boundary of Missouri, and which reach an elevation exceeding five thousand feet above sea level in the foothills of the Rocky Mountains, were washed very heavily, with much surface material being distributed to the central valley and filling the lower Mississippi basin. These surface deposits contained considerable loam and chemical material required for plant growth and resulted in the rich alluvial river-bottom lands along the western rivers. Successive deposits of vegetable growth and decay over thousands of years on the prairies and in the forests collected a vast reserve of organic remains, which would provide fertile fields for later agricultural pursuits by man in the valley basin.

THE MOUND BUILDERS AND THEIR SUCCESSORS

The earliest remains of mankind in the Mississippi Valley have been found in geological deposits left by the action of the melting glaciers. That these early men were contemporary with the mammoths and other large, now extinct animals is confirmed by arrowheads and human remains found buried at the same levels as the bones of prehistoric mammals in the Osage Valley of Missouri. The oldest evidence of continuous human habitation in the Mississippi Valley, by a semicivilized people, are the works of the Mound Builders. Their ancestors may have migrated to America from Asia over a land bridge across the Bering Strait at a remote period in prehistoric time.

Mound Builder cultures appear to be divided into two distinct groups. The earliest are the Hopewellians, named after a site in southern Ohio. The Hopewellians occupied the northern valley and introduced agriculture to the region before 500 B.C., reaching their greatest development between 300 B.C. and A.D. 400. They built great burial mounds and earthwork systems in riverside ceremonial centers, chiefly at Fort Ancient on the Little Miami River north of Cincinnati and near Newark, Ohio. The Hopewellian culture apparently disappeared about A.D. 1300, victim of savage Indian tribes.

The second group were the Mississippians, so called because they came up the valley from the south. Their temple mounds resemble the pyramids of the Aztecs, and they may have been an offshoot of the Mexican Indian civilization. The great mound at Cahokia, Illinois, east of Saint Louis, rose in several tiers to a height of a hundred feet. This culture spread out over the valley in a system of city-states built along rivers, and featured pyramidal mounds. The group reached its peak between A.D. 1300 and 1500 and appears to have suffered a fate similar to that of their predecessors. As their culture declined, survivors reverted to the barbarism of the surrounding Midwestern Indian tribes. An isolated example of the survival of this culture was the Natchez tribe, which worshipped the sun and maintained a caste system. They were scattered by the French in 1730, after the massacre at Fort Rosalie, Mississippi.

The Indian tribes of the Mississippi Valley at the

Burial mounds erected about A.D. 800 by the Hopewellians, near Marietta, Ohio. *From Archaeological History of Ohio, 1902*

Monks Mound, Saint Clair County, Illinois, example of the largest temple mounds built by the Mound Builders of the Mississippian culture. About A.D. 1400. *From The Valley of the Mississippi Illustrated, John Casper Wild, 1841*

A typical Indian river encampment, painted by Carl Bodmer. These are Poncas on the banks of the Missouri River. *Courtesy Saint Louis Mercantile Library Association*

Marietta Mound, near Marietta, Ohio. *From Prehistoric America, Marquis de Nadaillac*

The Great Serpent Mound, near Locust Grove, Ohio. *Courtesy Ohio State Development Board*

beginning of European exploration were distributed in linguistic groups. Predominant was the Algonquian family, which occupied both banks of the Mississippi above its junction with the Ohio and spread eastward into Ohio and northward into Michigan, Wisconsin, Minnesota, and Canada. West of the Algonquians were the Sioux, the Indians of the Great Plains; and the Crow, Mandan, and Osage tribes. To the southeast of the confluence of the Ohio with the Mississippi were the Muskogean family of tribes. These were the Chickasaws, Creeks, Choctaws, and Natchez. The principal tribes in Louisiana, Arkansas, and Texas, as we know these today, were the Caddo, Tunica, and Attacapa. In the extreme western reaches of the valley were the Comanches (Texas), Kiowas (Oklahoma and also Kansas) and Pawnees (Nebraska).

Painting by Carl Bodmer of Mandan Indians beside the frozen Missouri River. *Courtesy Saint Louis Mercantile Library Association*

The Algonquian tribes in the Middle West were constantly at war with each other, despite the similarity in their dialects, which indicates a common bond of ancestry. Neither were they able to confederate against harassment from the Sioux, from the west, and the Iroquois, from the east. The strongest tribes among the Algonquins were the Chippewa, or Ojibway, around the Great Lakes, and the Shawnees in the Ohio River valley. But the most aggressive Algonquians were the Sauk and Fox in Wisconsin and northern Illinois. While the war parties of raiding Sioux were a menace to the arboreal Algonquians, the Mississippi was a natural boundary

Painting by Carl Bodmer of Crow Indians near Fork Clark on upper Missouri River. *Courtesy Saint Louis Mercantile Library Association*

Piasa Rock, near Alton, Illinois, on the Mississippi River. Indians believed it was the home of Thunder Bird, a monstrous creature, half bird and half reptile, that attacked unwary river travelers. *From The Valley of the Mississippi Illustrated, John Casper Wild, 1841*

Painting by Carl Bodmer of Gros Ventres Indians along the upper Missouri. *Courtesy Saint Louis Mercantile Library Association*

Restored Indian painting of the Thunder Bird, Piasa Rock. *Courtesy State of Illinois, Department of Conservation*

between them; the horse-riding Sioux were not familiar with travel by canoe on the rivers and lakes in the valley.

Although the Mississippi was christened with various French and Spanish names, such as Rivière de St. Louis and Rivière de Colbert or Rio Grande del Espiritu Santo, it is the Indian name that has endured. The names of most of the midwestern rivers are Indian. *Mississippi* theoretically derives from the Algonquian "Mech-e" (great) and "Se-be" (river) and was revered by the Indians as the Father of Waters. *Missouri* means Big Muddy, and *Ohio* comes from the Iroquois "Ohiyo" (grand river). A glance at a map of the Midwest will indicate a great many place names of obvious Indian origin. Indian traditions have had a lasting influence on the Mississippi Valley.

On the eve of European exploration the valley was a vast undeveloped land inhabited by Indians of varying peaceful and warlike characteristics. The valley awaited the touch of development by civilized man—a long, arduous task that would require more than two hundred years.

EXPLORATION AND COLONIZATION OF THE MISSISSIPPI VALLEY

The first European explorations of the Mississippi Valley were impelled by a strange combination of forces: cities of gold, a route to Cathay, missionaries seeking converts to Christianity.

The earliest explorers came from Florida, which had been claimed for Spain by Juan Ponce de Leon in 1513. Francisco de Garay's expedition in 1518 was the first to reach what later became the Louisiana Territory, and in the following year the Mis-

The earliest known map showing the mouth of the Mississippi River, shown at the extreme left center. Called the "Admiral's Map," after Columbus, it appeared in a geographical work in 1513. *From History of the Louisiana Purchase Exposition, 1904*

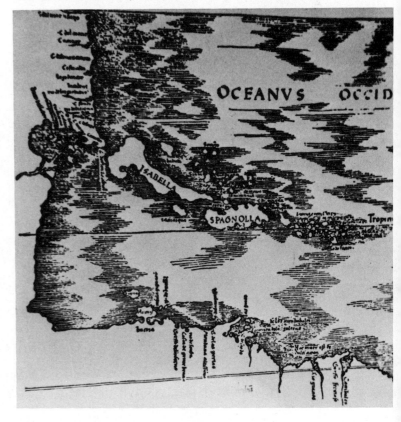

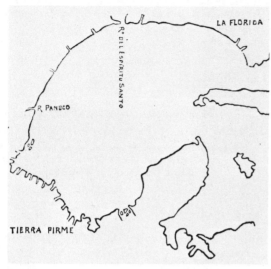

Earliest map assigning a name to the Mississippi River, here called "Rio del Espiritu Santo." Dated 1520, it illustrates de Pineda's explorations of the north shore of the Gulf of Mexico in 1519. *From History of the Louisiana Purchase Exposition, 1904*

Portrait of Francisco Vásquez de Coronado (1510–1554), Spanish explorer of the American Southwest. *Drawing by the author*

Below:
Hernando de Soto, from Herrera's *Historia Generale de las Indies*, 1601. Herrera was the official historian of the Spanish Crown. To make this portrait he probably drew upon information from contemporaries who knew De Soto. *From History of the Louisiana Purchase Exposition, 1904*

sissippi River was entered, from the Gulf of Mexico, by Alonzo Alvarez de Pineda, the first white man to do so. In 1527 Panfilo de Narvaez led an expedition to investigate reports of a rich land north of the Gulf of Mexico. His quest proved futile, and subsequent travels took him past the mouth of the Mississippi to the present site of Galveston, Texas.

Francisco Vasquez de Coronado was the first European to explore the valleys of the Platte and Arkansas rivers. He was in search of the fabulous land of Quivira, but in 1542, Coronado, like de Narvaez, returned empty handed.

The first white man to view the Mississippi River at a point far above its mouth was Hernando de Soto, who while with Pizarro had made a fortune in the conquest of the Incas. His fortune squandered in two years of dissolute living, in 1539 de Soto returned to Florida in search of riches where de Narvaez had failed over a decade earlier. After wandering through the present southern states east of the Mississippi, de Soto came upon the mighty stream in 1541, near the present site of Memphis.

Following subsequent travels on the Red River, which flows into the Mississippi in Louisiana, de Soto died of a fever and was buried on May 21, 1542, in the river he had discovered. After de Soto there were no further attempts to explore the valley from the Gulf for a century and a half. Spain did not pursue exploration of the valley and directed her efforts at colonizing the West Indies and Central America.

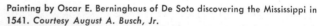

Painting by Oscar E. Berninghaus of De Soto discovering the Mississippi in 1541. *Courtesy August A. Busch, Jr.*

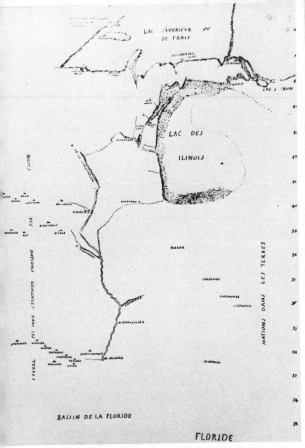

Father Jacques Marquette's map of the Mississippi Valley in 1673, drawn after his voyage of discovery. *From History of the Louisiana Purchase Exposition, 1904*

Painting by Oscar E. Berninghaus of Marquette and Joliet descending the Mississippi River in 1673. *Courtesy August A. Busch, Jr.*

While Great Britain was colonizing the Atlantic seaboard, France laid claim to the Louisiana and Illinois country in the present American Middle West. The first French expeditions into the Mississippi Valley came from French eastern Canada through the Great Lakes. These expeditions included a military man, Louis Joliet, and a priest, Father Jacques Marquette. They set out from Green Bay on Lake Michigan and, by way of the Fox and Wisconsin rivers, reached the Mississippi

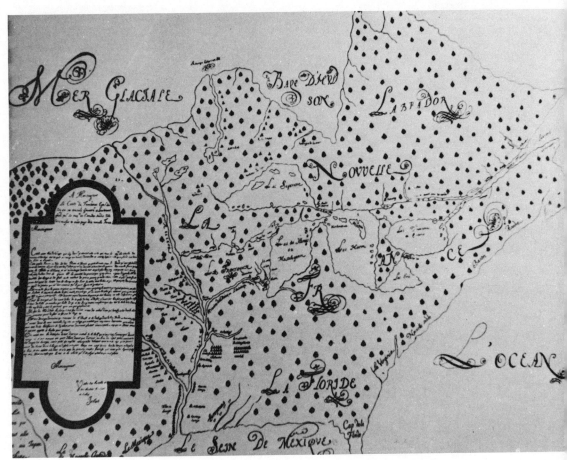

Louis Joliet's map of explorations. When his original map was lost, following the return from his voyage on the Mississippi, Joliet drew this one from memory in 1674. *From History of the Louisiana Purchase Exposition, 1904*

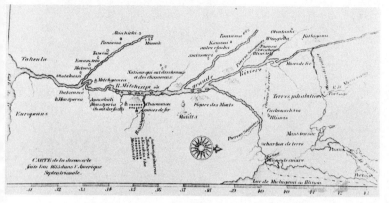

Marquette's 1675 map, published with his journal that year. *From History of Saint Louis City and County, J. Thomas Scharf, 1883*

on June 17, 1673. They continued down the great river to a point below the mouth of the Arkansas and then returned, convinced that this was the same river that de Soto had discovered over a century earlier.

Robert Cavelier, Sieur de La Salle, seeking a route to China through the Great Lakes, led an expedition with Father Louis Hennepin in 1679. Hennepin was sent to explore the upper Mississippi and discovered the Falls of Saint Anthony at the present site of Minneapolis. La Salle led an expedition down the Illinois and Mississippi rivers, reach-

ing the Gulf of Mexico on April 9, 1682, and thereupon claimed the Mississippi Valley for France. He named it Louisiana in honor of King Louis XIV. In 1684 La Salle led another expedition in an attempt to rediscover the mouth of the Mississippi. Landing at Matagorda Bay, Texas, he set out overland to Quebec and after extensive wanderings was assassinated by members of his own party in 1687. La Salle's devoted lieutenant, Henri de Tonti, made a persistent search for his commander in an expedition down the Mississippi, reaching the mouth of the Arkansas in 1688–1689.

Marquette, Joliet, La Salle, and Hennepin opened the way for French fur traders and missionaries into the valleys of the upper Mississippi and Ohio rivers. A mission at Kaskaskia, established by Marquette in 1678, had become a considerable village by 1700, as had Cahokia, nearly opposite the present site of Saint Louis. A mission at Vincennes, on the Wabash River, was founded in 1702, while others were scattered far apart along the rivers in the valley. Missionary fathers held these primitive settlements together, for they acted as teachers and law-givers as well as priests.

Since navigation on the Saint Lawrence River, their most direct route, was restricted by ice for

La Salle's party building his ship, the *Griffin,* from Hennepin's *Description de la Louisiane,* 1683. The little ship took La Salle through the Great Lakes during his expedition to the upper Mississippi in 1679. *From History of the Louisiana Purchase Exposition, 1904*

The La Salle and Hennepin expedition on the Mississippi, drawn by Hennepin after the voyage for his *Description de la Louisiane, 1683. From History of the Louisiana Purchase Exposition, 1904*

Robert Cavelier, Sieur de la Salle. From Voyages des Français *by Pierre Margry*

Painting by J. N. Marchand of La Salle at the mouth of the Mississippi River in 1682.

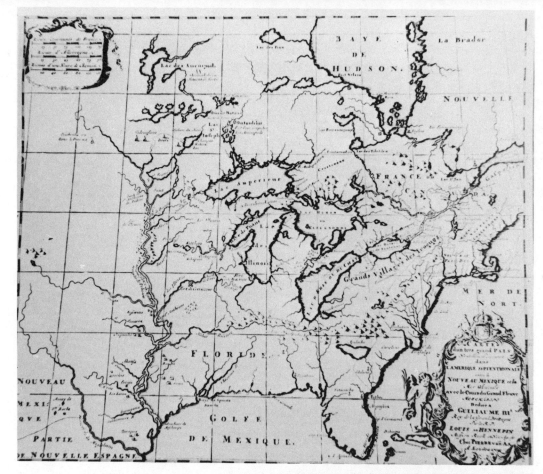

Father Hennepin's map of the Mississippi Valley and eastern North America, 1704. *From History of the Louisiana Purchase Exposition, 1904*

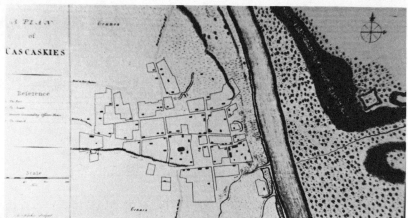

Map of Kaskaskia, Illinois, in 1770, by Thomas Hutchins. *Courtesy Saint Louis Mercantile Library Association*

Kaskaskia State Memorial's "Liberty Bell of the West," rung on the night that George Rogers Clark and his band of "Kentucky Long Knives" captured Kaskasia and Illinois from the British in 1778. *Courtesy State of Illinois, Department of Conservation*

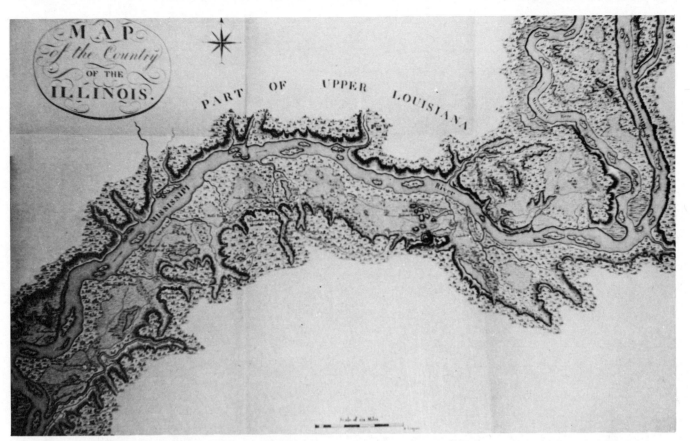

Map of the country of the Illinois. *From A Journey in North America—1796, General Victor Collot. Courtesy Saint Louis Mercantile Library Association*

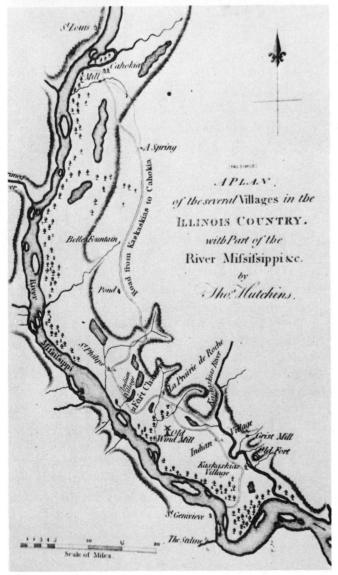

Villages in the Illlinois country along the Mississippi mapped by Thomas Hutchins. *about 1775. Collection of the author*

French quarters in the Illinois country. *From A Journey in North America—1796, General Victor Collot. Courtesy Saint Louis Mercantile Library Association*

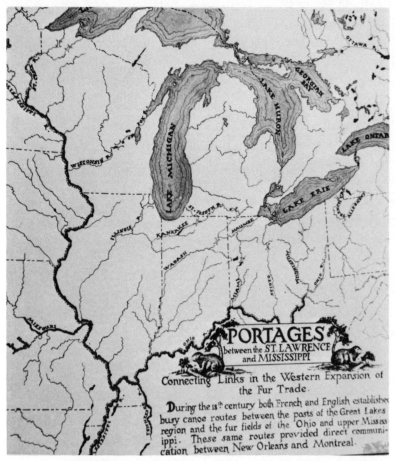

Portages between the Saint Lawrence and Mississippi rivers during the eighteenth century. *Courtesy Jefferson National Expansion Memorial, National Park Service*

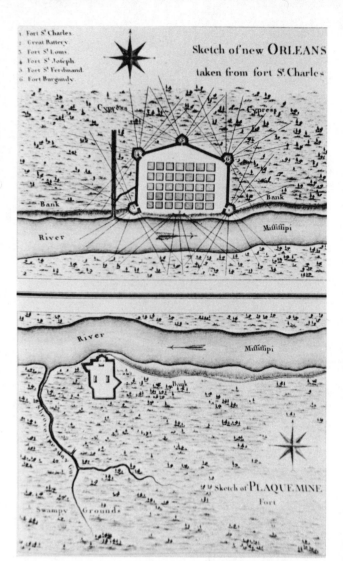

Sketch maps of early towns on the river—New Orleans and Plaquemine Fort, Louisiana. *From A Journey in North America—1796, General Victor Collot. Courtesy Saint Louis Mercantile Library Association*

Jean Baptiste le Moyne, Sieur de Bienville, the founder of New Orleans in 1718, was the most famous of the French governors of Louisiana. *From History of the Louisiana Purchase Exposition, 1904*

about five months each year, it became obvious to the French that in order to colonize the Mississippi Valley, expeditions would have to be sent out from posts established at the mouth of the Mississippi. Such posts were set up by Pierre le Moyne, sieur d'Iberville, in early 1699, the principal post being at Biloxi on the Gulf of Mexico. Iberville explored the Mississippi up to the mouth of the Red River and returned through lakes Maurepas and Ponchartrain. He returned to France for more colonists in May, 1700, leaving his younger brother, Jean Baptiste le Moyne, sieur de Bienville in charge of further explorations. On one of his trips, Bienville encountered an English expedition ascending the river at a point below the present site of New Orleans. Bienville forced the English to retreat, and the site became known as "the English Turn."

Among the new arrivals returning with d'Iberville in 1701 was a geologist named Lesueur, who ascended the Mississippi to the Falls of Saint Anthony to collect ores. Lesueur left a small garrison at Fort Thuilier on the Blue Earth River in Minnesota, which remained until 1704, when it was driven off by the Sioux.

Bienville had moved his headquarters to Mobile in 1702, but soon learned that the best location for the chief town was on the Mississippi River. This eventually led to his founding New Orleans in 1718.

A wealthy French merchant, Anthony Crozat, acquired, a trade monopoly in the Louisiana country in 1712 and named Antoine de la Mothe Cadillac as governor. After five years of unproductive effort, Crozat surrendered his grant in 1717. In 1718 the control of Louisiana commerce was given to John Law's company, known for its "Mississippi Scheme." Law's company was bound to send 6,000 white colonists and three thousand Negro slaves to Lousiana. Hundreds of German and other colonists were sent over to cultivate twelve square miles of land on the Arkansas River and other lands in the province. Two hundred white miners from France, led by François Renault, along with five hundred slaves from San Domingo, arrived in 1719 to work the La Motte lead mines in Missouri. The cultivation of rice and sugar in lower Louisiana and of cereal grains in the upper province soon assured the permanance of many communities before the downfall of Law's scheme in 1720.

Military outposts were established at key points on the major rivers. Among these were Fort Chartres near Kaskaskia in 1718 and Fort Orleans founded on the Missouri at the mouth of the Osage by de Bourgmond in 1721. Kaskaskia became the capital of the new district of Illinois in 1721 and in the following year New Orleans became the location of the provincial government. After the collapse of the Law company, efforts to develop the

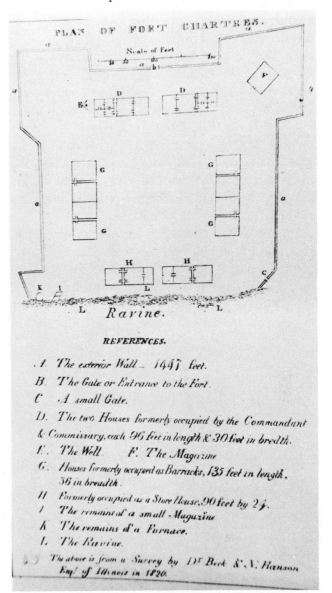

Plan of Fort Chartres, 1718. From The Valley of the Mississippi Illustrated, John Casper Wild, 1841. Courtesy Saint Louis Public Library

Ruins of Fort Chartres, built in 1718. *From The Valley of the Mississippi Illustrated, John Casper Wild, 1841. Courtesy Saint Louis Public Library*

Restored powder magazine at Fort Chartres State Park, Illinois. Courtesy State of Illinois, Department of Conservation

Louisiana country diminished because of a financial depression in France.

In 1727, flood control work was started in the form of a thirty-six mile-long levee to protect New Orleans.

At New Madrid, Missouri, a fur-trading post was established, in 1740, following the founding of the town of Sainte Geneviéve in 1735. By the time that Bienville retired as governor in 1742, French trading posts extended from the Great Lakes to the Yellowstone River and northward into the Winnipeg country.

While the French and Indian Wars were remote from the Louisiana settlements, an English victory in 1763 led to the dismemberment of the old Province of Louisiana and to English control of the land east of the Mississippi. The territory west of the Mississippi was ceded by France, as a gift, to Spain,

which agreed with England that navigation on the river should be equally free to both. News of the transfer of the territory to Spain's Charles III, cousin of the French king, was very slow in reaching upper Louisiana, so that when Saint Louis was founded by Pierre Laclede in 1764 as a French post, the French villagers from Cahokia fled to the west-bank town to avoid English dominion. The last French governor at New Orleans, D'Abbadie, granted fur-trade privileges on the Missouri River to Maxent, Laclede and Company, and Saint Louis became the base for a trade that would last for over a century.

The French had not explored the Ohio Valley until about 1730, but soon thereafter they estab-

Map of New Madrid, Missouri, and vicinity, founded in 1740 by the French as Anse à la Graisse, or Greasy Bend. *From A Journey in North America—1796, General Victor Collot. Courtesy Saint Louis Mercantile Library Association*

Old Spanish fortification tower at the foot of Mullanphy Street in Saint Louis, about 1845. *Courtesy Saint Louis Mercantile Library Association*

Painting by Oscar E. Berninghaus of Pierre Laclede's landing party at the present site Saint Louis, February 14, 1764. *Courtesy August A. Busch, Jr.*

Pioneers in flatboats drifting down the Ohio River in the early nineteenth century. *Courtesy Saint Louis Public Library*

An American settler's log cabin in the Ohio River valley. *From A Journey in North America—1796, General Victor Collot. Courtesy Saint Louis Mercantile Library Association*

Clearing the land, the beginning of a western settlement. *From Eighty Years of Progress in the United States, 1868*

lished a series of posts down the river to the Wabash. Purportedly the Ohio was traveled by La Salle in 1670 when he descended it to the falls at presentday Louisville. This voyage established French claims to the Ohio Valley for almost a century. However, the river was hardly known to the French early in the eighteenth century, and was shown as a small stream on their maps. They had formed their alliance with the Indians in the Ohio Valley in 1749 in an effort to restrict English progress westward from the thirteen seaboard colonies.

An English grant of six hundred thousand acres of choice land along the Ohio River to the Ohio Company, composed of wealthy Virginians, was a countermeasure.

After preliminary explorations by Christopher Gist in 1748, the Ohio Company set up a post near the present site of Dayton, Ohio, which was soon destroyed by the French. In 1753 the English governor of Virginia dispatched young George Washington to remonstrate with the French at Fort Le Boeuf on Lake Erie. The English claim to territorial rights through royal charters did not impress the French, whose claim had been based upon exploration and possession. An English attempt to enforce their sovereignity by erecting a fort on the present site of Pittsburgh ended in surrender to the French in 1754, after which the French strengthened the fortification and renamed it Fort Duquesne. There followed an ambuscade defeat of General Braddock's army against the fort in 1755, the taking of the fort by the English after it was abandoned by the French, its renaming, Fort Pitt, by General Forbes in 1758 in honor of the English prime minister, and the turning of the war in favor of the English, ending with the complete capitulation of the French after the fall of Montreal in 1760.

Soon after the Treaty of Paris in 1763, which led to English control of all land east of the Mississippi, control of the Ohio country was enforced by military occupation of all former French forts. Settlement of the Ohio Valley proceeded rapidly, with settlers migrating over the Alleghenies from the eastern colonies. After 1770 towns were founded along the river, such as Wheeling in 1770 and Louisville in 1773.

The English claim to the Northwest Territory, north of the Ohio and east of the Mississippi, was ceded to the new United States of America by the peace treaty of September 3, 1783. Since Indian title to the Ohio country had been ignored, Congress passed laws for the survey and sale of the land.

Old Fort Pitt blockhouse, Pittsburgh, Pennsylvania. *Collection of the author*

Replica of Fort Nashborough, Nashville, Tennessee, build originally by James Robertson in 1780 for English defense of the Mississippi Valley. *Courtesy State of Tennessee, Conservation Department*

The Ohio Company of Associates from New England purchased a large tract along the Ohio River and began settlement at Marietta in 1788 and at Columbia later in that year. Trouble with the Indians restricted settlements until the tribes were completely defeated by General Anthony Wayne near the present site of Toledo in 1794. The end of Indian hostilities led to a flood of settlements in the Ohio Valley, raising the question of American rights to navigation on the Mississippi. Americans used the river route to New Orleans to market their produce but were denied access by Spain. This had caused resentment against the Spanish authorities there. From 1784 to 1788 Spain halted American use of the river completely. In 1788 the Spanish relented partially, allowing trade to go through on payment of duties. In Pinckney's treaty of 1795, Spain was forced to grant more favorable terms, allowing Americans free navigation and the "right of deposit" at New Orleans. The right of deposit was the privilege of unloading river barges and storing the cargo on shore, free of duty, until an American seagoing ship came to carry it away.

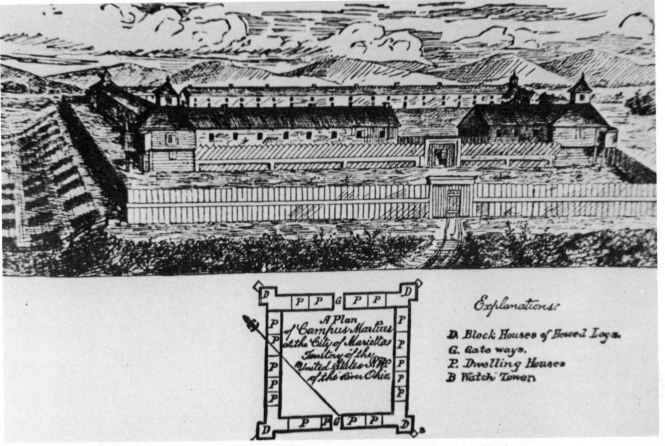

Campus Martius fortification at Marietta, Ohio, built in 1788. *Courtesy Saint Louis Public Library*

Spanish rule of the Louisiana territory west of the Mississippi was marked by dissension among the French settlers. The Spanish governor Antonio de Ulloa arrived in New Orleans in March, 1766, and in 1768 sent Captain Rios with Spanish troops to Saint Louis to assume the government of upper Louisiana. Meanwhile, Ulloa had been forced by French loyalists under Lafreniere, the former French attorney-general, to leave New Orleans. Spain retaliated by sending a second governor, Don Alessandro O'Reilly, with a fleet of twenty-four ships and five thousand soldiers to force Louisiana into submission. O'Reilly occupied New Orleans in August, 1769, and later sent the French Loyalist leaders to face a firing squad. The cruelty of O'Reilly led to his recall and the succession of a milder governor, Don Luis Unzaga. Lieutenant-Governor Pedro Piernas arrived in Saint Louis in May, 1770, to accept authority from French Captain Saint Ange de Bellerive.

A period of progress began at this time, with co-operation between the Spanish and the French in-

Nicholas Chauvin de Lafreniere, former French attorney general and leader of a French loyalist movement against Spain in 1768 at New Orleans. Lafreniere and the other French leaders in the movement were subsequently shot by order of the Spanish governor, Don Alessandro O'Reilly. *From* History of the Louisiana Purchase Exposition, *1904*

Don Alessandro O'Reilly, the second Spanish governor of Louisiana, is remembered for the cruelty with which he suppressed the French citizens of New Orleans in 1769. *From* History of the Louisiana Purchase Exposition, *1904*

habitants, who were encouraged to proceed with their fur trading and settlement west of the Mississippi.

The sympathies of the French in the Louisiana Territory were with the American colonists during the Revolutionary War, which came closest at St. Louis with the Kaskaskia and Vincennes campaigns of Colonel George Rogers Clark in 1778–1779. Spain declared war against England in 1779, and Don Bernardo de Gálvez, the fourth Spanish governor of Louisiana, invaded British West Florida and swept the English from the lower Mississippi by capturing Fort Manchac, about 115 miles above New Orleans. Later, garrisons at Baton Rouge and Natchez were forced to capitulate, as was Fort Charlotte at Mobile. Hostilities ended with the surrender of the British at Pensacola in March, 1781.

During the regime of Spain's Baron de Carondelet in New Orleans, beginning in 1792, French unrest in Louisiana continued. Any sign of sympathy with French republican movements was dealt with severely. Spain increased her efforts, through liberal land grants, to attract American settlers to the west bank of the river. Daniel Boone of Kentucky thereby acquired a large tract in Saint Charles County, Missouri. Spanish control of Louisiana retroceded, secretly, to France by the Treaty of San Ildefonso in 1800. The treaty proved to be a poorly kept secret. In 1802 President Thomas Jefferson expressed concern that French occupation of New Orleans by Napoleon's army would endanger the good relations between the two nations; American commerce on the Mississippi River would be a source of contention. Shortly after it was announced that Napoleon had secured Louisiana by treaty, the Spanish officers who were still in charge suddenly withdrew the right of deposit at New Orleans. Jefferson figured that if America controlled West Florida and New Orleans—the east bank of the river all the way to the Gulf—the Spanish could not halt American use of the river, so he sent diplomats to France to buy these. Bonaparte, convinced that the British would try to take Louisiana from him, decided to sell not part but all of the Territory to the Americans. The Louisiana Purchase treaty was signed on April 30, 1803; the land became American territory for fifteen million dollars and twelve years of duty-free admission of French and Spanish commerce to Louisiana ports. Thus ended foreign domination of the Mississippi Valley.

Don Bernardo de Galvez became governor of Louisiana in 1777. He aided the American colonies against England during the Revolutionary War and later was appointed Viceroy of Mexico, where he died in 1786. *From History of the Louisiana Purchase Exposition, 1904*

Daniel Boone Rock. According to legend, Daniel Boone in 1769 used this great rock on the South Fork of the Kentucky River near Beattyville as a reference point to mark one boundary of timberlands which he surveyed for himself. A change in the river's course reportedly erased Boone's name and the date he had carved on the rock. *Courtesy State of Kentucky, Department of Public Information*

Denial of the right of deposit at New Orleans in 1802, as shown in a diorama in the Jefferson National Expansion Memorial Museum in Saint Louis. *Courtesy Nies-Kaiser Printing Company, Saint Louis*

Signing the Louisiana Purchase Treaty, sculpture by Karl Bitter, showing James Monroe and Robert Livingston watching the Marquis de Barbe-Marbois signing the treaty in behalf of the French Republic. *From History of the Louisiana Purchase Exposition, 1904*

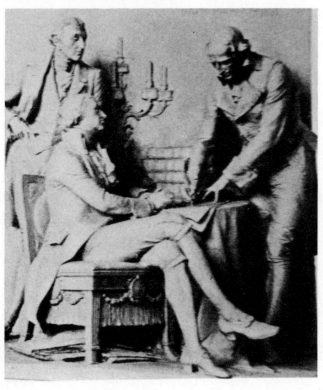

The Louisiana Purchase more than doubled the area of the United States and gave it complete control of the entire Mississippi Valley. Transfer ceremonies took place at New Orleans on December 20, 1803, and those for upper Louisiana were held at Saint Louis on March 9, 1804.

Jefferson was anxious to explore the new American land acquisition and to confirm his suspicions of a great river in the Oregon country flowing to the Pacific. At his request, Congress authorized an expedition to proceed from Saint Louis up the Missouri River to its source and thence across the continental divide to reach the Pacific Ocean. The expedition consisted of about fifty volunteers under the command of Captains Meriwether Lewis and William Clark. It departed on May 14, 1804, and, after descending the Columbia River, reached the Pacific on November 15, 1805. After being given up for lost, the Lewis and Clark expedition returned to Saint Louis on September 23, 1806, laden with much valuable data and material from the new land.

The first American effort at government was not well received by the inhabitants of the Louisiana Territory. The area was divided into upper and lower territories under a governmental arrangement—which was seen as a continuation of the colonial administrations used by France and Spain.

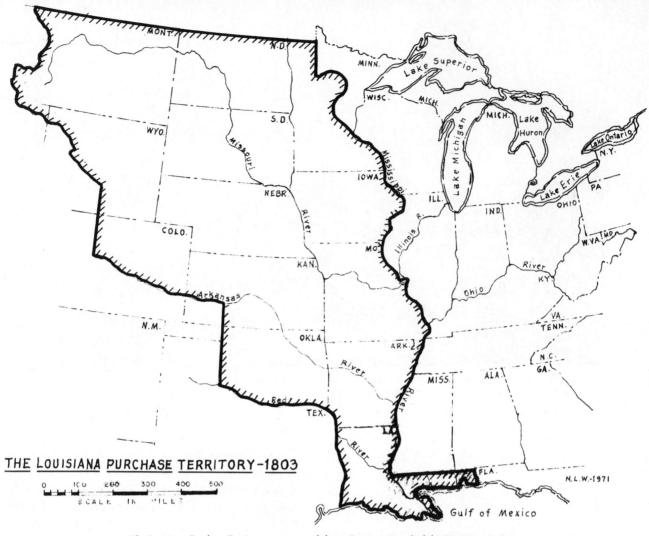

THE LOUISIANA PURCHASE TERRITORY—1803

0   100   200   300   400   500
SCALE IN MILES

N.L.W.-1971

The Louisiana Purchase Territory encompassed the entire western end of the Mississippi Valley.

The Ceremony of the Three Flags at Saint Louis, transferring the Upper Louisiana Territory to American dominion, March 9, 1804. *Courtesy Jefferson National Expansion Memorial, National Park Service*

Progress of the Lewis and Clark Expedition. Painting by Oscar E. Berninghaus. Courtesy August A. Busch, Jr.

Lewis and Clark encountering the Indians. From St. Louis Globe-Democrat, 1902

Meriwether Lewis, leader of the Lewis and Clark Expedition, participated in the Indian campaigns with General Anthony Wayne. He was appointed governor of the Louisiana Territory after his return from the expedition. From History of the Louisiana Purchase Exposition, 1904

Into the Unknown. Painting by J. K. Ralston of Lewis and Clark meeting with the Shoshone Indians in Montana on August 17, 1805. Courtesy Jefferson National Expansion Memorial, National Park Service

William Clark was the partner of Meriwether Lewis on the famous expedition to the Pacific after the Louisiana Purchase. He was territorial governor of Missouri until statehood was achieved in 1821. From History of the Louisiana Purchase Exposition, 1904

A scene that would have greeted Lewis and Clark on their way up the Missouri—Indians with their bullboats. Painted by Carl Bodmer. *Courtesy Saint Louis Mercantile Library Association*

Pierre Chouteau's residence on the east side of Main Street, south of Washington Avenue in Saint Louis, 1848. It was headquarters for his Missouri Fur Company. *Photo by Emil Boehl*

Auguste Chouteau of Saint Louis wrote to Governor William Henry Harrison at Vincennes, whose Indiana territorial government was to administer the new Territory of Louisiana, protesting the lack of a provision for self-government. A reply from Congressman John W. Eppes gave assurance that Congress would favor a representational form of territorial government, with the possibility of eventual statehood.

The first state formed from the Territory was Louisiana in 1812, followed by Missouri in 1821. American dominion over the Mississippi Valley resulted in the westward migration of new settlers from the eastern states, the Ohio River being the principal avenue of travel, via flatboats and rafts.

The value of the new lands inspired Aaron Burr, disgraced politically after his duel with Alexander Hamilton, to engineer a conspiracy to separate these rich western lands from the Union and to

Cordelling a keelboat upstream, with the crew on the riverbank pulling the craft by means of a rope attached to the mast. These boats were widely used on the western rivers before the introduction of the steamboat. *Courtesy Missouri Historical Society*

Fur traders on the Missouri River attacked by Indians, typical of the difficulties experienced by early expeditions of the American Fur Company. Painting by William Cary. *From* Harper's Weekly, *1868*

Traffic on the Ohio River passing Cave-in-Rock. Painting by Carl Bodmer. *Courtesy Saint Louis Mercantile Library Association*

Entrance of Cave-in-Rock, once the lair of desperate pirates who preyed upon passing river traffic. It was later used as a base of operations by the infamous Harpe gang of outlaws. *Courtesy State of Illinois, Department of Conservation*

Interior of the pirate's cave. It penetrates 108 feet into the riverbank. *Courtesy State of Illinois, Department of Conservation*

Views of Fort Benton, Montana, about 1900, an early outpost on the upper Missouri settled in the great westward migration. *From Siler's Historical Photographs, 1904*

Restoration of Fort Osage on the Missouri River at Sibley, Missouri, an important center in the early fur trade. *Walker-Missouri Tourism photo*

Tower of Fort Snelling, at the point where the Mississippi and Minnesota rivers meet. This fort established control in the north country after 1819. *Courtesy State of Minnesota, Department of Economic Development*

Historic Blennerhasset mansion, situated on an island in the Ohio River near Parkersburg, West Virginia, was the scene of Aaron Burr's conspiracy with Harman Blennerhasset for a western empire in 1805. The house was later destroyed by fire and flood. Drawing by Henry Howe. *Courtesy Saint Louis Public Library*

Chief Tecumseh of the Shawnee Indians, 1768–1813. He aided the British in the War of 1812, in which he tried to unite the Indian tribes against the United States. But the plan failed with the defeat of Tecumseh's brother, the Shawnee "Prophet," at the Battle of Tippecanoe in 1811. Tecumseh was killed in the Battle of the Thames, in southern Ontario, Canada, on October 5, 1813. This victory restored American control in the Northwest Territory. *Courtesy Saint Louis Public Library*

Painting by Carl Bodmer of battle at Fort McKenzie, a far-western outpost, on August 28, 1833. *Courtesy Saint Louis Mercantile Library Association*

join them to Mexico. The scheme received a fatal blow in December, 1806, when a fleet of boats carrying arms and provisions, along with Burr's confederates, was captured on the Muskingum River in Ohio.

In 1810, Indian uprisings, led by Tecumseh, created havoc among the new settlers. These were finally put down when the tribes were defeated by General Harrison at Tippecanoe, Indiana, during the next year.

The following year marked the first steamboat voyage on the western rivers, that of the *New Orleans* from Pittsburgh to New Orleans.

The second American war with Great Britain was declared on June 15, 1812, and the west became its principal theater, with British-inspired Indian attacks on frontier outposts. Although the early battles were disastrous for the Americans, the end was a triumphant display of arms—Jackson's victory at New Orleans on January 2, 1815. The development of the West resumed with renewed vigor, accompanied by the rapid use of the steamboat as an important means of transportation and commerce. Without the steamboat, the growth of the western country unquestionably would have been much slower.

Chief Black Hawk, leader of the Indian uprisings in the Black Hawk War of 1832. *Courtesy Saint Louis Public Library*

II
The River System

SCOPE OF THE MISSISSIPPI VALLEY

The extreme length of the Mississippi Valley from north to south is about twenty-five hundred miles, with a maximum descent of more than sixteen hundred feet. The descent is gradual, about three-fourths occurring in the upper half of the valley, from the head of the Mississippi in northern Minnesota to the mouth of the Missouri. From there the slighter degree of fall to the Gulf is one of the

The Mississippi River system. *Collection of the author*

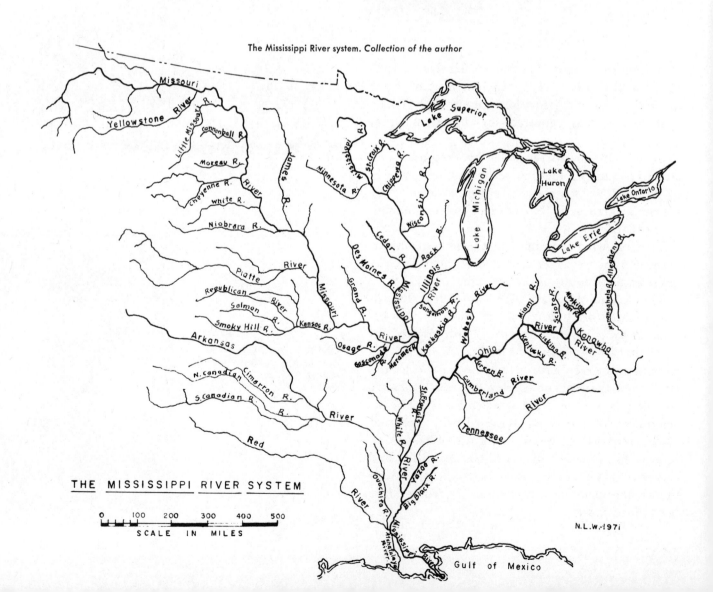

THE MISSISSIPPI RIVER SYSTEM

0 100 200 300 400 500
SCALE IN MILES

N.L.W.-1971

valley's most significant features. The greatest width of the basin, from the heights of the eastern watershed to the crest of the Rocky Mountains, is nearly sixteen hundred miles. The basin's western rim is by far the higher, although varying in elevation from ten thousand feet at the headwaters of the Arkansas River to about seven thousand feet for those of the Missouri, to about twenty-five hundred feet for the source of the Red River farther south. The descent is gradual through vast, grassy plains in the west, while the region inward to the river from the older Appalachian Mountains is much more broken. In parts of West Virginia, Kentucky, and Tennessee, a mountain slope meets the general southward descent in the bed of the Ohio. A ridge across the eastern center of the basin has prevented the extreme "washing" of the surface such as took place west of the Missouri River on the plains.

The area of the combined basins of the great central river and its branches is about 1,256,000 square miles, including the delta; the Missouri River basin accounts for nearly half of this drainage area.

During the steamboat era, this vast network of rivers provided a total of nearly nine thousand miles of navigable inland waterways. Among the major ones, the Mississippi was navigable from its mouth to Saint Paul, a distance of 1,944 miles, and beyond Saint Anthony's Falls at Minneapolis, for eighty miles farther. The Missouri was navigable for almost two thousand miles, and for six hundred miles more during periods of high water. The Ohio River's navigable length from Cairo to Pittsburgh was 980 miles, a distance that could be nearly doubled by including its tributaries. The Arkansas and Red rivers were both navigable for several hundred miles under normal conditions, and considerably farther during the spring and summer floods. Branches of the Mississippi in Minnesota could be traversed for about 350 miles, while the Illinois River could be navigated for 220 miles above its mouth.

About two-thirds of the Mississippi basin lies west of the central stream, with approximately half of this area well endowed with good soil, climate, and location. From the Missouri River westward are treeless plains, and for six hundred miles east of that river, in the upper valley, there is a large proportion of prairie, with forests usually bordering streams. These plains suffer from a relative lack of rainfall, being cut off from the Pacific by the Rock-

ies, and from the diminishing rainfall moving west from the well-watered eastern and southern portions of the Mississippi basin.

THE MISSISSIPPI RIVER

The Mississippi River, the main stem of the system of western rivers, rises near Lake Itasca in northern Minnesota and, flowing in a generally southerly direction, serves as the boundary for the states of Minnesota, Wisconsin, Iowa, Illinois, Missouri, Kentucky, Tennessee, Arkansas, Mississippi, and Louisiana in its 2470-mile course to the Gulf of Mexico. Its principal tributaries are the Missouri, Ohio, Arkansas, Illinois, and Red rivers.

After leaving its source, which was discovered by Henry Rowe Schoolcraft in 1832, the Mississippi flows northward and eastward through a series of lakes, until it begins its southward course above Grand Rapids, Minnesota. At Minneapolis, the river tumbles over a limestone ridge at the Falls of Saint Anthony, the beginning or the head of navigation for large boats. Below the Twin Cities, the Mississippi flows through a scenic country of wooded

Source of the mighty Mississippi, Lake Itasca, Minnesota. *Courtesy State of Minnesota, Department of Economic Development*

Lithograph by Henry Lewis of the Falls of Saint Anthony, on the Mississippi, 1835. *Courtesy Saint Louis Mercantile Library Association*

Minnesota's first flour mill, on the Mississippi, built at Fort Snelling in 1822. Painted from a photograph taken in 1857. *From* St. Louis Globe-Democrat, 1902

Typical of the scenic country near Minneapolis are the Falls of Minnehaha, made famous in Longfellow's poem of Hiawatha. *From* Down the Great River, 1887. *Courtesy Saint Louis Public Library*

Lithograph by Henry Lewis of the mouth of a tributary, the Saint Croix River, at the Mississippi, on the boundary between Minnesota and Wisconsin. *Courtesy Saint Louis Mercantile Library Association*

Closeup of a log raft on the upper Mississippi. *From* Down the Great River, *1887. Courtesy Saint Louis Mercantile Library Association*

A log boom and sawmills along the upper Mississippi. *From* Down the Great River, *1887. Courtesy Saint Louis Mercantile Library Association*

Life along the Saint Croix River approaching the Mississippi, about 1850. *From The United States Illustrated, 1855. Courtesy Saint Louis Mercantile Library Association*

Lake Pepin, on the Mississippi. *From Picturesque America, 1872. Courtesy Saint Louis Mercantile Library Association*

Read's Landing, Minnesota, 1867, where steamboats bound for Lake Pepin in winter waited for the ice to break in the spring thaw. This town started as a trading post in 1840, and during the 1850s fifteen hundred river travelers could be found in its seventeen hotels. Later Read's Landing was one of the nation's greatest grain-shipping ports. *Courtesy Saint Louis Public Library*

bluffs and rocky cliffs in Minnesota and Wisconsin. South of Red Wing, Minnesota, the river widens out into Lake Pepin, which is about twenty-five miles in length and more than two miles in width. Its surface is quite smooth and reflects the surrounding picturesque bluffs along the shore.

The Mississippi flows for four hundred miles to delineate the western boundary of Wisconsin amid wooded islands and castellated bluffs. Several large tributaries enter the Mississippi from Wisconsin, including the Saint Croix, Chippewa, and Wisconsin rivers. The Wisconsin, which is six hundred miles long, was navigable to Portage City, Wisconsin, during steamboat days. The limestone bluffs continue along the river as it wends its way between Iowa and Illinois.

View of the bluffs at Eagle Rock, Wisconsin, on the Mississippi. *From The United States Illustrated, 1855. Courtesy Saint Louis Mercantile Library Association*

Sketch of Chimney Rock, near Fountain City, Wisconsin, by A. R. Waud. *From Picturesque America, 1872. Courtesy Saint Louis Mercantile Library Association*

Approach to Trempealeau, Wisconsin, sketched by A. R. Waud. *From Picturesque America, 1872. Courtesy Saint Louis Mercantile Library Association*

Genoa, Wisconsin, on the Mississippi, scene of an Indian raid, the Battle of Bad Axe, in 1832. *From Genesis of Steamboating on Western Rivers, George B. Merrick, 1912*

Lithograph by Henry Lewis of Battle of Bad Axe. This was the Black Hawk Indian War. *Courtesy Saint Louis Mercantile Library Association*

Monument to Chief Black Hawk at Black Hawk State Park, Rock Island, Illinois. *Courtesy State of Illinois, Department of Conservation*

At Keokuk, Iowa, the largest dam and locks on the Mississippi have created Lake Keokuk, a recreation spot for the tri-state area. An interesting feature of the Mississippi as it forms the western boundary of Illinois is the American Bottom, an area of low-lying plains and grasslands, which averages six miles in width and extends for ninety miles from Alton to Kaskaskia. Two major tributaries enter the Mississippi above Saint Louis, Missouri, the Illinois River at Grafton and the Missouri River below Alton. After its junction with the Missouri, the waters of the Mississippi become yellow and turbid, although the clearer upper Mississippi current refuses for miles to mix with the flow of the Big Muddy.

A similar mixture of waters occurs where the clearer Ohio joins the Mississippi at Cairo, Illinois.

Passing Selma, Missouri, along the American Bottom, about 1840. Lithograph by John Casper Wild. *Courtesy Saint Louis Public Library*

Lithograph by John Casper Wild of Kaskaskia, Illinois, at the terminal of the American Bottom, about 1840. *Courtesy Saint Louis Public Library*

Painting by Carl Bodmer of Tower Rock on the Mississippi, 1835. *Courtesy Saint Louis Mercantile Library Association*

The Mississippi at Grand Tower from the Missouri shore. *Courtesy Saint Louis Public Library*

Stern quarter of an Ohio River steamboat on the Mississippi in 1828, moored at Grand Tower Rock, sixty miles above the confluence of the Ohio and Mississippi rivers. This is the first stone bluff seen on a trip upriver from New Orleans. Etching by Captain Basil Hall, 1829. *Courtesy Ardell Thompson Collection*

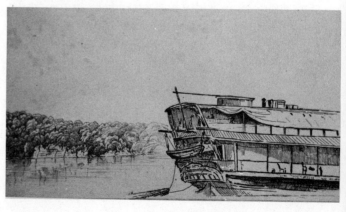

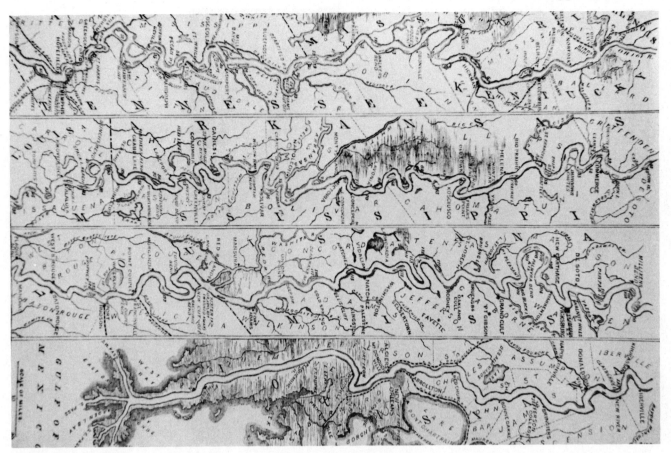

These four strips compose a map of the Mississippi River from Cairo to the Gulf of Mexico. *From Harper's Pictorial History of the Civil War. Courtesy Saint Louis Mercantile Library Association*

Peculiarly, the Mississippi's volume does not appear augmented after absorbing the Ohio, and a clear demarcation between the waters of the two rivers is visible for many miles. Below Cairo the scenery of the alluvial plain is almost uniformly flat, broken occasionally by a few bluffs, with levees and flood works prominent features. There are no dams on the lower Mississippi because the land is so flat that any impounded pools would flood the countryside.

It is therefore an open river, unlike the upper river, above Saint Louis, which is canalized by a series of twenty-seven locks and dams up to Minneapolis. The river's course south of its junction with the Ohio is a continuous series of bends, with new courses being cut through the bends and islands being created and disappearing intermittently.

About two hundred miles, by river, below Memphis, Tennessee, the Arkansas River enters the Mississippi from the west, and farther south a junction is effected with the Yazoo River above Vicksburg.

The flat, monotonous plain can be seen here along the Mississippi at West Memphis, Arkansas. *Courtesy Arkansas Publicity and Parks Commission*

The ground rises a bit here, approaching Greenville, Mississippi. *Courtesy State of Mississippi Agricultural and Industrial Board*

On the Yazoo River, the steamer *Katie Robbins* which ran in the cotton trade under the Parisot Line, 1884–1889. *Courtesy Boatmen's National Bank, St. Louis*

Supplying the cotton trade was the planter, such as in this drawing by A. R. Waud of a typical scene in Louisiana. *From Picturesque America, 1872. Courtesy Saint Louis Mercantile Library Association*

Lithograph by Henry Lewis of a Louisiana cotton plantation, 1840. *Courtesy Saint Louis Public Library*

Drawing by A. R. Waud of Cypress Swamp, Louisiana. *From Picturesque America, 1872. Courtesy Saint Louis Mercantile Library Association*

As the great river's mouth at the Gulf of Mexico is approached, the vegetation becomes more tropical in character and the river loses itself in a wilderness of bayous and swamps, reaching the Gulf through several outlets below New Orleans.

The entire length, including the tributaries, became the waterways for the great tide of westward settlement into the valley, first by flatboat, keelboat, and raft, followed by the steamboat. The earliest steamboats were of the Robert Fulton design and were not adapted to navigation of the shallow western rivers; a suitable craft was the *Washington,* developed by Henry M. Shreve at Wheeling

Sherman's troops on the Mississippi at Vicksburg. During the long siege, Union troops under General William T. Sherman occupied the heights above the Mississippi north of Vicksburg. *From Harper's Pictorial History of the Civil War*

in 1815, which became the prototype for the western river steamboat.

The Mississippi's commercial value for steamboats peaked in the years preceding the Civil War. During the conflict, most civilian shipping ceased, but the river was widely used for troop movements and important military engagements. Union control was finally secured after the fall of Vicksburg in 1863.

River traffic experienced a brief revival after the war, until in the 1870s railroad competition began to make inroads. A long dispute between rail and

Drawing of Eads Bridge from Compton and Dry's *Pictorial Saint Louis,* 1875. This bears the notation by Eads, "I consider this an excellent and faithful representation of the bridge." *Collection of the author*

Drawing by A. R. Waud of site of the future South Pass jetties, Southwest Pass at the mouth of the Mississippi River. *Courtesy Saint Louis Mercantile Library Association*

Both sail and steamboats made their way up the mouth of the Mississippi. Lithograph by Henry Lewis, 1840. *Courtesy Saint Louis Mercantile Library Association*

river interests over bridges began in the 1850s, when the first bridge across the Mississippi was built at Rock Island, Illinois. In 1874 railroad dominance was symbolized by the Eads Bridge at Saint Louis, which provided direct rail communication with the East. James Buchanan Eads, who had built river ironclads for the Union during the Civil War, also helped preserve New Orleans as a seaport; his South Pass jetties at the mouth of the Mississippi, completed in 1879, widened and deepened the entrance.

A portion of the modern delta of the Mississippi River, looking south from above the Head of Passes: Southwest Pass (right), the major navigation artery maintained to a minimum depth of forty feet by the U.S. Army Corps of Engineers; South Pass (center), the secondary navigation artery, maintained to a minimum depth of thirty-five feet; and (left), a natural artery. *Courtesy U.S. Corps of Engineers, New Orleans District*

The old-style river steamboat had all but disappeared from the western rivers by 1910. The rivers became primarily a medium for freight haulage on vast tows of barges propelled by diesel-powered towboats. Government river-control work by the Army Corps of Engineers continues to provide significant aid to navigation on the Mississippi. In the nineteenth century such work was principally concerned with channel maintenance and levee construction under supervision of the Mississippi River Commission. Canalization of the upper Mississippi between Alton, Illinois, and Minneapolis was completed in 1939. The lower Mississippi, below Cairo, is open all year and has no locks or dams. A partially completed project is the Great River Road, which ultimately will provide a scenic highway route for the full length of the Father of Waters.

The old U.S. Corps of Engineers sternwheeler *Tuscumbia*, used for inspection work early in the twentieth century. *Courtesy U.S. Corps of Engineers, Saint Louis District*

The Great River Road along the Mississippi north of Alton, Illinois. *Courtesy State of Illinois, Department of Conservation*

The Mississippi River. U.S. Corps of Engineers boats constantly check the river channel and reset buoys when drifting sand changes the depths. *Courtesy Arkansas Publicity and Parks Commission*

THE MINNESOTA RIVER

Rising in Big Stone Lake at the western boundary of Minnesota, the 332-mile-long Minnesota River flows southeast to Mankato, Minnesota, then in a northeasterly direction to join the Mississippi at Mendota, above St. Paul. In its earlier years the river was called the Saint Pierre or Saint Peter and was a favored route for explorers and fur traders.

Steamboat navigation began on the Minnesota River about 1850. The opening of its valley to settlement, after the relocation of Indian tribes, gave river traffic a great impetus. However, because of the war, commerce declined after 1862. Shipping was necessarily by small boat, few ascending above Mankato, about one hundred miles above the river's mouth. The death knell for Minnesota River traffic sounded in 1871, when the Chicago and Northwestern Railroad reached New Ulm on the river. A small number of steamboats ventured on other tributaries of the upper Mississippi, such as the Wisconsin, Des Moines, Saint Croix, Chippewa, and Rock rivers during the 1850s. These essentially engaged in local trade only. Navigation on the Mississippi above Minneapolis by small steamboats of light draft was principally in the lumber trade.

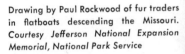

Drawing by Paul Rockwood of fur traders in flatboats descending the Missouri. *Courtesy Jefferson National Expansion Memorial, National Park Service*

THE WISCONSIN RIVER

The Wisconsin River rises in northeastern Wisconsin and flows generally southwest for 430 miles, before emptying into the Mississippi below Prairie du Chien. It is navigable to Portage City, Wisconsin, where a short canal connects it with the Fox River, and thence into Lake Michigan. Rapids and falls, called dalles, occur at several places, where the river passes through deep gorges between rocky bluffs as high as four hundred feet. The best known of these is the eight-mile scenic gorge known as the Wisconsin Dells in the central part of the state.

Here sandstone has been carved by the river into unusual forms, many of them spectacularly colored.

The Fox-Wisconsin river system was widely used as a waterway by early French explorers in the upper Mississippi Valley. Marquette and Joliet used this route to reach the Mississippi on their voyage in 1673. In presteamboat days, great rafts of timber were a common sight on the Wisconsin River, on their way downstream to the Mississippi. Steamboat navigation on the Wisconsin began in the 1830s and by the mid-1850s had attained an ex-

Lithograph by Henry Lewis of the mouth of the Wisconsin River. *Courtesy Saint Louis Mercantile Library Association*

Closeup of Starved Rock. *Courtesy State of Illinois, Department of Conservation*

tensive status. After the Civil War, as rails tapped the lucrative sources of waterways commerce, general river traffic on the Wisconsin declined. Timber rafting remained active, however, until the northern Wisconsin forests became exhausted in the early twentieth century.

THE ILLINOIS RIVER

The Illinois River is the most important tributary of the upper Mississippi (above the mouth of the Missouri). It is formed in northeastern Illinois by the junction of the Des Plaines and Kankakee rivers, and flows southwestwardly for 273 miles to enter the Mississippi at Grafton. During the steamboat era, the sluggish, placid Illinois was navigable for over 200 miles to La Salle, Illinois. The river flows through a rich, level country and receives the waters of the Fox, Sangamon, Spoon, and Vermilion rivers. The Illinois was ascended by Marquette

and Joliet and was further explored by La Salle in the late seventeenth century.

Steamboating on the Illinois River began in 1828 with the steamer *Criterion,* and experienced a slow increase for the next ten years. Packet-line operations began about 1848, after completion of the Illinois and Michigan Canal, which gave Chicago and the Great Lakes a waterways link to the Mississippi. It also provided a more direct route for midwestern products to the East.

Peoria and other Illinois River towns became busy river ports during the 1850s, when any point on the navigable Illinois was less than a week from New Orleans by steamboat. Railroads brought a swift decline to waterways use and the Illinois and Michigan Canal was eventually abandoned. The lower Illinois River was canalized, beginning in 1872, with locks and dams at various points. The

Starved Rock State Park, a geological paradise, rising 125 feet above the Illinois River. *Courtesy State of Illinois, Department of Conservation*

Site of a fort established by La Salle in 1680 on the Illinois River, near Peoria. *Courtesy State of Illinois, Department of Conservation*

Chicago Sanitary and Ship Canal, completed in 1900, again made parts of the old canal route practical for large volumes of river traffic, and the Illinois Waterway has been considerably improved since that time. Its channel is maintained with a nine-foot minimum depth and will eventually have sixteen locks for navigation.

Waterways improvements contemplated in Illinois include a new Illinois and Mississippi Canal to replace a presently unused canal from the Illinois River to the Mississippi at Rock Island, Illinois. Improvement of the lower Kaskaskia River and development of the Wabash River with a system of canals is also planned.

This New Salem sawmill, near Petersburg, on the Sangamon River, which feeds into the Illinois, once was the principal source of milled lumber for New Salem's settlers. *Courtesy State of Illinois, Department of Conservation*

Lock & Dam
Kaskaskia River, Illinois

Diagram of a lock and dam to be built on the lower Kaskaskia River in southern Illinois as part of a navigation project. *Courtesy U.S. Corps of Engineers, Saint Louis District*

Lithograph by John Casper Wild of Kaskaskia, Illinois, about 1840, showing covered bridge and rope ferry crossing the Kaskaskia River. This town, founded by the French in 1703, passed to the British in 1765. It became the territorial capital of Illinois and was the first state capital until 1820. No sign of the old town remains, as it was washed away by a shift in the Mississippi River. A state memorial now marks the site. *Courtesy Saint Louis Public Library*

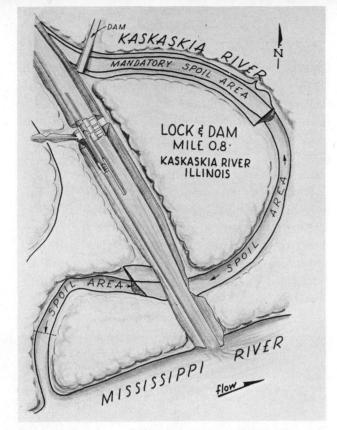

Map showing how the mouth of the Kaskaskia River will be straightened as part of the Kaskaskia project. *Courtesy U.S. Corps of Engineers, Saint Louis District*

View showing a typical oxbow that must be bypassed for the navigation project on the Kaskaskia River in southern Illinois. *Courtesy U.S. Corps of Engineers, Saint Louis District*

THE ARKANSAS RIVER

Rising in the Rocky Mountains near Leadville, Colorado, the 1,460-mile-long Arkansas River follows an irregular eastward course across the states of Colorado and Kansas, before turning southeastward at Great Bend, Kansas. The river then flows across Oklahoma and Arkansas to a junction with the Mississippi River above Greenville, Mississippi. Its principal tributaries are the White River, which joins it near its mouth after a three hundred-mile course southward from the Ozark plateau, and the Canadian and Cimarron Rivers, which meet the Arkansas in Oklahoma.

The Arkansas River has had an unpredictable existence for many years and was subject to serious flooding periodically. During the great flood of 1927, half of the state of Arkansas was under water from the overflowing river and its tributaries.

The Arkansas River Navigation Route. It begins at the juncture of the White and Mississippi rivers and proceeds ten miles up the White before entering the Arkansas via the ten-mile Arkansas Post Canal. The route crosses Arkansas and enters Oklahoma at Fort Smith. Leaving the Arkansas at Muskogee, the last fifty miles of the navigation route is on the Verdigris River, terminating at Catoosa, fifteen miles east of Tulsa, the headwaters of the Arkansas River Navigation system. *Courtesy U.S. Corps of Engineers, Little Rock District*

Drawing by A. R. Waud of Napoleon, an Arkansas town swallowed by the Mississippi River. *From Every Saturday Magazine, 1868*

Lithograph by Henry Lewis of the mouth of the Arkansas River, 1840. *Courtesy Saint Louis Public Library*

Painting by G. C. Widney of Arkansas Post, Arkansas, 1719, founded by Henri de Tonti of La Salle's 1686 expedition. It was the first permanent settlement in the Louisiana Purchase Territory. *From St. Louis Globe-Democrat, 1902*

President Madison's message to Congress in 1815 suggested the necessity of improvements for roads, canals, and waterways. This was implemented by a Congressional resolution in 1818, which stated that Congress had the constitutional right to appropriate money for such improvements. River traffic had increased in volume to such an extent by 1824, that Congress authorized the Army Corps of Engineers to engage in river-control work.

One year after Arkansas became a territory in 1819, the steamboat *Comet* navigated the Arkansas River to Arkansas Post, sixty miles from the mouth. A second boat, which was a combination sailing vessel and steamboat, the *Maid of Orleans,* reached

Lock and Dam No. 1, the first step in the Arkansas River navigation program. It is located at the downstream end of the Arkansas Post Canal near the juncture with the White River. The canal connects the Arkansas and White rivers for a more direct route to the Mississippi. *Courtesy U.S. Corps of Engineers, Little Rock District*

Arkansas Post in 1820. Early steamboaters took chances on the treacherous river, where any miscalculation meant disaster. The first steamboat to reach Little Rock, the *Eagle,* arrived there in 1822 and a few months later the *Robert Thompson* ascended the river to Fort Smith. Navigation during high water was found to be feasible as far as Fort Gibson in the Indian Territory.

The first money for Arkansas River improvement was $15,000, voted in 1832, for channel main-

Lock and Dam No. 7, the first upstream lock above Little Rock, Arkansas, on the Arkansas River navigation project. The lock is one of seventeen in the 436-mile project. It raises and lowers river traffic eighteen feet at normal pool levels and measures 110 feet wide by 600 feet long, as on all the system's locks. The dam forms a thirty-mile navigation pool reaching to Lock and Dam No. 8 at Conway, Arkansas. *Courtesy U.S. Corps of Engineers, Little Rock District*

tenance 465 miles upstream to the mouth of the
Neosho River. In 1833 Henry M. Shreve began
snag removal on the Arkansas River with several
snag boats. Shreve reported that some snags in the
river weighed as much as one hundred tons. Several
small shipyards flourished on the Arkansas during
the 1840s and 1850s, building hulls that were
floated down to New Orleans for outfitting. Shallow-draft boats became a specialty of Little Rock
boatyards.

The Government river-control efforts continued
throughout the nineteenth century, and were extended into tributaries of the Arkansas as well.
Small annual appropriations precluded any great
amount of work being accomplished, even for such
important functions as snag and wreck removal. In
1881 a Corps of Engineers district office was established at Little Rock. One of the first problems attacked by the new office was erosion of the riverbank, which threatened the town of Pine Bluff.

During the high water of 1882, when tracks were
under water, the railroads were forced to charter
steamboats to maintain service between Memphis
and Little Rock. A bad flood in 1898 wiped out river-control works at Pine Bluff and caused extensive
damage from flooding. A protracted dry spell for
the next few years interrupted river traffic and
caused heavy financial losses. During the winter of
1904–1905, the Arkansas was frozen over completely. Railroad competition made itself felt on
the river traffic during the late 1890s, when their
bridges began to impede the waterways. By 1910
river traffic was practically abandoned because of
railroad competition, which was considered more
efficient despite higher rates.

David D. Terry Lock and Dam (No. 6) on the Arkansas River near Little
Rock, Arkansas, was the site for ceremonies in October, 1968, to herald
the coming of modern navigation to the Arkansas River. Courtesy U.S.
Corps of Engineers, Little Rock District

Typical barge at the port of Little Rock. These shipments of steel arrived
from Wheeling, West Virginia, Pittsburgh, Pennsylvania, and Chicago,
Illinois. Courtesy U.S. Corps of Engineers, Little Rock District

Privately owned port of Jones-Kirby in North Little Rock. Steel piling
(foreground) has been offloaded, and barges of fertilizer are moved
into position for offloading. Courtesy U.S. Corps of Engineers, Little Rock
District

The great flood of 1927 produced these boatloads of mules rescued by
the ferries Vicksburg and Charles J. Miller. Photo by Limerick McRae of
Vicksburg. Courtesy Waterways Journal

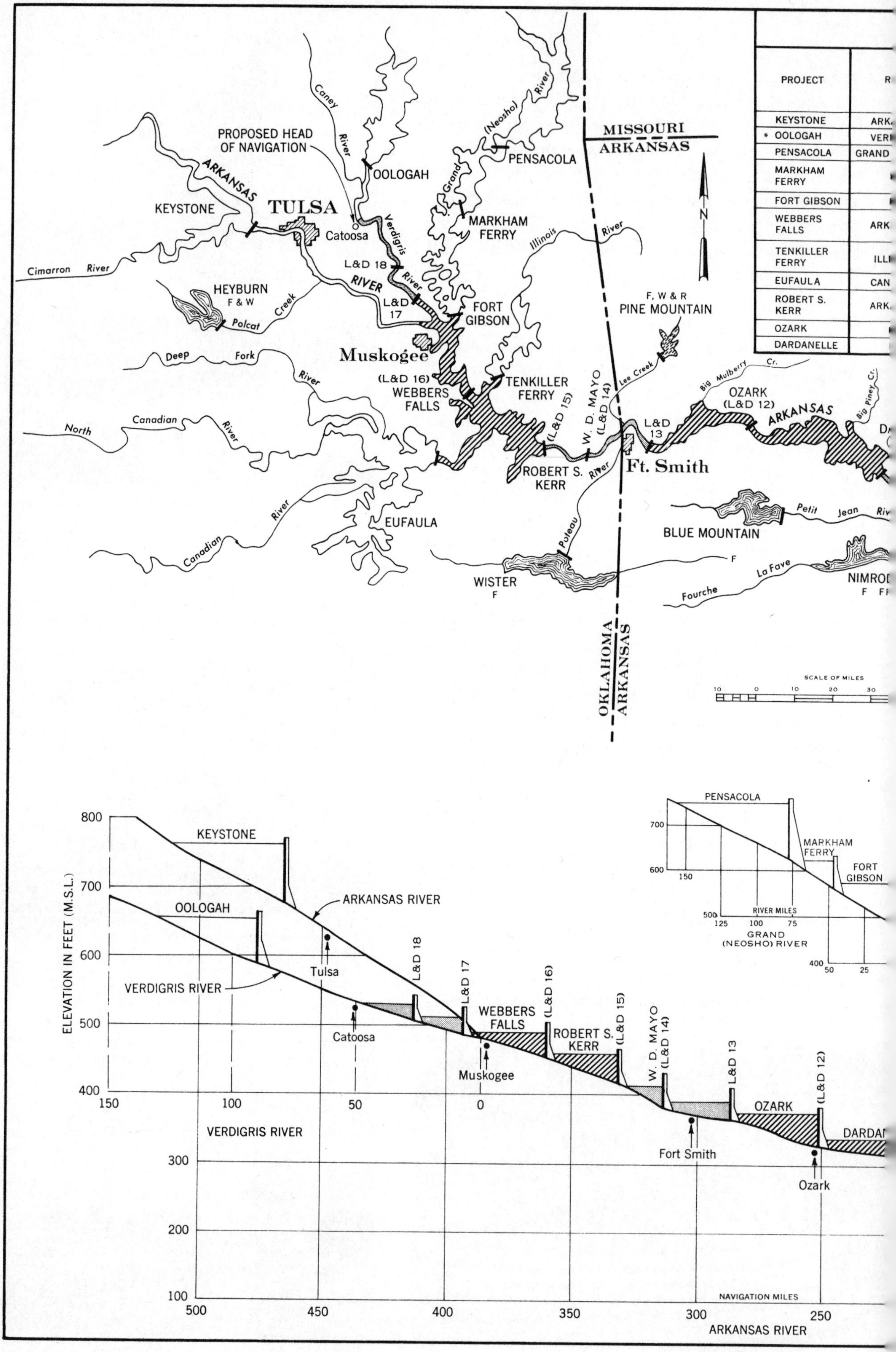

PROJECT	R
KEYSTONE	ARK.
* OOLOGAH	VER
PENSACOLA	GRAND
MARKHAM FERRY	
FORT GIBSON	
WEBBERS FALLS	ARK
TENKILLER FERRY	ILL
EUFAULA	CAN
ROBERT S. KERR	ARK.
OZARK	
DARDANELLE	

RESERVOIR PROJECTS

MILE SOUTH RIVER PT ED	PURPOSE	ELEVATION (M.S.L.)			F. C. CAPACITY (ACRE-FEET)	POWER PLANT CAPACITY (KW.)
		TOP FLOOD CONTROL POOL	BOTTOM OF POWER POOL	TOP POWER POOL		
8	F, N, P, W, & FW	754.0	706.0	723.0	1,216,000	70,000
2	F, N, W, FW & FP	651.0	608.0	638.0	963,000	.
0	F, P & W	756.1	731.1	746.1	525,000	86,400
4	F, P & W	636.0	.	619.0	244,000	100,000
7	F, P & W	582.0	551.0	554.0	919,200	67,500
3	N, P, R, & FW	.	487.0	490.0	.	66,000
8	F, P & W	667.0	594.5	631.0	600,000	34,000
0	F, N, P & W	597.0	565.0	585.0	1,470,000	90,000
3	N, P, R, & FW	.	458.0	460.0	.	110,000
0	N, P, R, & FW	.	370.0	372.0	.	100,000
2	N, P, R, & FW	.	336.0	338 0	.	124,000

* ULTIMATE DEVELOPMENT
** 1940 SURVEY

PURPOSE

F - FLOOD CONTROL
N - NAVIGATION
P - HYDROELECTRIC POWER
FP - FUTURE POWER
W - WATER SUPPLY
FW - FISH AND WILDLIFE
R - RECREATION

NAVIGATION PROJECTS
(River and Harbor)

STRUCTURE	NAVIGATION MILE (EXCEPT AS NOTED)	UPPER POOL ELEVATION (FEET M.S.L.)	LOWER POOL ELEVATION (FEET M.S.L.)
DAM NO. 18	412.9 VERDIGRIS R.	532.0	511.0
LOCK NO. 18	412.9 DO	532.0	511.0
DAM NO. 17	393.2 DO	511.0	490.0
LOCK NO. 17	393.2 DO	511.0	490.0
WEBBERS FALLS (L&D NO. 16) (1)	359.3 ARKANSAS R.	490.0	460.0
ROBERT S. KERR (L&D NO. 15) (1)	330.3 DO	460.0	412.0
W. D. MAYO (L&D NO. 14)	313.7 DO	412.0	392.0
L&D NO. 13	286.8 DO	392.0	372.0
OZARK (L&D NO. 12) (1)	251.0 DO	372.0	338.0
L&D NO. 11	(DELETED)		
DARDANELLE (L&D NO. 10) (1)	201.2 DO	338.0	284.0-287.0
L&D NO. 9	173.4 DO	284.0-287.0	265.0
L&D NO. 8	152.9 DO	265.0	249.0
L&D NO. 7	123.0 DO	249.0	231.0
DAVID D. TERRY (L&D NO. 6)	106.3 DO	231.0	213.0
L&D NO. 5	85.0 DO	213.0	196.0
L&D NO. 4	65.0 DO	196.0	182.0
L&D NO. 3	49.3 DO	182.0	162.0
DAM NO. 2	(2) 40.5 DO	162.0	ARKANSAS R.
LOCK NO. 2	13.2	162.0	142.0
L&D NO. 1	10.4	142.0	112 (WHITE R.)

(1) MULTIPLE PURPOSE.
(2) 1943 SURVEY.

LEGEND

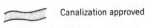 Canalization approved

Navigation lock & dam

Navigation - power reservoir

Reservoir included in multiple - purpose plan

Reservoir in operation (not included in multiple - purpose plan)

Reservoir approved (not included in multiple purpose plan)

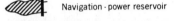

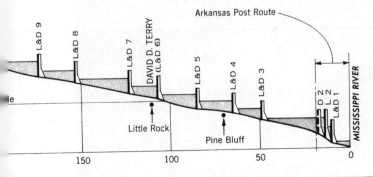

ARKANSAS RIVER AND TRIBUTARIES
ARKANSAS AND OKLAHOMA

NAVIGATION FEATURES
GENERAL PLAN AND PROFILE

SCALE AS SHOWN

LITTLE ROCK DISTRICT. CORPS OF ENGINEERS
LITTLE ROCK. ARKANSAS. FEBRUARY 1970

DRAWN: DGB
TRACED: DGB
CHECKED: SH

Navigation features of the Arkansas River and its tributaries in Arkansas and Oklahoma. *Courtesy U.S. Corps of Engineers, Little Rock District*

A serious flood in 1912 for the first time resulted in government aid for levee reinforcement and transport of flood-relief supplies. Very little river-control work was done until the need was graphically shown by the great flood of 1927. Flood losses along the Arkansas exceeded forty-three million dollars and over fifty thousand animals were drowned in that great disaster. A direct result was the Flood Control Act of 1928, but work was suspended during the Depression. Government aid began again after floods in 1936 and 1937, but was interrupted by World War II and not resumed until 1946.

A series of locks and dams to permit navigation on the Arkansas as far as Muskogee, Oklahoma, was proposed by the Army Engineers in 1907, but was not considered feasible because of high construction costs. The importance of Arkansas River development gained increasing recognition, and in 1946 the present program of locks and dams was authorized. Initial work began in 1949, but was suspended between 1950 and 1955 because of the Korean War. Construction began again in 1956 on various phases of the project, culminating in the completion of the first lock and dam in June, 1967. The navigation channel was declared open to Little Rock on December 31, 1968, by the Little Rock district engineer Colonel Charles L. Steel.

The head of navigation for the nine-foot channel of the Arkansas River system is at Catoosa, Okla-

The Mississippi River at Arkansas City carries heavy barge traffic in gasoline. Large pipeline-pumper stations are located along the entire eastern Arkansas border. *Photo by Harold Phelps. Courtesy Arkansas Publicity and Parks Commission*

homa, on the Verdigris River, near Tulsa. The Verdigris is used for the upper end of the channel because of the higher costs involved in improving the Arkansas below Tulsa. Ceremonies dedicating the $1.2 billion Arkansas River project were held at Catoosa in 1971. The 440-mile-long navigation route has 12 locks in Arkansas and five in Oklahoma. These raise the water level 420 feet in steps ranging from 14 to 54 feet. The project also includes the generation of electric power at ten plants, implementing a tremendous industrial potential in the Arkansas Basin.

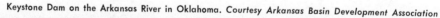

Keystone Dam on the Arkansas River in Oklahoma. *Courtesy Arkansas Basin Development Association*

THE RED RIVER

The Red River, which is about thirteen hundred miles in length, rises in the Texas Panhandle, southwest of Amarillo, and flows in a southeasterly direction between Texas and Oklahoma and between Texas and Arkansas, and then across Louisiana to the Atchafalaya and Mississippi rivers. It enters the Mississippi about 240 miles above New Orleans, after receiving the Ouachita River a few miles above its mouth. The Red River is currently navigable to a point near the eastern boundary of Oklahoma. The Denison Dam, completed in 1944 on the river at Denison, Texas, impounds Lake Texoma, which is one of the largest artificial lakes in the nation. Along its course in Louisiana, many lakes and bayous are tributary to the river.

Captain Henry M. Shreve's steamboat *Enterprise* made the first trip up the Red River in 1815, carrying a company of soldiers to the rapids at Alexandria, Louisiana. Normal river commerce began in 1820, when several boats reached Alexandria, and the *Beaver* went another hundred miles upstream to Natchitoches. Above that point navigation was precluded for many years by the so-called Red River Raft, which was a natural mass of tangled timber blocking the river for more than a hundred miles. It could be by-passed by a circuitous route through lakes and bayous, but these trips were rare and uncertain ventures. Removal of part of the Raft by the U.S. Engineers under Captain Shreve in 1836 allowed steamboats to reach Shreveport, which became the head of navigation for most boats. The Raft was ultimately removed between 1837 and 1873 by the Engineers at great expense.

In the years following the Civil War, the cotton trade became a prosperous traffic on the Red River, in boats ranging up to eight hundred tons capacity. Steamboats navigated still other lower Mississippi River tributaries—in Arkansas, Louisiana, and Mississippi—such as the White, Ouachita, and Yazoo rivers, as well as on numerous large bayous. The Atchafalaya River in Louisiana, which branches off from the Red River near its junction with the Mississippi and flows southward for 170 miles to the Gulf of Mexico, is still used by river traffic.

Lithograph by Henry Lewis of the mouth of the Red River, Louisiana, 1840. *Courtesy Saint Louis Public Library*

Bird's-eye view of the meandering Red River, which is once again a navigation artery. *Courtesy U.S. Corps of Engineers, New Orleans District*

Mississippi River Flood Control model. Guide points out to group of visitors the plan to prevent capture of the Mississippi River by the Atchafalaya River as tested on the Mississippi River Flood Control model which has been in use since construction in 1936 to study flood-control measures. The scale is 1:100 vertical and 1:2000 horizontal. The densely folded screen wire is to obstruct overbank flow on the model as trees, fences, and vegetation do in nature. Group is standing in the vicinity of Angola, Louisiana, on east bank of Mississippi River. *Courtesy U.S. Army Engineer Waterways Experiment Station, U.S. Corps of Engineers, Vicksburg District*

A portion of the model showing the river control structures for studies of cutoffs, floodways, backwater areas, protection levees, and main-line levee grades. It represents about five hundred miles of the Lower Mississippi River. *Courtesy U.S. Army Engineer Waterways Experiment Station, U.S. Corps of Engineers, Vicksburg District*

Forming the Missouri River at Three Forks, near Sterling, Montana: the junction of the Gallatin, Madison, and Jefferson rivers. *From The Mississippi Valley in Prehistoric Times by G. H. Walker*

THE MISSOURI RIVER

The Missouri River has its source in springs in the Rocky Mountains, on the Continental Divide. The first five hundred miles of its course is nearly north, then turning northeast it reaches its extreme northern bend at its junction with the White Earth River. After this, its general course is to the southeast to its mouth at the Mississippi River above Saint Louis. At a distance of eighteen miles east of Helena, Montana, is the Gates of the Rocky Mountains, a canyon named by Lewis and Clark. The river narrows to three hundred feet as it flows between its precipitous rock walls, twelve hundred feet high, for nearly six miles.

The bed of the Missouri begins at the confluence of three small streams, the Jefferson, Madison, and

Painting by Carl Bodmer of the Stonewalls on the upper Missouri, about 1835, typical northern scenery. *Courtesy Saint Louis Mercantile Library Association*

The same view of the Stonewalls on the upper Missouri in the 1850s by an unknown artist. *From The United States Illustrated, 1855. Courtesy Saint Louis Mercantile Library Association*

Painting by Carl Bodmer of Citadel Rock on the Missouri River, 1835. *Courtesy Saint Louis Mercantile Library Association*

Paintings by Carl Bodmer, 1835, of additional remarkable eminences on the upper Missouri. *Courtesy Saint Louis Mercantile Library Association*

Painting by Carl Bodmer, 1835: Shortly after crossing into North Dakota at the confluence of the Missouri and Yellowstone rivers. *Courtesy Saint Louis Mercantile Library Association*

Gallatin rivers at Three Forks, Montana. The Great Falls of the Missouri commences three miles below the mouth of the Sun River and descends 450 feet in fifteen miles. Below the falls, at a point thirty-five miles upstream from Fort Benton, was the head of navigation on the Missouri during the steamboat era. Below Fort Benton the river flows first over a gravelly bed and then between high and arid bluffs. In this area is the Fort Peck Dam, which has created a vast reservoir 175 miles long.

Shortly after crossing the state boundary into North Dakota, the Missouri is joined by the 850-mile-long Yellowstone River, which was once navigable as far as Billings, Montana. This river traffic ceased after railroads entered the Yellowstone Valley in 1881. Several major tributaries enter the Missouri in its course across the Dakotas, including the Little Missouri and Cheyenne rivers. An interesting topographical feature of this area is the Plateau du Coteau du Missouri, which is a great grassy tableland running southward between the Missouri and James rivers. It is treeless and has masses of boulders crowning its odd-shaped hills and ridges. The Missouri slope sinks away in waves of rich soil from the crest of the Coteau to the level of the great river, 250 feet below.

The swirling and turbulent course of the Missouri through the Dakotas was beset with numberless sandbars, from which steamboats had to extricate themselves by "climbing" up on poles ingeniously arranged for the purpose. The practice was known as "grasshoppering." The crooked and shifting Missouri forms the eastern boundary of Nebraska, through rolling country. Its chief tributary here is the Platte River, which rises in its North and South forks in the Rockies and flows eastward for twelve hundred miles before joining the Big Muddy below Omaha. The Missouri at Council Bluffs, Iowa, flows at an elevation 425 feet higher than the Mississippi River at Davenport.

In its course along the eastern edge of Kansas, the Missouri varies in width from a thousand feet to half a mile. The Kansas or Kaw River joins the Missouri at Kansas City, four hundred miles east of its source at the confluence of the Republican and Smoky Hill rivers at Junction City, Kansas. The Big Muddy runs eastward for 436 miles across the State of Missouri as a broad, deep, and turbid stream, with bottoms of incredibly rich soil. It is entered from the north by the Grand and Chariton rivers, while from the south it is joined by the Gas-

Aerial view of sandbars on the Platte River in Nebraska. *Nebraska Game Commission photo*

Pathway of the pioneers—Nebraska's rambling Platte River. It became famous as the historic route of westbound wagon trains a century ago. Today, scenic vistas, like this one near Lewellen, still beckon travelers. *Nebraska Game Commission photo*

The Missouri River bluffs, just below the mouth of the Platte River. Lithograph by E. Robyn, 1855. *Courtesy State Historical Society of Missouri*

The Missouri River valley, Nebraska. *Nebraska Game Commission photo*

Water-level control dams upstream and navigational aids make the Missouri usable throughout the shipping season. *Nebraska Game Commission photo*

At the Brownville Historical Society Museum, displays trace the settlement of the area from discovery through the days when this community was a bustling port on the Missouri River. *Nebraska Game Commission photo*

Indian Cave State Park, newest and largest in the state, will soon arise from the past. Astride Richardson and Nemaha counties, the 4,200-acre treasure of history is a giant step forward. Development is included in the ten-year park program. Legend records that John Brown hid escaped slaves in this cave overlooking the winding Missouri. The cave's history dates back to early Indians, evidenced through drawings on the cave walls. *Nebraska Game Commission photo*

Drawing by Henry Howe of Lawrence, Kansas, on the Kansas River on its way to meet the Missouri, 1855. *Courtesy Saint Louis Public Library*

Running eastward, the Missouri River enters Missouri. These are the bluffs above Saint Joseph, Missouri. *From Annual Report of the Missouri Geological Survey, 1855. Courtesy Missouri Historical Society*

Drawing by R. B. Rice of a steam mill below the bluffs at Weston, Missouri, 1853. *Courtesy Missouri Historical Society*

conade and the Osage. The latter has been dammed at Bagnell, Missouri, creating the Lake of the Ozarks, a favorite Missouri recreational center. The 2,714-mile Missouri is the longest river in North America and drains a basin of 518,000 square miles. It reaches a width of 3,000 feet at its mouth, where its rate of water discharge is 120,000 cubic feet a second.

The Missouri River basin was first explored by Coronado for Spain in 1541, but it was the French who pioneered its development in the eighteenth century. French explorers from Canada ascended the Missouri as far as the Kansas River in 1705, confirming the report of French-Canadian traders in 1659 of a "great river that divides itself in two." Etienne de Bourgmond led an expedition up the Missouri to its junction with the Platte in 1714 in a successful effort to establish friendly relations with the Indians. This proved to be beneficial to the French when in 1720 these same Indians massacred a hostile Spanish expedition. To prevent further Spanish incursions from Santa Fe, de Bourgmond installed a French garrison at Fort Orleans, on the Missouri, in 1723.

French fur trading was greatly expanded after the founding of Saint Louis in 1764. The post set up there by Maxent, Laclede and Company became the base for numerous trading expeditions up the Missouri. The upper reaches of the valley had been explored in 1742 by Pierre Gaultier, Sieur de La Vérendrye, assuring French dominion despite Spanish control of the territory under the treaty of San Ildefonso in 1762.

Auguste and Pierre Chouteau made a fortune in

Lithograph by John Casper Wild of the mouth of the Missouri River, 1841. Courtesy *Saint Louis Public Library*

The confluence of the Missouri (left) and Mississippi (right) rivers, above Saint Louis, today. Courtesy *U.S. Corps of Engineers, Saint Louis District*

Pierre Chouteau, Jr., partner of John Jacob Astor in the western fur trade and a dominant figure in commercial enterprises in the upper Mississippi Valley. *From* History of the Louisiana Purchase Exposition, *1904*

Manual Lisa was the first fur trader to penetrate the upper Missouri Valley. His influence among the Indians succeeded in keeping them under control during the War of 1812, despite activity by British agents. *From* History of the Louisiana Purchase Exposition, *1904*

western fur trading in the late eighteenth century from their headquarters at Saint Louis. After control of the territory passed to the United States in 1803, the Missouri Fur Company was founded by the Chouteaus, Manuel Lisa, William Clark, and others. Clark had become well acquainted with the country through his expedition with Meriwether Lewis in 1804–1806. During this period the only method of traversing the river upstream was by the cordelling of keelboats, and returning by keelboats, mackinaws, or bullboats.

The introduction of the steamboat on the Missouri in 1819 revolutionized fur-trading operations. This first steamboat was the *Independence,* which went upriver to Franklin, Missouri. In the same year an expedition under Stephen H. Long reached the present site of Omaha. Long's boat, the *Western Engineer,* was a most unusual craft. On its bow was a black serpent's head, with a red tongue, which spewed forth smoke and steam, much to the consternation of the Indians.

Fur traders were responsible for founding posts that later became some of the Midwest's leading cities. Kansas City dates its beginning in 1821 from a trading post founded by François Chouteau; Joseph Robidoux, a fur company agent, started Saint Joseph in 1826; and a trader's cabin was erected in 1825 at the present site of Omaha. The Missouri River became the principal route for migrating settlers to the West.

In 1830 Kenneth McKenzie, Chouteau's agent on the upper Missouri, persuaded his employer to send a steamboat to try to reach the posts far up the river. The new company sidewheeler *Yellowstone* was dispatched to Fort Pierre in 1831. Low water prevented the 130-foot craft from proceeding farther upstream. However in 1832, during the June rise, the boat penetrated as far as Fort Union, at the mouth of the Yellowstone River. Below the Platte, the Missouri was generally navigable during normal rainfall, but above there advantage had to be taken of the April and June rises, fed by melting

The *Independence,* the first steamboat to ascend the Missouri River, at Franklin, Missouri, 1819. Mural by Victor Higgins in the Missouri State Capitol at Jefferson City

Painting by Carl Bodmer of Fort Pierre, South Dakota, on the Missouri River in the 1830s. *Courtesy Saint Louis Mercantile Library Association*

Painting by Carl Bodmer of the American Fur Company sidewheeler *Yellowstone* on the upper Missouri River, 1833. *Courtesy Missouri Historical Society*

Painting by Carl Bodmer of Fort Union, on the Missouri. Assiniboine Indians are breaking camp, 1835. *Courtesy Saint Louis Mercantile Library Association*

snow, in order to reach Fort Union in even the lightest-draft riverboats.

Fur-trade boats set records for navigation and resulted in better steamboat design. Boatbuilders learned that shallower drafts, broader beams, and lighter-weight construction and machinery contributed to greater ease in steamboat handling. The principal lesson learned, however, was that sternwheel boats were much more maneuverable in shallow water than were side-wheel boats.

Among the unique problems encountered by steamboats on the Missouri was that the abundant

Etching by Captain Basil Hall of banks of the Missouri falling in, 1829. *Courtesy Ardell Thompson Collection, Saint Louis*

river silt soon clogged boiler valves and pipes, a condition that resulted in many sinkings. Another trouble was the steamboat's inability to travel the treacherous river at night and the consequent loss of time. Raids by hostile Indians, when the boats tied up to take on fuel wood, required constant vigilance by armed boatmen.

In 1834 Pierre Chouteau, Jr., purchased the western department of the American Fur Company from John Jacob Astor and established control as the dominant fur operator in the West. In order to improve their image with the public, the company hired John C. Frémont and the famous French geologist Joseph Nicolas Nicollet to make a scientific expedition into the Missouri Valley to further the general knowledge of the area. This resulted in other expeditions, by missionaries such as Father De Smet, surveyors, artists, and tourists to visit the fur country.

Painting by Carl Bodmer of snags on the Missouri River, 1835. These obstructions took the life of many boats—and passengers. *Courtesy Saint Louis Mercantile Library Association*

A favorite stopping place for westward-bound travelers on the Missouri River and the Santa Fe Trail was old Arrow Rock Tavern built in 1834. It is preserved in Missouri's Arrow Rock State Park. *Walker-Missouri Tourism photo*

Steamboats did not navigate the Missouri above Fort Union until well after 1850, necessitating the use of mackinaw batteaux to bring hides and pelts to Fort Union for transfer to the steamboats. These mackinaw boats were cheaply built and were shaped like a scow, averaging forty feet in length and ten feet in beam, with a draft of under twenty inches. Their crews consisted of a steersman, who perched high in the stern, and several oarsmen, who were grouped fore and aft. The cargo rode in the center of the boat, covered by animal skins tightly drawn over a crude wooden framework. These boats were broken up or abandoned at their downriver destination and the return trip was usually made overland.

The sandy, silt-laden character of the river gave way, about halfway across Montana, to a rocky section that extended to Fort Benton. In later years when Indian trade with the Blackfeet and Crows increased, and after pilots learned to respect the sandy river and its violent windstorms during the brief ice-to-ice navigation period, the fur-company steamboats began to venture into Montana. It was not until 1860 that the steamer *Chippewa* reached Fort Benton, and finally in 1865 the *Tom Stevens* penetrated to the ultimate head of navigation at Portage Creek, five miles below the Great Falls.

Changes in the fur market meant a change in the commodities shipped downriver; beaver pelts were replaced by buffalo robes as the most important item. Deer and muskrat were also trapped in greater quantities due to accelerated demand.

The route along the Missouri to the Platte and then westward along the Oregon Trail on the Platte's south bank was followed by most of the California-bound gold seekers in 1849, and, until the advent of the railroad, by western wagon trains of settlers. This was also the route of the Overland Trail and the Pony Express. Most of the westward-moving settlers bypassed the upper Missouri until after the Civil War, resulting in slow settlement of the Nebraska and Dakota territories. The discovery of gold in Montana in 1861 sent a rush of prospectors and settlers up the river and caused a disorganization in the fur trade, from which it never fully recovered.

After the death of Pierre Chouteau, Jr., in 1865, the American Fur Company relinquished its Upper Missouri Outfit, causing a decrease in the importance of Saint Louis as a fur-trading center, but the city turned to other business activity to strengthen its commercial position.

The extension of the railroads had the same diminishing effect upon the steamboat traffic on the Missouri that it had on the Mississippi and the other western rivers. The boat lines merely became feeders to the railheads, and as the rails reached more and more upriver ports, the packet business declined and by 1900 had disappeared. The river traffic is now all freight, carried as far as Sioux City, Iowa, on barges propelled by towboats in a channel maintained by dredging by the Army Engineers.

The U.S. Corps of Engineers inspection boat *Sergeant Floyd* and passenger barge on the Missouri River. *Missouri Tourism Commission photo*

A barge tow on the Missouri River, once a highway to the West. Today, water-level control dams upstream and navigational aids make the river usable throughout the shipping season. *Nebraska Game Commission photo*

Light-draft boats operate above there to Yankton, South Dakota, below the Gavin Point Dam. A revival of river traffic on the Missouri, in the form of barge-line operations, began after 1912 when Congress appropriated twenty million dollars to improve the river from Kansas City to its mouth.

In recent years, several large hydroelectric dams have been built in the Missouri River basin by the U.S. Bureau of Reclamation and the Army Corps of Engineers. Among these are the dams at Fort Peck and Canyon Ferry, Montana, Garrison, North Dakota, and Oahe and Fort Randall, South Dakota. The power produced at these and other installations in the basin is marketed by the Department of the Interior through a network of more than nine thousand miles of transmission lines. Storage dams constructed in the basin provide irrigation for millions of acres.

The Missouri, whose name comes from the Algonquian *missui* (big) and the Dakota *souri* (muddy), plays an important part in the nation's economy today, matching its illustrious past.

Gavin Point Dam near Crofton, Nebraska, on the Missouri River. *Nebraska Game Commission photo*

THE OHIO RIVER

The Ohio River is formed by the junction of the Allegheny and Monongahela rivers at Pittsburgh, Pennsylvania. Flowing westward and then southwestward, the 981-mile-long river and its banks form boundaries for the states of West Virginia, Ohio, Kentucky, Indiana, and Illinois before its waters enter the Mississippi River at Cairo, Illinois. The Ohio is the chief tributary of the Mississippi from the east and its principal tributaries are, from the south, the Kanawha, Big Sandy, Licking, Kentucky, Green, Cumberland, and Tennessee rivers,

Drawing by A. R. Waud of the Ohio River, below Pittsburgh. *From Picturesque America, 1872. Courtesy Saint Louis Mercantile Library Association*

A dock on the Ohio today, Wellsville, Ohio, for unloading petroleum. *Courtesy State of Ohio, Department of Industrial and Economic Development*

Wellsville's River Museum, built in 1811 when the town was a famous port between Pittsburgh and Wheeling. *Courtesy State of Ohio, Department of Industrial and Economic Development*

Junction of the Ohio River (right) and the Mississippi River (left) at Fort Defiance State Park, Cairo, Illinois. *Courtesy State of Illinois, Department of Conservation*

and, from the north, the Muskingum, Scioto, Miami, and Wabash rivers. It drains a large, productive, heavily populated valley, with many large cities along its course. Frequent costly floods have resulted in the construction of extensive river-control works, such as locks and dams to aid navigation and to furnish hydroelectric power. The river was characterized by a shallowness that permitted navigation only during high-water periods, until the completion of a nine-foot channel through canalization in 1929. The present channel is from four hundred to six hundred feet wide and remains

Drawing by A. R. Waud of an early lock and dam on the Muskingum River at Marietta, Ohio, which emptied into the Ohio. *From Picturesque America, 1872. Courtesy Saint Louis Mercantile Library Association*

Above Marietta was Long Reach on the Ohio River. *From A Journey in North America—1796, General Victor Collot. Courtesy Saint Louis Mercantile Library Association*

Drawing by A. R. Waud of the Ohio at Marietta. *From Picturesque America, 1872. Courtesy Saint Louis Mercantile Library Association*

open for twelve months a year. The Ohio, for most of its course, flows through scenic hilly country, which earned it the sobriquet *La Belle Rivière* (Beautiful River) by early French explorers. The name Ohio is derived from the Iroquois Indian *O-he-yo* (Great River), later Anglicized by the English.

Although the State of Ohio is named for the river, no part of the stream is within the state's boundaries; agreements establishing the Northwest Territory in the eighteenth century gave West Virginia and Kentucky control over the river to its low-water mark on the north side. The use of steam

On the Ohio River, at Point Pleasant, is the birthplace of President U. S. Grant. *Courtesy State of Ohio, Department of Industrial and Economic Development*

to navigate the Ohio first occurred to James Rumsey of Virginia in 1785. His proposal was for a boat that would be propelled by water being pumped out at the stern, an idea which proved unfeasible. It was much later that Robert Fulton, with others, built his steamboat *New Orleans* at Pittsburgh, in 1810. The *New Orleans* traveled downstream to New Orleans but was unable to return upstream, a feat first accomplished by Henry Shreve's *Washington* in 1816.

The steamboat brought prosperity to the Ohio Valley. Steamboat arrivals at Cincinnati tripled to a thousand between 1825 and 1829, and increased to four thousand by 1848. Steam furnished the motive power to colonize the West and to build some of her towns into metropolises. Here, too, though, the steamboat began to be eclipsed by the railroad in the decade before the Civil War, when Ohio River traffic diminished after 1856. During the war the Ohio remained an important waterway for the movement of troops and supplies, although no military action of importance took place on the river. After the war, coal towing supported river traffic on the Ohio as packet lines decreased in importance.

Painting by Carl Bodmer of Cave-in-Rock, c. 1835, on the Ohio River, shows the steamboat at this time to be fairly well developed in design. *Courtesy Saint Louis Mercantile Library Association*

Since the first River and Harbor Act of 1824, the Army Corps of Engineers had been engaged in snag and wreck removal work on the Ohio. Shortly after the Civil War, the Engineers were made responsible for river survey work as well. W. Milnor Roberts, chief engineer at Pittsburgh, recommended a slack-

Veteran troops moving up the Ohio to Louisville and Cincinnati. The Ohio River was used extensively during the Civil War as a marine route for the transport of Union troops in both directions. Boatyards along the river were the scene of wartime construction activity for river vessels of all types, since the Ohio Valley was practically untouched by military engagements. *From Harper's Pictorial History of the Civil War*

Large group of steamboats assembled at the Monongahela Wharf in Pittsburgh during the celebration of the completion of the Ohio River canalization system in 1929. *Courtesy U.S. Corps of Engineers, Pittsburgh District*

water system of locks and dams on the Ohio in 1868. This system was finally adopted in 1875, when three hundred thousand dollars was appropriated for Lock and Dam Number One at Davis Island, below Pittsburgh. This project was completed in 1885 and was the first in a series of fifty-three watery stairsteps that was to reach from Pittsburgh to Cairo by 1929. Increasing river traffic after World War II made the Ohio's system of locks and dams inadequate, which for large tows meant double lockage, or the breaking up of the line of barges to duplicate the effort. In 1954 the Army Engineers began construction of nineteen new locks and dams, with lock chambers twelve hundred feet long. This billion-dollar project, which is still underway, will carry river traffic from an elevation of 700 feet above sea level at Pittsburgh to 275 feet at Cairo.

The motor vessel *Frank C. Rand* leaving Lock No. 10 on the Ohio River in August, 1951. *Courtesy U.S. Corps of Engineers, Pittsburgh District*

THE ALLEGHENY RIVER

The Allegheny River rises in northern Pennsylvania and flows northwestward into New York State. Turning southwest, it again enters Pennsylvania to complete its 325-mile course at Pittsburgh, where it joins the Monongahela to form the Ohio River. Its name comes from the Indian and means "stream of the cave people."

During the early nineteenth century, the rocky course of the Allegheny precluded the growth of steamboating on the river, except for very shallow-draft boats. Steamboats ran on the river as early as 1828, but most navigation was by raft and flatboat. By the late 1830s, small boats could operate as far upstream as Warren, Pennsylvania, during high water.

A flourishing trade for steamboats on the Allegheny was created by the discovery of oil, in its upper valley, in the early 1860s. Little progress in river improvement on the Allegheny was made until the 1890s when canalization work began. It was completed in 1938, when the slack-water system extended for seventy-two miles, ending in the Brady's Bend area. In such a system, the river is impounded in pools above the dam to slacken the river's normal flow. Low bridges obstructing navigation were a problem on the lower river for many years. These bridges were finally modified in 1917, under the pressure of shipping during World War I.

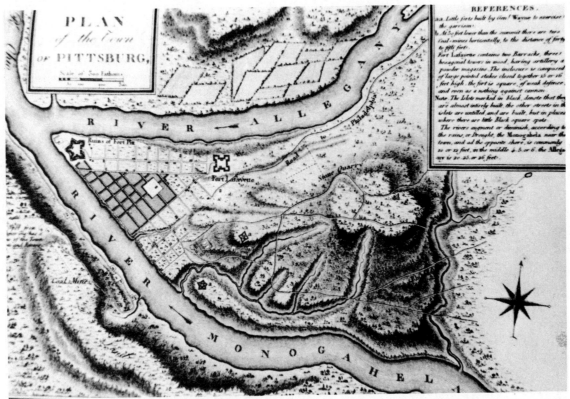

Plan of Pittsburgh showing conjunction of the Allegheny and Monongahela rivers. From A Journey in North America—1796, General Victor Collot. Courtesy Saint Louis Mercantile Library Association

Following the devastating flood of 1936 at Pittsburgh, flood-control work began on the Allegheny and its tributaries, as well as on the Monongahela system. The resulting creation of thirteen flood-control reservoirs in the Pittsburgh Engineer District has prevented flood damage far exceeding their cost. The present system of locks and dams on the Allegheny, with its nine-foot channel, is considered adequate for projected tonnage volumes averaging five million tons per year.

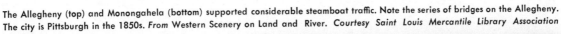

The Allegheny (top) and Monongahela (bottom) supported considerable steamboat traffic. Note the series of bridges on the Allegheny. The city is Pittsburgh in the 1850s. From Western Scenery on Land and River. Courtesy Saint Louis Mercantile Library Association

THE MONONGAHELA RIVER

The Monongahela River is formed by the junction of the West Fork and Tygart rivers near Fairmont, West Virginia, and flows northward into Pennsylvania for 128 miles to join the Allegheny at Pittsburgh. Also of Indian derivation, Monongahela means "high banks falling down."

The Monongahela Valley was a center for the building of thousands of flatboats to take the pioneer settlers westward down the Ohio. One of these boats was the first of its kind to descend the Mississippi. It was launched at Brownsville, Pennsylvania, in 1782 by Jacob Yoder, who took several months to reach the Gulf of Mexico over two thousand miles away.

Before the nineteenth century, enterprising shipbuilders at Monongahela River ports were constructing sea-going vessels to carry midwestern exports to foreign points. In 1798–1799 they launched two armed galleys, when it seemed that war was inevitable because of clashes between French, Spanish, and American interests in the Mississippi Valley. These vessels were two masted and lateen rigged, and each carried a twenty-four-pound gun for possible service in the first American inland navy.

After the Louisiana Purchase assured American control of the Mississippi Valley, the importance of river improvements became readily apparent in the Ohio Valley. State legislators in 1808 drafted bills to protect all river-control works, and the Monongahela Navigation Company was chartered in

A scenic bend in the Monongahela River at Newell, Pennsylvania. *Courtesy Pennsylvania Scenic and Historic Commission*

Pennsylvania to build dams on the river. Although the company failed in 1822, valley residents raised money to clear the river from Brownsville to Pittsburgh. The Pennsylvania Assembly appropriated ten thousand dollars to remove snags and boulders from the Monongahela in 1822. A state survey of the Monongahela was made in 1828, followed by a federal survey in 1833, which proposed a system of locks and dams. A second Monongahela Navigation Company was organized in 1836, for the purpose of building a slack-water system from Pittsburgh to the state line. In 1844 the company's six locks and dams were opened, creating a link with the Cumberland Road at Brownsville, Pennsylvania. A similar enterprise was completed on the Monongahela's chief tributary, the Youghiogheny River in 1848. However, it was an ill-starred project whose dams broke in 1854 and were not rebuilt. The Monongahela Navigation Company operated successfully and collected over two million dollars in tolls in its first ten years of operation serving the coal trade. A clash between the company and the federal government developed in 1886, when Congress stipulated that no tolls could be charged by the company on river traffic that originated above government dams on the Monongahela. Coal operators were paying the company an average toll of six and a half cents a ton, whereas West Virginians were shipping coal toll-free as the result of government improvements on the Kanawha. After a year of condemnation litigation, the government purchased the Navigation Company in 1897 for $3,761,615. With the abolition of tolls, traffic increased from four and a half million tons in 1896 to over twenty million tons annually by 1920. In the period between 1902 and 1932, nine of the Monongahela River's locks and dams were rebuilt to more modern standards. In later years the Corps of Engineers completed canalization of the Monongahela to its headwaters and rebuilt all of the Navigation Company's original locks. Continuing replacement of obsolete navigation dams is in progress on the Monongahela, in an effort to achieve a nine-foot channel depth.

THE MUSKINGUM RIVER

The Muskingum River is formed in eastern Ohio by the union of the Walhonding and Tuscarawas rivers. It flows about 112 miles in a southerly direction to meet the Ohio River at Marietta. The lower

On the banks of the Muskingum River at Malta-McConnelsville, Ohio. *Courtesy State of Ohio, Department of Education*

Confluence of the Kanawha and Ohio rivers at Point Pleasant, West Virginia. *Photo by Dave Cruise. Courtesy State of West Virginia, Department of Commerce*

part of the river is followed by the Ohio and Erie Canal as far as Zanesville.

Steamboats began navigating the Muskingum as early as 1824, but expansion of traffic on the river did not occur until after the completion of river improvements in the 1840s. At that time steamboats operated from Zanesville to Ohio River ports such as Parkersburg, West Virginia, and Pittsburgh.

The canalization of the Muskingum, known as the Muskingum Improvement, was part of an extensive system of canals in Ohio. Work began in 1837 and was completed in 1842, extending sixty-eight miles from Marietta to Dresden, Ohio. The system was well used until the coming of the railroads in the 1850s.

THE KANAWHA RIVER

The Kanawha River is formed in Fayette County, West Virginia, by the junction of the Gauley and New rivers, and flows ninety-seven miles northwest to join the Ohio River at Point Pleasant, West Virginia. The Kanawha was extensively improved by the federal government during the nineteenth century with a lock and dam system. The Kanawha Valley once was an important natural source for salt and contains many coalfields in the area above its chief port at Charleston. A nine-foot channel is maintained on the Kanawha, with three locks, each fifty-six by three hundred feet. The river is open to navigation year-round. Other navigable rivers in West Virginia include the Little Kanawha, which could be traversed by steamboat on slack-water navigation from its mouth at Parkersburg, on the

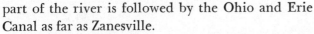

Construction work on a guide wall for a lock on the Little Kanawha River, West Virginia, about 1910. *Courtesy Waterways Journal*

On the Kanawha River, near its mouth, at Point Pleasant, West Virginia, about 1900. *Courtesy Waterways Journal*

Ohio, to the oil regions of Burning Springs, West Virginia. During the nineteenth century, the Big Sandy and Guyandot rivers were much used by flatboats and lumber rafts.

On the Big Sandy River, West Virginia, 1909, at Lock No. 2, the steamer *Enquirer*. This boat was named after the Cincinnati newspaper. *Courtesy Waterways Journal*

The Kentucky River's palisades of birds-eye limestone. *Courtesy Kentucky Department of Public Information*

THE KENTUCKY RIVER

The Kentucky River is formed by two forks rising in the Cumberland Mountains. After a winding northwestern course of 260 miles, it enters the Ohio at Carrollton, Kentucky. The river flows for many miles through a picturesque gorge in the bird's-eye limestone, and has fine canyon scenery between Frankfort and Boonesborough.

Steamboats began to operate on the Kentucky River about 1816, but navigation was restricted to a few small boats, which could run as far as Frankfort during high water periods only.

Improvement work on the Kentucky began in 1836, but was discontinued in 1842 after the completion of five dams below Frankfort, about sixty-six miles above its mouth. By the late nineteenth century, the U.S. Government had spent about $1,500,000 for navigation improvements on the Kentucky, which during flooding could be ascended by small boats as far as Beattyville, 261 miles from the Ohio. Now the Kentucky is controlled by a series of fourteen locks and dams that provide a channel to Beattyville.

An old arsenal at Frankfort, on the Kentucky, makes a strange contrast with the junk passing by. *Courtesy Kentucky Department of Public Information*

After 1841 such steamboats were a common sight on the Green River seen here near Owensboro, Kentucky. *Courtesy Saint Louis Public Library*

Miss Green River has replaced steamboating on the Green River. *Courtesy Kentucky Department of Public Information*

A "flatboat" of today, strictly for pleasure. Kentucky River, at Frankfort. *Courtesy Kentucky Department of Public Information*

Boonesborough State Park, Kentucky's newest, most popular state park, located on the Kentucky's shores just below Lock No. 10. *Courtesy Kentucky Department of Public Information*

THE GREEN AND BARREN RIVERS

The 350-mile Green River rises near the center of Kentucky and flows north and northwest, passing near Mammoth Cave, and enters the Ohio River nine miles above Evansville, Indiana. In 1831 a steamboat managed to ascend the Green and its chief tributary, the Barren River, to Bowling Green, Kentucky, a distance of 180 miles. But steamboating was irregular until the completion of a slack-water system in 1841.

In 1863, on July 4, the Green River was the site of a severe defeat inflicted upon Morgan's Confederate raiders by entrenched Union forces at Tebbs Bend.

Mining is the principal industry served by the Green River, whose lower course is through the coalfields of western Kentucky. A nine-foot channel maintained by several locks and dams runs over a hundred miles.

On the Wabash River, about 1905, the steamboat *Clarence Thorn*, built at Mount Carmel, Illinois. She was typical of the smaller boats which operated in short trades. *Courtesy Waterways Journal*

THE WABASH RIVER

The Wabash River originates in west-central Ohio. After following a winding course across Indiana it becomes the boundary between Ohio and Illinois until emptying into the Ohio River below Mount Vernon, Indiana. The Wabash, which is about 475 miles in length, at one time was navigable by steamboat, for three or four months of the year as far as Lafayette, Indiana.

Steamboating began on the Wabash before 1820 and, despite impediments such as rapids, increased to sixty arrivals at Lafayette during 1832. Other principal ports on the river were Terre Haute and Vincennes. Completion of a lock and dam at Grand Rapids, near Vincennes, in 1849 eliminated the worst navigational obstruction. During the 1850s, an active commerce between Wabash River ports and Ohio River cities developed, as did some commerce between the Wabash and New Orleans. After the Civil War, government appropriations contributed substantially to the improvement of the Wabash and other Ohio River tributaries. River traffic on the Wabash declined as a result of railroad competition after 1900, following the general trend that beset all western river commerce.

THE CUMBERLAND RIVER

The Cumberland River rises in eastern Kentucky, winds for seven hundred miles down into Tennessee, swings back north through western Kentucky, and enters the Ohio River at Smithland, Kentucky.

During the steamboat era it was navigable to Nashville during the whole year, and as far as the head of Smith's Shoals (529 miles) in periods of high water. The Cumberland was the Ohio tributary on which steamboating developed to the greatest extent. The first attempt at steamboat operation occurred at Nashville in 1816, when local interests formed a navigation company. The first boat to reach Nashville was the *General Jackson* in 1818, and by 1825 regular service to New Orleans and Louisville was maintained. This led to the exchange of greater amounts of produce and a considerable drop in prices, creating a much improved economic climate in the Cumberland Valley.

During the Civil War, Fort Donelson, on the Cumberland, was taken by Union forces under General Grant and Commodore Foote in a short but severe battle.

In the 1890s a large freight-steamboat traffic flourished on the Cumberland, carrying grain, tobacco, and lumber. At that time the government was improving the stream for navigation from Burnside to Pineville, near the Cumberland Gap. Today there are several TVA dams on the Cumberland and a nine-foot channel is projected from the mouth to Celina, Tennessee, with locks and dams for navigation and irrigation. The river, discovered by a party of Virginians in 1748 and named for the Duke of Cumberland, plays an important role in the economy of the Southeast.

THE TENNESSEE RIVER

The largest tributary of the Ohio River is the Tennessee, which is formed four miles above Knoxville by the junction of the Holston and French Broad rivers. It is 650 miles long, traversing eastern Tennessee to Chattanooga, sweeping around through northern Alabama, and turning northward to again cross Tennessee, and on to Kentucky before entering the Ohio at Paducah. The Tennessee River drains forty-one thousand square miles and falls two thousand feet along the way. Its chief tributaries are the Clinch, Little Tennessee, Hiwassee, Elk, and Duck rivers. Despite its size, the Tennessee was not commercially important in the early nineteenth century, because of the lack of towns in its lower valley and the navigational obstructions at Muscle

Commodore Foote's gunboat flotilla on the Mississippi. *From Harper's Pictorial History of the Civil War*

Norris Dam, situated in the foothills of the Cumberlands, was the first to be completed and is possibly the best-known unit of the giant T.V.A. system. *Courtesy State of Tennessee, Division of State Information*

The Cumberland today, at South Fork, is especially noted for its walleye pike, judging by the number of fishermen. *Courtesy Kentucky Department of Public Information*

Drawing by Harry Fenn of the Tennessee River at Chattanooga. *From Picturesque America, 1872. Courtesy Saint Louis Mercantile Library Association*

This wharf at Clifton, Tennessee, on the Tennessee River was visited by every type of riverboat afloat. *Courtesy Webster Groves Book Shop*

The Bloody Pond at the battlefield of Shiloh, Tennessee. *Courtesy State of Tennessee Conservation Department*

Shoals, Alabama. Except for a few weeks of high-water stages, it was necessary to transship all cargoes at the Shoals for points on the upper Tennessee.

Steamboating began on the lower river about 1817, but the head of navigation, below the Shoals at Florence, Alabama, was not reached until 1821. Trade later developed to Louisville and New Orleans.

Efforts were made to organize a steamboat company at Knoxville, on the upper river, in 1825, but proved unsuccessful. Three years later, the first boat to force its way past the Shoals reached Knoxville. Limited operations with small boats between Decatur, Alabama, and Knoxville, on the upper river, and on the Clinch and other tributaries were reported during the 1850s. As late as the early nineties, several steam freight boats plied the upper Tennessee, and many laden flatboats came down the upper tributaries from Virginia and North Carolina, bearing produce for Knoxville.

The Tennessee played an important part in the Civil War, as both sides realized its strategic significance. After the fall of Fort Henry and the occupation of Nashville, Union control of the lower Tennessee Valley was assured by bloody victory at Shiloh. After a succession of defeats, the Confederates, under General Bragg, turned at bay at Chickamauga and inflicted a severe beating on the Federals, whom they besieged in Chattanooga. In October, 1863, control of the upper Tennessee passed to the Union, when armies under Grant and Sherman won brilliant victories at Lookout Mountain and Missionary Ridge, driving the Southerners into Georgia. The mountain counties of eastern Tennessee refused to join the secession movement and remained loyal to the Union.

After the war steamboat traffic enjoyed a resurgence because of the lack of railroads here, but continued to be impeded by Muscle Shoals. A canal around the Shoals was started in 1836 and improved in 1876 but was never used commercially.

The government began construction of the Wilson hydroelectric dam and two nitrate plants at the Shoals in 1916, to meet demands of World War I. During the 1920s, the project was expected to come under private industry but became the nucleus for the Tennessee Valley Authority in 1933. The T.V.A. has canalized the Tennessee River through the construction of a series of locks and dams to provide a nine-foot channel from Knoxville to its mouth. During World War II, T.V.A. supplied

Steamboats at Pittsburg Landing, Tennessee, after the Battle of Shiloh. The steamer farthest upstream (right) is the *Universe*. The next steamer, the *Tigress*, was General Grant's headquarters boat. On the opposite shore is the gunboat *Tyler*. *Courtesy Boatmen's National Bank of St. Louis*

power for the atomic energy plant at Oak Ridge, Tennessee.

River commerce has increased considerably in recent years, principally in petroleum, steel, chemicals, grain, and automobiles. Eight T.V.A. dams maintain a series of broad pools that are heavily used for recreation and flood control, and to operate hydroelectric plants, which provide cheap power. Other T.V.A. activities include conservation and the development of natural resources.

A section of the mile-long Pickwick Dam of the T.V.A. system adjacent to Shiloh, Tennessee. The tailwaters of the dam constitute excellent year-round fishing waters. *Courtesy State of Tennessee, Division of State Information*

This chart represents pictorially how the Tennessee River is controlled and stepped down by dams. The map below shows the area geographically. *Courtesy Tennessee Valley Authority*

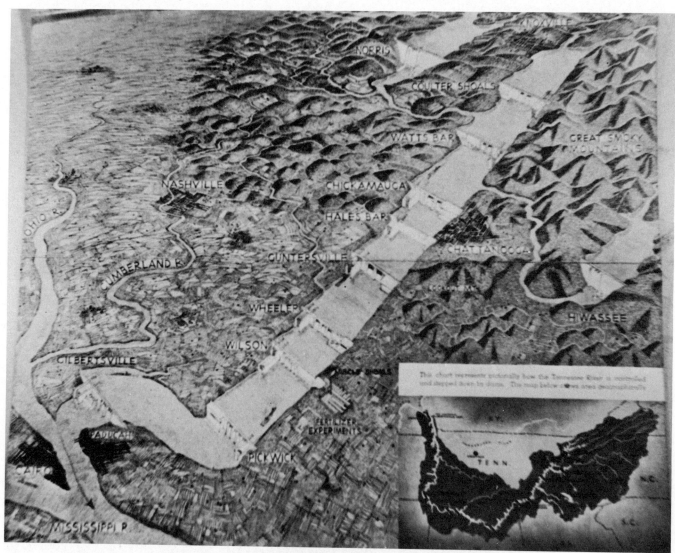

III
The River Cities

HOW RIVER TRAFFIC INFLUENCED URBAN GROWTH

The western river system has been the lifeline of civilization in America's grand westward migration, which developed our great nation. After the explorers, missionaries, and trappers, came the settlers. They established the first outposts in the wilderness, some of which became the populous river cities of today. Many of these settlements never developed beyond the village or town stage, while others completely disappeared, either deserted by their citizens or destroyed by the menacing river. Those that prospered, either through the happy circumstance of fate or knowledgeable use of assets, are now the metropolitan centers of the Mississippi Valley.

The river cities, regardless of origin, tradition, culture, or size, owe their existence to their riverside locations. The diverse stories of these communities are described here in geographical sequence, from the upper reaches of the principal rivers to their mouths.

MISSISSIPPI RIVER CITIES

MINNEAPOLIS, MINNESOTA

The Falls of Saint Anthony, at the present site of Minneapolis, were discovered and named by the French missionary Father Louis Hennepin in 1680. In 1805, after the Louisiana Purchase, Lieutenant Zebulon M. Pike purchased land from the Indians and established a military reservation, where Fort Snelling was built, in 1819. The town of Saint Anthony was founded on the east bank of the Mississippi, at the falls, in 1838, and a town called Min-

Drawing by A. R. Waud of Minneapolis and the Falls of Saint Anthony. *From Picturesque America, 1872. Courtesy Saint Louis Mercantile Library Association*

Minneapolis in 1882, showing suspension bridge and the falls. *From* Down the Great River, 1887. *Courtesy Saint Louis Mercantile Library Association*

neapolis was settled on the west bank in 1849; the name is derived from the Indian *minne* (water) and the Greek *polis* (city). Minneapolis was chartered as a city in 1867, and in 1872 absorbed Saint Anthony to form the basis for the present metropolis.

Because of water power, developed at the falls, and the rich grain lands nearby, Minneapolis has become the largest milling center in the world. It had long been a major lumber production center.

As the head of navigation on the Mississippi, only small boats were able to reach the city until completion of a nine-foot channel in 1939. Since then, a large upper-river harbor has been built and barge traffic has accelerated rapidly.

SAINT PAUL, MINNESOTA

The earliest permanent white settlement in Minnesota was a fur-trading post at Mendota in 1819. Located across the Mississippi from the present site of Saint Paul, Mendota grew into a village by 1834, when it was known as Saint Peter's. A Jesuit mission dedicated to Saint Paul, from which the city takes its name, was established on the site in 1841. Experiencing a steady influx of Irish and German

Lithograph by Henry Lewis of Saint Paul, Menesotah Territory, in the 1840s. *Courtesy Saint Louis Mercantile Library Association*

Lock and Dam No. 24, Clarksville, Missouri, on the upper Mississippi River, part of the canalization project completed in 1939. *Courtesy U.S. Corps of Engineers, Saint Louis District*

Fort Snelling, near Saint Paul, about 1850, shortly after the city's founding. *From The United States Illustrated, 1855. Courtesy Saint Louis Mercantile Library Association*

View of Saint Paul in 1881. *From Down the Great River, 1887. Courtesy Saint Louis Mercantile Library Association*

Drawing by A. R. Waud of Saint Paul seen from Dayton's Bluff. *From Picturesque America, 1872. Courtesy Saint Louis Mercantile Library Association*

immigrants arriving by steamboat, the town had a population of 642 in 1849, when it was chosen as the territorial capital of Minnesota. The city was incorporated in 1854, when it had grown to nearly ten thousand inhabitants.

Saint Paul owes a great part of its modern development to James J. Hill, who arrived in 1856 and began building his railroad empire from his Saint Paul headquarters. By 1884 Saint Paul's population passed the hundred thousand mark, and the city became the major transportation and distribution center of the north-central states. River traffic there has experienced a renaissance since the present upper Mississippi canalization project was opened in 1939.

A closer view of Saint Paul, 1873. Drawing by Henry Howe. *Courtesy Saint Louis Public Library*

RED WING, MINNESOTA

An Indian village named for Chief Red Wing by French explorers was formed here by Father Hennepin in 1680. A Swiss mission to the Indians operated in 1836–1840, and in 1852 the present community of Red Wing was begun. Picturesquely situated on the Mississippi at the head of Lake Pepin, Red Wing has a long history as a river town and is the location of Lock and Dam Number Three of the upper Mississippi River navigation system.

Drawing by A. R. Waud of Steamboat Landing at La Crosse, Wisconsin, and view of Mississippi River scenery above the city. *From Picturesque America, 1872. Courtesy Saint Louis Mercantile Library Association*

Lake Pepin from the river bluffs. *From Down the Great River, 1887. Courtesy Saint Louis Mercantile Library Association*

wooded valleys. The name came from an Indian game that reminded early French travelers of the French game *la crosse*. Founded in 1842, La Crosse was entirely dependent upon river traffic until the coming of the railroads. An average of two hundred steamboats a month docked there at the peak of the river era in 1856–1857. Lumbering became the dominant industry by the late fifties, but when the forests were depleted the city turned to diversified manufactures.

PRAIRIE DU CHIEN, WISCONSIN

Prairie du Chien, on the Mississippi just above the mouth of the Wisconsin River, is one of the oldest cities in Wisconsin. In 1686 Nicolas Perrot built a fort on the site, which was situated on the early ex-

WINONA, MINNESOTA

Winona is located on an island between Lake Winona and the Mississippi River. It was once the site of a Sioux Indian village. Winona was founded in 1851 by Captain Orrin Smith, whose steamboat was the *Nominee*. In 1852, after the Indians withdrew from the region, Winona began its growth as a river town. It experienced a boom in the late 1850s, when lumbering and milling became its chief industries. Today Winona is notable for its fine old homes from its river days and contains a fine river museum in the old wooden-hulled sternwheeler *Julius C. Wilkie*.

Lithograph by Henry Lewis of a trading post at Prairie du Chien, Wisconsin, in the late 1830s. *Courtesy Saint Louis Mercantile Library Association*

LA CROSSE, WISCONSIN

La Crosse is located at the confluence of the Black, La Crosse, and Mississippi rivers, in an impressively scenic region with high river bluffs and

plorers' waterway route from Lake Michigan to the Mississippi River. The site was named for a Fox chief whom the French called *Le Chien* (the dog). An American Fur Company post was established in 1835, and a river town soon grew up around it. A fortune in furs was made here by Hercules Dousman, agent for John Jacob Astor; Dousman's Victorian mansion, *Villa Louis,* is now a museum. Doctor William Beaumont conducted his experiments here, at Fort Crawford, built in 1816.

CASSVILLE, WISCONSIN

Cassville was settled in 1829, and in 1836 two eastern land speculators platted the village as the future state capital. When the seat of government was located elsewhere, the village became a lead and wheat shipping port, and later a farmer's trading center. Cassville is the site of Stonefield Village, a replica of a frontier village.

Lithograph by Henry Lewis of Dubuque, Iowa, in the 1840s. *Courtesy Saint Louis Mercantile Library Association*

Lithograph by Henry Lewis of Cassville, Wisconsin, on the Mississippi, as it appeared during the early 1830s. *Courtesy Saint Louis Mercantile Library Association*

DUBUQUE, IOWA

Julien Dubuque, a French-Canadian trader and miner, built a cabin in 1788 on a river bluff near the site of the city that now bears his name. He began to mine lead ore from the bluffs and acquired a great influence among the Fox Indians. In 1833, when troops from Fort Crawford, Wisconsin, withdrew, the site was opened to settlement. Between 1833 and 1860 Dubuque grew into Iowa's largest city, with a prosperous river trade and lum-

ber mills busy processing great rafts of timber from upriver. When the Illinois Central Railroad reached the Mississippi, opposite the city, in the late fifties, Dubuque interests formed their own railroad to run westward, across Iowa. Today Dubuque has one of the nation's few inland shipbuilding yards and is an important port in the upper Mississippi barge-line operations.

Drawing by A. R. Waud of Dubuque from Kelly's Bluff. *From Picturesque America, 1872. Courtesy Saint Louis Mercantile Library Association*

Galena, Illinois, 1850. *From Western Scenery on Land and River, 1851. Courtesy Saint Louis Mercantile Library Association*

Industrial Galena amid busy Fevre River shipping, about 1855. *Courtesy Saint Louis Public Library*

Old Market House State Memorial, Galena, built in 1846, last of the old community trading centers preserved in Illinois. *Courtesy State of Illinois, Department of Conservation*

Ulysses S. Grant Home State Memorial, Galena, presented to Grant by the grateful citizens of Galena as a token of their esteem, after his return home from the Civil War. *Courtesy State of Illinois, Department of Conservation*

GALENA, ILLINOIS

Galena, on the Fevre River, near the Mississippi, is a picturesque old town built upon lofty bluffs. It was the site of Indian lead mines and was named for its principal product, sulphide of lead. The diggings, which attracted miners as early as 1717, fell under government regulation in 1807. By the 1820s, Galena had become a sizable town, reaching its peak between 1840 and 1860, when the region produced over eighty percent of the nation's lead supply. The Fevre River, navigable for steamboats, was used for lead shipments down the Mississippi. Galena became the western terminus of a railroad out of Chicago, and at one time appeared destined to become the principal city in Illinois. However, with the exhaustion of most of the lead diggings, the city declined. It is currently notable for its fine old architecture. General U. S. Grant's home here is preserved as a state memorial.

CLINTON, IOWA

The first settler at Clinton was Elijah Buell, who established a ferry crossing in 1835. Three years later a town was laid out and named New York. It was replatted in 1855 and renamed in honor of De Witt Clinton. A river town with boatbuilding yards soon emerged. After the establishment of sawmills, Clinton grew rapidly and by 1880 was recognized as the world's largest lumber-producing city. After the arrival of the last raft of timber in 1906, the city turned to railroads and other industries.

DAVENPORT, IOWA

The present site of Davenport's business district was given to Antoine Le Claire, a French half-breed who had served as an interpreter in the Black Hawk Treaty of 1832. In 1836 Le Claire sold his land to Colonel George Davenport and others, who founded the town bearing Davenport's name.

The city was incorporated in 1851 and soon experienced a rapid growth due to river traffic and heavy immigration of German refugees. One of the first railroads west of the Mississippi was begun at Davenport in 1853, and in 1855 the first bridge over the Mississippi was built across from Rock Island, Illinois.

After the Civil War, when log rafts were floated down the river, Davenport became a great lumber-mill center. Davenport is now Iowa's third largest city and is an important river port serving its many industries.

The Mississippi River bridge between Rock Island, Illinois, and Davenport, Iowa, seen from Iowa, 1855. *Courtesy Saint Louis Public Library*

Davenport, Iowa, from the river bluffs. *From the United States Illustrated, 1855. Courtesy Saint Louis Mercantile Library Association*

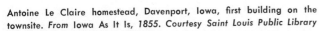

Antoine Le Claire homestead, Davenport, Iowa, first building on the townsite. *From Iowa As It Is, 1855. Courtesy Saint Louis Public Library*

ROCK ISLAND AND MOLINE, ILLINOIS

Rock Island and Moline are located on the Mississippi at its junction with the Rock River. Marquette and Joliet visited the Illini Indians in this area in 1673. The Illini were driven out by the Sauk and Fox tribes in 1680. Zebulon M. Pike led the first American expedition to this region in 1805, and the first American settler in the vicinity was Colonel George Davenport, who arrived in 1815. In 1816 the American Army established Fort Armstrong on the rocky island that gave the city its name. The Indians were finally cleared from the area in the Black Hawk War of 1832. Settlers then arrived in large numbers, and Rock Island was

The Mississippi River at Moline, Illinois. *From the United States Illustrated, 1855. Courtesy Saint Louis Mercantile Library Association*

Lithograph by Henry Lewis of Fort Armstrong, c. 1835, on Rock Island in the Mississippi River. *Courtesy Saint Louis Public Library*

Drawings by A. R. Waud of Rock Island (top) and Davenport (below). *From Picturesque America, 1872. Courtesy Saint Louis Mercantile Library Association*

founded in 1841, followed by Moline which was platted in 1843.

The towns became busy river ports during the steamboat era, and lumber mills prospered from the large timber rafts that were floated down the Mississippi. The first bridge built at Rock Island was deemed a hazard by steamboat owners, but railroad interests, for whom the bridge was built, were successful in a case involving a collision with the bridge pier by the steamboat *Effie Afton*. They were represented by Abraham Lincoln. Rock Island Arsenal, established on the island during the Civil War, at one time housed twelve thousand Confederate prisoners. Today, by virtue of its large payroll, the arsenal is a prominent factor in the local economy, along with several large industries in both cities.

MUSCATINE, IOWA

Situated on the west bank of the Mississippi, about a hundred miles above Keokuk, Muscatine derives its name from the Mascouten Indian tribe. An Indian trading post there was known as Manatheka, before James W. Casey staked a claim in 1835 and set up a wood yard for steamboats. The site was surveyed and named Bloomington in 1836. It received its present name in 1849. The settlement quickly became an important steamboat landing and was incorporated as a city in 1853. In the late fifties, Muscatine's two steam sawmills turned out four million board feet of lumber annually from logs rafted downriver from Minnesota. After railroads were built in the area, local industry became more diversified, although lumbering remained dominant until after 1890.

Lithograph by Henry Lewis of riverfront of Muscatine, Iowa, during the 1840s. *Courtesy Saint Louis Public Library*

BURLINGTON, IOWA

Burlington's site was known as Sho-ko-kon (flint hills) to the Indians who established a village there in 1820. The first white families arrived in 1833, and it was named in honor of the Vermont hometown of one of the first settlers. Burlington served as a temporary seat of government for Iowa from 1837 until the capital was moved to Iowa City in 1839. The town grew rapidly during the 1840s when hundreds of steamboats docked there annually to load pork, lard, and produce at the "Porkopolis of Iowa." The completion of a railroad from Peoria in 1855 made Burlington a busy railroad center, although the river was not bridged until 1868. During the seventies it became a sawmilling hub and later developed into a prominent industrial city.

Lithograph by Henry Lewis of Burlington, Iowa, about 1840. *Courtesy Saint Louis Public Library*

A safe, peaceful harbor, Burlington, Iowa, 1850. *From* The United States Illustrated, *1855. Courtesy Saint Louis Mercantile Library Association*

FORT MADISON, IOWA

Fort Madison received its name from a trading post set up there in 1808, shortly after President James Madison's inauguration. The post was abandoned in 1813 when under siege by Chief Black Hawk. A trading post was established at Fort Madison in 1833, and in 1847 S. D. Morrison began an extensive farm-tool industry. Steamboats brought business to the town, which became an extensive depot for pine lumber. The Santa Fe Railroad later built a large drawbridge and established a division point at Fort Madison.

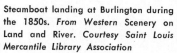

Steamboat landing at Burlington during the 1850s. *From Western Scenery on Land and River. Courtesy Saint Louis Mercantile Library Association*

Fort Madison, Iowa, burning during the War of 1812, while under siege by Indians led by the British agent Dixon, in the summer of 1813. The small American garrison, under Lieutenant Thomas Hamilton, tunneled out of the fort and then set it afire, before escaping downriver to Saint Louis. *From St. Louis Globe-Democrat, 1902*

NAUVOO, ILLINOIS

Nauvoo is on the site of a former Indian village, where a town known as Venus was founded in the late 1820s. It was absorbed by nearby Commerce in 1834 and chosen as a haven for the Mormons in 1839 after they were driven out of Missouri.

Joseph Smith, leader of the Mormon Church, renamed the town Nauvoo, which means "pleasant land" in Hebrew. A city of twenty thousand was developed by the Mormons, who began construction of a great temple there. In five years Nauvoo was the largest city in Illinois. Smith became powerful in state politics and formed his own militia. Fearful non-Mormons leveled charges against

Nauvoo from the Iowa bluffs during the 1850s, showing ruined Mormon temple (top). *From The United States Illustrated, 1855. Courtesy Saint Louis Mercantile Library Association*

Lithograph by Henry Lewis of Nauvoo, Illinois, 1840. *Courtesy Saint Louis Public Library*

Mormon leader Joseph Smith's first home in Nauvoo, built in 1823 and bought by Smith in 1839. It is in restored condition. *Courtesy Illinois Department of Business and Economic Development*

The *Times and Seasons* Mormon newspaper building at Nauvoo, Illinois. *Courtesy State of Illinois Department of Conservation*

Lithograph by Henry Lewis of Keokuk, Iowa, during the 1840s. *Courtesy Saint Louis Mercantile Library Association*

Smith's group, which was opposed by a splinter faction of the Church. When Smith destroyed an opposition press, he and his brother were jailed at nearby Carthage. An anti-Mormon mob broke into the jail and murdered the Smiths in 1844. The next year the Mormons, under Brigham Young, began their migration to Utah, leaving Nauvoo and its uncompleted temple. In 1849 the deserted town was resettled by French Icarians in a communal experiment. This soon failed, and the remaining residents began to plant grapes and make wines and cheese, for which Nauvoo became famous. An extensive restoration of old Nauvoo is now being undertaken by a branch of the Mormon Church.

KEOKUK, IOWA

Keokuk is located on the Mississippi near the mouth of the Des Moines River, at the former foot of the Lower Rapids. The first white settler built a cabin here in 1820, and in 1828 the American Fur Company opened a trading post on the site, which was named for Chief Keokuk of the Sac and Fox tribes.

The town was platted in 1837 by an agent of the New York Land Company. During the 1840s, it became the trade headquarters for an extensive area. Keokuk's location at the foot of the Rapids made it necessary for all steamboat passengers and freight to be unloaded for transfer around the obstruction.

The steamers *G. W. Hill* (left) and *Sidney*, the first boats to pass through the new Keokuk Lock at Keokuk, Iowa, on June 12, 1913. The *Hill*, built in 1909 for use as a packet in the Saint Louis-Calhoun County, Illinois, apple trade, became an excursion boat in 1912 and was put in service between Cincinnati and Coney Island as the *Island Maid* in 1922. The *Sidney* was completed at Wheeling in 1880 for the Cincinnati-Wheeling trade and was originally painted yellow instead of the traditional white. She ran on the upper Mississippi as a Diamond Jo Line packet from 1883 until sold to the Streckfus Line in 1911. Rebuilt as an excursion boat, *Sidney* tramped the rivers until 1921, when she was again rebuilt as the *Washington*. She was dismantled at Saint Louis in 1938 after years of service on the upper Ohio. *Courtesy Waterways Journal*

This obstacle to navigation was finally conquered by a government canal opened in 1877. The canal and its locks were submerged under the waters of Lake Keokuk. The lake was impounded by the hydroelectric dam and lock completed in 1913. Among Keokuk's many attractions is the former sternwheel towboat *George M. Verity,* now a steamboat museum.

Lithograph by Henry Lewis of Quincy, Illinois, 1840. *Courtesy Saint Louis Public Library*

Lithograph by Henry Lewis of Hannibal, Missouri, as it appeared during Mark Twain's boyhood in the 1840s. *Courtesy Saint Louis Public Library*

Boyhood home of Mark Twain and Tom Sawyer's whitewashed fence at Hannibal, Missouri. *Walker-Missouri Tourism photo*

QUINCY, ILLINOIS

Favorably situated on limestone bluffs above the Mississippi, Quincy was originally settled in 1822 by pioneers who came to explore the Military Bounty Tract. Others followed and built a small town, which was named Quincy, in Adams County, both names in honor of President John Quincy Adams.

Steamboat traffic brought prosperity to Quincy, which became Illinois's second city between 1850 and 1870. The city is now the trade center of a three-state area and has developed interesting riverfront tourist attractions.

HANNIBAL, MISSOURI

Hannibal was established in 1819 but did not grow much until the town's incorporation in 1838, when more settlers arrived. Hannibal developed a thriving lumber trade, whose mills processed logs floated downriver from Wisconsin and Minnesota. A local paper boasted in 1847 that steamboats had transported over one million dollars' worth of freight from Hannibal during the previous season. In 1856 construction began on the Hannibal and Saint Joseph Railroad, which was destined to transform the town industrially.

River commerce practically ceased during the Civil War, but its place was soon taken by the railroads. The lumber boom collapsed when the northern timber supply was exhausted, and other industries supplanted it.

Hannibal is famous as the boyhood home of Mark Twain and as the scene of the adventures of Tom Sawyer and Huckleberry Finn.

A quiet nocturnal river scene, the *River Queen* moored at Hannibal, Missouri. *Walker-Missouri Tourism photo*

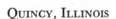

Lithograph by Henry Lewis of the riverfront at Alton, Illinois, about 1835. Courtesy Saint Louis Public Library

Lithograph by John Casper Wild of Alton from the Missouri shore in 1841. Courtesy Saint Louis Mercantile Library Association

LOUISIANA, MISSOURI

Louisiana is a former river town that is now an agricultural and industrial center. It was founded in 1818 and named for the State of Louisiana. It is notable for its Victorian architecture, in both waterfront structures and fine residences. Louisiana is located in the center of a large apple-growing region.

ALTON, ILLINOIS

Alton lies on the east bank of the Mississippi, about three miles above the mouth of the Missouri River. A trading post was established by the French on its townsite in 1785 but was abandoned in 1807. The town's continuous existence dates from 1817, when it was founded by Rufus Easton, a Saint Louis lawyer who named it after his son. In 1837 Alton was incorporated as a city, absorbing two other nearby settlements.

Elijah Lovejoy and his abolitionist press moved to Alton in 1835 from Saint Louis, because of adverse public sentiment. In August, 1837, after three of his presses had been destroyed by local mobs, Lovejoy was murdered when he emerged

Looking downstream at Alton, Illinois, showing the installation at Lock and Dam No. 26 of the upper Mississippi system. Courtesy U.S. Corps of Engineers, Saint Louis District

Locks and Dam No. 26, Mississippi River. Section of Mississippi River at Alton, Illinois, showing outdated structure which will be left partially in place to improve flow conditions downstream where the new twin twelve-hundred-foot locks are proposed for construction. Tows pushing barges are operated by remote control to test navigation conditions at this location. Scale of the model is 1:120. *Courtesy U.S. Army Engineer Waterways Experiment Station, U.S. Corps of Engineers, Vicksburg District*

from the burning warehouse that sheltered his fourth press. The last Lincoln-Douglas debate was held in Alton in October, 1858.

Although river traffic diminished after the Civil War, Alton flourished as a railroad center and became the nucleus of a populous urban area. Lock and Dam Twenty-six of the upper Mississippi River system is located here. It has become inadequate and plans are underway for its replacement.

EAST SAINT LOUIS, ILLINOIS

The earliest activity at the present site of East Saint Louis was a ferry crossing operated by Captain James Piggott in 1797. He also cleared timber and erected a few houses on the site. Growth was negligible until the 1850s, when railroads reached the east bank of the Mississippi opposite Saint Louis.

The town was incorporated as Illinoistown in 1859, and in 1861 it was merged with the newer town of East Saint Louis. The city grew considerably after the first stockyards were established in 1872, and the Eads Bridge across the river to Saint Louis was finished two years later. To avoid floods, the grade level of the main part of the city was raised from eight to fifteen feet in 1888, in conjunction with new levees. The proximity of abundant coalfields in southern Illinois has made East Saint Louis into a rail center, with most of its riverfront under railroad ownership.

Lithograph by John Casper Wild of Bloody Island in Illinoistown (later East Saint Louis) in 1841. The island was so named because of the many early duels fought there. *From The Valley of the Mississippi Illustrated. Courtesy Saint Louis Public Library*

SAINT LOUIS, MISSOURI

Saint Louis, one of the oldest cities of the Mississippi Valley, was founded by Pierre Laclede in 1764. The city is well situated on the Mississippi, below the Missouri and Illinois rivers, and occupies a strategic position with regard to river commerce. It was here that a break in steamboat traffic occurred: cargoes from the large lower-river boats

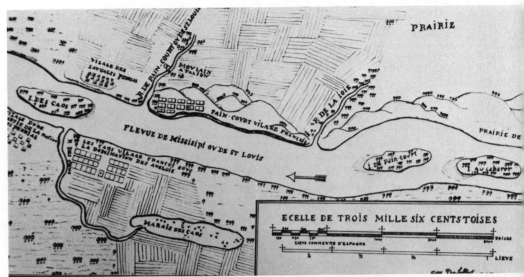

Earliest known map showing the location of Saint Louis, then called Pain-court Vilage Francois. This map was made in 1767 by Lieutenant Guy Dufossat of Captain Rui's Spanish expedition, only three years after the founding of Saint Louis by Laclede. *Copy in collection of the author*

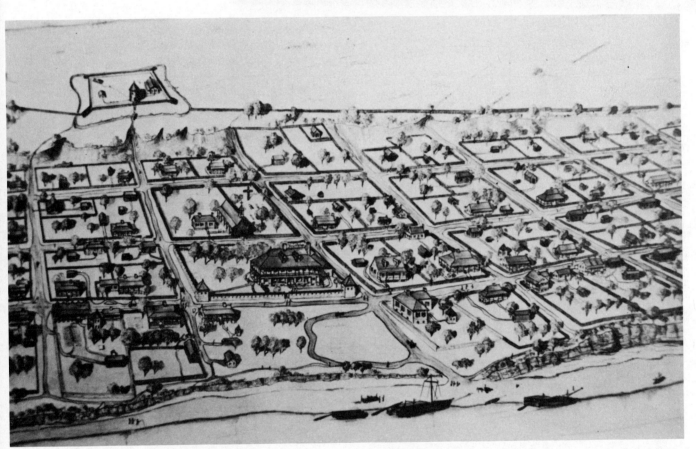

The French colonial village of Saint Louis as it appeared in 1794. Watercolor by the author

required reloading on lighter-draft vessels for transport upriver above Saint Louis.

Saint Louis's early growth was primarily from the fur trade, and it became the gateway to the West, the starting point for western exploration and settlement. Saint Louis's first steamboat, the *Zebu-* *lon M. Pike,* reached Saint Louis in 1817, the forerunner of a vast armada of riverboats that moored at its levee for more than a century.

Saint Louis experienced a boom period in the antebellum years, when its population grew from sixteen thousand in 1840 to ten times that in 1860.

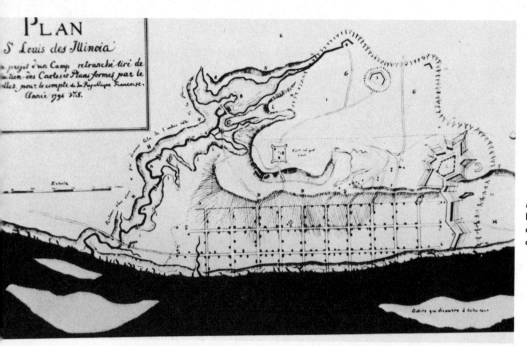

Map of the village of Saint Louis made in 1796 by General Victor Collot, to show plans for changes in the fortifications. *Copy in collection of the author*

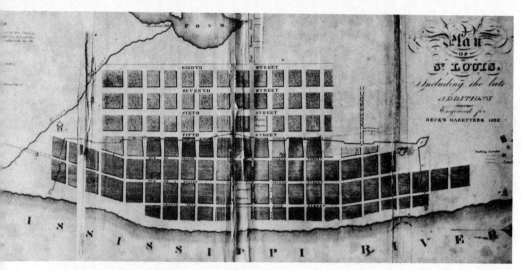

Map of Saint Louis in 1822 from Lewis Beck's gazetteer of Missouri and Illinois. *Courtesy Saint Louis Mercantile Library Association*

Bird's-eye view of Saint Louis in 1841, soon after its population began to boom. *Watercolor painting by the author*

The city's prosperity was reflected in its extensive river trade, which soon made it the leading river port and largest city in the Middle West. Its trade suffered a setback in the panic of 1857, as a prelude to the ominous approach of the Civil War. The war caused a cessation of civilian river traffic and consequent destruction of Saint Louis's sources of trade. The city's large German population directed its sentiments toward the North during the war, saving Missouri for the Union.

The postwar period witnessed a brief revival of packet-boat activity, which fell before the competition of the railroads by the turn of the century. The time was also marked by the defeat of Saint Louis in its contest with Chicago for midwestern commercial dominance. After the World's Fair of 1904 Saint Louis business experienced a renaissance, which was based upon railroad commerce rather than river traffic. At present, river trade at Saint Louis shares in extensive barge-line activity,

Advertisement for a popular hostelry for rivermen. *From The Shipping Guide and Directory, 1870. Courtesy Ardell Thompson Collection*

Lithograph by John Casper Wild of Front Street, Saint Louis, showing Market House in 1841 and the river trade. *Courtesy Saint Louis Public Library*

View of Saint Louis from Illinois in 1855, just before its setback in 1855. Painting by Frederick Piercy. *Courtesy Saint Louis Mercantile Library Association*

which began increasing during the 1950s. The last packet-boat line at Saint Louis ceased operations in 1947, and passenger river trade now is restricted to excursion boat trips and occasional visits by the tourist boat *Delta Queen.*

Saint Louis's bluff-top site precluded damage from floods, which only reached to the entrance of riverfront warehouses. A large government flood-wall project, which will protect other low-lying areas on the city's northern riverfront, is now nearing completion. However, Saint Louis's worst river-connected disaster was the fire of 1849, which began on the steamer *White Cloud.* It destroyed twenty-two other steamboats and laid waste to many blocks of riverfront businesses.

The city, long accused of turning its back on the river, is revitalizing its riverfront as a tourist attraction. Riverboat museums and restaurants vie with the *Golden Rod* showboat and excursion trips for the visitor's attention. Many blocks of dingy riverfront warehouses have been cleared for a vast riverside national park—the Jefferson National Expansion Memorial, with its great Gateway Arch. An underground museum of westward expansion will portray the story of the nation's western growth, in which Saint Louis played such an important part.

The Saint Louis riverfront, 1875. *From Compton and Dry's Pictorial Saint Louis*

The Gateway Arch and Saint Louis skyline today. This 630-foot stainless steel arch, symbolizing the Gateway to the West, is located in the Jefferson National Expansion Memorial National Park on the Saint Louis riverfront. *Walker-Missouri Tourism photo*

SAINTE GENEVIEVE, MISSOURI

The oldest known settlement in Missouri is Sainte Genevieve, believed to be founded in 1735 by settlers from Kaskaskia. The town was forced to move to higher ground by a severe flood in 1785, and by 1822 only a few houses remained on the old site.

Sainte Genevieve was blessed with a surrounding farmland of rich soil and nearby sources of salt and lead. The leisurely village life changed after the Americans assumed control in 1804, with a complex system of laws and codes. For a brief period, Sainte Genevieve was a rival of Saint Louis in the

River landing at Sainte Genevieve, Missouri, in French colonial times. Mural by Oscar E. Berninghaus in the Missouri State Capitol in Jefferson City. *Courtesy State Historical Society of Missouri*

French Creole colonial architecture in Sainte Genevieve: the restored Bolduc House. *Walker-Missouri Tourism photo*

river trade, but the village declined with the removal of the fur trade and the cessation of lead mining. Iron ore was diverted from nearby Iron Mountain to Saint Louis by the railroad, and the town came to rely solely upon its agricultural heritage. At present, the town, which is well served by railroads, has become a center of the lime and marble industries. As evidence of its historical importance, many old French houses have been restored to re-create Sainte Genevieve's original Creole charm.

CAPE GIRARDEAU, MISSOURI

Cape Girardeau is built upon the Mississippi River bluffs about 150 miles below Saint Louis. The city

Plan of Cape Girardeau, Missouri, 1796. From A Journey in North America—1796, General Victor Collot. *Courtesy Saint Louis Mercantile Library Association*

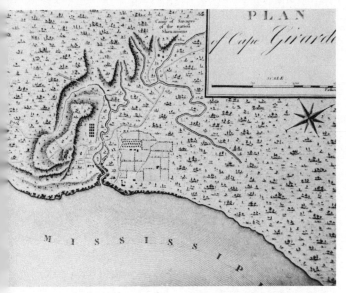

takes its name from a French ensign named Girardot, who is said to have settled on Cape Rock in the 1730s. In 1792 Don Louis Lorimier, the Spanish government's Indian agent, founded a trading post on the present townsite. Lorimier aided American settlement by offering free land. After the Louisiana Purchase, Lorimier's title was rejected by the U.S. Land Commission, invalidating all town-lot titles. This caused the town's development to cease until 1836, when the American government confirmed the titles.

Incorporated as a city in 1843, Cape Girardeau soon became a busy river port with saw- and gristmills.

The town's locale on the first high point above the mouth of the Ohio River gave it a strategic importance as a communications post during the Civil War. It was occupied by Union forces in 1861 and repulsed a Confederate attack in 1863. River traffic ceased during the Civil War and was later restricted at Cape Girardeau by the Iron Mountain Railroad, which tapped the hinterlands. A railroad reached the city in 1881, furthering its growth. Barge traffic currently plays an important part in Cape Girardeau's economy.

Levee at Cape Girardeau, about 1910. *Courtesy Webster Groves Book Shop*

NEW MADRID, MISSOURI

New Madrid is descended from a fur-trading post established in 1783 by François and Joseph Le Sieur. In 1789 the Spanish rulers of the Louisiana Territory granted fifteen million acres of land to Colonel George Morgan, an American Revolutionary War veteran. The buffer colony was intended

Lithograph by Henry Lewis of New Madrid, Missouri, about 1835. From *Das Illustrirte Mississippithal,* 1853 Courtesy State Historical Society of Missouri

Drawing of Memphis from the Arkansas shore, by Frederick Piercy, 1855. Courtesy Saint Louis Mercantile Library Association

by the Spanish to discourage American expansion west of the Mississippi. An ambitious town plan proposed here failed to materialize, and the settlement continued as a trading post. The site was at the center of the great earthquake of December, 1811, which destroyed the town and greatly altered the topography and course of the river. New Madrid was moved about four times before the Civil War because of the shifting river. During the war, the area was the scene of an attack on nearby Island Number Ten by Union gunboats and a siege by Union Army forces under General Pope in 1862. The town is now protected from the river by a great earthen levee.

MEMPHIS, TENNESSEE

Memphis, the largest city in Tennessee, is situated on the Fourth, or Lower, Chickasaw Bluff on the Mississippi's east bank. It was from these bluffs that Hernando de Soto discovered the river in 1541.

Spain, France, and England contested for the area before it became a part of the United States in 1797. General James Robertson established a depot on the bluffs in 1782 to trade with the Chickasaw Indians, and John Overton built a trading post there in 1794.

However, the site remained under Indian control until 1818 when General Andrew Jackson settled their claims by a treaty. Jackson and Overton owned the site in 1819 and had a townsite platted, which was named Memphis because of the location's similarity to that of the ancient Egyptian city.

Memphis grew rapidly following its incorporation in 1826, becoming an important cotton-shipping point for steamboat traffic. Chartered as a city in 1849, its population exceeded twenty thousand on the eve of the Civil War. The city was occupied by Union forces in 1862 and remained in Northern hands for the duration of the War.

Memphis river scenes before the Civil War. From Harper's Pictorial History of the Civil War. Courtesy Saint Louis Mercantile Library Association

Memphis, Tennessee, 1850. From Western Scenery on Land and River. Courtesy Saint Louis Mercantile Library Association

While recovering from the economic aftermath of the war, Memphis was stricken by yellow fever epidemics, which caused many to flee the city. Between 1879 and 1891 municipal government suspended in favor of state control. During this period a sewer system was built and artesian wells were installed, and by 1890 the city almost doubled in population.

Memphis became one of the nation's railroad centers, and in 1892 a bridge was built to link Tennessee with Arkansas. This brought increased trade with the Southwest, making Memphis the world's greatest inland cotton market and hardwood-lumber center. The city has developed a new harbor and industrial area on President's Island on the Mississippi and is a busy regional port for barge commerce.

Drawing by A. R. Waud of Arkansas River Packet Company wharfboat opposite Memphis. *From Every Saturday Magazine, 1871. Courtesy Saint Louis Mercantile Library Association*

Memphis riverfront during the visit of President Theodore Roosevelt on October 27, 1909. The sidewheelers *Grey Eagle* and *Alton* are visible in the foreground. *Courtesy Waterways Journal*

Aerial view of President's Island and harbor, Memphis. *Courtesy Memphis and Shelby County Port Commission*

Drawing by A. R. Waud of Helena, Arkansas. From Every Saturday Magazine, 1871. Courtesy Saint Louis Mercantile Library Association

HELENA, ARKANSAS

Helena is an old river town on the Mississippi about midway between Memphis and the mouth of the Arkansas River. It was named about 1820 after an early settler's daughter and was a center of culture in antebellum days. Helena was an important river port for packet boats during the steamboat era.

The town was occupied by Union forces during the Civil War and was unsuccessfully attacked by the Confederates in 1863.

The Mississippi River is still an important factor to Helena, which is an essential rail center and distribution point.

GREENVILLE, MISSISSIPPI

The first settlement on the present site of Greenville was the Blantonia Plantation, on Bachelor's Bend. It was founded in 1828 by Colonel W. W. Blanton and sold by his widow in 1866 as a site for the town. Greenville is the third county seat of Washington County. The first was destroyed by flooding from the river, and the second was demolished by fire from Federal gunboats in 1863. Greenville was incorporated in 1870, and is northeast of the second county seat site, which eventually fell into the river. Much of the present city suffered a similar fate, until the 1927 flood, when the city was under water for seventy days. After that, higher levees were built and, in 1935, the troublesome Mississippi was banished to a new course west of Greenville. The present Lake Ferguson was created on the city's western boundary.

Greenville is now one of the principal ports on the lower Mississippi and has a large trade in cotton and lumber.

VICKSBURG, MISSISSIPPI

Vicksburg, which is about a hundred miles north of Natchez, lies in the western declivity of the Walnut Hills and presents a picturesque appearance from the Mississippi River.

A French fort was built near here in 1719, and in 1791 Fort Nogales was built by the Spanish regime. The area became American territory in 1798, with the present city dating from 1812, when it was founded by Newitt Vick, a Methodist minister. Vicksburg was incorporated in 1825 and experienced rapid growth as a river cotton port.

Upstream view of the new harbor at Greenville, Mississippi. Since the 1930s, when the town was plagued by floods, Greenville has developed one of the finest slack-water harbors on the inland waterways. Its ten-mile harbor, on a former arm of the Mississippi, can now provide as much as thirty feet of water for shipping from the Gulf, as well as facilities for barge-line activity. A new seaport-type deep-water dock is near completion. *Courtesy Waterways Journal*

Vicksburg, Mississippi, 1850. *From Western Scenery on Land and River. Courtesy Saint Louis Mercantile Library Association*

Drawing by Frederick Piercy of Vicksburg from the Louisiana shore of the Mississippi River, about 1855. *Courtesy Saint Louis Mercantile Library Association*

Vicksburg before the river changed course. *From Down the Great River, 1887. Courtesy Saint Louis Public Library*

Vicksburg landing in 1863 just before hostilities began. Steamboats *Des Moines* in foreground and *Emerald* in the rear. *Courtesy Jefferson National Expansion Memorial National Park Service*

The city's location at the mouth of the Yazoo River made it strategically important during the Civil War. In 1862 the South still held the city and the Mississippi River below it. The capture of Vicksburg was necessary for General Grant to control the river and to split the Confederacy. After several unsuccessful attempts, Grant reached the city in May, 1863, and failing to take it by storm, laid siege. This was successful after six weeks, and the beleaguered city fell on July 4, 1863. Gunboat activity was especially brisk on the Mississippi and

Vicksburg wharf, 1883, with business as usual. The steamboats *Leflore,* *Will S. Hays,* and *Ed Richardson* are the largest boats visible in this view. *Courtesy Boatmen's National Bank of St. Louis*

Carrying an estimated twenty-five-hundred Union troops bound to Saint Louis from Vicksburg after the end of the Civil War is the sidewheeler *Sultana,* built at Cincinnati in 1863, showing her overcrowded condition shortly before her tragic explosion. Many of the men had just been released from Confederate prison camps. More than three-fifths of them perished in this disaster, caused by strain on the boilers from the overload. *Courtesy Boatmen's National Bank of St. Louis*

Yazoo, as several naval attacks were mounted against Vicksburg.

The Mississippi River changed its course in 1876, leaving Vicksburg high and dry. The Army Engineers later diverted the Yazoo into the old riverbed and the U.S. Waterways Experiment Station at Vicksburg now conducts continual tests to tame the Father of Waters. The extensive Vicksburg National Military Park and Cemetery is of great historic interest.

An artist's impression of the fire that consumed the *Sultana,* following the explosion of her boilers on April 27, 1865, above Memphis. The official death toll in this disaster was 1,547, making it one of the worst marine catastrophes in history. *From Harper's Weekly, May, 1865. Courtesy Saint Louis Mercantile Library Association*

NATCHEZ, MISSISSIPPI

Located on the high bluffs overlooking the Mississippi River, Natchez, one of the oldest cities in the South, is named for the Natchez tribe of Indians. Its area was visited by La Salle in 1682. Bienville, the founder of New Orleans, established Fort Rosalie here in 1716, naming it after the Duchess of Ponchartrain. In 1729 the entire garrison was massacred by the Natchez Indians, who were later driven out by the French. The Natchez area passed to the English in 1763 and to the Spanish in 1779. A Spanish engineer designed the town on the

Lithograph by Henry Lewis of upper and lower Natchez about 1835. Courtesy St. Louis Mercantile Library Association

Fort Rosalie at Natchez, Mississippi. *From A Journey in North America— 1796, General Victor Collot. Courtesy Saint Louis Mercantile Library Association*

bluffs, which came under American jurisdiction in 1798.

River traffic caused the town to flourish in its strategic location at the end of the Natchez Trace. The town divided into two distinct parts, the lower part, on the riverfront, became the infamous Natchez-under-the-hill, known for its crime and profligacy. The upper town, which became rich and elegant, is noted for its fine old antebellum mansions.

Natchez was captured by Federal forces during the Civil War, but regained some of its prewar eminence as a cotton port during Reconstruction.

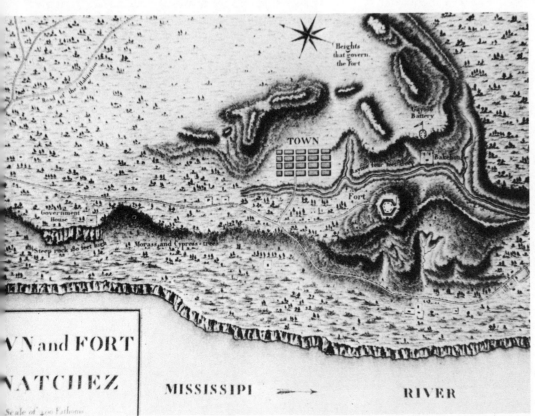

Map of the town and fort of Natchez. *From A Journey in North America—1796, General Victor Collot. Courtesy Saint Louis Mercantile Library Association*

Drawing by Frederick Piercy of the lower part, or Natchez-under-the-hill, looking downriver, 1855. *Courtesy Saint Louis Mercantile Library Association*

Natchez was the home of Captain Tom Leathers, who built the series of steamboats bearing the city's name.

The city's old homes are open for public inspection annually in March, during the Natchez Pilgrimage.

The port of Natchez, with direct rail access, was opened in 1861.

BATON ROUGE, LOUISIANA

Baton Rouge (red stick), the capital of Louisiana, is on the first spur of high land that reaches the Mississippi River above its mouth. A fort was established at the site in 1719 by the French, who gave it its name, which referred to a red post that marked the boundary between Indian lands. The area became British in 1763 but was captured by

the Spanish in 1779. American residents rebelled and captured the fort and its settlement in the second battle of Baton Rouge in 1810. The area was annexed to Louisiana by Governor Claiborne, and in 1817 Baton Rouge was incorporated.

After becoming a river port and commercial center, the city became the state capital in 1849. At the

Lithograph by Henry Lewis of Baton Rouge about 1835. *Courtesy Saint Louis Public Library*

outbreak of the Civil War, Baton Rouge had a population of about fifty-five hundred. It was captured by Union troops pressing northward after the fall of New Orleans in 1862. The capitol burned during the Union occupation and was not rebuilt until 1882, when the seat of government returned from Shreveport.

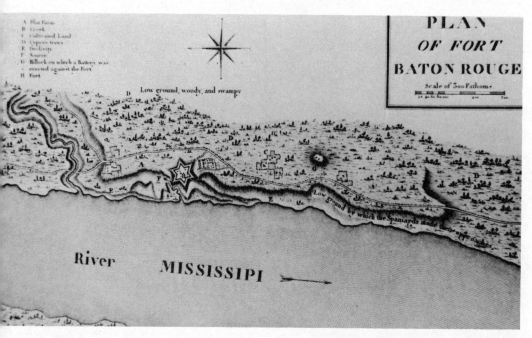

Plan of the fort at Baton Rouge, Louisiana. *From A Journey in North America—1796, General Victor Collot. Courtesy Saint Louis Public Library*

Drawing by Frederick Piercy of Baton Rouge from the river, showing the original state capitol building completed in 1850. *Courtesy Saint Louis Mercantile Library Association*

Baton Rouge is the eighth largest port in the nation today. View is from Port Allen looking toward the capital city. *Courtesy U.S. Corps of Engineers, New Orleans District*

After the wartime problems were solved, the deep-water port of Baton Rouge became a large distributing center, with considerable industry. The city is a hub for oil refineries, chemical plants, and other factories, as well as the market for a large surrounding agricultural region.

DONALDSONVILLE, LOUISIANA

This town began as a trading post shortly after 1750 and, because of a church so dedicated there by a Capuchin missionary in 1781, was known for many years as Ascension.

LAKE PROVIDENCE, LOUISIANA

A prosperous river town during the steamboating days, it is best known for an uncompleted canal, intended by General Grant as a shortcut for Union gunboats during the Civil War.

Lithograph by Henry Lewis of Bayou Sara, Louisiana, as it appeared during the 1830s. *Courtesy Saint Louis Public Library*

BAYOU SARA, LOUISIANA

A twin town of present-day Saint Francisville, it was founded in 1790 and was disenfranchised in 1926.

NEW ORLEANS, LOUISIANA

New Orleans, the Crescent City, is located on a sharp bend of the Mississippi River about 107 miles from the Gulf of Mexico. Bienville, after founding it in 1718, named it in honor of the Duc d'Orleans, Regent of France. The original town was the area still known as the Vieux Carré (old square). In 1723 the new town superseded Biloxi, Mississippi, as the capital of the French colonial empire of Louisiana. During the regime of the Marquis de Vaudreuil, between 1743 and 1753, the town developed into a social center of culture, in

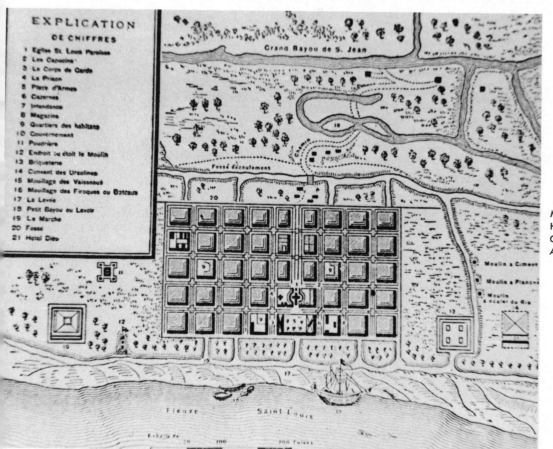

EXPLICATION
DE CHIFFRES

1 Eglise St. Louis Paroisse
2 Les Capucins
3 Le Corps de Garde
4 La Prison
5 Place d'Armes
6 Casernes
7 Intendance
8 Magazin
9 Quartiers des habitans
10 Gouvernement
11 Poudrière
12 Endroit où étoit le Moulin
13 Briqueterie
14 Convent des Ursulines
15 Mouillage des Vaisseaux
16 Mouillage des Piroques ou Bateaux
17 La Levée
18 Petit Bayou ou Lavoir
19 Le Marché
20 Fossé
21 Hotel Dieu

Map of New Orleans in 1728. *From A History of the Mississippi Valley, 1903. Courtesy Saint Louis Mercantile Library Association*

Bird's-eye view of New Orleans in 1850. Judging by the two center steamboats, the wind is going in both directions. The Vieux Carré is to the right. *Courtesy Saint Louis Public Library*

Passing New Orleans's old square, about 1850. *From Western Scenery on Land and River. Courtesy Saint Louis Mercantile Library Association*

Drawing by Frederick Piercy of New Orleans harbor about 1855. *Courtesy Saint Louis Mercantile Library Association*

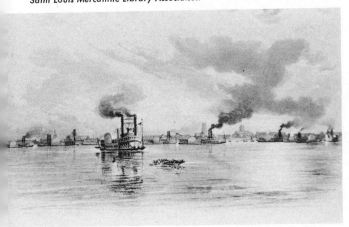

the manner of Versailles. It also became known as a rough river town as well. After the partition of the old Province of Louisiana between England and Spain in 1763, New Orleans became the capital of Spanish Louisiana. The town, which was nearly destroyed by two great fires in 1788 and 1794, assumed a Spanish character in its reconstruction period. In 1794 a nearby plantation owner succeeded in producing sugar from cane, marking the beginning of a prosperous period for the area.

Louisiana was transferred from Spain to France by the Treaty of San Ildefonso in 1800, and became a part of the United States in 1803, after the Louisiana Purchase. A city charter was granted to New Orleans in 1805, and in 1812 it was made the

River traffic boomed after the Civil War. Drawing by A. R. Waud of New Orleans harbor. *From Picturesque America, 1872. Courtesy Saint Louis Mercantile Library Association*

Heavy commerce resulted in considerable construction along the New Orleans riverfront district by 1874. *From Jewel's Crescent City Illustrated, 1874. Courtesy Saint Louis Mercantile Library Association*

Steamboat landing at New Orleans in the 1870s. *From Jewel's Crescent City Illustrated, 1874. Courtesy Saint Louis Mercantile Library Association*

state capital upon Louisiana's admission to the Union, at about the time when the first steamboat, the *New Orleans,* came downriver to the city, marking the start of its preeminence as a river port. The final battle of the War of 1812 was won in January, 1815, when a motley army of Americans under Andrew Jackson defeated the British near New Orleans.

As river traffic increased after 1820, the city boomed commercially and became the nation's fourth largest city in 1840. New Orleans enjoyed an era of peaceful prosperity, with only fear of floods and epidemics to cause worry. The city is now protected from flooding by the Bonnet Carré spillway, built by the U.S. Army Engineers. It removes any threatening flood crests from the river by shifting them to Lake Ponchartrain.

At the start of the Civil War, New Orleans was an important military and naval center for the Confederacy. It was forced to surrender to Admiral Farragut's Union fleet in April, 1862. A repressive rule was in effect until the end of the war, suc-

Floods were a constant fear at New Orleans. This view shows a major levee break, or crevasse, at Bonnet Carré, Louisiana. The irresistible rush of flood waters would sweep all before it. *From Leslie's Illustrated Newspaper, 1871. Courtesy Saint Louis Mercantile Library Association*

The force of the crevasse at Bonnet Carré, Louisiana, during the flood of 1871, is apparent in this drawing by A. R. Waud. *From Every Saturday Magazine, June, 1871. Courtesy Saint Louis Mercantile Library Association*

The Saint Charles Hotel was an exquisite piece of architecture and a favorite among the more prosperous rivermen. *From Jewel's Crescent City Illustrated, 1874. Courtesy Saint Louis Mercantile Library Association*

Drawing by A. R. Waud of a steamboat picking up flood refugees near Bonnet Carré during the flood in 1871. *From Every Saturday Magazine, 1871. Courtesy Saint Louis Mercantile Library Association*

Drawing by A. R. Waud of activity on a busy day at the La Fourche packet landing in New Orleans. *From Every Saturday Magazine, July 22, 1871*

ceeded by a period of racial and political strife between 1865 and 1877. Construction of jetties at the mouth of the Mississippi, by James B. Eads, made it possible for larger ships to reach the city, preserving its status as a seaport. New Orleans is a modern metropolis and the nation's second port, with an international free-trade zone. A vast new harbor improvement plan is underway to further augment the city's commercial position.

New Orleans today. A N.A.S.A. barge makes its way downriver past the port—the second largest in the United States. *Courtesy U.S. Corps of Engineers, New Orleans District*

Modern New Orleans, across the river. *Courtesy Chamber of Commerce of the New Orleans Area*

MISSOURI RIVER CITIES

SIOUX CITY, IOWA

Sioux City sits on the bluffs at the mouth of the Big Sioux River and is at the head of navigation on the Missouri River. Sergeant Charles Floyd, a member of the Lewis and Clark expedition, who

A Corps of Engineers' contractor's dredge working at New Orleans to insure a channel depth adequate for oceangoing ships. In the background the International Trade Mart building marks the head of world-famous Canal Street.

The Missouri River from Stone Park at Sioux City, Iowa. Courtesy Saint Louis Public Library

Floyd Monument at Sioux City, erected in 1901 in memory of Sergeant Charles Floyd of the Lewis and Clark Expedition. Courtesy State of Iowa Conservation Commission

died here in 1804, has a tall monument on his grave recalling the first appearance of white men in the area. A pioneer, William Thompson, settled here in 1848 and platted a town, Thompsonville, on Floyd's bluff. In 1849 a French-Canadian trader, Theophile Bruguier, settled at the mouth of the Big Sioux. Bruguier's claim was purchased in 1855 by Dr. John K. Cook, who platted it as Sioux City.

The first steamboat arrived in 1856, and the following year the city was incorporated. The surrounding network of waterways played an important part in the growth of the city in this period before the coming of the railroads in 1868. The railroads doomed the steamboat activity but led to the industrial development that marks the city today. Through-barge-line service from Sioux City to New Orleans and other river ports is available on the Missouri and Mississippi rivers.

107

OMAHA, NEBRASKA

Lewis and Clark camped near the present site of Omaha in 1804, preceding the first-known fur trader's cabin by some twenty years. The city was begun by the Council Bluffs and Nebraska Ferry Company, organized in 1853 to ferry travelers to California across the Missouri River. The ferry company platted a town on the Nebraska side of the river, and named it Omaha, after a local Indian tribe. When the area was opened to settlement by a treaty with the Indians in 1854, Omaha was established as the territorial capital. The city became an outfitting point for westward-bound emigrants and a lively river port, and was incorporated as a city in 1857. Omaha profited from the gold discovery in Colorado in 1859, when another influx of prospectors brought much business to the town's merchants. A telegraph line from Omaha to California was opened in 1861, followed in 1865 by the start of construction of the transcontinental railroad. Completion of the railroad in 1869 started Omaha on its way to becoming a railroad center and a principal grain and livestock market. The city is now an important port for river shipments by barge on the Missouri.

Drawing by Henry Howe of Omaha, Nebraska, about 1860. *Courtesy Saint Louis Public Library*

Bird's-eye view of Omaha in 1867. *Courtesy Saint Louis Mercantile Library Association*

Omaha is the center of Nebraska's financial and agricultural backbone, home of the world's largest stockyards, and cultural center of the Midwest. *Nebraska Game Commission photo*

Near Omaha is Bellevue, seen about 1862. Drawing by Henry Howe. Courtesy Saint Louis Public Library

Saint Joseph, Missouri, during the early 1850s. From The United States Illustrated, 1855. Courtesy Saint Louis Mercantile Library Association

COUNCIL BLUFFS, IOWA

The Missouri River bluffs, on which Council Bluffs sits, witnessed early meetings between Indians and French fur traders. Lewis and Clark camped nearby during their expedition in 1804. In 1827 François Guittar, an agent of the American Fur Company, set up a trading post on the bluffs. Federal troops established a fort here in 1837, and in the next year Father De Smet arrived and conducted a mission for several years. During the winter of 1846–1847, migrating Mormons settled in the town, which became known as Hanesville. After the departure of the Mormons in 1852 the town was renamed Council Bluffs. The town benefited from an extensive traffic on the Missouri River before the coming of the railroads. President Lincoln officially designated Council Bluffs as the eastern terminus of the Union Pacific Railroad in 1862, a move that brought subsequent prosperity to Council Bluffs as well as to Omaha, its neighbor across the river.

SAINT JOSEPH, MISSOURI

Joseph Robidoux, the agent of the American Fur Company of Saint Louis who established a trading post at the present site of Saint Joseph in 1826, lived on peaceful terms with neighboring Indians after he purchased the post from the fur company in 1834. The northwestern corner of Missouri, including Saint Joseph, was added to the state in 1836 by the Platte Purchase, the result of a treaty between several Indian tribes and the United States government. This brought an influx of settlers, many of them slaveholders from southern states. The town was platted in 1843 and was named by Robidoux after his patron saint. In 1846 it had 350 houses and several public buildings.

The immigrant tide to the Oregon Territory flowed through Saint Joseph, which was the farthest western town in Missouri with river communication to Saint Louis. By 1849 a daily average of

Council Bluffs and the Missouri River from an elevation. Drawing by Frederick Piercy, 1855. Courtesy Saint Louis Mercantile Library Association

Pony Express Monument at Saint Joseph, Missouri. Walker-Missouri Tourism photo

twenty steamboats, bringing staples in exchange for furs and hides, docked at Saint Joseph. The city was an outfitting point for California-bound pioneers after the discovery of gold there in 1849, and also benefitted from the diversion of immigrants from cholera-ridden Westport and Independence. River traffic on the Missouri diminished following completion of the Hannibal and Saint Joseph Railroad in 1859. Saint Joseph became the eastern terminus for the Pony Express, but a similar distinction for the City for the transcontinental railroad was denied to Saint Joseph because of its pro-Southern sentiment during the Civil War. Like Kansas City, Saint Joseph experienced a railroad-based prosperity after the war, when river traffic practically disappeared. Today, Saint Joseph is an important distribution point and port for barge-line cargoes on the Missouri River.

Drawing by Henry Howe of Leavenworth, Kansas, in the late 1850s. Courtesy Saint Louis Mercantile Library Association

LEAVENWORTH, KANSAS

Spreading over rolling hills above the west bank of the Missouri River, Leavenworth traces its beginning to the establishment of a fort by Colonel Henry H. Leavenworth, in 1827, to protect traffic on the Santa Fe trail. A town gradually developed next to the fort, and after passage of the Kansas-Nebraska Bill of 1854, a town was platted and incorporated in 1855. It grew rapidly with the aid of

steamboat traffic, and by 1860 with eight thousand inhabitants it became the largest city in Kansas. Leavenworth lost that distinction after 1880, when Kansas City came to be preferred as a railroad terminus.

WESTON, MISSOURI

An old town nestled between Missouri River bluffs, Weston is well known for its antebellum architecture. It was founded in 1837 and developed into an important river port, until cut off by a shift in the river in 1857. Since the 1890s, Weston has

Painting by Curtis Gandy of Colonel Henry H. Leavenworth's fort on the Missouri River, founded in 1827. *From St. Louis Globe-Democrat, 1902*

Weston, Missouri, about 1855, before the river shifted. *From The United States Illustrated, 1855. Courtesy State Historical Society of Missouri*

become the largest loose leaf-tobacco market west of the Mississippi.

KANSAS CITY, KANSAS

Located at the point where the Kansas or Kaw River empties into the Missouri, Kansas City was the site of a camp of the Lewis and Clark expedition in 1804. The future townsite became part of a Delaware Indian reservation in 1818, and in turn was purchased in 1843 by the Wyandotte tribe, which migrated from Ohio. They founded a town at the site and disposed of it in 1857 to white settlers, who named it Wyandotte. A rival town named Quindaro was set up on the Missouri River to the north in 1856. A flourishing river traffic soon

made Wyandotte a prominent gateway to the West, aided by the start of Union Pacific Railroad construction in Kansas in 1863. The city's career as a major livestock and packing-house center began during the 1860s. In 1886 Wyandotte, Quindaro, and several other adjacent towns were merged into the present Kansas City.

KANSAS CITY, MISSOURI

The first settlement at the Kansas City site was the fur-trading post set up in the Kansas River bottoms in 1821 by François Chouteau. The trading post was destroyed by a flood in 1830 and Chouteau relocated it at the foot of what is now Grand Avenue, where a ferry had been established in 1828. Here supplies were unloaded from steamboats for transport to Westport, a town founded in 1833, at a site four miles south. The riverside settlement was known as Westport Landing until 1839, when the townsite was platted and the name changed to Kansas City.

Trade on the Santa Fe Trail brought prosperity to the new town. Progress was halted for six years after a cholera epidemic in 1849, and the population diminished by half. However, the town was incorporated as a city in 1853 and in two years much of the trade had returned, causing Kansas City to vie with Saint Joseph and Leavenworth as the "commercial capital of the far West."

In the late 1850s Kansas City became a base for Southern sympathizers who launched forays into neighboring Kansas. This trouble was intensified

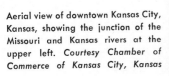

Aerial view of downtown Kansas City, Kansas, showing the junction of the Missouri and Kansas rivers at the upper left. *Courtesy Chamber of Commerce of Kansas City, Kansas*

On the present site of Kansas City, Westport Landing, Missouri, as it appeared about 1839. *Courtesy Jefferson National Expansion Memorial, National Park Service*

Kansas, on the right bank of the Missouri River, one mile below the mouth of the Kansas River, in the 1840s. *From The United States Illustrated, 1855. Courtesy Saint Louis Mercantile Library Association*

The levee at Kansas City, Missouri, 1858. *From The Kansas City Daily Journal of Commerce, 1876. Courtesy State Historical Society of Missouri*

by the outbreak of the Civil War, which caused further inroads into the city's business, halting river commerce. Local trade went to Leavenworth under protection of the Union fort there. After Confederate raiders, under Quantrill, sacked Lawrence, Kansas, Union General Ewing issued his famous Order Number Eleven, which depopulated Kansas City and adjoining Missouri counties of pro-Southerners. The Battle of Westport in 1864 decided the fate of the city in favor of the Union. After the war, in 1866, completion of the interrupted Pacific Railroad from Saint Louis was accomplished. This marked the beginning of a new era of commercial prosperity for Kansas City, with the growth of a rail network in all directions, making the city a center for meat packing and grain trade. With the expansion of the railroads, diminution of river commerce occurred, although intermittent efforts were made to operate packet lines from Saint Louis until after 1900. Barge traffic on the Missouri increased after World War I and by 1940 over one hundred thousand tons of freight were shipped annually at Kansas City. Today, the city shares in the barge-line activity on the Missouri, with its navigable channel to Sioux City, Iowa.

LEXINGTON, MISSOURI

The establishment of a Missouri River ferry at its site in 1819 marked the beginning of Lexington, which was platted in 1822 and named for the former Kentucky hometown of many early settlers. Its rich farm territory was responsible for the town's development into a prosperous river port, which is noted for classic-revival architecture. In 1852 the steamboat *Saluda* exploded at Lexington, with over 150 fatalities. The town was the scene of a Confederate victory on a nearby battlefield in September, 1861.

BRUNSWICK, MISSOURI

Brunswick was laid out in 1836 and between 1840 and 1856 grew rapidly as a river port. In the late fifties, construction of railroads cut off its markets, and in 1875 the capricious Missouri River changed course and left the town a mile inland.

Just east of Kansas City is Independence. This is the town square about 1850. *From The United States Illustrated, 1855. Courtesy Saint Louis Mercantile Library Association*

Aerial view of Lexington, Missouri, 1861. *Courtesy State Historical Society of Missouri*

View of the Missouri River from the Civil War battlegrounds at Lexington, Missouri. *Courtesy State Historical Society of Missouri*

Brunswick, Missouri, on the Missouri River, viewed from Missouri in 1867. *Courtesy Saint Louis Mercantile Association*

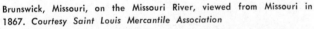

had a population of several thousand, a race track, a library, and a landed gentry. By 1843 Franklin had almost disappeared, displaced by river ports farther upstream.

JEFFERSON CITY, MISSOURI

Jefferson City, on the south bank of the Missouri a short distance above the mouth of the Osage River, was chosen as the site for the Missouri state capital in 1821 and was occupied as such in 1826. Early growth was slow, until hastened by the arrival of German immigrants in the 1830s. By the time of its incorporation in 1839, Jefferson City had become important as a stagecoach stop and steamboat landing. The Pacific Railroad reached the capital from Saint Louis in 1855.

Pro-Southern Governor Claiborne F. Jackson at-

FRANKLIN, MISSOURI

Established on the Missouri River in 1816, Franklin was the debarkation point for steamboats and was considered the "last outpost of civilization." It

Steamboat landing and state capitol building at Jefferson City, Missouri, after the arrival of the German immigrants. *From The United States Illustrated, 1855. Courtesy Saint Louis Mercantile Library Association*

German immigrants in the 1830s also continued farther west to Hermann, Missouri, which they founded in 1837. The colonists, sent out by the German Settlement Society of Philadelphia, found the countryside reminiscent of their Rhine Valley homeland. Local vineyards made Hermann famous as a wine-producing center and an active commerce was built up on the Missouri River. The town is known for its annual German Mai-Fest and contains a fine river museum in its old German school building. *Lithograph by E. Robyn, about 1855. Courtesy State Historical Society of Missouri*

tempted to secede Missouri from the Union, but the capital was soon occupied by Union troops under Colonel Frank P. Blair. An era of industrial expansion began after 1880, and despite an effort to remove the capital to Sedalia in 1896, Jefferson City remained the seat of government, confirming its position when the new state capitol was completed in 1917.

Jefferson City's state capitol and the Missouri River, 1965. *Walker-Missouri Tourism photo*

Washington, Missouri, in the 1860s. *Courtesy State Historical Society of Missouri*

Saint Charles, in the 1850s. *From The United States Illustrated, 1855. Courtesy Saint Louis Mercantile Library Association*

Saint Charles's restored original state capitol building, dedicated as part of the Missouri sesquicentennial celebration in February, 1971. *Walker-Missouri Tourism photo*

WASHINGTON, MISSOURI

A quiet German-American town, Washington was first platted in 1828 and received its first German settlers five years later, when it was little more than a tavern and a ferry crossing. The Germans organized a *Turnverein,* or athletic club, and dramatic groups, and later they proved to be a Missouri bulwark for the Union during the Civil War. A vigorous river trade developed the town's industries. Today Washington is notable for its corncob pipe and zither factories.

SAINT CHARLES, MISSOURI

The original settlement at Saint Charles was made by French-Canadians after 1769, and called Les Petites Côtes (the little hills). Under Spanish dominion the name later changed to San Carlos, which was Anglicized to Saint Charles after the Louisiana Purchase, when the town attracted many American

Lithograph by John Casper Wild of Saint Charles, Missouri, about 1840. *Courtesy Saint Louis Public Library*

settlers. Saint Charles was designated the first state capital of Missouri in 1821, and still contains the first state capitol building.

A wave of German settlers began to arrive in Saint Charles during the 1830s and continued until after the Civil War. The city experienced a healthy commercial and industrial development during this period, which was accompanied by a prosperous river trade. In later years, a similar growth was sustained through the railroads and highways.

Saint Charles, where the Sesquicentennial of Missouri's statehood was held in August, 1971, is developing a historical district of architectural restorations and antique shops.

OHIO RIVER CITIES

PITTSBURGH, PENNSYLVANIA

Pittsburgh, the metropolis of western Pennsylvania, is located at the strategic point where the Allegheny and Monongahela rivers merge to form the

Ohio. George Washington is said to have selected the river junction as a site for a fort.

In 1754 the British began to build a fort but were driven off by the French, who completed it as Fort Duquesne. It later became Fort Pitt under British forces. A settlement there was named Pittsburgh and grew slowly until after the Revolutionary War.

The discovery of iron ore nearby, and the final subjugation of the Indians by Anthony Wayne, led to the incorporation of the village as a borough in 1794 and as a city in 1816. River traffic played an important role in Pittsburgh's history, and the city became the leading boatbuilding center of the West. The city's industrial potential developed rapidly and by 1850 her manufactured products were valued at fifty million dollars.

Pittsburgh's metal industries benefitted greatly from Federal munitions orders during the Civil War. Before the war, Pittsburgh had been reached by trackage of the Pennsylvania and B&O railroads, thereby strengthening her industrial might

Pittsburgh, 1829, soon after it became incorporated. *From The Western Pilot, Samuel Cumings. Courtesy Saint Louis Public Library*

Drawing by A. R. Waud of Pittsburgh, from the Soldiers Monument, emerging as an industrial power. *From Picturesque America, 1872. Courtesy Saint Louis Mercantile Library Association*

Pittsburgh, at the junction of the Allegheny and Monongahela rivers forming the Ohio River. *From A Journey in North America—1796, General Victor Collot. Courtesy Saint Louis Mercantile Library Association*

Map of Pittsburgh, 1805. The Ohio is at the extreme upper left. *Courtesy Saint Louis Mercantile Library Association*

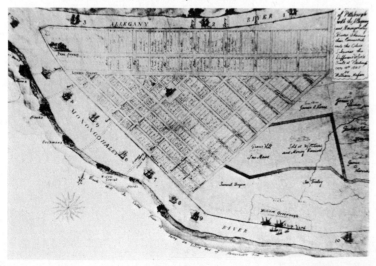

but causing a decline in river-packet activity. River commerce maintained a significant part in Pittsburgh's economy through extensive barge transport of coal and steel products. Extensive government river improvements in the Pittsburgh district have definitely aided the port's tonnage in reaching a volume that has made it the nation's leading inland river-commerce center.

The rivers have dealt harshly with Pittsburgh in the past, particularly in the memorable flood of 1936, which inundated the business district. Floods

Within Pittsburgh's confines are South Pittsburgh (top) and Allegheny City (below). Drawings by A. R. Waud. *From Picturesque America, 1872. Courtesy Saint Louis Mercantile Library Association*

are now controlled by a major system of government-built dams and reservoirs on rivers and creeks in the area. Pittsburgh conquered its smoke problem and has subsequently emerged as a city with a spectacular skyline, in the Golden Triangle, and has many fine cultural and educational institutions.

STEUBENVILLE, OHIO

On a hilly site on the Ohio River, west of Pittsburgh, is Steubenville, founded as a military post in 1786 during a time of Indian warfare. The fort was named for Baron von Steuben, a Prussian who aided the Colonies during the American Revolution. A settlement called La Belle grew up around the fort and was later named Steubenville. The townsite was platted in 1797 by Bezaleel Wells and James Ross and soon became an industrial center with considerable river traffic. After 1820 Steubenville's boatyards built many Ohio River steamboats during the riverboat era.

The dominant industry in the city is steel, which had its beginnings here before the Civil War. Other important local activities include coal mining and pottery making. Completion of the nine-foot Ohio River channel in 1929 permitted cheap transport for bulky products of the area, increasing its industrial potential.

WHEELING, WEST VIRGINIA

Wheeling, at the center of the north panhandle of West Virginia, extends along the east bank of the Ohio River at the mouth of Wheeling Creek. The name of the city is derived from the Delaware Indian *weeling,* meaning skull. The Indians purportedly decapitated slain early white settlers and placed their heads on poles here. The area was first visited by French explorers in 1749 and was settled by the Zane family in 1769. Fort Fincastle, built here by the British in 1774, was renamed Fort Henry by the Americans in 1776. The fort figured prominently as a frontier outpost during the Revolutionary War and witnessed the last battle of the conflict in 1782. The town was platted as Zanesburg in 1793 and became the county seat in 1797. It was chartered as Wheeling in 1806 and became a thriving commercial center after the opening of the National Road in 1818. Wheeling was the

Drawing by Henry Howe of Market Street, Steubenville, Ohio, about 1850. *Courtesy Saint Louis Public Library*

Wheeling, Virginia, about 1855. It became West Virginia in 1863. *From The United States Illustrated, 1855. Courtesy Saint Louis Mercantile Library Association*

The suspension bridge across the Ohio River at Wheeling that provoked a fight with Pittsburgh. *From Lloyd's Steamboat Directory, 1856. Courtesy Saint Louis Public Library*

point of transshipment for the river voyage down the Ohio, which made it a port of entry, by Federal declaration, and in 1836 the city was incorporated.

A long fight with Pittsburgh concerning a bridge across the Ohio was finally decided in favor of

Wheeling by the Supreme Court, and a suspension bridge was completed there in 1856. Pittsburgh had contended that a bridge would make Wheeling the head of navigation on the river. Wheeling was the first capital of West Virginia following separation from Virginia in 1863, holding that honor until 1870 and again between 1875 and 1885, when the capital was permanently established at Charleston.

In March, 1936, the Ohio inflicted serious damage when Wheeling Island was completely inundated and boats were the only means of travel in the business district of the city. Wheeling today is the trade center of a rich coal area and has extensive mills and industries.

MARIETTA, OHIO

Marietta, the pioneer settlement of Ohio, is situated at the junction of the Muskingum and Ohio rivers. From its inception, the town has been identified with river traffic and was a prominent boat-building center before the Civil War. It was part of a land purchase by the Ohio Company from Congress in 1787. Marietta had its origin with the arrival of settlers under General Rufus Putnam in April, 1788. It was named after Queen Marie Antoinette out of gratitude for French aid during the Revolution. A fortified village was built on a bluff above the Muskingum, near the Ohio River. The fort was named Campus Martius after its Roman counterpart, and was finally abandoned after the Treaty of Greenville assured frontier peace with the Indians. Marietta's cultural heritage is manifested in its fine old homes and the Campus Martius Museum, the latter containing a fine collection of steamboating memorabilia. Nearby is the former sternwheel towboat *W. P. Snyder, Jr.,* permanently moored as a floating marine exhibit.

PARKERSBURG, WEST VIRGINIA

Situated at the confluence of the Ohio and Little Kanawha rivers, the site of Parkersburg was visited by George Washington in 1770 to locate his land grants. Founded in 1785, the village was named in 1810 for Alexander Parker, an early settler. Parkersburg began to assume commercial importance about 1820, when steamboats came into general use. By the 1840s, when a system of locks

Marietta, Ohio, built on a bluff. *From A Journey in North America—1796,* General Victor Collot. *Courtesy Saint Louis Mercantile Library Association*

River museum: sternwheel towboat *W. P. Snyder, Jr.,* at Marietta, Ohio. *Courtesy State of Ohio, Department of Industrial and Economic Development*

and dams on the Little Kanawha was built and new turnpikes opened, Parkersburg was one of the busiest ports on the Ohio. A boom period started with the discovery of oil in the vicinity about 1859, resulting in incorporation as a city in 1863. Only slightly affected by the Civil War, Parkersburg's industrial development increased after 1890 when nearby gas fields supplied fuel for manufacturing.

POMEROY, OHIO

Pomeroy lies along the Ohio River at the great Pomeroy Bend, in a coal-mining area. It was named for a Boston merchant who purchased the townsite in 1804. With the advent of steamboats, Pomeroy became an important coal producing and shipping point. Salt wells have also been a major local industry.

GALLIPOLIS, OHIO

Gallipolis is an old river town settled by French immigrants in 1790. Agents of the Scioto Land Company in Paris sold the land on the eve of the French Revolution. The name, means "city of the Gauls." Most of the original settlers eventually abandoned the townsite to the privations of the wilderness. Gallipolis later became an important river town when resettled by Americans, who shipped coal and produce. A tourist attraction here is Our House, an early inn once patronized by Lafayette.

HUNTINGTON, WEST VIRGINIA

Huntington, at the junction of the Ohio and Guyandot rivers, is the largest city in a three-state industrial complex covering West Virginia, Kentucky, and Ohio. The first settlement in the area was the village of Guyandotte in 1810. Its growth was stimulated by the opening of the James River and Kanawha Turnpike in 1830, and it became a flourishing river town. Because of Southern sympathizers, the town was burned by Union troops in 1861. Restored after the war, Guyandotte hoped to become a railroad center.

However, Collis P. Huntington, head of the Chesapeake and Ohio Railway, decided to build a new town for the terminus of the railroad. The town of Huntington was laid out in 1871 and named after its founder. With later extension of the C&O, Huntington began a period of growth, leading to its present position as the principal city of West Virginia. A city charter adopted in 1910 provided for the inclusion of several surrounding towns, including Guyandotte, into the present municipality. Huntington has suffered from periodic floods of the Ohio River, the worst being in 1937 when four-fifths of the habitable area was under water. A flood wall has since been built to prevent a disastrous recurrence. The city today is one of the principal river ports on the Ohio for barge-line activity.

Lafayette also popularized Lafayette Spring, on the Ohio River, near Tell City, Indiana. He camped here during his fourth visit to the United States, when the steamer *Mechanic*, on which he was traveling, struck a rock and sank near the spring. Lafayette lost his carriage, baggage, and $8,000 in gold in the calamity. *Photo by Ken Williams. Courtesy State of Indiana, Department of Natural Resources*

Aerial view of Huntington, West Virginia, and the Ohio River, 1941. *Courtesy Huntington Chamber of Commerce*

ASHLAND, KENTUCKY

The principal city of eastern Kentucky is Ashland, located on the Ohio River, near the mouth of the Big Sandy River. The city stretches for seven miles along the Ohio following the contours of the river bluffs. The city's industrial waterfront is protected from flooding by a high riverbank, lined with steel mills and industrial plants.

Ashland was first settled in 1815 and was called Poage Settlement after its founders. Lumbering, the first important industry, was superseded by

View of three states, Kentucky, West Virginia, and Ohio, from Ashland, Kentucky. Mouth of the Big Sandy River is at left center. *Courtesy Saint Louis Public Library*

mining after the discovery of iron ore in the area in 1826. Ashland was platted in 1850 and named for Henry Clay's home in Lexington. It was incorporated as a village in 1858. Its iron production increased considerably during the Civil War. Ashland's industrial activity boomed following the war, when many blast furnaces and steel mills were built. Accessibility of clay deposits soon made brickmaking important, and later the discovery of oil and gas resources launched a new industrial era for the town. River traffic is an essential factor in Ashland's economy, and for the highly industrialized three-state area, as well.

PORTSMOUTH, OHIO

Portsmouth, on the Ohio River at the mouth of the Scioto, is a busy industrial center with a river-town background. Originally settled as Alexandria in 1803 on low-lying land, but it was soon relocated to its present site and given its present name. It had attained a population of three hundred by 1815 after its incorporation. The town's strategic river location made it a flourishing river port and boatbuilding center. Portsmouth became a commercial hub of south-central Ohio after the opening of the Ohio and Erie Canal in 1832. Chief local industries are iron and steel production, clay products, and sandstone quarrying. With the decline of river traffic, Portsmouth became an active railroad shipping point. The city is located in a region rich in prehistoric Indian mounds and archaeological artifacts.

Maysville, Kentucky, about 1850. From Western Scenery on Land and River. *Courtesy Saint Louis Mercantile Library Association*

MAYSVILLE, KENTUCKY

Maysville is built in terraces above the Ohio River, at the mouth of Limestone Creek. First known as Limestone, the town, established by the Virginia legislature in 1787, had become a principal port of entry by 1792. The wealth of Maysville was due to river traffic, as the town was a distribution point for goods destined for central Kentucky. It was named for John May, the original owner of the townsite.

NEWPORT, KENTUCKY

Newport was begun in 1790 by Hubbard Taylor, a

young soldier from Virginia who planned a town named after Christopher Newport, commander of the first ship to reach Jamestown in 1607. It was not much more than a clearing in its first years, but it became the county seat in 1796, a year after its incorporation as a village. Newport was incorporated as a city in 1835 and attracted many German immigrants during the 1840s. The city was the scene of much dissension between the North and South before the Civil War. During the late decades of the nineteenth century, Newport enjoyed a mild industrial boom but has grown little since. Its nearness to Cincinnati has drawn many Newport residents across the river for employment.

COVINGTON, KENTUCKY

Covington is located at the junction of the Licking

View of Covington (left) and Newport (right), Kentucky, about 1855. Cincinnati, Ohio, is in the background. *From Voyage Pittoresque et Anecdotique dans le Nord et Sud des Etats-Unis d' Amérique. Courtesy Saint Louis Mercantile Library Association*

and Ohio rivers, across the Ohio from Cincinnati. It was originally founded by Thomas Kennedy as a ferry crossing and tavern in 1801. The town was chartered in 1815 and named for General Leonard Covington, a hero of the War of 1812. Growth was slow until 1830. River traffic and western emigration made Covington a trade center during the next decade, and after 1840 the population was increased by a large number of German settlers. Construction of a bridge to Cincinnati was authorized by the Kentucky legislature, in 1846, but was stopped, periodically, until after the Civil War. The Suspension Bridge was finally completed on January 1, 1867, at a cost of $1,800,000. Covington has long suffered from Ohio River floods beginning in 1832 and climaxing with the disastrous inundation of 1937. Modern Covington has diversified industries, but its economic and social life are strongly influenced by Cincinnati.

CINCINNATI, OHIO

The second oldest settlement in Ohio, Cincinnati was founded in November, 1788, a few months after the establishment of Marietta. Originally named Losantiville, the city received its present name in 1790 in honor of a military society of Revolutionary War officers. Early growth was slow, but after its incorporation in 1814, the city began a boom period, accelerated by completion of the Miami Canal northward to Toledo. Cincinnati's central location on the Ohio River made it a transshipment point for cargoes during the steamboat era. The city experienced great population growth before the Civil War, due to massive immigrations of Germans. By 1860 its population had risen to

Floods plagued the river towns. This is a scene on the lower Mississippi. From a drawing by A. R. Waud in *Harper's Pictorial History of the Civil War. Courtesy Saint Louis Mercantile Library Association*

Fort Washington was the beginning of Cincinnati, built on the present site in 1790. *From Cincinnati, 1851. Courtesy Saint Louis Public Library*

Cincinnati in 1802. *From The Queen City, 1869. Courtesy Saint Louis Mercantile Library Association*

Map of Cincinnati, 1815, just after incorporation. *From Drake's Natural and Statistical View of Cincinnati, 1815. Courtesy Saint Louis Mercantile Library Association*

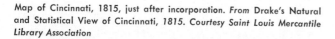

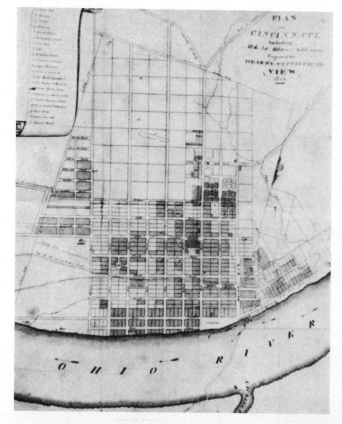

Public Landing, Cincinnati, 1841. *From Cincinnati, 1841. Courtesy Saint Louis Public Library*

Cincinnati riverfront, from the Kentucky shore, about 1848, a transshipment point on the Ohio. *Courtesy Saint Louis Public Library*

Opposite Cincinnati, the mouth of the Licking River, about 1850. *From Western Scenery on Land and River, 1851. Courtesy Saint Louis Mercantile Library Association*

161,044 and Cincinnati became known as the Queen City of the West. Sentiment was divided during the war but was finally resolved by the pro-Union stand of the German populace. River traffic, which had dwindled during the fifties, took on new life in the postbellum period, when packet passage was obtainable to all principal river ports.

A prominent feature along Cincinnati's levee at this time was a row of huge posts at its summit. These were used to anchor steamboats during high-water periods, when the boats were level with riverfront warehouses. Floods have been disastrous to Cincinnati on numerous occasions, significantly in 1883 and 1937. Another river-borne menace was ice, causing severe damage to steamboats when it broke up. One of the worst ice jams occurred in January, 1918, when several of the river's few large surviving packet boats were crushed and sunk. In the early twentieth century, river trade at Cincinnati suffered from the general decline resulting from railroad competition, but it has shared in the revival of waterway commerce since World War II created by barge-line activities.

Cincinnati is the headquarters of the last river-packet company, the Greene Line, operators of the *Delta Queen*. For many years the city was the home of the famous Louisville and Cincinnati Packet Company and of excursion boat runs to the nearby Coney Island amusement park. The Ohio is

Cincinnati about 1870, when river traffic was spurred by the packet boats. *From Harper's Weekly. Courtesy Saint Louis Mercantile Library Association*

Cincinnati Public Landing from the deck of a steamboat, about the middle 1930s. *Courtesy Jefferson National Expansion Memorial, National Park Service*

The Ohio also sustained agriculture at Cincinnati. This scene is at Grandin Road. *From Cincinnati Illustrated, 1875. Courtesy Saint Louis Mercantile Library Association*

Drawings by A. R. Waud of Ohio River scenes near Cincinnati. *From Picturesque America, 1872. Courtesy Saint Louis Mercantile Library Association*

The *Delta Queen,* still in service, docked at Memphis. *Courtesy State of Tennessee Conservation Department*

Drawing by A. R. Waud of Cincinnati from Mount Adams, 1872, showing the newly completed suspension bridge. *From Picturesque America, 1872. Courtesy Saint Louis Mercantile Library Association*

crossed at Cincinnati by several bridges, including the famous Suspension Bridge completed in 1867.

MADISON, INDIANA

Madison, situated on the Ohio River about halfway between Cincinnati and Louisville, has a Southern atmosphere with fine old antebellum structures. The first settlement was in 1805, but the town was not platted until 1809 by Colonel John Paul, a Revolutionary War veteran. He named it in honor of President James Madison. As

Drawing by A. R. Waud of Jeffersonville, Indiana, 1872, a famous steamboat-building town. *From Picturesque America 1872. Courtesy Saint Louis Mercantile Library Association*

Madison, Indiana, nestled under the bluffs, from the Kentucky side of the Ohio River. *Photo by Ken Williams. Courtesy State of Indiana, Department of Natural Resources*

the nearest port to the interior of Indiana, Madison grew rapidly until by 1850 it became one of the state's largest cities. Madison was an important boatbuilding center during the nineteenth century and is a distribution point for tobacco grown in the area.

JEFFERSONVILLE, INDIANA

One of the oldest towns in Indiana, Jeffersonville was originally settled with the construction of Fort Steuben in 1786. The town was platted in 1802 by William Henry Harrison at the suggestion of Thomas Jefferson. It prospered during the river-

boat period and was the location of the well-known Howard Shipyards, where many famous steamboats were built between 1834 and 1942. Jeffersonville probably sustained the most damage of any city on the Ohio in the 1937 flood, when ninety-five percent of its area was inundated.

LOUISVILLE, KENTUCKY

Louisville, the largest city in Kentucky, may well owe its existence to the Falls of the Ohio River, which interrupted navigation at this point. The falls were visited by Spanish missionaries and French explorers during the seventeenth and eigh-

Map of the Falls of the Ohio at Louisville. *From A Journey in North America—1796, General Victor Collot. Courtesy Saint Louis Mercantile Library Association*

George Rogers Clark, author of the successful plan to capture the Northwest Territory from the British. He was the elder brother of William Clark of expedition fame. *From History of the Louisiana Purchase Exposition, 1904*

Shippingport, on the Ohio, the present site of Louisville. Etching by Captain Basil Hall, 1829. *Courtesy Ardell Thompson Collection*

Louisville a generation later, seen from the Public Landing, 1850. *From Western Scenery on Land and River. Courtesy Saint Louis Mercantile Library Association*

teenth centuries. The first settlement was attempted in 1773 by Captain Thomas Bullitt and a band of frontiersmen who remained only a year. George Rogers Clark established a base of operations here in 1778 against the British Northwest Territory. About twenty families accompanied the soldiers and settled on Corn Island, across from the present site of Louisville. After a successful campaign against the British and Indians, Clark's men built a fort on the Kentucky shore in 1778–1779. This was Clark's headquarters until the completion of Fort Nelson in 1782, in what is now the business district of Louisville. The town was named in 1780 in honor of King Louis XVI, for French aid during the American Revolution.

Louisville's location at the portage point for Ohio River traffic around the falls was responsible for its early growth and commercial importance. The first steamboat to navigate the Ohio River, the *New Orleans*, arrived at Louisville in 1811, and after 1820, Louisville's prosperity was dependent upon steamboat traffic. Louisville was incorporated in 1828. Through-navigation to bypass the falls was achieved in 1830 when the Portland Canal was completed and Louisville became a city of wealth and commerce. An influx of Yankees and Germans settled during this period and were later responsible for the city's Union support during the Civil War.

After the War, a duel for commercial preemin-ence developed between Louisville and Cincinnati, which was eventually resolved in a peaceful division of Southern trade. Louisville became a principal rail center following the decline of river traffic after 1880, increasing its position as the market and industrial hub of a wide area. Today barge-line activity is a significant force in the city's diversified economy. Louisville is a leader in tobacco, whiskey, paint, and many other industries.

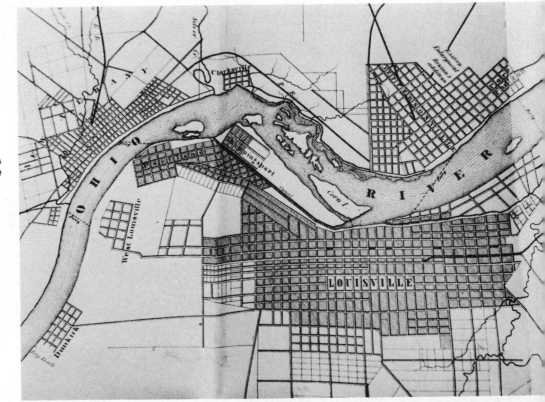

Map of Louisville in 1852. *From Casseday's History of Louisville, 1852. Courtesy Saint Louis Public Library*

Louisville on its way to becoming a principal rail center. The railroad bridge spans the Ohio. Drawing by A. R. Waud. *From Picturesque America, 1872*

Louisville levee, about 1900. *From Historic Towns of the Southern States. Courtesy Saint Louis Public Library*

New Albany, Indiana

New Albany was platted in 1813 by the Scribner brothers from New York, who foresaw the commercial potential of a townsite below the Falls of the Ohio. The falls were the only break in navigation between Pittsburgh and the mouth of the Ohio River at Cairo. The strategic location of the town caused a remarkable growth in population and importance, due to river traffic in the western migrations. Boatbuilding yards were established here soon after the introduction of steamboats on the Ohio. The first boat built at New Albany was the *Ohio* in 1817, followed by the *Volcano* in 1818. Boat construction was especially active between 1847 and 1867. Such famous steamboats as the *Eclipse* and the *Robert E. Lee* were built at New Albany yards. By 1850 New Albany was the largest

Drawing by A. R. Waud of New Albany, Indiana, once a great shipyard. *From Picturesque America, 1872. Courtesy Saint Louis Mercantile Library Association*

New Albany's *Peytona*, built in 1859. She was destroyed in the Yazoo River in 1863. *From American Steam Vessels, 1895*

The *Eclipse*, built at New Albany, Indiana, in 1852, was probably the largest, fanciest, and most luxurious of all antebellum steamboats. She cost $375,000 and measured 365 feet by 40 feet by 9 feet and had a cabin 330 feet long. *Courtesy Waterways Journal*

The *Robert E. Lee,* winner of the race with the *Natchez* in 1870, was built at New Albany in 1866. She was later succeeded by another, even more ornate boat bearing the same name. She was dismantled in 1876. *From a drawing by the author*

city in Indiana and its boatbuilders reached a peak year in 1856, when they turned out twenty-two packets. It was second in rank, behind Pittsburgh, as the chief city for marine construction in the Ohio Valley. The end of the steamboat-building era came shortly after the Civil War, and New Albany developed many other industrial pursuits to continue its growth. The construction of the famous *Robert E. Lee* was completed in 1866 and the boat's name affixed only after it was moved to the Kentucky side of the river; reports had Union sympathizers planning to burn the *Lee* because it bore the Confederate general's name.

OWENSBORO, KENTUCKY

Owensboro, in the center of an agricultural and oil-producing area, was first known as Yellow Banks because of an unusual stretch of yellow clay on the nearby bank of the Ohio River. Yellow

Banks was chosen as the seat of Daviess County in 1815 and was renamed Rossborough. When it was chartered as a city in 1866, it received its present name in honor of Colonel Abraham Owen, an early Kentucky hero in the Indian wars. Owensboro became an important river port by 1850 and was the scene of several skirmishes during the Civil War. Present-day Owensboro is a tobacco-processing center and the home of large distilleries and electronics industries.

EVANSVILLE, INDIANA

Located on the Ohio River about midway between Louisville and Cairo, Evansville has a fine harbor and was a prominent river port during the steamboat era. The earliest settler at Evansville was Colonel Hugh McGary, who operated a ferry about 1812. In 1815 McGary sold a section to General Robert Evans, who replatted the town, which was called Evansville. The town was incorporated in 1819 and grew with the westward migration of settlers traveling down the Ohio on flatboats. With the advent of steamboats, river traffic at Evansville increased tremendously, reaching a peak in the mid-1850s. An exception was the winter of 1831–1832, when the Ohio froze solid to a depth of twenty-two inches. Evansville was incorporated as a city in 1848, and in 1853 the long-deferred Wabash and Erie Canal was completed. That same year, the first train arrived in the city, closing the canal in 1860 and causing the eventual decline of the packet lines. After the Civil War, Evansville became the industrial and commercial center of southwestern Indiana. Floods interfered with local commercial activities at various times, notably in 1913 and 1937. After the 1937 calamity, when forty-six percent of the city was submerged, a huge levee was

Owensboro, Kentucky, along the Ohio, an important port in 1850. *Courtesy Saint Louis Public Library*

Evansville, Indiana, riverfront about 1900. *Courtesy Saint Louis Public Library*

Riverfront at Evansville, Indiana, today. *Courtesy Neare-Gibbs and Company and the Waterways Journal*

Junction of the Tennessee and Ohio rivers viewed from the levee at Paducah, Kentucky. *Courtesy Saint Louis Public Library*

Paducah harbor, 1850s. *Courtesy Saint Louis Public Library*

built to protect the city. Growth has been steady, however, and the city today is a busy barge-line port.

PADUCAH, KENTUCKY

Paducah lies on the Ohio River flood plain, where the Ohio is joined by the Tennessee River. The first settlers arrived in 1821 and named their village Pekin. The area was part of a grant made by Virginia to George Rogers Clark in 1795 as a reward for his valor in the Revolutionary War. After Clark's death in 1818, his claim was revived by his brother William, of Lewis and Clark expedition fame. William Clark laid out a townsite here in 1827 and renamed it Paducah, in honor of his friend Chief Paduke of the Chickasaw tribe. The community prospered from heavy river traffic to such an extent that it was incorporated in 1830 and became a city in 1856. The location, near four great rivers, made Paducah a busy transshipment port. A flourishing lumber industry developed here during the 1840s and 1850s from log-rafting on the Tennessee and Cumberland rivers. The city was important strategically to the Union during the Civil War and was the scene of a desperate, unsuccessful Confederate attack by General Nathan B. Forrest in 1864. With the revival of river traffic after the war, Paducah became a boatbuilding center. It later became an important railroad hub and, with the growth of barge-line activity after 1920, Paducah attained new prominence as a river port. Extensive damage was sustained here in the 1937 Ohio River flood, when over ninety percent of the

city's buildings were made untenable and the damage amounted to thirty million dollars. The city is known as a great tobacco-producing center and as the home town of Irvin S. Cobb, the great American humorist.

CAIRO, ILLINOIS

The southernmost point in Illinois is Cairo, at the junction of the Ohio and Mississippi rivers. The first settlement there was made by the French,

Lithograph by Henry Lewis of Cairo, Illinois, 1835, junction of the Ohio and Mississippi rivers. *Courtesy Saint Louis Public Library*

Lithograph by John Casper Wild of Cairo about 1840. *Courtesy Saint Louis Public Library*

under Charles Juchereau de Saint Denis in 1702, but was soon abandoned because of the prevalence of disease. The next attempt was by John Comegys, a Saint Louis merchant who established the town in 1818 and named it Cairo because the country resembled the Nile delta. After Comegys' death in 1820, the community languished until 1837, when the Cairo City and Canal Company was organized by Darius Holbrook, of Boston. A levee was built, and the population increased to over a thousand, before the failure of the company in 1840. Among those losing money in the failure was Charles Dickens, who critically characterized Cairo in later novels. Cairo's prosperity began with completion of a rail link to Chicago, which led to the city's incorporation in 1857. It was a Union Army center during the Civil War, and after the war it became the most important city in southern Illinois. There were sixty-seven hundred steamboat arrivals at

Cairo in 1867, at which time it was also a connection point for rail-river shipping. Cairo was the only city on the lower Ohio River that was not submerged in the great 1937 flood, because of its high levee. Modern barges and towboats have replaced the packets at Cairo's old waterfront.

ARKANSAS RIVER CITIES

TULSA, OKLAHOMA

Oklahoma's second city, Tulsa, known as the Oil Capital of the World, was originally settled about 1836 by Creek Indians from Georgia. The name Tulsa was the Creek word for town or community. The village remained essentially the same until 1882 when the present Frisco Railroad arrived. By 1889, when the Oklahoma Territory was opened for settlement, Tulsa was a thriving cattle town. It was first surveyed in 1900. In 1905 oil was discovered across the river and the boom began.

Tulsa's phenomenal rise in population went from more than 18,100 in 1910 to more than 141,000 in 1930, when the city began to assume its metropolitan aspect of today. With the opening of

Tulsa, 1893, from Standpipe Hill. The First Methodist Episcopal Church stands at what is now the corner of Main and Brady streets. *Courtesy Metropolitan Tulsa Chamber of Commerce*

Tulsa today. *Courtesy Metropolitan Tulsa Chamber of Commerce*

The Ohio River flood of 1937. This is Old Shawneetown, Illinois, seen from the Ohio River. Shawneetown, dating from the early nineteenth century, was the gateway to the Illinois country. At the time, according to legend, local bankers had turned down a thousand-dollar loan to a group of Chicagoans because "Chicago was too far away from Shawneetown ever to amount to anything." After the disastrous flood a new town was established in the hills bordering the river. *Courtesy State of Illinois, Department of Conservation*

the Arkansas River Waterway to Catoosa, Tulsa's port on the Verdigris River, the city and its trade territory will enter into another period of commercial prosperity.

MUSKOGEE, OKLAHOMA

Muskogee, near the confluence of the Arkansas, Grand, and Verdigris rivers, began with the arrival of the M.K.&T. Railroad in 1872, and was named after the Muskogee Indian tribe. It became the headquarters of the U.S. Indian Agency in 1875 and experienced its greatest growth after the opening of the oil fields in 1901. Muskogee is expected to benefit well, commercially and industrially, thanks to the Arkansas River Waterway.

FORT SMITH, ARKANSAS

Fort Smith was established as a military post in 1817 to keep peace among the Indians. A town later took form at the fort, at the junction of the Arkansas and Poteau rivers. It was an important departure point for California-bound gold seekers in 1849. Fort Smith was the practical head of navigation during the steamboat era on the Arkansas River. Although it is now an agricultural center, Fort Smith is highly industrialized and will be a busy port on the new Arkansas River Waterway.

The old fort, Fort Smith, Arkansas, about 1900. *Courtesy Saint Louis Public Library*

LITTLE ROCK, ARKANSAS

Little Rock received its name from a rock promontory jutting out from the south bank of the Arkan-

sas River. It was so named by explorer Bénard de la Harpe in 1722 to distinguish it from a large bluff upriver. The spot later was a fort on the Great Southwest Trail and attracted its first settler

The "little rock" from which Little Rock, Arkansas, takes its name. *From Arkansas Yesterday and Today, 1917. Courtesy Saint Louis Public Library*

Little Rock levee, about 1900, victim of the railroads. *Courtesy Saint Louis Public Library*

An excursion boat still plies the Arkansas River at Little Rock. *Courtesy Arkansas Publicity and Parks Commission*

in 1812. Seven years later a land speculator laid out the town of Arkopolis at the site. In 1821 it was chosen as capital of the Arkansas Territory and officially named Little Rock. Steamboat activity began as early as 1822 and reached its zenith during the 1850s. The city was occupied by Northern forces in 1863 after retreat by Confederates. Railroad expansion in the 1880s brought a rapid increase in Little Rock's population. One of the city's outstanding landmarks is the Old State Capitol, a fine example of Greek Revival architecture, which is now a war memorial.

PINE BLUFF, ARKANSAS

Pine Bluff is located on a bluff along a deep bend of the Arkansas River. It was started as a trading post in 1819, and a settlement developed slowly, attaining a population of only 460 in 1850. By 1860 Pine Bluff became a busy cotton-shipping port for steamboats and the center of a wealthy plantation district. A Confederate attack was repulsed by entrenched Union troops in October, 1863. During Reconstruction, the city was the leading cotton port in the state. Pine Bluff is now a center for lumbering, chemicals, and livestock, as well as cotton.

RED RIVER CITIES

SHREVEPORT, LOUISIANA

Shreveport, Louisiana's second city, is on the Red River about eighteen miles east of the Texas border. Bienville found a Caddo Indian village here, on the Red River bluffs, in 1700. Larkin Edwards, from Tennessee, settled on the site in 1803, acting as an Indian interpreter. In 1835 his lands became the location of a small settlement. The townsite was sold by Edwards to Henry M. Shreve and others in 1837, and in 1839 it was incorporated as Shreveport. Shreve had succeeded in breaking through the Great Raft of jammed timber in the Red River to open the town to river commerce. By 1863, the town was of sufficient importance to become the Confederate capital of Louisiana. Steamboat traffic dwindled toward the end of the nineteenth century because of railroad competition. The discovery of oil nearby in 1906 led to a boom

The old Caddo Parish Court House at Shreveport, Louisiana, about 1910. *Courtesy Saint Louis Public Library*

Texas Street, Shreveport, 1907. *Courtesy Saint Louis Public Library*

period for Shreveport, which is also a center for cotton and lumber processing.

NATCHITOCHES, LOUISIANA

Natchitoches, pronounced "Nak-a-tosh," is the oldest settlement in the Louisiana Purchase. The region was explored by La Salle in the seventeenth century. It was established as a fort in 1715 with Juchereau de Saint Denis as commandant. Its location at a junction of important water and land routes made it a busy center until 1832, when a shift in the Red River left it on the bank of a quiet lake. Natchitoches lost much business during the Civil War, but later recovered and is now a prime point for the processing and shipping of cotton products.

ALEXANDRIA, LOUISIANA

Alexandria is located on the Red River at a rapids where during the late eighteenth century a fort was built to protect the portage. A settlement grew up on the site, which was formally platted in 1810 by Alexander Fulton, who named it after his daughter. The town became a busy port during the steamboat era, with exports of cotton, lumber, and sugar. A railroad was begun here as early as 1837, and in 1849 a steam ferry operated across the Red River to Pineville. Alexandria was occupied by Federal troops in 1864. Union forces dammed the river in order to circumvent the rapids to get their gunboats upstream, but troops retreating from their defeat at Mansfield set fire to Alexandria, largely destroying the town. The city's industry is now principally based upon agricultural products, chiefly cotton, as well as on woodworking and chemicals.

TENNESSEE RIVER CITIES

KNOXVILLE, TENNESSEE

Knoxville is located in eastern Tennessee, on the Tennessee River, which is formed by the nearby confluence of the Holston and French Broad rivers. The first settler in the area was Captain James White, who built a cabin on the future townsite in 1786. White had received land grants in the area as a reward for his Revolutionary War service. A town was soon platted and named in honor of General Henry Knox, Secretary of War in Washington's cabinet. Knoxville was twice the state capital of Tennessee, between 1796 and 1812 and again from 1817 to 1819. Although the town was of considerable commercial importance, its growth was slow prior to the Civil War. It was important as a river port on the upper Tennessee, and was first reached by rail in 1852. Eastern Tennessee was loyal to the Union during the Civil War and so Knoxville was occupied by Confederates until August, 1863. Later that year, Union forces in the city were besieged by Southerners under General Longstreet. This move failed and the Union remained in control. After 1880 Knoxville's growth became quite rapid, with a population of more than thirty-two thousand being attained by 1900. Knoxville is the seat of the University of Tennessee, and is near the great T.V.A. development at Norris Dam.

CHATTANOOGA, TENNESSEE

Chattanooga lies on the sharp Moccasin Bend of the Tennessee River, near the Georgia border. The earliest settlement at the site was Ross's Landing in 1815. A town was laid out and named Chattanooga in 1838, when steamboat traffic on the upper Tennessee began to develop. The town was connected to the eastern seaboard by rail in 1849.

Lookout Mountain, a Civil War battleground, from the Tennessee River at Chattanooga, Tennessee. Rising to a height of twenty-three hundred feet, it is one of the most historic peaks in America. *Courtesy Saint Louis Public Library*

Bridge over the Tennessee River at Knoxville, Tennessee, in the horse and buggy days. *Courtesy Saint Louis Public Library*

North of Lookout Point is Signal Mountain, near Chattanooga. Looking east from Brady's Point. *Courtesy Saint Louis Public Library*

Nashville, about 1850, showing the old state capitol building. *Courtesy Saint Louis Public Library*

Chattanooga was a center of strategic importance in the Civil War, when several key battles were fought at nearby Chickamauga, Lookout Mountain, and Missionary Ridge. Today, Chattanooga is a tourist hub of scenic and historic interest and is a principal headquarters for T.V.A. activities.

CUMBERLAND RIVER CITIES

NASHVILLE, TENNESSEE

Nashville, the capital of Tennessee, is situated on both banks of the Cumberland River, in the central part of the state. The first settlers, led by James Robertson, arrived in 1779 and established a fort named for General Francis Nash of North Carolina. The town was located at the northern end of the Natchez Trace, a much used road traveled by

boatmen returning northward in pre-steamboat days. The town grew to prominence as a cotton center and river port, with considerable industries. The town was incorporated by the North Carolina legislature in 1784, and after Tennessee's statehood, Nashville was chartered as a city in 1806. Steamboating began at Nashville in 1818 and reached its peak during the decade before the Civil War. The city was chosen as the state capital in 1843 and about ten years later it was linked by rail with Chattanooga. During the Civil War, Nashville was occupied by Federal forces in February, 1862, and was the scene of a decisive defeat to Confederates under General Hood in December, 1864. Nashville is called the Athens of the South, because of a replica of the Parthenon in Centennial Park, site of the Tennessee Exposition of 1897. Today Nashville is an important educational center and has a widely diversified commerce and industry.

On the Cumberland River, at Nashville, in 1855, with the old suspension bridge in the background. *From Lloyd's Steamboat Directory, 1856*

KANAWHA RIVER CITIES

CHARLESTON, WEST VIRGINIA

Charleston, capital of West Virginia, is in the narrow Kanawha River valley at its junction with the Elk River. The origin of Charleston may be traced to the construction of Fort Lee, for protection of the Great Kanawha Valley, in 1788. The fort's commander, Colonel George Clendenin, was authorized by the Virginia Assembly to plat a town there in 1794. He named it Charles Town, after his father. The present name was adopted later

The Kanawha River reflects the lights of Charleston, West Virginia's capital city. *Courtesy State of West Virginia Department of Commerce*

through usage. Daniel Boone resided here for seven years, until 1795 when he returned to Kentucky.

The Kanawha Turnpike reached Charleston in 1804, making the town a point of transfer from overland to water transport. The local salt industry was stimulated by the advent of the steamboat in 1824. Coal, oil, and gas deposits created new industry in the area when salt production declined. The town was held by the Union during the Civil War and was relatively untouched by military activity. Charleston was the state capital from 1870 to 1875, when it was returned to Wheeling. However, Charleston was made the permanent capital after a special election in 1885. Railroad connections and river improvements on the Kanawha led to increased coal mining, greatly aiding the town's growth. Establishment of the chemical industry in Charleston occurred about 1913, marking the beginning of modern industrial development in the Kanawha Valley.

WABASH RIVER CITIES

VINCENNES, INDIANA

Vincennes, the oldest city in Indiana, is one of the most historic towns in the Mississippi Valley. A French fur-trading post was established on its site in the late seventeenth century, followed by a fort which was commanded by François Morgane de

Fort Sackville at the present site of Vincennes, Indiana, on the Wabash River, captured by George Rogers Clark in 1779. From Historic Towns of the Western States

Vincennes in 1732. The settlement was named in his honor after he was burned at the stake by the Indians in 1736. The fort was ceded to the British by the Treaty of Paris in 1763, and named Fort Sackville. It was captured by Americans under George Rogers Clark in 1779, with aid from the Creole villagers of Vincennes. The village began to lose its French flavor with the arrival of large numbers of Germans in the 1840s. Beginning in the 1820s, steamboat navigation on the Wabash River made Vincennes a busy port. The railroad from Cincinnati to Saint Louis was completed through Vincennes in 1857, inaugurating a new industrial era for the city. Growth has since been steady, with the German and American population gradually supplanting the French. Modern Vincennes is the seat of agriculturally rich Knox County and is the home of a diversified group of industrial plants.

NEW HARMONY, INDIANA

New Harmony, on the Wabash River, is notable as the home of two communal experiments. The town was founded in 1815 by followers of George Rapp, who originally came from Germany. Their beliefs dictated celibacy and common ownership of property. After starting crops and vineyards, the Rappites sold "Harmonie" to Robert Owen, a Welsh philanthropist, in 1825. Owen sought to create a "new moral world," founded upon common cooperation and progressive educational ideas. One of the better-known instructors was William Maclure, the "father of American geology." Owen abandoned his colony in 1827, but New Harmony continued as a center of culture and as the predecessor of liberal colonies elsewhere.

Many of the early nineteenth-century buildings are still preserved in New Harmony, which has become a tourist attraction of the Middle West.

ILLINOIS RIVER CITIES

PEORIA, ILLINOIS

Peoria lies on the right bank of the Illinois River at the south end of Lake Peoria. Marquette and Joliet crossed the lake on their voyage in 1673. La Salle established Fort Creve Coeur on the bluffs of the east bank, two miles below the future townsite, in 1680. This fort was abandoned in La Salle's absence, but was rebuilt in 1691 by La Salle's lieutenant, de Tonti. A French village was started on the present townsite in 1725, but was abandoned in 1796. In 1813 the Americans erected Fort Clark on the site of the former Indian village of Au Pe. An influx of Yankee settlers around the fort became the nucleus of present-day Peoria, which was incorporated as a town in 1835 and chartered as a city in 1845. Peoria became the busiest port on the Illinois

New Harmony, Indiana, on the Wabash. *From The United States Illustrated, 1855. Courtesy Saint Louis Mercantile Library Association*

Painting by Carl Bodmer of New Harmony viewed through the brush, about 1840. *Courtesy Saint Louis Mercantile Library Association*

Fort Creve Coeur, near the present site of Peoria, Illinois, was established by La Salle and De Tonti in 1680. *From The Streckfus Line Magazine, 1931*

River during the steamboat era, especially after the opening of the Illinois and Michigan Canal in 1848. The first steamboat had arrived at Peoria in 1828, and in 1850 the number of steamer arrivals was 1,286. Peoria later became a railroad and industrial center that grew into one of the largest cities in Illinois.

DES MOINES RIVER CITIES

DES MOINES, IOWA

The name Des Moines is believed to be traceable to the Indian *moingona,* or river of mounds. The area was explored by a man named Kearny in 1835 and by Frémont in 1841, and in 1843 a fort was built there at the confluence of the Des Moines and Raccoon rivers. The former Sac and Fox Indian land was thrown open to white settlement on October 11, 1845, and a ferry was soon placed in operation. Steamboats made their way up the sluggish Des Moines River by means of a state-built slackwater system in the 1850s. The town became a way

station on the western stage route and when it reached five hundred population in 1853, it was incorporated as a city. Des Moines was selected as the state capital in 1857, succeeding Iowa City. Modern Des Moines, surrounded by rich agricultural lands, is a central distribution point and the largest city in the state.

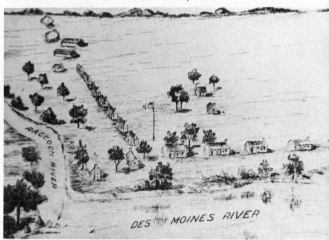

Settlement at Fort Des Moines, Iowa, 1844, beginnings of the present city. *From Historic Towns of the Western States, 1901*

IV
The Riverboats

THE ADVENT OF THE STEAMBOAT

The beginnings of American steam navigation occurred on rivers of the North Atlantic seaboard, but activity was soon transferred to the inland waterways of the West. In its role as the principal agent in the development of the Mississippi Valley, the steamboat soon became recognized as an American creation. Its readily accessible waterways made overland modes of transport seem crude and expensive by comparison.

Etching by Captain Basil Hall, 1829, of an early American stage, the alternative to steamboat travel in the 1820s and 1830s. *Courtesy Ardell Thompson Collection*

Growth in transportation: 1788 to 1868. Overall, the waterways were more comfortable and cheaper. *From Eighty Years of Progress in the United States, 1868*

EVOLUTION OF WESTERN RIVERBOAT DESIGN

The earliest water-borne transport on the western rivers was via Indian canoe. On the upper reaches

139

of the rivers, lightweight birchbark canoes were used because of the frequent need to carry them over portages between streams. The more durable pirogue or dugout canoe was used on the deeper, lower rivers. These were made from hollowed-out halves of large tree trunks. Some of them were over thirty feet long, with a beam of four feet or more, with a mast and sail amidships. On rivers where wood was not plentiful, bullboats made of a willow frame covered with buffalo hides were used. The arrival of white fur trappers brought the introduction of a larger version of the Indian bullboat. The construction was similar, but these craft were oval in shape and about twenty-five feet in length and twelve feet wide. They carried large cargoes of hides and pelts. Another large boat of this type was the mackinaw boat, made entirely of wood. In the latter half of the eighteenth century,

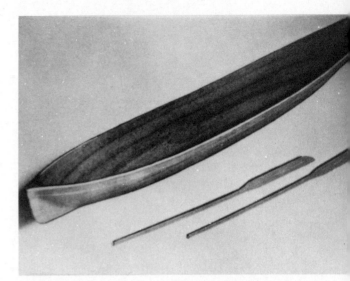

Model of a pirogue, or dugout canoe, hollowed out of a tree trunk. Originated by the Indians, these canoes were later used by early explorers and fur trappers on the western rivers. *Courtesy Jefferson National Expansion Memorial, National Park Service*

Drawing by Paul Rockwood of fur trappers using an enlarged version of the Indian bullboat to transport pelts and hides down the Missouri River. *Courtesy Jefferson National Expansion Memorial, National Park Service*

Flat-bottomed boat used to descend the Ohio and the Mississippi. *From A Journey in North America—1796, General Victor Collot. Courtesy Saint Louis Mercantile Library Association*

a utilitarian craft made its appearance on the rivers. This was the flatboat or barge, used for hauling freight and passengers during the great westward migration. They were rectangular, boxlike boats with sides about five feet high and varying in length from twenty to sixty feet. From ten to twenty-five feet in width, they would draw about two feet of water when fully loaded. Flatboats were decked over, with living quarters in the stern, complete with hearth and chimney. These clumsy craft, which were navigated by three long sweeps, or oars, one at the stern and one on each side, like horns, were later known as "broad-horns." These boats were usable only for downstream trips, and were broken up for lumber salvage after arrival at their lower river destination. The return trip overland was over the dangerous Natchez Trace, the northern trail from Natchez to the Ohio Valley. It was frequented by murderous highwaymen, much to the peril of an unsuspecting traveler. The only alternative for a return trip was expensive passage on a keelboat, which could travel upriver as well as down.

Keelboats represented a considerable improvement over flatboats. They were well-built vessels about seventy feet long and up to eighteen feet in beam. The depth of hold was from three to four feet. The boats had roofs for protection from the weather, and a pointed bow and stern. Running along each side was a narrow gangway. This was used for a walkway for a crew of four or five men on each side, who would thrust poles into the river bottom and, on command, walk toward the stern while leaning on the poles, thereby propelling the boat forward in shallow water. In deeper water, a

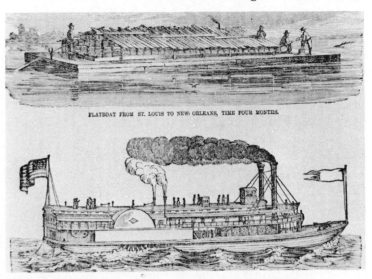

FLATBOAT FROM ST. LOUIS TO NEW ORLEANS, TIME FOUR MONTHS.

The flatboat above took four months to travel the Mississippi from Saint Louis to New Orleans, compared with this 1840 steamboat which could make several such trips in that time. *From* Eighty Years of Progress in the United States, *1868*

Shanty flatboats of the 1880s drifting down the Mississippi. *From* Down the Great River, *1887*

Painting by Oscar E. Berninghaus, *The Itinerant River Merchant*, showing commercial use of a flatboat in the late nineteenth century. *Courtesy Boatmen's National Bank of St. Louis*

A drawing of a Mississippi River keelboat. This was a considerable improvement over the flatboat. *From* The Crockett Almanac, *1838. Courtesy Saint Louis Mercantile Library Association*

Cordelling a keelboat on the upper Missouri. Drawing by Paul Rockwood, 1935. *Courtesy Jefferson National Expansion Memorial, National Park Service*

Keelboatmen in the early years of the nineteenth century. *From* Incidents and Sketches of the West, *1851. Courtesy Saint Louis Mercantile Library Association*

Mike Fink, known as the most boastful, strongest fighter, and best rifle shot among keelboatmen on the western rivers. His river career lasted from about 1790 until his death in 1822. Like all boatmen, Fink was skilled in navigating the keelboats through rapids, a feat in which boatmen took professional pride. For amusement, men engaged in dancing, fighting, drinking, and rough horseplay among themselves, and in playing practical jokes on others. *From The Crockett Almanac, 1838. Courtesy Saint Louis Mercantile Library Association*

Mike Fink à *la* William Tell. Deadly accuracy with the rifle was an ability in which Fink took the utmost pride, but it led to his ultimate downfall. Fink shot the apple from the man's head, the man fell stunned, but before he arose, unharmed, his brother, believing him dead, shot Mike through the heart, not realizing the true circumstances. *From The Great West, 1847. Courtesy Saint Louis Mercantile Library Association*

towrope was used. This was called a cordelle and was tied to the top of the boat's mast to clear it above the brush along the bank. The cordelle was as much as a thousand feet long and was used by a towpath crew to pull the boat against the current. It was sometimes used in a warping process—tying the rope end to a tree upstream and then hauling the line to pull the boat up to the anchorage point, and then repeating this same procedure until past the dangerous place. Depending on conditions, keelboats could also be navigated by oars or by sails if the wind was favorable. Keelboat men were a lusty lot, exceptionally muscular from poling and rowing, and threw their weight around. They were generally honest but were heavy drink-

ers and great fighters, such as one of the greatest boatmen of all, the notorious Mike Fink. These men were constantly looking for a contest. Among their favorite haunts was Natchez-under-the-hill. After the advent of the steamboat many of these keelboatmen became pilots and crewmen aboard the steamers.

Who the actual inventor of the steamboat was has long been a matter of debate. However, the *New Orleans,* the uncontested first steamboat on the western rivers, was built at Pittsburgh in 1810 by Robert Fulton and Robert Livingston, with Nicholas J. Roosevelt. In the next year, Roosevelt and his family embarked on a long adventurous trip to New Orleans aboard the new steamboat. They managed to survive the cataclysmic disaster of one of the worst earthquakes ever in North America as they passed New Madrid, Missouri, in December,

Pioneer steamboat, 1: Experimental steamboat (the second) of John Fitch, using oars as paddles. It ran four miles an hour on the Delaware River in May, 1787. *From* Eighty Years of Progress in the United States, *1868*

Pioneer steamboat 3: First steam propeller-driven boat, built experimentally by John Fitch in 1796. *From* Eighty Years of Progress in the United States, *1868*

Pioneer steamboat 4: *Oruktor Amphibolus* steamboat of Oliver Evans, built in 1804. *From* Eighty Years of Progress in the United States, *1868*

1811. When the *New Orleans* reached Natchez, with a spurt of energy, an old Negro on the bank said, "Ole Mississippi done met her master now!"

The Fulton-designed boats proved to be much too deep drafted and underpowered for the Mississippi River system. The first successful light-draft riverboat was Captain Henry M. Shreve's *Washington*. Shreve was the one who cleared the channels of snags and wrecks, which impeded navigation. The *Washington,* built in 1815, had a shallow hull, and the machinery and boilers were mounted on the main deck rather than in the hold, as in the Fulton boats. The engines were a revolutionary design,

Pioneer steamboat, 2: John Fitch's Philadelphia and Trenton packet, on the Delaware River, 1790. *From* Up the Heights, *1873*

Pioneer steamboat 5: The *New Orleans,* Robert Fulton's first steamboat, early nineteenth century. *Courtesy Jefferson National Expansion Memorial, National Park Service*

Pioneer steamboat 6: Robert Fulton's *Clermont,* on the Hudson River, between New York and Albany, 1807. *From Eighty Years of Progress in the United States, 1868*

using horizontal cylinders with oscillating pitmans, or connecting rods.

Initial steamboat voyages on the western river system were on the Ohio and lower Mississippi. The first boat to reach Saint Louis, the *Zebulon M. Pike,* in 1817, was followed two years later by the earliest attempt to navigate the Missouri River when the *Independence* steamed from Saint Louis to Chariton and back in twenty-one days. In 1823

the *Virginia* reached Fort Snelling, Minnesota, the head of navigation on the upper Mississippi, and by the mid-1820s steamboats had penetrated to most of the navigable tributaries. These early boats were small by later standards, seldom exceeding 120 feet in length and of extreme shallow draft. Some were humorously described as able to "navigate on the dew." The shallow draft was predicated upon the minimum depths of the river channels.

Pioneer steamboat 7: The first steamboat to reach Saint Louis, the *Zebulon M. Pike*, arriving from Louisville on July 27, 1817. *Drawing by the author*

The *Paragon*, a sidewheeler built in Cincinnati in 1819, was 156 feet long, 27 feet in beam, and 9 feet of hold, with a low-pressure engine. She was described as "a first class running boat." *From* Up the Heights, *1873*

Two types of propulsion were developed, the side and the stern paddle wheel. The sidewheelers were more efficient in steering, as the paddle wheels could augment the rudders for maneuvering. The sternwheelers originally were used primarily for pushing barges, and since the design permitted a very shallow draft to the hull, they were adapted for packet operations on tributaries.

The *Caledonia*, launched at Cincinnati in December, 1823, with dimensions similar to the *Paragon*. Her original low-pressure engine was replaced by a high-pressure one in 1827. The *Caledonia* ran until 1832, when she was converted into a towboat. *From* Up the Heights, *1873*

After the introduction of a second deck on Shreve's *Washington,* multidecked boats became common by the 1830s. The lower deck, known as the main deck, contained the boilers, engines, fuel, and space for heavy cargoes. However, the second deck was called the boiler deck, but was primarily for passenger use, as it carried the main cabin with its line of staterooms on each side. Meals were served in the main cabin, which was also used for dancing and social events. The main cabin ran fore and aft, continuous and unobstructed, but was "divided" by a midship gangway, into a forward cabin and a ladies' cabin, aft. Kitchens and washrooms were adjacent to the wheelhouses. The roof of the boiler deck was called the hurricane deck, particularly the portion forward of the smokestacks. Atop the longitudinal skylight above the main cabin was

Lithograph by Henry Lewis of an 1835 steamer, the *Martha,* at Quincy, Illinois. *Courtesy Saint Louis Public Library*

A common design—an Ohio River steamboat, 1837. *From Sketch of Civil Engineering, London, 1838*

A typical Mississippi River steamboat of the early 1840s. *From Lloyd's Steamboat Directory, 1856*

The *Princess* shows the classic features after the 1830s and 1840s. The lower or main deck; the boiler deck; the hurricane deck; the texas deck; the pilot house; and the twin stacks. She was built at Cincinnati in 1855 and was typical of the Mississippi River steamboats of the antebellum decade. She featured a statue of an Indian princess atop her pilothouse. The *Princess's* boilers exploded below Baton Rouge, Louisiana, in 1859. Seventy lives were lost. Drawing by the author. Courtesy Missouri Historical Society

The texas deck looking aft aboard the palatial steamboat *J. M. White III* (1878–1886). *Courtesy Missouri Historical Society*

The texas deck and pilothouse of the steamboat *City of Providence.* Painting by William T. Smedley for *Harper's Monthly,* 1893

the texas deck, which was the crew's quarters, purportedly so named because Texas became a state at about the time the deck came into use. Staterooms were called thus because on early craft rooms were identified by the states of the Union. On the roof

of the texas deck was the pilothouse, from which the boat was navigated. This elevated room, with windows on all sides, afforded an uninterrupted view of the river. It contained the large wheel for steering the rudder and controls for operating the engines. The twin stacks found on western riverboats provided each boiler with draft, and escape pipes aft of the pilothouse were used for exhausting the steam. A novel feature on some boats was the steam calliope, on which tunes were played when approaching a river town. A steam whistle and a large bell on the top deck were used for signaling. American ingenuity soon provided fast, practical boats well adapted to the western rivers. They were crowded with emigrants moving west, and on their lower decks reposed tons of farm produce and ore from riverside mines. These boats

One of the few "three deckers" ever built, the *Mayflower,* completed at Saint Louis in 1855. The additional deck, midway between the main and boiler decks, was later removed to increase cargo space. This short-lived boat burned at Memphis on December 3, 1855. By Fanny E. Palmer, a Currier and Ives artist. *Courtesy Saint Louis Public Library*

The *John Simonds* was a large, luxurious, three-decked boat of the 1850s. Built by Saint Louis interests, she is shown here leaving that city's waterfront in 1854. She was reported destroyed during the Civil War. *From* Thoughts about St. Louis, 1855

traveled on streams that now seem navigable only by canoe, reaching every possible place where business could be found.

The steamboats grew larger and more luxurious, reaching their zenith during the "Golden Age" of steamboating in the decade before the Civil War. Their main cabins were splendidly appointed with carved furniture, crystal chandeliers, heavy carpeting, and large mirrors. The dining accommodations were equally fine, with exquisite china, shining silver, and sparkling cut glass. During this period the boats ran on regular schedules and speed became a most important factor. Racing became popular, sometimes at the sacrifice of safety and common sense. Western-river steamboats of the largest size were well over three hundred feet in length with accommodations for hundreds of passengers. The *Grand Republic* and the *Eclipse* were about 365 feet long, and the *Thompson Dean* was reported to have cost $400,000. The pinnacle of luxury was reached in the *J. M. White III,* believed to be faster than the *Robert E. Lee.* It was the most splendidly appointed steamboat ever to grace the Mississippi.

The boats in the last decades of the nineteenth century began to decline in splendor, as well as size, although some packets made a valiant effort to compete with the railroads by furnishing good accommodations. This proved a losing cause in the modern age of speed; only one packet boat survives from the vast armada of beautiful boats that once sailed the western rivers.

Advertising poster. The M. S. Mepham, built in 1864, operated in the postwar trade. *Courtesy Boatmen's National Bank of St. Louis*

The ever larger, more commodious boats soon dominated traffic, as seen in this Currier and Ives print of the Mississippi during the 1870s. *Courtesy Saint Louis Mercantile Library Association*

At the turn of the century. The river packet *Kate Adams III*, built at Jeffersonville, Indiana, 1899, for the Memphis and Arkansas City Packet Company. "Lovin' Kate" was used in the movie made of *Uncle Tom's Cabin* in the twenties. The *Kate* burned at Memphis in January, 1927. *From Life on the Western Rivers, 1901. Courtesy Saint Louis Mercantile Library Association*

STEAMBOAT BUILDING—STRUCTURAL DEVELOPMENT

The steamboat was an important American technological advance in the early nineteenth century, and attracted international attention regarding adaptation to European waterways. The American steamboat devolved into two basic classes, the eastern and the western. The eastern, or Hudson River style, based upon Robert Fulton's *Clermont*, featured a low-pressure engine, deep hull, and fine lines necessary for speed. The walking beam and arched hogframe above the superstructure were identifying features.

Unlike the eastern design, the western-river steamboat carried freight as well as passengers, was shallow in draft, and noisy in the operation of its high-pressure engine. It was humorously characterized as "expensive jigsaw carpentry, with an engine on a raft."

Usually, boatbuilders on the western rivers worked by a system of trial and error, being at a disadvantage on an industrial frontier, where engineers and skilled artisans were at a premium. Beginning with a makeshift combination of a stationary engine in a seagoing hull, the western steamboat became a well-adapted mode of travel for inland river commerce by the early 1840s. Innovative changes in its design and construction were encouraged in the pioneering atmosphere of the frontier, where the low cost and short lives of the boats were conducive to experimentation. On the negative side, western riverboats wore out quickly, wasted fuel, and had a high accident rate. These attributes were due as much to poor handling as to faulty construction.

The sailing-vessel design of these riverboats prevailed as late as 1830, when some of them still featured bowsprits, masts, and figureheads. Sails were used, in favorable winds, as an auxiliary means of power, as they had been on keelboats. After 1830 the typical western design became more apparent—enclosed upper-deck cabins, dictated by needs of passenger comfort, producing the boxlike superstructure more practical than esthetic, twin smokestacks, and pilothouses, shal-

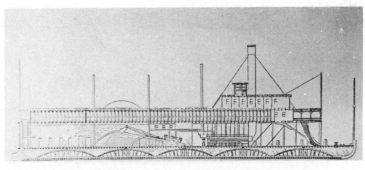

Longitudinal section of a typical western-river sidewheeler of the 1850s. *From Transactions of the Institute of Naval Architects, London, 1861*

Sternwheel freight boats *Elk* and *Mandan* on the Missouri, at Williston, North Dakota, about 1900. *Photo by Miller Studio. Courtesy Waterways Journal*

lower hulls, and a keel that all but disappeared. The ratio of hull length to width later increased, and the side paddle wheels grew and were enclosed in semicircular wheelhouses. Chimneys were moved aft and emerged from within the superstructure,

Crew loading fuel, or wooding up a steamboat, at night, about 1850. *Courtesy Boatmen's National Bank of St. Louis*

Sketch by A. R. Waud of figurehead on the jackstaff of the famous *Robert E. Lee*, with roustabout in the foreground. *From* Every Saturday Magazine, *September 2, 1871. Courtesy Missouri Historical Society*

instead of forward of it. The jack staff on the bow was a navigation aid for the pilot to judge the boat's position and direction. With longer and narrower hulls, with flat bottoms and straight sides, the boats weighed less, increasing buoyancy and stability. By 1850 keels disappeared and their structural function taken over by keelsons built along the inside of the hull. Landings without docks were facilitated by giving the stem of the boat a long rake, or angle. This made it possible for an approaching boat to strike the mud and sand of the sloping river bank, close enough to reach shore by gangplanks. Such contact required no further mooring, and a slowly turning paddle wheel was sufficient to counteract the current.

The size and capacity of steamboats increased during the antebellum years and culminated in the 365-foot *Eclipse* of 1853. Long, narrow hulls were found to be faster as well as easier to handle in shoal water and in the swift current of the rapids. As the boats grew, so did their superstructures. Main decks were made higher, and wider guards were extended full length on each side of the hull. Guards were the extensions of the main deck beyond the hull, on the sides, and their original function was to protect the protruding wheelhouses. Wide guards were commonplace on western riverboats

Front and rear elevations of a typical western-river sternwheeler. *Courtesy Missouri Historical Society*

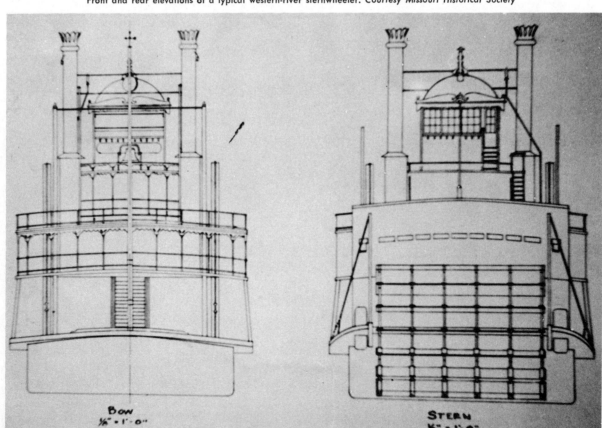

BOW
½" = 1'-0"

STERN
½" = 1'-0"

and quite often the overall width exceeded that of the hull by seventy-five percent. They not only increased the deck space but provided passageways fore and aft. During the mid-1840s, texas decks began to appear atop the superstructures of some boats. These were narrower and shorter than the main cabin and provided quarters for the boat's officers. The height of three-deck steamboats created an illusion of top-heaviness. Actually, the decks were countered by the weight of machinery and cargo on or below the main deck.

A common structural problem was the prevention of "hogging," or the arching of the hull. This was caused by a distortion from the weight of the machinery and cargo, or from shocks when grounding or snagging occurred. The solution was a combination of hog chains, trusses, and bulkheads, or a series of small, arched hogframes tied by rods. Hog chains were iron rods made fast to hull timbers at bow and stern and carried over a series of struts rising from keelsons. These could be adjusted for rigidity to tighten the hull, to prevent

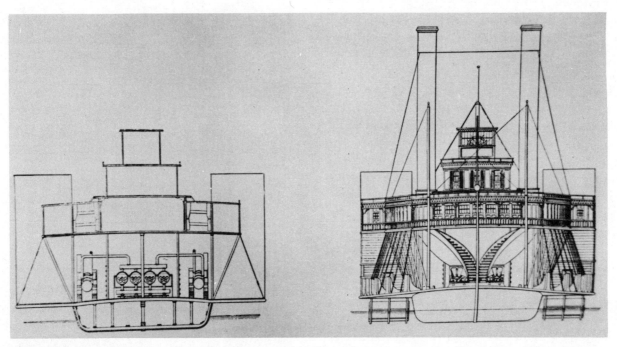

Midship section and bow view of a typical western-river sidewheeler of the 1850s. *From Transactions of the Institute of Naval Architects, London, 1861*

Ohio River sternwheel towboat W. W. O'Neil, a model on exhibit at the River Museum at Wellsville, Ohio. *Courtesy State of Ohio, Department of Industrial and Economic Development*

arching or sagging. Cross chains were used in a similar manner to support the wide guards overhanging the hull.

The short lives of western-river steamboats were lengthened in later years by technical advances and the steamboat-inspection system. By 1880 their average age about doubled an earlier twenty years. Poor longevity was attributed to navigational dangers such as snags and bars, to hazards such as fires and explosions, and to ignorance and rough handling by crew members.

Steamboats on the Mississippi River system over several decades gradually evolved from traditional boat designs through the boxlike forms of the 1830s into the graceful designs of the antebellum years. The lines of the hull, obscured by the wide overhanging guards, made necessary the decoration of the superstructure. During this period of Victorian gingerbread architecture, the rise of the jigsaw-carpentry ("steamboat Gothic") style was natural. Gaudily painted wheelhouses, feathered chimney tops, and elaborately carved decorations on pilothouses and in cabin interiors became commonplace. The overall effect, in most cases, was of elaborate grandeur on a scale not seen ashore.

The construction, equipment, and repair of western steamboats grew into an important industry in the Ohio Valley. Between 1820 and 1880, about six thousand vessels were built at yards in Pittsburgh, Cincinnati, Louisville, and smaller towns along the Ohio. The early barges and keelboats of the presteamboat era were built along the

Lithograph by Henry Lewis of Carondelet about 1835. Carondelet was founded by Clement DeLore DeTreget in 1767, and given its present name in 1794 in honor of the Spanish Governor-General in New Orleans. It became a town in 1832, a city in 1851, and in 1870 was annexed to Saint Louis. *Courtesy Saint Louis Public Library*

Lithograph by John Casper Wild of Carondelet's Main Street, 1841. *Courtesy Saint Louis Public Library*

General views of a Carondelet, Missouri, shipyard and river front during the 1890s. This was the yard where ironclad riverboats were built by James B. Eads during the Civil War. *From Siler's Historical Photographs, 1904*

lower Monongahela. By 1840 the Pittsburgh area became the dominant boatbuilding center, followed in later years by yards in Marietta, Wheeling, and Portsmouth. Cincinnati yards accounted for a large proportion of the construction, as did the Louisville area, where the principal yards were located on the Indiana shore at New Albany and Jeffersonville. The chief center for steamboat building outside the Ohio Valley was Saint Louis. The boatyards tended to locate at industrial centers, where foundries and machine shops could turn out machinery and where rolling mills were available for boiler-plate and bar-iron production. Plentiful supplies of timber were readily available for the lumber requirements. Efficient production

The Howard Shipyard and Dock Company at Jeffersonville, Indiana, 1893, on the Ohio River. *Courtesy Jefferson National Expansion Memorial, National Park Service*

Sternwheeler under construction at Howard's shipyard. *Courtesy Jefferson National Expansion Memorial, National Park Service*

Launching a small sternwheeler at Howard's. *Courtesy Jefferson National Expansion Memorial, National Park Service*

The sternwheeler *Natchez* under construction at Howard's shipyard. *Courtesy Jefferson National Expansion Memorial, National Park Service*

Construction scene at Howard's shipyard about 1890. *Courtesy Jefferson National Expansion Memorial, National Park Service*

Launching of the steamer *Shiloh* at Howard's shipyard. This sternwheeler was a short-trade boat of the Saint Louis and Tennessee River Packet Company. *Courtesy Jefferson National Expansion Memorial, National Park Service*

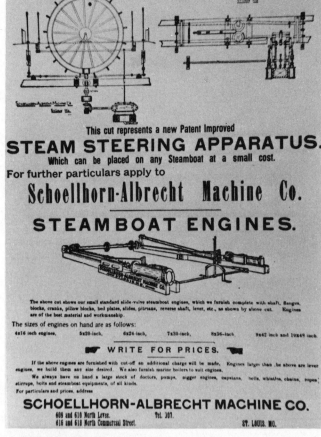

This cut represents a new Patent Improved

STEAM STEERING APPARATUS.

Which can be placed on any Steamboat at a small cost.

For further particulars apply to

Schoellhorn-Albrecht Machine Co.

STEAMBOAT ENGINES.

The above cut shows our small standard slide-valve steamboat engines, which we furnish complete with shaft, flanges, blocks, cranks, pillow blocks, bed plates, slides, pitmans, reverse shaft, lever, etc., as shown by above cut. Engines are of the best material and workmanship.

The sizes of engines on hand are as follows:

4x16 inch engines,   5x20-inch,   6x24-inch,   7x30-inch,   8x36-inch,   9x42 inch and 10x49 inch.

WRITE FOR PRICES.

If the above engines are furnished with cut-off an additional charge will be made. Engines larger than the above are lever engines, we build them any size desired. We also furnish marine boilers to suit engines.

We always have on hand a large stock of doctors, pumps, nigger engines, capstans, bells, whistles, chains, ropes, stirrups, bolts and steamboat equipments, of all kinds.

For particulars and prices, address

SCHOELLHORN-ALBRECHT MACHINE CO.

609 and 610 North Levee.   Tel. 307.
616 and 618 North Commercial Street.   ST. LOUIS. MO.

Advertisement for steam-steering machinery and steamboat engines, built by the Schoellhorn-Albrecht Machine Company of Saint Louis during the 1890s. *Courtesy Waterways Journal*

Detail of a wooden side paddle wheel. This is a view of the *Arkansas City* after its destruction in the Saint Louis tornado of 1896. *Courtesy Waterways Journal*

needs led to certain yards specializing in boat-machinery production, while others concentrated on building the hulls and superstructures. The most durable parts of steamboats were the engines, which could be salvaged from wrecked or dismantled boats. Their reuse was a common practice. Salvaged hulls were frequently used as wharf boats, but cabins seldom had much value for reinstallation.

Wood continued to be used for most phases of steamboat construction, even in later years when iron and steel were commonly used in other forms of building. Wooden paddle wheels and connecting rods, known as pitmans, were used because they were easily replaced, compared with metal members, which required refabrication. Comparatively few iron-hulled boats were built for western-river use, despite favorable publicity regarding their durability. Their use was confined chiefly to government snag boats and to commercial towboats and barges. Metal-clad hulls came into more general use during the early decades of the twentieth century on packet and excursion boats.

A method of tonnage measurement for rate-making was established in 1789 by government act and was continued until 1865. Unfortunately, corrective changes introduced by the act of May 4, 1864, were adapted to seagoing ships, rather than to the shallow-draft hulls of riverboats. Some relief was obtained in 1865, when amendments provided that no deck above the hull was to be measured for tonnage purposes. Nevertheless, tonnage figures for steamboats were still about forty-five percent greater under the new rules than they had been under the old.

The metal-clad Streckfus Line excursion boat *President*. Completed in 1924, she began her career as the Ohio River packet *Cincinnati*. Sold to Streckfus in 1932, the boat was remodeled into the all-steel, oil-burning excursion boat *President*, which opened the 1933 season at Saint Louis. She was superseded at Saint Louis by the *Admiral* in 1940 and since then has operated out of New Orleans. *Courtesy Streckfus Steamers, Inc.*

MECHANICAL DEVELOPMENT OF THE WESTERN
RIVER STEAMBOAT

The development of machinery to run western steamboats was contemporary with experimental phases of the steam engine itself. The earliest boats, such as Fulton's *Clermont,* were powered by low-pressure engines using a vertical cylinder from which steam was exhausted into a condenser, in which the action of a jet of cold water created a partial vacuum. The steam was used principally to produce this vacuum, which created more power to drive the piston than did the steam pressure of about fifteen pounds a square inch.

The high-pressure engine, which later came into general use on western river steamboats, was a non-condensing type, using the steam directly to drive the piston. Pressures of a hundred pounds a square inch were commonly used by 1840. The cylinder was much smaller in diameter than the low-pressure type and was mounted horizontally, with the steam exhausted into the air. Credit for its introduction goes to Oliver Evans, one of the ablest inventors of his time. Seeking a compact, powerful design, he established the first steam-engine factory

Machinery used in the *Clermont. From Eighty Years of Progress in the United States, 1868*

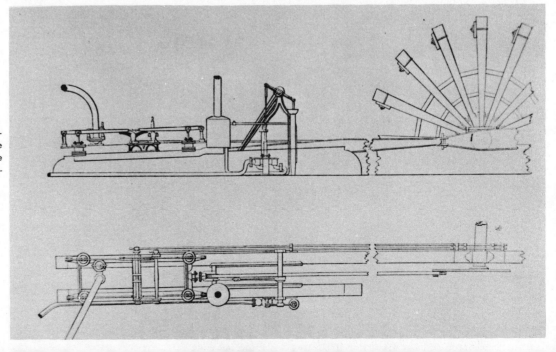

An early example of a standard western-river steamboat engine, built for the steamer *Merrimack of 1837. From The Steam Engine, P. R. Hodge, 1840. Courtesy Saint Louis Public Library*

Maze of pipes and machinery in the engine room of an upper Mississippi riverboat. *Courtesy Waterways Journal*

Advertisement for a lightweight compound condensing engine for river steamboats, designed and built by D. M. Swain, of Stillwater, Minnesota, in 1898. *Courtesy Waterways Journal*

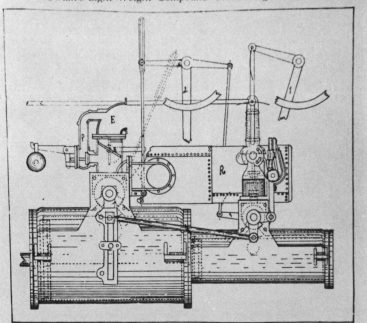

Swain's Light-Weight Compound Condensing Engine.

The above cut is D. M. Swain's Light-weight Compound Condensing Engine for river steamboats, showing valve gear, receiver and levers to manipulate the same, noted for its light weight and simplicity.

The main valve is controlled by means of round-pointed cams; has one cam for forward motion and one for back-ward motion. The exhaust ports are held open full port 19-20 of the stroke of the piston. The travel of the H. P. valve is during the time that it is subjected only to the terminal pressure, and the ports and clearance are filled with steam—that of the terminal pressure before the steam is exhausted and used over again, making the expense of steam used to fill the ports and clearance practically nothing.

Lever 1 is employed to adjust the point of cut-off while the engines are in motion.

When the engines are at rest lever 2 is employed to close valve B in exhaust pipe leading to condensor, its continued movement lifts the main valves off their seat then steam can be blown through to relieve the boilers of their pressure and to prevent the accumulation of condensation in the cylinders and receiver, and provides steam for the compound cylinder for starting the engine. Valve B is closed. Valve P is a by-pass and pressure valve. The steam that is blown through is, by valve B being closed, compelled to pass through by-pass pressure valve P, thus preventing vacuum from entering both cylinders, receiver and connec-

tions; also, accumulation of condensation. By these means the engines are as easily and as readily manipulated as the ordinary high-pressure engine. While these engines are at rest, the steam that is blown through by means of pressure valve P, the receiver and both cylinders have a pressure of 15 pounds of steam. This prevents an accumulation of condensation in the cylinders.

In starting, lever 2 lowers the valves to their seats; its continued motion opens valve B in exhaust pipe leading to condensor. This device of lifting these valves off their seats and closing valve B and opening the same is very simple, is no greater than change valves in the ordinary exhaust pipes of the high-pressure engines.

These engines, as shown in the cut, are but little heavier than one high-pressure lever engine to develop the same power. These two engines, as shown, have less mechanism and cost less to maintain than the engines now commonly employed. This alone recommends their general use. Besides a guarantee of the saving of one-half the cost of fuel to develop corresponding power, the small consumption of fuel enables the vessel to fuel where fuel is the cheapest and the most convenient on each voyage, besides the space occupied for fuel.

I am prepared to build these engines any size required. Estimates on entire outfits made on application.

D. M. SWAIN, Stillwater, Minn.

in the West, at Pittsburgh, in 1812. Evans was not directly connected with the application of the high-pressure engine, owing to his involvement in other affairs. However, engines of this type were used in several early boats designed by Daniel French and Henry M. Shreve at Brownsville, Pennsylvania, from 1813 to 1816. The *Washington*'s engine, designed by Shreve, was connected to the paddle wheel by a pitman connecting rod, rather than by a beam or flywheel. This was the forerunner of the high-pressure horizontal engines later used on most western riverboats.

The contest between the low- and high-pressure designs was largely resolved by 1825 in favor of the latter, since it was so well adjusted to the shallow navigation conditions on the inland waterways. It also occupied much less space, was considerably lighter, and much less expensive. The high-pressure engine also had more reserve power, with its limits being governed by the strength of its components. Excessive pressures obtained by misuse, ignorance, or a lust for speed, were responsible for many fatal boiler explosions before the steamboat-inspection service act of 1852. Advantages claimed for low-pressure engines were increased safety and greater economy of operation. The Cincinnati and Louisville Mail Line attempted to popularize the low-pressure engine in the *Jacob Strader* of 1853. The boat proved unsuccessful, in spite of her speed, and eventually her troublesome boilers were replaced by the conventional flue type. For either type of engine, silt from muddy water continued to be pumped into the boilers and grit from sand still fouled the valves and condensers.

While western steamboat engines were unrefined in appearance and noisy in operation, they provided the desirable objectives of low cost, ease of repair, and sufficiency of power desired by their engineers. Its long, slow stroke of about twenty revolutions a minute was well suited to operation of the large paddle wheels. Later, increases in power were first obtained through enlargement of the diameter of the cylinders, and then, after about 1840, through the use of two engines instead of one. Among the largest engines ever built were those of the steamer *Eclipse* (1117 tons), with thirty-six-inch cylinders and an eleven-foot stroke. Cylinder sizes and the number of boilers and flues were the criteria of engine power; horsepower ratings were seldom used because few could make the calculation. The use of two separately connected engines to independent side paddle wheels popularized the sidewheeler by clearing machinery from the center of the boat, providing additional cargo space. Independent engines also permitted paddle wheels to be run at varying speeds or in opposite directions for increased maneuverability.

To improve the standardized high-pressure engine, compound or double-expansion engines, called Clipper engines, after the boats they propelled, were tried at various times. The first attempt was in 1843, with a horizontal tandem engine featuring two cylinders, one twice the diameter of the other. Steam acting under high pressure in the small cylinder passed into the larger one to activate a second piston before exhausting. The effort was not as successful as a second one, made in 1865 with the steamer *Dictator,* in which an engine designed by Andrew Hartupee of Pittsburgh was used. This engine featured a sixteen-inch high-pressure cylinder and a thirty-six-inch low-pressure cylinder, from which steam passed to a condenser, creating a partial vacuum. At least twenty boats were equipped with these engines until the mid-seventies, when their use was questioned because of high maintenance costs.

Steamboat boilers were generally placed lengthwise, in batteries side by side, across the forepart of the main deck, where they counterbalanced the weight of the engines and wheels aft. They were connected underneath by a water pipe to maintain a common level in each boiler, and their tops were joined by a steam line to the engines. The furnace end was built up with firebrick encased with sheet

Loading coal aboard a steamboat at Cairo, Illinois. Sketch by Alfred R. Waud, July 30, 1871. *Courtesy Missouri Historical Society*

iron. They stood free of the deck on brackets. The smoke and gas, after returning through flues to the furnace end of the boilers, were exhausted through twin chimneys rising on each side, affording the pilot an uninterrupted forward view from the pilot-house. Boilers were usually about thirty-six to forty inches in diameter and up to about thirty-five feet in length; their number was governed by the size of the boat. The *J. M. White* of 1878 had ten steel boilers, all necessary to drive the engines of such a large steamboat. However a trend toward fewer boilers was evident in normal-sized craft.

Increased draft was obtained by heightening the chimneys, from the maximum of fifty feet above the river surface, standard in 1840, to a hundred feet in such huge boats as the *Grand Republic* of 1867. The great clouds of smoke and sparks from

Engine room of a steamboat, about 1900. *Courtesy Waterways Journal*

the smokestacks and the violence of the exhausted steam were evidences of fuel waste. Poor boiler design and condensation from unjacketed surfaces required excessive firing to maintain sufficient pressure. Maintenance of an adequate water supply for the boilers was a vexing problem on the earlier boats. The water was supplied only when the engines were running the feed pumps. This proved awkward at landings when the engines were not running, with steam pressure continuing to build in the boilers, creating a safety hazard. Eventually this problem was solved by the use of a small auxiliary, or "doctor," engine, installed solely to run the pumps to provide a supply of water to the boilers and to pump the bilge as well.

Steam gauges did not come into general use until after adoption of the steamboat-inspection act of 1852, which required their installation. Water gauges were in more general use by 1850, and safety valves were standard equipment on boilers from the earliest times, but were usually inefficient because of poor design. An added hazard was the placing of weights on the safety valve to prevent its opening while building higher pressures, as it was considered to waste steam. By 1850 the use of inexpandable cast iron for boiler heads and steam pipes was discontinued in favor of more flexible wrought iron and copper.

Stoking the boilers of a typical western-river steamboat of the mid-nineteenth century. *From Harper's Weekly. Courtesy Saint Louis Mercantile Library Association*

Ad for an auxiliary, or doctor engine, for steamboats of the nineties. *Courtesy Waterways Journal*

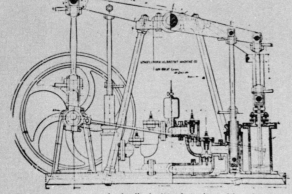

SCHOELLHORN-ALBRECHT MACHINE CO.

NEW IMPROVED
Steamboat Doctor.

These doctors are principally built of steel, making them strong and light, as the old style doctors are made of cast-iron, which make them very heavy and is dead weight for boats.

We build them all sizes to suit.

For particulars and prices address

Schoellhorn-Albrecht Machine Co.,
609 and 610 North Levee.
616 and 618 Commercial Street.   Telephone 107.   St. Louis Mo

SCHOELLHORN-ALBRECHT MACHINE CO.

SIDEWHEELS VS STERNWHEELS

Paddle wheels were the traditional method of propulsion for western-river steamboats because the screw propeller was ill adapted for shallow channels. The rugged construction of paddle wheels usually survived the punishment from obstructions, and repairs could be readily made by the crew. Enlarging the wheel's diameter and increasing the length and width of its blades, known as buckets, could furnish higher circumferential speeds to propel large packets without alteration of engine speed. A change in the position of sidewheels from amidships to about two-thirds of the distance aft occurred in the 1840s, most notably in the case of the record-setting *J. M. White* of 1844.

The sidewheelers were the favorites of riverboat travelers throughout the steamboat era. Sidewheels

Sternwheel churning water while underway. *Courtesy Waterways Journal*

The earliest sternwheelers were built by Daniel French and Henry Shreve, probably to counter Fulton patents, which used sidewheels in their designs. Sternwheel boats had almost completely disappeared by 1830, not to reappear until the early forties, when they became popular for freight hauling in the Pittsburgh area. They remained a favorite on the Ohio River, where they outnumbered sidewheelers three to one by 1880. Until the Civil War, they were primarily small, for use on tribu-

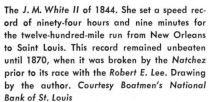

The *J. M. White II* of 1844. She set a speed record of ninety-four hours and nine minutes for the twelve-hundred-mile run from New Orleans to Saint Louis. This record remained unbeaten until 1870, when it was broken by the *Natchez* prior to its race with the *Robert E. Lee*. Drawing by the author. *Courtesy Boatmen's National Bank of St. Louis*

had a more solid foundation than sternwheels, in addition to furnishing necessary weight amidships to counteract excessive buoyancy, thereby reducing hull stresses. Shorter pitmans reduced vibration, and less length in steam lines, reducing the distance between engine and wheel, meant a minimal heat loss through condensation. The greatest superiority for sidewheelers remained maneuverability, its independently run wheels increasing handling and steering. Compared with the plodding, stolid sternwheelers, sidewheelers had speed, performance, and grace, and were especially well adapted for passenger service. The last factor led to their almost exclusive use for packet-line operations, particularly on the Mississippi River, where the sidewheeler attained its most elegant and beautiful examples in such fine boats as the *Grand Republic*, *J. M. White*, *Natchez*, and *Robert E. Lee*.

Daniel French's sternwheeler *Enterprise*, on the Ohio River, 1814. *From Up the Heights, 1873*

taries and for harbor work. After the problem of supporting sternwheels aft of the stern instead of within the hull lines was solved, they came into general use on larger boats. The emergence of towboats after the Civil War brought about technical improvements that made the sternwheeler adaptable to heavy freight work. In that field, the superiority of the sternwheeler over the sidewheeler was unquestioned. Their pushing power made them ideal for propulsion of fleets of barges, and with their greater cargo-carrying ability, they soon replaced the flashy sidewheelers.

The rear position of the paddle wheel protected it from floating debris, and the guards could be minimized and the hull made wider and shallower, so reducing overall width. This not only enabled them to run in shallow tributaries, but also permitted more operating days during the periods of low water on the principal rivers. Other innovations that greatly improved the practicality of the sternwheeler were cranks at right angles at each end of the wheel shaft to give a smoother power flow from the two engines, and the incorporation of hog chains in the paddle-wheel assembly to give added support, enabling the design of much larger sternwheelers. The problem of steering was solved by the advent of the multiple-balance rudder. The blade extended under the paddle wheel as well as forward under the stern rake of the hull, greatly increasing its area and turning power. It steered better in reverse than forward, as the wheel action drove water against the rudder to accentuate its turning ability. This aided development of the navigational technique known as "flanking," which enabled a normal-sized sternwheeler to handle extremely large tows in difficult channels.

Detailed view of the paddle wheel of a sternwheeler. *Courtesy Waterways Journal*

NAVIGATION—PERSONNEL AND TECHNIQUES

CAPTAIN

The captain of a riverboat, unlike his seagoing counterpart, was often not supreme in matters concerning navigation. The captain, who was usually part owner of the boat, left details of navigation and operation to the pilot and the mate, being more concerned with the boat as a business enterprise. Any man with sufficient capital could set himself up as captain of a boat, without the benefit

The sternwheeler *Homer Smith* on the Ohio River, built in 1914 for excursion and packet services. *Courtesy Jefferson National Expansion Memorial, National Park Service*

William T. Smedley's sketch of a Mississippi River steamboat captain during the 1890s. *From Harper's Monthly, 1893*

Officers of the steamer *J. M. White III* seated on the boiler-deck guard. *Courtesy Jefferson National Expansion Memorial, National Park Service*

Old-time steamboat captains Sam and "Steamboat Bill" Heckman, of Hermann, Missouri. *Courtesy Missouri Conservation Commission*

of a master's license. However, many captains came up through the ranks and were familiar with the duties of the various crew members. The captain was the legal authority of the boat after leaving port, having dominion over passengers and crew alike.

MATE

The mate was the captain's deputy in the boat's management and was not required to have the knowledge of navigation that characterized mates on ocean vessels. Among his chief duties on the riverboat was the direction of the deckhands in their labors. In boat handling, the mate's responsibilities included supervision of emergency activities, such as warping the boat across a bar, and repair work. The mate directed the stowage of the cargo and the loading of cordwood for fuel. Cargo distribution required skill in loading to maintain proper balance of the boat and could have a bearing upon the efficient use of the paddle wheels.

The mate of a Mississippi River steamboat. Painting by William T. Smedley. *From Harper's Monthly, 1893*

Deckhands at rest on the forecastle of the steamboat *Golden Eagle*. *Courtesy Jefferson National Expansion Memorial, National Park Service*

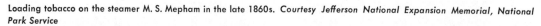

Loading tobacco on the steamer M. S. Mepham in the late 1860s. *Courtesy Jefferson National Expansion Memorial, National Park Service*

PILOT

The actual navigation of the boat was the responsibility of the pilot, who reigned supreme in the pilothouse. He has been proclaimed as the most skilled of all boatmen and was accordingly compensated. The pilot was a full-time officer who established and maintained the boat's course and was accountable for the safety of all aboard. His constant vigilance was needed in dangerous waters, where a slight inattention could lead to an accident. On easier stretches of the river the pilot could delegate the steering to an apprentice, if he was well advanced. The pilot's education was gained through actual practice and observation of the river. Some were licensed only for certain stretches of the streams, those with which they were familiar. His knowledge required learning the myriad details of water depth, current speed, configuration of river bed, and location of snags and other obstacles. He needed a detailed familiarity with landmarks along the banks to aid his navigation by day and by night, and had to interpret all visible symptoms of the current and wind that affect the boat's progress. Stringent regulations for pilots came into effect with the steamboat-inspection act of 1852, which established the first licensing system.

In the early days of steamboating, many pilots who had learned their trade at the helm of flatboats or keelboats became navigators of steamboats. While the handling characteristics were different, their knowledge of the river obviously was placed first. In later years, pilots were trained as steersmen during their cub-pilot years, before advancing to the status of apprentice and finally to pilot rating. Pilots generally had to rely on their own resources to learn the river, as navigation

The pilothouse of the *Bald Eagle* of the Eagle Packet Company. *Courtesy Saint Louis Public Library*

Pilothouse interior—U.S. Corps of Engineers snag boat *Horatio G. Wright*. *Courtesy Jefferson National Expansion Memorial, National Park Service*

Navigation charts such as this one of the Falls of the Ohio were indispensable to a pilot. *From The Western Pilot, Samuel Cumings, 1829. Courtesy Saint Louis Public Library*

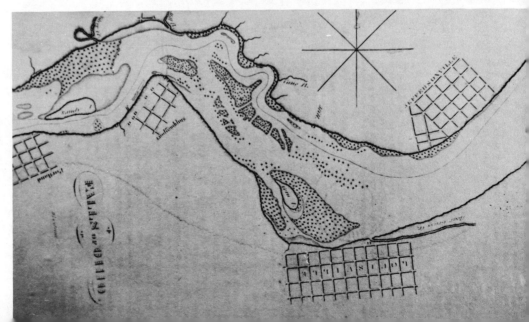

Steamboat pilot and crewmen on the steamer *Philadelphia* on passage from New Orleans to Louisville in 1827. Etching by Captain Basil Hall, 1829. *Courtesy Ardell Thompson Collection*

charts were crude and of little value. Several publications purporting to be navigating guides were available but were not reliable. These were unable to keep up with channel changes. Pilots on downstream runs usually held to the channel, keeping to the outside on bends to take advantage of depth and faster currents. This required making crossings where the channel ran diagonally across the river. Rounding bends going upstream, the pilots would hold to shallow slack water on the inside of the bends. A weaving course avoided the strong current and saved fuel and wear on the machinery.

Government river charts, based on earlier surveys, were first published in the 1880s, but inexpen-

Pilothouse of a nineteenth-century western-river steamboat. *From Harper's Weekly. Courtesy Saint Louis Mercantile Library Association*

The pilot had to keep a steady watch at crucial points. This is the pilothouse of the towboat *Sprague. Courtesy Waterways Journal*

sive, convenient maps were not made available until 1916. Nineteenth-century steamboat pilots obtained information from newspaper reports of river conditions. Telegraphic reports became available by 1850, and pilot associations encouraged the exchange of information among their members. Locked boxes along the river were used to deposit navigation data for the pilots' use. Steamboat courtesy on a reciprocal basis furnished free travel for off-duty pilots to make observation trips on the riv-

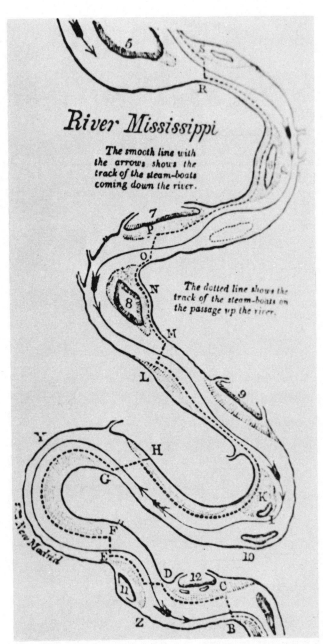

River Mississippi

The smooth line with the arrows shows the track of the steam-boats coming down the river.

The dotted line shows the track of the steam-boats on the passage up the river.

The upstream and downstream tracks of steamboat courses on the Mississippi charted for pilots. *From Travels in North America, 1830. Courtesy Saint Louis Public Library*

was not attempted on the Missouri River, because of difficult conditions, until beacons were placed late in the nineteenth century.

The value of beacon lights for the guidance of pilots was realized in the late 1860s and in 1869 the Louisville Pilot's Association set up lights at Grand Chain on the lower Ohio. By the mid-seventies, Congress had authorized a Federal beacon-light system for the western rivers, and by 1875 several hundred lights and buoys had been placed along the Ohio and the Mississippi. Nighttime navigation was revolutionized by the introduction of the electric-arc searchlight in 1875 on the Ohio River steamer *General Lytle*. Piloting ceased to be a mysterious art, and a great gain in navigation safety resulted.

Adequate rules of river practice were long a controversial subject among boatmen. Western river characteristics did not permit the adoption of any general rules for passing an approaching boat or on matters of precedence. Most collisions were caused by a lack of understanding of passing rules or by failure to observe them. After years of fruitless discussion and disagreement, the steamboat-inspection act of 1852 authorized the establishment of rules

One of the most esteemed pilots on the Mississippi was Isaiah Sellers. This is the captain's monument in Bellefontaine Cemetery, Saint Louis. Captain Sellers was said to have used the pseudonym "Mark Twain" when he wrote river news for the New Orleans *Picayune*. After Sellers's death in 1864, the pen name was adopted by Samuel L. Clemens. Clemens tells the story that Sellers ordered his tombstone before he died and carried it with him on his river trips. *Photo by the author*

ers. In 1871 the Federal government began to issue river reports, and about ten years later a forecasting system began to give predictions several days in advance.

In the beginning, boats could only be operated by daylight. Later, after pilots had become experienced in handling steamboats, nocturnal operation was tried, usually on clear moonlit nights. After 1830 it had become a general practice, except in low water in snag-ridden areas. Night operation

This tombstone of Captain Pleasant Devinney (1818–1895), a Saint Louis riverman, with its bas-relief of a steamboat signifies his livelihood. It is located in Bellefontaine Cemetery, Saint Louis. *Photo by the author*

A bell meant the difference between life and death at times. Bells were also used for signaling arrivals and departures. Dated 1887. *Courtesy Missouri Historical Society*

governing the passing of boats. These rules of the river became the subject of debate for years among rivermen and steamboat inspectors, and were frequently amended. Eventually, a strict code emerged that merited general observance. Among early rulings by the inspection board was an order to use a steam whistle for signaling. This replaced the large steamboat bell mounted on the forward hurricane deck. Bell signals were subject to misinterpretation, depending upon weather conditions, and could be a factor in collisions. Whistles, which had been in use for some years on a partial basis, gave a more audible and authoritative warning sound and were commended as a safety agent.

LOW-WATER NAVIGATION

Navigation difficulties were minimized during periods of moderate flood stage. There was sufficient depth to avoid most underwater hazards, and secondary cutoffs could be taken to shorten the distance around the bends. One authority estimated that this technique could save a hundred miles of the twelve-hundred mile distance from Saint Louis to New Orleans. This could be offset by delays caused by increased vigilance to avoid driftwood, and the strain on the machinery induced by the faster current. An interesting sidelight on a rising river is that it is higher in the center of the stream than at the sides, causing boats to drift toward the

Roof bell on the steamer *Chris Greene* of the Greene Line. *Courtesy Jefferson National Expansion Memorial, National Park Service*

banks. When the stream is subsiding, the opposite is true. In a falling river, navigational obstructions reappeared and a constant state of alertness had to be maintained, calling for continual depth soundings. The advent of the low-water period caused the withdrawal of all but the smallest boats, which profiteered at inflated rates. Boat owners tried to make a profitable season last as long as possible, and boats were run in minimum depths, which occasioned delays in crossing bars. As a boat came closer to literally scraping bottom, water resistance slowed its progress considerably. In difficult places, a boat would be run at full speed into the most likely areas, and if successful, would scrape across with only some slowing. If the boat grounded lightly, it could be removed by various maneuvers of the paddle wheel or by temporarily removing cargo to lighten the load. More serious cases of grounding could be met by warping. Sparring could be used also. Colloquially described as "grass-hoppering," sparring consisted of the sinking of large spars at a forty-five degree angle into the riverbed just ahead of the boat. These were placed on each side of the bow, with their heads overhanging the forecastle. A system of block and tackle was run from the head of the spar to the bow and then back to a capstan. Manual winding of the capstan produced a forward lifting motion, which, aided by the paddle wheels, raised the boat off the bar as though it were on crutches. This would be repeated until the boat was free of the obstruction. These methods of low-water navigation were slow and laborious, usually delaying the trip far beyond any normal duration, and could cause many unforeseen mishaps to both boat and crew.

Steamboat engineer's license for an Erasmus Allison, September, 1848. Courtesy Boatmen's National Bank of St. Louis

ENGINEER AND ENGINE ROOM

Unfamiliarity with the newly developed steam engine created a shortage of engineers for the first western-river steamboats. Some were brought from

High Water on the Mississippi, a Currier and Ives print by Fanny E. Palmer, depicting hardships incurred by river flooding in low lying areas. Courtesy Saint Louis Public Library

the East, but most had to be trained from the start, and engineers were in short supply for years. Their job was a greasy one, performed behind the scenes in hot engine rooms, with little public contact. The work required a knowledge often beyond the competence of men hired in a short labor market, with the result that breakdowns and disasters were more prevalent than necessary.

Apprentice engineers, or "strikers," began their training by oiling and cleaning the machinery and tending the boiler. Later, they progressed to adjustment and operation of the machinery under supervision. Unlike stationary steam engines, those on

Whistles of various types and sizes used on western-river steamboats. *Courtesy Missouri Historical Society*

Bells used for signaling from the pilothouse to the engine room and other parts of a river steamboat. *Courtesy Missouri Historical Society*

Engine room of a small sternwheeler, showing throttle, switchboard, and old-fashioned electric plant. *Courtesy Jefferson National Expansion Memorial, National Park Service*

boats were subject to stresses of the hull while running, thereby causing breakage not found in land-based machinery. The frequent signals requiring changed engine speeds or reversals created strain on engine and engineer. The hardworking machinery was operated almost continuously, with no opportunity for needed adjustments. Most importantly, the engineer had to contend with the ever-present danger of a boiler explosion, and constant vigilance was needed to control the steam pressure. The engineer was usually the victim of an explosion, and at least was held responsible for the catastrophe. The difficult job was lightened after passage of the steamboat act of 1852, which required the installation of proper gauges and safety devices. It also increased the standards for the job and provided for a licensing system for qualified personnel.

The muddy character of the river water used in the boilers left behind deposits of mud, which necessitated frequent, disagreeable cleaning jobs. The problem was solved by the introduction of blowout valves, and mud drums caught silt deposits under the boilers. Also, steam drums were placed above the boilers to prevent the passage of muddy water into the cylinders, reducing the incidence of valve wear by river sand.

Wood was almost exclusively used as a fuel and tremendous quantities of it were consumed, sometimes quite wastefully in inefficient operations. While timber was in plentiful supply along the rivers, there was no problem in maintaining a sufficient amount. It was the usual practice to take on a fresh supply twice daily at regularly established woodyards. The cutting of cordwood for steamboats became the prime business of many backwoodsmen. Wood quality varied, with beech, oak, ash, or chestnut the most favored. The ever-present cottonwood was not desirable, because it did not give a lasting fire. A resinous pine wood was found most satisfactory for some on the lower Mississippi. While wood was a quick, clean fuel, producing a hot fire, it came into short supply as timber near the rivers was cleared. This led to an eventual turn to coal, beginning in the 1840s. Coal required less space for storage on decks and was low in cost, particularly in the coal-laden Ohio River valley. By 1880 coal had superseded wood on the Ohio and upper Mississippi. The last stronghold for wood as a fuel was on the upper Missouri River, which was distant from sources of coal supply.

The starboard engine of the snag boat *Horatio G. Wright. Courtesy Missouri Historical Society*

A steamboat operating-control standard. *Courtesy Missouri Historical Society*

The steamboat *Philadelphia* at a wooding station in the Arkansas Territory, 1828. Etching by Captain Basil Hall, 1829. *Courtesy Ardell Thompson Collection*

Lithograph by Henry Lewis, about 1850, of the *Grand Turk* wooding at night. *Courtesy Saint Louis Mercantile Library Association*

At the Arkansas Territory wooding station the price of a cord of wood for fuel was between $1.50 and $3.00 each. A cord was a stack of wood about eight feet long by four feet high. Etching by Captain Basil Hall, 1829. *Courtesy Ardell Thompson Collection*

A Currier and Ives print of the *Princess* wooding up on the Mississippi. *Courtesy Saint Louis Public Library*

V
The Packet Lines

REGULAR PASSENGER LINE STEAMBOAT OPERATIONS

Not long after the introduction of the steamboat on the western rivers, it became apparent that the traveling public could not rely on the irregular services provided by transient boats. To meet this deficiency, a new type of operation, the packet line, was inaugurated. The word "packet" derives from the French *paquet,* which was applied to vessels that carried mail and passengers on regularly

Packet lines evolved out of a need for regular, reliable service. This is the Memphis and Arkansas River Packet Company's ad for service to Little Rock and to points on the White River. *From The Shipping Guide and Directory, 1870. Courtesy Ardell Thompson Collection*

MEMPHIS & ARKANSAS RIVER
PACKET COMPANY.
U. S. MAIL LINE.

The Elegant Passenger Packets of this Line will
Leave MEMPHIS every
Monday, Wednesday & Friday
At 5 o'clock P. M., for
HELENA, MOUTH WHITE RIVER, PINE BLUFF,
And all points on ARKANSAS RIVER through to
LITTLE ROCK.
AND THE ELEGANT PASSENGER PACKETS OF THE
White River U.S. Mail Line
OF THIS COMPANY.
Will leave MEMPHIS every
Tuesday, Thursday & Saturday
At 5 o'clock for
CLARENDON, DeVALS BLUFF,
And all Points on White River through to Jacksonport.
and to West Point and Searcey Landing
on Little Red River.
The Packets of both the above Lines will make connections at
Little Rock with LIGHT DRAUGHT BOATS for
FORT SMITH and Stages for HOT SPRINGS.
ALL FREIGHTS CONSIGNED TO
"MEMPHIS AND ARKANSAS RIVER PACKET COMPANY,
will be received and forwarded to all points on both Arkansas and
White Rivers, FREE OF CHARGE at Memphis for transfer.
JNO. D. ADAMS, Pres't,
Office, No. 3 Madison Street, Stanton Block, MEMPHIS.
34

The Cincinnati–New Orleans trade was one of the more reliable routes. The *Thompson Dean II* (1872–1882) ran in that trade. *Courtesy Saint Louis Public Library*

Meeting the packet boat. This omnibus is typical of the vehicles from hotels that met boats during the mid-nineteenth century. The Wheeling and Parkersburg packet *Express* is at the wharf at Wheeling, West Virginia. *Courtesy Waterways Journal*

A popular lodging place for river travelers, the old Rose Hotel, Elizabethtown, Illinois, one of the earliest hostelries in the state. *Courtesy State of Illinois, Department of Conservation*

scheduled trips. The term here designated boats making fairly regular trips on some semblance of a schedule. A line consisted of two or more boats engaged in this regular service, operated by the same management.

The development of packet lines had a tendency to limit competition among independent operators and to provide more frequent service on short and medium runs. The larger lines, operating more

Ship Southern Freight via. Memp. & Charleston R. R. (p. 96.)

DEE.   SHIPPING DIRECTIONS.   385

Ship Freight by MEMPHIS & ST. LOUIS PACKET CO. to all points South. (See p. 26.)

DEER RIVER, Iowa; ship by Northern line or Northwestern Union packets to Davenport, Mississippi river, thence by Chicago, Rock Island & Pacific railroad to Victor station.

DEER PARK, Ill.; ship by Northern line or Northwestern Union packets to Rock Island, Mississippi river, thence by Chicago, Rock Island & Pacific railroad to Utica station.

DEER PARK, Ill.; ship to Lasalle station on Illinois Central railroad, via St. Louis & Vandalia railroad.

DEER PARK, Ark., Mississippi river; ship by Vicksburg packets.

DEER CREEK, on Yazoo river; ship to Vicksburg, via Vicksburg packets, thence via Yazoo river packets.

DEER PARK, La.; ship via St. Louis & New Orleans packets.

DEERPARK, Ala., on Mobile & Ohio railroad; ship via Memphis packets to Columbus, Ky., thence via Mobile & Ohio or St. Louis & Iron Mountain railroad.

DEER PLAIN, Ill.; ship by Illinois river packets.

DEERINGS, Mo., on Missouri river; ship via Missouri packets.

DEERSVILLE, Ind.; ship to Washington station on Mobile & Ohio railroad.

DEETH, Nev., on Central Pacific railroad; ship via "O" line or connecting railroads to Omaha, thence via Union Pacific railroad to Promontory, Utah, via Central Pacific railroad; or via Far West Freight line, through bill.

DE KALB, Ill., on Chicago & Northwestern railroad; ship via Northern line or Northwestern Union packets to Clinton, thence via Chicago & Northwestern railroad.

DE KALB, Miss., on Mobile & Ohio railroad; ship via Memphis packets to Columbus, Ky., thence via Mobile & Ohio or via St. Louis & Iron Mountain railroad.

DELACROIX PLANTATION, La.; ship to New Orleans by New Orleans packets, thence by Lower Coast packets.

DELOCHES, J., La.; ship by New Orleans packets to mouth of Red river, thence via Kouns' line.

DELOCHES ROCKS, La.; ship by New Orleans packets to mouth of Red river, thence via Kouns' line.

DELASSUS, Mo., St. Louis & Iron Mountain railroad.

DELAVAN, Ill.; ship to Rock Island, Mississippi river, by Northern line or Northwestern Union packets, thence by Western Union railroad.

Phillips & St. John. { Dealers in all kinds of Steamboat Coal—Three Whistles will always call their Tug at Memphis. See Adv. inside of back cover Page.

49

Typical page from the 1870 *Shipping Guide and Directory*, describing freight routings via river packets and railroads. *Courtesy Ardell Thompson Collection*

The wharfboat of the Atlantic and Mississippi Steamship Company at Saint Louis. The steamer *Thompson Dean I* is in the background. Wharf-boats were for the distribution of goods coming and going via steamboat. *Courtesy Boatmen's National Bank of St. Louis*

St. Louis & New Orleans Packet Co.

OFFICE, ON COMPANY'S WHARF-BOAT,

Foot of Market Street, St. Louis, Mo.

DAYS OF DEPARTURE

From ST. LOUIS and NEW ORLEANS,

TUESDAYS, THURSDAYS & SATURDAYS, AT 5 O'CLOCK P.M.

COMPOSED OF THE FIRST CLASS PASSENGER STEAMERS

RICHMOND,
THOMPSON DEAN,
MOLLIE ABLE,
COMMONWEALTH,
W. R. ARTHUR,
PAULINE CARROLL,
OLIVE BRANCH,
BISMARCK,
DEXTER.

Through Bills of Lading

SIGNED TO

GALVESTON AND ALL TEXAS PORTS,

MOBILE, MONTGOMERY and ALABAMA RIVER PORTS on the

New Orleans, Jackson, & Great Northern Alabama & Georgia R. R's.

TO POINTS ON RED RIVER,

To AND FROM NEW YORK AND BOSTON,

Via STEAMSHIPS.

COMPANY'S AGENTS:

J. EAGER, 41 Broad Street, New York.
J. HENRY SEARS, 99 State Street, Boston.
J. B. WOODS, 104 Common Street, New Orleans.

OFFICERS, ST. LOUIS.

JOHN N. BOFINGER, President.   WALKER R. CARTER, Secretary.
J. W. CARROLL, Superintendent.   WM. F. HAINES, Freight Agent.

The Saint Louis and New Orleans Packet Company fell on hard times at the start of the Civil War. *From The Shipping Guide and Directory, 1870. Courtesy Ardell Thompson Collection*

boats, were able to provide more frequent departures on the longer trips, such as from Cincinnati to New Orleans. An unfavorable factor in packet-line operations was the laying up of boats during periods of low water, when these large packets were unable to negotiate the shallow rivers. Occasionally, lighter-draft boats were pressed into service at such times, but only among the older and better-established lines. Packet boats generally were individually owned and operated. Their participation in the line consisted of being bound, rather loosely, to making departures at scheduled hours and at reasonable frequencies. There was a rare pooling of receipts, generally in later years when organizations became more complex.

Some of the lines maintained ticket and freight agencies at principal ports and occasionally would have their own wharfboats—if the line was sufficiently large. Agreements among the various boat owners were informal and usually unwritten, generally carrying no provision for penalties, even in written contracts. Not many of these loosely organized lines remained in service for more than a few years in the antebellum period. Packet-line failures were common during times of economic upheaval, and many lines failed to survive even a single season. Differences among line members over schedules or rates were the principal reasons for disruptions in the routine. The transient boats did not cause much worry to the packet lines; their chief competition came from nonline boats that were their equals in speed and accommodations. Such independents were owners who either had been

"Squeeze Play." Competition for passengers and freight caused pilots to be foolhardy, to take risks to outspeed each other. Getting into a lock ahead of another packet was a big advantage, but not this time. They jammed the lock. *Courtesy Waterways Journal*

The sternwheeler *General Pike*, built at Cincinnati in 1818, the first boat in the West designed solely for the accommodation of passengers. The Cincinnati city directory of 1820 states: "She measures 100 feet of keel, 25 feet of beam and draws 3 feet-3 inches of water. The cabin is 40 feet long, with staterooms at each end, and is divided by a commodious hall capable of accommodating 100 passengers. Her accommodations are ample, her apartments spacious and superb, her machinery and apparatus perfectly safe and in fine order, and her commander, Captain Bliss, is always attentive and obliging." *From* Up the Heights, *1873*

refused line membership or did not join because of disapproval of packet-line practices. A strong attack by a powerful independent could play havoc with the loosely knit line organizations and frequently brought about their end. After the Civil War conditions were more formal among participants in packet-line agreements. Efforts were made to strengthen agreements, through penalties and forfeits, to prevent dissension among the line members.

The more successful lines were those that owned all the boats in their line. Organizers of such lines

The *Grand Turk*, built at Freedom, Pennsylvania, in 1848, was one of the better-known early-day boats on the lower Mississippi. She ran in trades to New Orleans from Louisville and Saint Louis. She burned in a disastrous steamboat fire at New Orleans, when the cotton-laden *Charles Belcher* caught fire and set the *Grand Turk* ablaze along with *Natchez III* and others, on February 6, 1854. *Courtesy Boatmen's National Bank of St. Louis*

raised capital to purchase the required boats, and then a central incorporated management was set up to operate them.

While the desirability of regular line service was recognized early in western-river steamboat operations, the first twenty years found scant use of packet lines. The reason was the many natural and mechanical troubles. With the exception of the Fulton-Livingston operation of line boats between New Orleans and Natchez, the origin of steamboat-line service appears to have taken place on the Ohio River, beginning with the Louisville and Cincinnati runs of the *General Pike* in 1819. Packet lines became numerous during the 1830s, when they began to appear on many tributary rivers. These lines usually consisted of only two boats, in relatively short trades. After 1840 the principle of packet-line operation came to be adopted on a large scale in all of the trades, and soon developed into steamboating's golden age. Steamboats represented the fastest and most luxurious mode of travel. The railroads, which had become numerous and were indisputably faster than the steamboats, with their crude cars, were rough-riding affairs compared with the smooth rides and superb appointments aboard the riverboats. Later improvements in railroad operation, chiefly through speed and the ability to reach inland market centers unattainable by waterways, led to the general demise

A busy levee scene at New Orleans in 1870. *Courtesy Jefferson National Expansion Memorial, National Park Service*

of passenger and freight packet lines during the nineties.

ON THE LOWER MISSISSIPPI

The earliest packet line on the lower Mississippi was the Mississippi Steamboat Navigation Company, organized by the Fulton-Livingston interests in 1810. It was designed to establish their claim to sole rights for steamboat operations on the Mississippi River. The line ran boats between New Orleans and Natchez for several years until the Fulton monopoly was broken by a legal verdict favorable

The New Orleans levee in the late 1850s featured many a packet boat. *From Harper's Weekly. Courtesy Saint Louis Mercantile Library Association*

Built in 1858 at Paducah, Kentucky, the *New Falls City* had dimensions of 311 feet by 45 feet by 7½ feet. She ran in the Saint Louis & New Orleans Railroad Line service until it was suspended on the eve of the Civil War. The line was so named because of its connections with railroads at river ports. This boat was purposely sunk in the Red River in Louisiana in 1864 to prevent an invading Union force from reaching the upper river valley. *Courtesy Boatmen's National Bank of St. Louis*

An intricately carved archway colonnade in the main cabin of the *Grand Republic*, 1876. *Courtesy Missouri Historical Society*

Built in 1867 at Pittsburgh (as the *Great Republic*), the *Grand Republic* measured 335 feet by 51 feet by 9½ feet, and cost $235,000. She was not a financial success and bankrupted her original owners by 1871. Her hull was lengthened to 350 feet with a 56-foot beam in 1872 at Carondelet, Missouri, where she was outfitted as the most luxuriously appointed boat on the river. Her name was changed to *Grand Republic* in 1876. In the following year she was totally destroyed in a fire at Carondelet. *Drawing by the author. Courtesy Boatmen's National Bank of St. Louis*

Built in 1871, the steamer *Katie* was completed for the New Orleans-Lake Providence trade. She was a fast boat and difficult to handle, hitting a snag and sinking opposite Helena, Arkansas, on her maiden voyage. The boat was not successful financially and was dismantled in 1878, with her engines going into the steamer *Ed Richardson*. *Courtesy Boatmen's National Bank of St. Louis*

Built in 1870 at Saint Louis, by Captain David Silver, who formed the Shreveport, New Orleans and Saint Louis Packet Company in 1872, the *Susie Silver* ran also to New Orleans from Louisville and Cincinnati. She was dismantled at Cincinnati in 1878. *Courtesy Boatmen's National Bank of St. Louis*

Built in 1878 in Cincinnati, the *Edward J. Gay* (right) ran in the New Orleans-Bayou Sara trade with the *John W. Cannon*. She burned at New Orleans in 1888. The *Yazoo Valley* (left) was a stern-wheeler completed at Howard's shipyard in 1876. She was owned by S. H. Parisot & Company of Vicksburg and was sold for the Red River trade in 1882. She sank thirty-five miles above New Orleans in 1883. *Courtesy Boatmen's National Bank of Saint Louis*

Built in 1878 at Howard's yard, the *John W. Cannon*, named for the captain of the famous *Robert E. Lee*, ran in the Bayou Sara trade. An unusual design feature was the extension of the boiler deck forward over the forecastle. She was luxuriously fitted as a private boat for wealthy planters but dismantled in 1886. *Courtesy Boatmen's National Bank of St. Louis*

Built in 1878 by Howard's yard, the steamer *J. M. White III* was probably the finest and fastest boat in the western-river trades. Her dimensions were 312 feet 7 inches in length and 47 feet 9 inches in beam, rated at 2027.76 tons. She was built for Captain John W. Tobin and was named for a Cloverport, Kentucky, river captain. After a short career, the *White* burned near Bayou Sara, Louisiana, on December 13, 1886. Drawing by the author. *Courtesy Missouri Historical Society*

Portrait of Captain John C. Swon, a well-known Saint Louis steamboat man and master of the *J. M. White* in the early 1880s. *From* History of Saint Louis City and County, *1883*

to their rival, Captain Henry M. Shreve, in 1818. The first large-scale packet service was the Ohio and Mississippi Mail Line, organized at Louisville in 1832 with sixteen boats. Its purpose was to establish thrice-weekly mail and passenger service to New Orleans. The line began running in the spring of 1833, when it announced that one of its boats would leave each terminus daily. Unfortunately, this progressive attempt at scheduled operation

Built in 1880 at Cincinnati, the sidewheeler *Belle of the Coast* ran for many years in the upper-coast trade. When she burned in 1897 there were only seventeen sidewheelers left on the Mississippi River system. *Courtesy Boatmen's National Bank of St. Louis*

ceeded in 1849 by a service composed of the steamers *Autocrat* and *Magnolia*. Infrequent packet service from Nashville to New Orleans was tried by two lines in 1848, and in 1854 a single line was making thrice-weekly departures to Memphis. In 1851 a line running three boats tried departures every four days from Louisville for New Orleans. By 1854 the Star Line was running three boats on weekly departures from Ohio River ports to New Orleans, and in 1858–1859 the New Orleans Express Line provided a ten-boat service from Cincinnati to the Crescent City. The Lightning Line served Ohio and lower Mississippi River points with a three-times-a-week schedule after 1858, until the outbreak of the Civil War. A Louisville-Memphis line was organized in 1857, and in 1859 a short-lived venture was tried between Pittsburgh and Memphis. As early as 1836, line service was tried between Pittsburgh and Saint Louis, but

failed before the end of its first season, owing to attacks by independents fearing a monopoly.

Service from the Ohio River to Memphis operated briefly on weekly departures in 1846. Regular runs between Memphis and New Orleans began in 1844 with a line of four boats. This line was suc-

Built in 1898 at Howard's yard, the well-known Vicksburg and Greenville packet *Belle of the Bends* was considered one of the best-proportioned sidewheelers ever built. After surviving two sinkings in 1909–1910, the *Belle* was withdrawn from the Greenville run in 1912 and sold to Saint Louis interests, who converted her into an excursion boat. She was operated as such at Saint Louis until 1918, when her name was changed to *Liberty*. She ran out of Cairo, Illinois, in 1918–1919 and was then sold and dismantled. *Courtesy Boatmen's National Bank of St. Louis*

Business resumed after the war—New Orleans during the 1870s. In the foreground is the Canal Street ferry *Louise*, with the sternwheeler *Kate Kinney* behind her. *Courtesy Waterways Journal*

The levee at Saint Louis about 1859, just before traffic vanished because of the Civil War. *From Harper's Weekly. Courtesy Saint Louis Mercantile Library Association*

Captain John A. Scudder of Saint Louis, who established the Memphis and Saint Louis Packet Company in 1859 and later founded the Anchor Line. *From History of Saint Louis City and County, 1883*

failed because of the panic of 1837. By 1852 service between these ports was resumed, and in 1860 direct packet service from Cincinnati to Saint Louis was provided by the Saint Louis Express Line's five boats, with two departures weekly in each direction. A two-boat independent line competed briefly before all service was suspended in 1861 because of the Civil War.

The Memphis and New Orleans Packet Line was operated jointly with the Memphis and Charleston Railroad for a few years after 1857. It was not a success and was liquidated with substantial losses. Line service from Saint Louis to lower Mississippi River points was run on an irregular basis until the late fifties. One of the first organized lines in this trade was the Memphis and Saint Louis Packet Company established in 1859 by John A. Scudder, Daniel Able, and others. This company survived wartime dislocations by running its boats in conjunction with the progress of Federal control on the lower river.

Painting by Oscar E. Berninghaus of the Saint Louis levee in the early 1870s. *Courtesy August A. Busch, Jr.*

Predecessor to Scudder's famous Anchor Line. *From The Shipping Guide and Directory, 1870. Courtesy Ardell Thompson Collection*

The Saint Louis levee in the 1880s. In the foreground is the wharfboat of the Saint Louis & New Orleans Anchor Line with the steamboat *City of New Orleans* behind it. *Courtesy Jefferson National Expansion Memorial, National Park Service*

The Anchor Line sidewheeler *James Howard*. She measured 320 feet by 53 feet by 10 feet, and was built in 1870 for Captain J. R. Pegram to run in the Saint Louis-New Orleans trade. Pegram sold out to the Anchor Line in 1878. This boat took Grand Duke Alexis of Russia on his trip down the Mississippi. The *Howard* burned at Saint Louis on March 13, 1881. *Courtesy Boatmen's National Bank of St. Louis*

The Anchor Line's *City of Alton*. She was originally built in 1868 at Saint Louis and in 1873 rebuilt to 1458 tons. She was later purchased by the Anchor Line and placed under the command of Captain Horace Bixby. The *Alton* burned at Saint Louis in January, 1884. *Courtesy Boatmen's National Bank of St. Louis*

The Anchor Line's *Belle Memphis III*. Built by Howard's shipyard in 1880, she was a fast boat and made a record run from Helena, Arkansas, to Memphis in five hours and fifty-six minutes in May, 1881. This beat the best time of the *Robert E. Lee* for this distance by thirty minutes. *Belle Memphis* snagged and sank at Crane's Island, below Chester, Illinois, in September, 1897. *Courtesy Boatmen's National Bank of St. Louis*

The Anchor Line's *City of Providence*. She had about the longest life of any Anchor Line boat, having been built in 1880 for the Saint Louis-Natchez trade. The boat was sold, when the Anchor Line was discontinued in 1898, to the Columbia Excursion Line of Saint Louis. She was long a favorite of Saint Louisans until she was crushed by ice in January, 1910. *Courtesy Boatmen's National Bank of St. Louis*

The saloon, or main-cabin interior, of the Anchor Line steamer *City of Providence*, with the water cooler in the foreground. Drawing by William T. Smedley for *Harper's Monthly*, 1893

Anchor Line's sidewheeler *City of Vicksburg* was built for them in 1881 and sold to the Columbia Excursion Company of Saint Louis in 1894. She was badly damaged by the Saint Louis tornado of 1896 but was sold and rebuilt as the *Chalmette* to run in the New Orleans trade. The boat sank at Legon's Landing, Louisiana, in 1904. *Courtesy Boatmen's National Bank of St. Louis*

The *City of Baton Rouge* was one of the Anchor Line's finest packets running in the Saint Louis-New Orleans trade. Built in 1881, she was 294 feet by 49 feet by 9½ feet. The packet sank at Hermitage, Louisiana, in 1890, with the loss of two lives. *Drawing by the author. Courtesy William Pagenstecher*

The *City of New Orleans* was one of the Anchor Line's better-known boats, enjoying a long career, from 1881 to 1898, when she was dismantled at Marietta, Ohio. *Courtesy Boatmen's National Bank of St. Louis*

Anchor Line packet *Arkansas City*, built at Jeffersonville, Indiana, in 1882 and wrecked in the Saint Louis tornado of May, 1896. Her dimensions were 273 feet by 44 feet by 7 feet—1236 tons. *Courtesy Boatmen's National Bank of St. Louis*

The Anchor liner *City of Cairo* was built at Howard's in 1882. She was 271 feet long with a beam of 44 feet. Running chiefly in the Saint Louis-Vicksburg trade, she was wrecked in the tornado at Saint Louis in 1896. *Courtesy Boatmen's National Bank of St. Louis*

The *Will S. Hays,* named for the noted Louisville songwriter and reporter, was built at Freedom, Pennsylvania, in 1882. Her cabin came from the *Thompson Dean II.* She ran in the Cincinnati-New Orleans trade until sold to the Anchor Line in the mid-eighties. The *Hays* was cut down by ice at Saint Louis in 1887. *Courtesy Boatmen's National Bank of St. Louis*

The Anchor Line steamer *City of Saint Louis* was completed in 1883. Her dimensions were 300 feet by 49 feet by 8½ feet. She ran in the Saint Louis to New Orleans trade until the end of her career as a packet in 1898. The boat was then sold to Captain W. H. Thorwegan of Saint Louis, who converted her into an excursion boat. The *City of Saint Louis* burned at Carondelet, Missouri, on October 29, 1903. Drawing by the author. *Courtesy Boatmen's National Bank of St. Louis*

The steamer *City of Bayou Sara* was built for the Anchor Line in 1884 at Howard's shipyard. She had a short life, being destroyed by fire at New Madrid, Missouri, on December 5, 1887, with the loss of eight lives. *Courtesy Boatmen's National Bank of St. Louis*

The Steamboat *Crystal City* of the Anchor Line was completed in 1887 for the Saint Louis-Grand Tower trade. She sank in 1889 but was raised and ran until she was cut down by ice below Jefferson Barracks, Missouri, in February, 1893. *Courtesy Boatmen's National Bank of St. Louis*

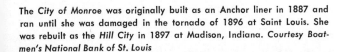

The *City of Monroe* was originally built as an Anchor liner in 1887 and ran until she was damaged in the tornado of 1896 at Saint Louis. She was rebuilt as the *Hill City* in 1897 at Madison, Indiana. *Courtesy Boatmen's National Bank of St. Louis*

The *City of Hickman* of the Anchor Line was completed in 1890 at Howard's shipyard in Jeffersonville, Indiana, where most of the line's steamers were constructed. She sank in the chute of Island No. 40, twelve miles above Memphis, on August 23, 1896. *Courtesy Boatmen's National Bank of St. Louis*

The Anchor Line's only sternwheeler was the *Bluff City*, built in 1896. She burned at Chester, Illinois, in November, 1897. *Courtesy Jefferson National Expansion Memorial, National Park Service*

The Anchor Line's *Hill City*, rebuilt from the *City of Monroe*. Sold by the Anchor Line, she sank near Memphis in 1900. She was raised and rebuilt into the excursion boat *Corwin H. Spencer. Courtesy Boatmen's National Bank of St. Louis*

Captain John N. Bofinger, who transported General Sherman's army during the Civil War. He founded the Atlantic & Mississippi Steamship Company and the Saint Louis & New Orleans Packet Company. Captain Bofinger also founded the Merchants-Southern Line Packet Company in 1870 for service in the Saint Louis and New Orleans trade. This line was in existence for several years but was finally abandoned for lack of profits. Another line, unconnected with Bofinger's, the Saint Louis, Cincinnati, Huntington and Pittsburgh Packet Company, formed in 1881, with good boats and management, withdrew after only a few months of operation—chiefly because of railroad competition and the long distances involved in its route. *From* History of Saint Louis City and County, *1883*

After the war the line extended operations to Vicksburg and later to New Orleans. The famous Saint Louis and New Orleans Anchor Line was an outgrowth of this line. The anchor symbol was adopted in 1874 at the suggestion of Captain Scudder. The Anchor Line was a successful operation until the 1890s, when it finally succumbed to railroad competition.

The veteran riverman Captain John N. Bofinger, who had been in charge of the movement of General Sherman's army of thirty-five thousand men from Memphis to Vicksburg during the Civil War, was instrumental in the establishment of the Atlantic and Mississippi Steamship Company in 1866. Its purpose was to fulfill the demand for trade with the South, and it included twenty of the finest riverboats afloat. The line had excellent connections with railroads and other steamboat lines, but in spite of its good management it only survived until 1869. Inflationary trends after the war led to extravagances in A. & M. operations, causing an insufficient profit margin, and the line fell victim to relentless competition. Also its fleet suffered several mishaps in fires and sinkings, lead-

The Saint Louis and New Orleans Packet Company's *Richmond*, built at Madison, Indiana, in 1867, was 340 feet long, with a beam of 50 feet. This boat featured low-pressure steam engines and had its own newspaper, the *Richmond Headlight*. Bought in 1869, she sank that year at Grand Chain on the Ohio River. The Saint Louis and New Orleans Packet Company was founded in 1858 and consisted of ten fine boats, separately owned but managed under a pooling agreement. Its profitable career slackened with the beginning of the war in 1861. Drawing by the author. *Courtesy Boatmen's National Bank of St. Louis*

One of Bofinger's boats, the *Ruth II*, built in 1865 at Jeffersonville, Indiana. She burned at Paw Paw Island, above Vicksburg, in March, 1869. *Courtesy Boatmen's National Bank of St. Louis*

Bofinger's advertisement. His company operated between Saint Louis and New Orleans from 1866 to 1869. *From the Saint Louis City Directory, 1866*

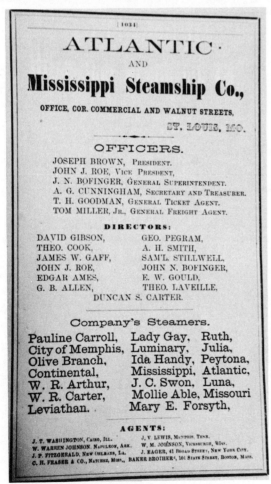

ing to damage awards the company could not meet.

One of the last regular lines to run on the lower Mississippi was the Lee Line of Memphis, which ran between Memphis and Cairo for some years. Their first boat to reach Saint Louis was the *Georgia Lee* in 1899, beginning a service that continued until World War I. The Lee Line merged with the former Memphis and Rosedale Packet Company, then known as the Delta Line, in 1924. The Lee Line name was changed to the Valley Line, which ceased operations in the late 1920s.

Passenger service on the lower Mississippi now is restricted to the occasional visits of the sternwheeler *Delta Queen*.

The Lee Line sternwheeler *Georgia Lee*, completed at Howard's in 1898, for the Cairo-Memphis trade. She sank in the Ohio River at Paducah in 1909, while being hauled up on marine ways. She was raised and ran in the Cincinnati-Memphis trade until 1914 and was lost in the ice in 1918. *Courtesy Jefferson National Expansion Memorial, National Park Service*

The Lee Line's *James Lee,* completed in 1898, ran in service between Memphis and Friar's Point, Mississippi, until she sank near Memphis in 1914. She was raised and rebuilt into the excursion boat *De Soto.* She was lost in the ice in 1918. *Courtesy Waterways Journal*

The Lee's sternwheeler *Ferd Herold,* named for a Saint Louis brewer, was built at Dubuque, Iowa, in 1890. She ran in Ouachita River service and also on the Saint Louis-Alton run before she was sold to the Lee Line, which ran her in the Saint Louis-Memphis service until it was discontinued in 1919. The *Ferd* was dismantled in 1920. *Courtesy Webster Groves Book Shop*

Captain John S. McCune, president of the Keokuk Packet Company, who was also operated steamboats on the Missouri River in the 1860s. *From St. Louis, the Fourth City, 1909*

The Keokuk's *Die Vernon II,* built at Saint Louis in 1850, replaced the first *Die Vernon,* which ran in 1842. The boat pictured here was involved in a collision with the *Archer* near the mouth of the Illinois River in 1851, sinking the *Archer* with the loss of forty-one lives. The *Die Vernon* was used as a freight boat until the late 1850s. *Courtesy Boatmen's National Bank of St. Louis*

Advertising cards of the Keokuk Line in 1870 and 1874, listing its fast steamers and stressing close connectons with all railroads. *Courtesy Saint Louis Public Library*

ON THE UPPER MISSISSIPPI

Regular packet-line service on the upper Mississippi River began with the formation of the Saint Louis and Keokuk Packet Line in 1842. John S. McCune and James E. Yeatman were the founders. Their first boat was the new *Di Vernon,* which made her initial run late in 1842. During the next season she operated in a daily line along with two transient steamers. An opposition line of three boats provided

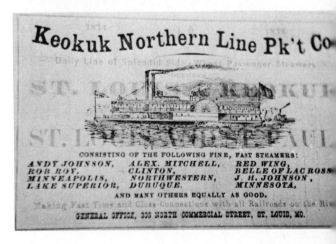

The *Rob Roy* was completed at Saint Louis in 1866. In 1871 she blew a mud drumhead, killing a fireman and two camels (a menagerie was on board). She sank in 1874, was raised, and sank again in 1880, and that year was dismantled. *Courtesy Boatmen's National Bank of St. Louis*

The *Andy Johnson*, built at Saint Louis in 1866, named for President Andrew Johnson, who made a trip on her from Alton to Saint Louis in 1867. After ten years in the Keokuk Line service, the *Andy Johnson* was crushed by an ice jam at Saint Louis in December, 1876, along with the *Bayard* and the *Davenport*. *Courtesy Boatmen's National Bank of St. Louis*

Advertisement from the *Shipping Guide and Directory*, 1870. *Courtesy Ardell Thompson Collection*

The *Lucy Bertram*, completed at Madison, Indiana, in 1863, measured 242 feet by 40 feet by 5½ feet. After a long career on the upper Mississippi, she was dismantled in 1876. *Courtesy Boatmen's National Bank of St. Louis*

competition in 1844 but capitulated during the summer of 1845. Another opposition attempt, in 1850, was withdrawn later in that year. A succession of various boats was operated by the Keokuk company during these prosperous years, and in 1852 the company established a separate line to Quincy, Illinois. This line later merged with the Northern Line.

The Northern Line was formed at Saint Louis in 1857 by a group of captains in the Saint Louis to Saint Paul trade. A joint stock company was formed in 1859 and was incorporated as the Northern Line Packet Company. The Northern Line admitted the boats of the Northwestern-Union Packet Company into its line in 1868, and soon

The Northern Line's *Davenport*, built in 1860, was rated at 340 tons and ran until 1873, when she began operating in the Cincinnati-Saint Louis trade. She was cut down by ice at Saint Louis in 1876. *Courtesy Boatmen's National Bank of St. Louis*

The Northern Line sidewheeler *Burlington* was completed in 1864 and measured 210 feet by 35 feet by 5½ feet. She sank in the upper Mississippi above Wabasha after a snagging in September, 1867. *Courtesy Boatmen's National Bank of St. Louis*

An ad of the Northern Line from the *Shipping Guide and Directory for 1870* before the Northern merged with the Keokuk Packet Line in the following year. *Courtesy Ardell Thompson Collection*

The Northern Line's *Sucker State*, completed at Pittsburgh in 1860. She made a fast trip from Saint Louis to Saint Paul in two days, twenty-three hours, and forty-eight minutes, in June, 1867. She was a sister boat of the *Hawkeye State* and was destroyed by fire in the Alton Slough in 1872. *Courtesy Boatmen's National Bank of St. Louis*

The Northern's steamer *Minneapolis*, whose wheelhouse carried a painting of the Falls of Saint Anthony, was built in 1869. She was one of their larger boats and was dismantled in the late 1870s. *Courtesy Boatmen's National Bank of St. Louis*

The Northern Line *Minnesota* was among the fleet in the late 1860s. *Courtesy Boatmen's National Bank of St. Louis*

The Keokuk-Northern Line sidewheeler *Golden Eagle,* built in 1876, using the machinery from the dismantled *J. H. Johnson. Courtesy Boatmen's National Bank of St. Louis*

The *Gem City I,* built for the Keokuk-Northern Line in 1881, was sold after the line's failure in the same year to the successor Saint Louis and Saint Paul Packet Company. The round-trip fare to Saint Paul then was twenty-four dollars, and this fast boat sometimes made the 1,532-mile round trip in five and a half days. She burned at Saint Louis in September, 1883. *Courtesy Boatmen's National Bank of St. Louis*

An announcement of the Keokuk Line after its merger with the Northern Line in 1871, advertising service to all important upper river ports. *From the Saint Louis City Directory, 1871*

Keokuk-Northern Line successor, Saint Louis and Saint Paul's *War Eagle,* was built at Saint Louis in 1876—279 feet long, with a 42-foot beam. She sank after striking the bridge at Keokuk in 1881. *Courtesy Boatmen's National Bank of St. Louis*

about twenty boats were running under the Northern Line banner. It proved such a strong rival to the Keokuk Line, that the two lines consolidated into the Keokuk-Northern Packet Line in 1871. Following the death of president John S. McCune in 1874, dissension among the stockholders resulted in extended litigation, and contributed to the line's demise in 1881. The Saint Louis and Saint Paul Packet Company was formed as a successor line, in that same year, with a capital of a hundred thousand dollars.

Railroads, which paralleled the river for long distances, and crossed it at numerous points, caused a decline in the business of the Saint Paul Line, as it had for its predecessor. The Saint Paul Line represented a last-ditch effort to keep packet operations alive on the Upper Mississippi; the decline in river traffic is reflected in the drop of steamboat arrivals at Saint Paul from 1,068 in 1858 to 218 in 1874. The Saint Paul Line finally abandoned operations in 1889, when it sold out to the Diamond Jo Line.

No account of steamboat activities on the upper Mississippi would be complete without reference to the career of Captain William F. Davidson. He was a shrewd Minnesota River steamboat operator

William P. Davidson, president of the Northwestern Packet Company. *Courtesy Saint Louis Public Company*

The Northwestern Line packet *Itasca*, running mate of the *Key City*, measured 230 feet by 35 feet by 5 feet and was rated at 560 tons. She was built at Cincinnati in 1857, and burned at La Crosse, Wisconsin, in 1868. *Courtesy Boatmen's National Bank of St. Louis*

Part of Davidson's fleet was the *Northern Belle*, built in 1856. She ran in the La Crosse-Saint Paul trade in the late 1850s, and was used as a transport during the Civil War. She ran in Davidson's line until she was abandoned in 1874. *Courtesy Boatmen's National Bank of St. Louis*

Davidson's *War Eagle I*, built at Cincinnati in 1854. She ran to Saint Paul from Galena in 1854–1856 and from Dunleith in 1857–1858. During the war, in 1862, she was used to transport supplies to troops on the Tennessee River. She returned to the Davidson line in 1863 and ran until the early 1870s. *Courtesy Boatmen's National Bank of St. Louis*

The sidewheeler *Key City* began running in the Dunleith-Saint Paul trade in 1857, teamed with the *Itasca*. She continued in Davidson line operations until 1870. *Courtesy Boatmen's National Bank of St. Louis*

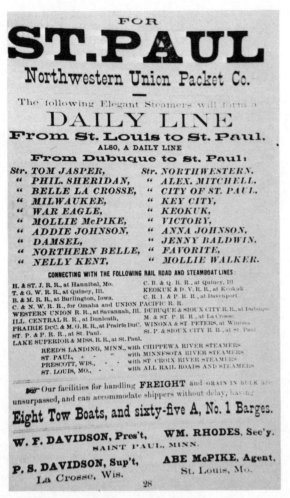

FOR

ST.PAUL

Northwestern Union Packet Co.

The following Elegant Steamers will form a

DAILY LINE

From St. Louis to St. Paul.

ALSO, A DAILY LINE

From Dubuque to St. Paul:

Str. TOM JASPER,	Str. NORTHWESTERN.
" PHIL. SHERIDAN,	" ALEX. MITCHELL.
" BELLE LA CROSSE,	" CITY OF ST. PAUL.
" MILWAUKEE,	" KEY CITY,
" WAR EAGLE,	" KEOKUK,
" MOLLIE McPIKE,	" VICTORY,
" ADDIE JOHNSON,	" ANNA JOHNSON,
" DAMSEL,	" JENNY BALDWIN.
" NORTHERN BELLE,	" FAVORITE,
" NELLY KENT,	" MOLLIE WALKER.

CONNECTING WITH THE FOLLOWING RAIL ROAD AND STEAMBOAT LINES:

H. & ST. J. R. R., at Hannibal, Mo.   C. B. & Q. R. R., at Quincy, Ill
T. & G. W. R. R., at Quincy, Ill.   KEOKUK & D. V. R. R., at Keokuk
B. & M. R. R., at Burlington, Iowa.   C. R. I. & P. R. R., at Davenport
C. & N. W. R. R., for Omaha and UNION PACIFIC R. R.
WESTERN UNION R. R., at Savannah, Ill. DUBUQUE & SIOUX CITY R. R., at Dubuque
ILL. CENTRAL R. R., at Dunleith,   M. & ST. P. R. R., at La Crosse
PRAIRIE DuC. & M. G. R. R., at Prairie DuC. WINONA & ST. PETERS, at Winona
ST. P. & P. R. R., at St. Paul.   St. P. & SIOUX CITY R. R., at St. Paul
LAKE SUPERIOR & MISS. R. R., at St. Paul.

REED'S LANDING, MINN., with CHIPPEWA RIVER STEAMERS
ST. PAUL, - - - with MINNESOTA RIVER STEAMERS
PRESCOTT, WIS., - - with ST. CROIX RIVER STEAMERS
ST. LOUIS, MO., - - with ALL RAIL ROADS AND STEAMERS

☞ Our facilities for handling **FREIGHT** and GRAIN IN BULK are unsurpassed, and can accommodate shippers without delay, having

Eight Tow Boats, and sixty-five A, No. 1 Barges.

W. F. DAVIDSON, Pres't,   **WM. RHODES**, Sec'y.
SAINT PAUL, MINN.

P. S. DAVIDSON, Sup't,   **ABE McPIKE**, Agent,
La Crosse, Wis.   St. Louis, Mo.

28

An advertisement of Davidson's two-line consolidation, the Northwestern-Union Packet Company. *From the Shipping Guide and Directory, 1870. Courtesy Ardell Thompson Collection*

The *Favorite I* ran in Davidson's White Collar Line on the Minnesota River in 1859–1862. The 252-ton boat continued to operate in various upper-river trades until 1870. *Courtesy Boatmen's National Bank of St. Louis*

Before the merger—the Northwestern Line's packet *Northern Light*, featuring a picture of the Aurora Borealis on her paddle-wheel boxes. She came out in 1857 and was considered the fastest boat on the upper Mississippi. She was sunk by ice in 1866. *Courtesy Boatmen's National Bank of St. Louis*

Completed at La Crosse in 1870, the steamboat *Alex. Mitchell* was named for the president of a railroad with which the packet line had connections. The steamer was dismantled in 1881. *Courtesy Boatmen's National Bank of St. Louis*

who began a packet line between La Crosse, Wisconsin, and Saint Paul on the Mississippi. Davidson's line was the La Crosse and Saint Paul Packet Company, which began operations in 1860, with assistance from the La Crosse and Milwaukee Railroad. Davidson soon obtained control of the older Galena Line, the principal line in the area during the 1850s. A minority group in the Galena Line formed the Northwestern Packet Company in 1864 as a countermove. Nevertheless, through pooling agreements, Davidson soon achieved a dominant position in the line. After the end of the Civil War, Davidson's White Collar Line and the Northwestern Line operated thirty boats and barges, as well as a shipyard. An antimonopoly movement that failed to dislodge Davidson's control resulted in the consolidation of his two lines into the Northwestern-Union Packet Line in 1866. This line had a capitalization of $1,500,000 and extended its operations downriver to Saint Louis. This is the competition that led to the Keokuk and Northern Line merger in 1871, with Davidson in control. The strong monopoly was not sufficient to prevent the decline in river traffic, and even before the death of McCune, in 1873 the Davidson line was bankrupt. Following the reorganization with the Saint Paul Line, the interests survived, in depleted form, until their 1889 demise.

The earliest line to operate in the most northern navigable sector of the upper Mississippi was the Minnesota Packet Company, organized in 1847 by Captain M. W. Lodwick, who purchased the steamboat *Dr. Franklin* at Cincinnati. He began operating in the Galena-Saint Paul trade in 1848. A rival line ran in this trade in 1850–1853, until they were consolidated in the last year as the Galena and Minnesota Packet Company. They opened the 1854 season with the *Nominee, War Eagle, Galena,* and *Royal Arch.* In 1855 the *Northern Belle,* under Captain Preston Lodwick, was used as a connecting boat with the newly completed Illinois Central Railroad at Dunleith, Illinois. During the next season the line added Dunleith to its name, and had about a dozen boats running in the profitable western-immigrant season.

Dubuque interests started an opposition line in 1856 and built two new boats for the 1857 season. This line merged with the Galena Line and added Dubuque to its long name. Special railroad connec-

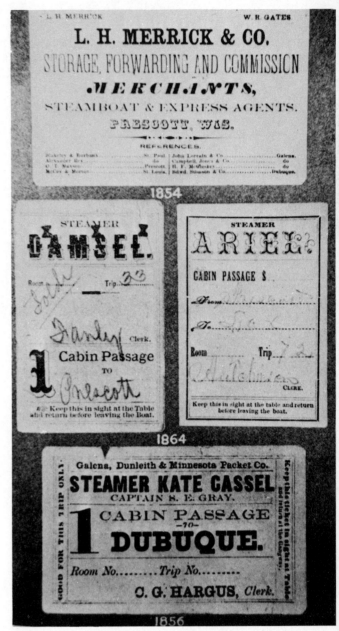

Business cards and tickets of upper Mississippi River packet lines and agents, 1854–1864. *From the Genesis of Steamboating on Western Rivers, George B. Merrick, 1912. Courtesy State Historical Society of Wisconsin*

tions were started by the line in 1857 at Prairie du Chien and at La Crosse in 1858. The former was known as the Prairie du Chien and Saint Paul Packet Company and proved to be a successful operation, until the railroads reached Saint Paul. It was the Galena Line that was sold to the Davidson combine, in 1863.

The Diamond Jo Line was the last line to operate between Saint Louis and Saint Paul. It was

Captain Lodwick's Minnesota Packet Company steamer *Grey Eagle* docked at Galena, Illinois. In the fall of 1858 this boat carried the first news of the completion of the transatlantic cable to Saint Paul. She made the 290-mile run from Dunleith in eighteen hours at an average record speed of 16.1 miles an hour. The *Grey Eagle* sank after hitting the Rock Island bridge in May, 1861. *From Captain Fred Bill's Scrap Book. Courtesy Saint Louis Public Library*

Captain Joseph Reynolds, founder of the Diamond Jo Line. *Courtesy Saint Louis Public Library*

fares, because frequent periods of low water made it impossible to handle heavy freight shipments. In 1909 they ran four boats in this long line trade, compared with thirty steamers that had run under the Davidson combine in 1875. The four boats were the *Quincy, Dubuque, Saint Paul,* and *Sidney.* The boats were sold in 1911 to the Streckfus Line of Saint Louis, which continued to run some of them as packets on the upper river as late as 1917. After that they were converted to excursion boats.

The Diamond Jo Line packet *Saint Paul* at Wabasha, Minnesota, about 1910. *Courtesy Streckfus Steamers, Inc.*

The Saint Louis and Alton Packet Company had several boats and barges in operation in 1889, engaged in towing lumber, rock, and building materials. It had been one of the first lines to run above Saint Louis and engage in a prosperous packet business before the extension of the railroads. In later years, it extended its line to Clarksville, Missouri. This is an advertisement of their steamer *Belle of Alton,* from the *Shipping Guide and Directory* for 1870. *Courtesy Ardell Thompson Collection*

ALTON AND GRAFTON PACKET.

THE

STEAMER BELLE OF ALTON,

WILL RUN REGULARLY DURING THE SEASON,

Leaving St. Louis for Alton every afternoon, except Sunday, at 4 o'clock,

And on Mondays, Wednesdays and Fridays will go through to Grafton.

Freight received on the Wharf-boat at the foot of Olive Street, at all times, for Grafton and all intermediate landings. Accommodations for passengers, freight and stock unsurpassed. JNO. A. BRUNER, Superintendent.

TUNSTAL & HOLME, Agents,

No. 100 N. Commercial Street.
19

founded in 1867 by Captain Joseph Reynolds, who had only one boat plying in the produce trade on the upper river. But by 1889, following its absorption of the Saint Louis and Saint Paul Packet Company, the Diamond Jo Line was operating five large steamers between Saint Louis and Saint Paul. Its headquarters were located at Dubuque, Iowa. At the turn of the century, about seventy-five percent of the line's revenue came from passenger

The *Belle of Alton*. Built in 1863, she ran in the Alton trade in the late 1860s and also on the Black and Ouachita rivers. She burned at New Orleans in 1871, but was rebuilt and operated until November, 1873, when she was destroyed by fire at Vicksburg, Mississippi. *Courtesy Boatmen's National Bank of St. Louis*

The Saint Louis-Alton packet *Altona*, was built at Memphis in 1851. She had what rivermen called "oval" wheels, with buckets of varying widths. The *Altona* pulled several boats to safety during a disastrous steamboat fire at Saint Louis in 1853. She was dismantled in 1855. *Courtesy Boatmen's National Bank of St. Louis*

Four famous steamboat operators. Captain W. H. "Buck" Leyhe of the Eagle Packet Company, Captain Jesse Hughes of the Greene Line, and Captain Mary B. Greene and her son, Captain Tom Greene, of the Greene Line. *Courtesy Waterways Journal*

The Eagle Packet Company was founded by Henry and William Leyhe of Warsaw, Illinois. In 1861 they built a small sternwheeler named the *Young Eagle,* which they operated on the short five-mile run from Warsaw to Keokuk, Iowa. Operations were expanded in 1865 when their new boat, the *Grey Eagle,* ran in a daily line from Canton, Missouri, to Quincy, Illinois. By 1873 their business was so successful that they had a new sidewheeler built at Madison, Indiana, at a cost of thirty thousand dollars. This boat, the *Spread Eagle,* was placed in the Saint Louis, Alton, and Grafton daily trade, and it was about this time that the Eagle Packet Company was organized, with offices at

One of the earliest boats in the Eagle Packet Company of Saint Louis was the small sidewheeler *Grey Eagle*, built at Warsaw, Illinois, in 1865. This boat was sold by the Leyhe brothers for service on the Illinois River about 1872. *Courtesy Waterways Journal*

Alton, Illinois. During subsequent years the Eagle Packet Line added several new boats and absorbed some of their competition. In 1891 the line purchased the Saint Louis, Naples and Peoria Packet Company, which ran on the Illinois River. This property included a wharfboat at Saint Louis, which then became the Eagle Packet Line's base of operations. The Leyhe brothers acquired the Saint Louis and Mississippi Packet Company in 1894, which expanded their line downriver in the Cape Girardeau and Commerce trade. During the flood of 1903, the Alton Railroad chartered two of the Eagle Packet boats to run as a daily connection from Saint Louis to trains at Alton. The Eagle Packet Company's passenger business received a great boost during the Saint Louis World's Fair of 1904, when the daily run of the *Spread Eagle* to Grafton

Spread Eagle, built in 1873, was dismantled in 1880, with her machinery going into a successor boat of the same name. *Courtesy Boatmen's National Bank of St. Louis*

The pride of the Eagle Packet Company fleet, the *Alton*, built at Jeffersonville, Indiana, in 1906. She made the fast time of one hour and forty-three minutes from Saint Louis to Alton and was a notable success in the daily excursion trade between those cities. The *Alton* was lost in a bad ice jam which destroyed three other fine packets of the Eagle Line near the mouth of the Tennessee River in January, 1918. *Courtesy Fred Leyhe*

A group of river men assembled in front of the Eagle Boat Store on the Saint Louis riverfront during the 1880s, including pilots, clerks, stewards, and engineers. Captain George Derrickson, the store's owner, is eighth from left. *Courtesy Waterways Journal*

became a favorite excursion. Boats of the Eagle Packet Company were prominent in a great marine parade staged at Saint Louis for the visit of President Theodore Roosevelt in October, 1907. The packets *Alton* and *Cape Girardeau* made the trip to Memphis, where the President attended a river convention stressing the need for a fourteen-foot channel on the lower Mississippi. But completion of paved roads along the river caused a slack in the packet trade after 1910, when the automobile and motor truck joined the railroads as competitors of steamboat lines. However, business on the Illinois River remained so good that the Leyhes had a new boat, the *Peoria,* built for that trade in 1914.

With the four finest packets of the Eagle Line crushed in an ice jam while in winter quarters at the mouth of the Tennessee River in 1917–1918, only two boats remained to begin the 1918 season. The Leyhes purchased the former cotton boat *William Garig,* which was remodeled and renamed the *Golden Eagle.* The last boat built for the Eagle

Packet Company was the sternwheeler *Cape Girardeau* in 1924, destined for the downriver trade.

The surviving founder of the line, Captain William Leyhe, died in 1930, and control of the company was assumed by his sons, Captains Henry and William H. (Buck) Leyhe. A tourist boat policy was begun in 1932, with trips to the Mardi Gras and tourist cruises during the regular season. Financial difficulties forced the sale of the *Cape Girardeau* to the Greene Line in 1935, which renamed her *Gordon C. Greene.* The remaining boat, the *Golden Eagle,* was renovated, and it made the first steamboat trips since the early years to Saint Paul and Chattanooga.

In a publicity stunt in 1939 the *Golden Eagle,* running from Saint Louis to Cape Girardeau, won a race against time with the *Delta Queen,* which

The *Cape Girardeau,* built at Howard's yard. She measured 210 feet by 38 feet by 6½ feet and, as the *Gordon C. Greene,* ran in Ohio River trades and as a tourist boat. Retired from service in 1949, she was converted into a floating museum-restaurant and moored at points in Kentucky, Florida, and New Orleans. The boat was moved to Hannibal, Missouri in 1962 and rechristened *River Queen.* Her final mooring was the Saint Louis waterfront, where she sank in December, 1967, and was broken up. *Courtesy Jefferson National Expansion Memorial, National Park Service*

The *Spread Eagle IV* built at Howard's yard in 1911 for the Saint Louis-Alton trade. She was lost in the ice near Paducah, Kentucky, in the tragic disaster of 1918, which almost decimated the Eagle Packet fleet. *Courtesy Saint Louis Public Library*

The *William Garig* (1904) replaced one of the Leyhe boats lost in the ice jam. She was renamed *Golden Eagle* and ran in Eagle Packet service until 1941, when she sank near Chester, Illinois. She was later raised and sold, and sank again at Grant Tower, Illinois in May, 1947. Drawing by the author. *Courtesy Boatmen's National Bank of St. Louis*

A contemporary of Captain Able was Captain Joseph La Barge who had a career of more than fifty years in the Missouri River fur trades and steamboating. He set a steamboat speed record on the Missouri when he piloted the *Saint Ange* from Saint Louis to the Yellowstone River in twenty-eight days in 1850. *Courtesy Missouri Historical Society*

ran an equal distance on the Sacramento River in California. After sinking at Chester, Illinois, in 1941, the *Golden Eagle* was raised, to run two more seasons before developing boiler trouble in 1944. Replacements were impossible because of wartime restrictions and the boat was laid up until 1946, when the Eagle Packet Company ceased operations. The *Golden Eagle* was sold and subsequently returned to service. It lost what was probably the last steamboat race on the Mississippi. The winner was the *Gordon C. Greene*. In 1947 the *Golden Eagle* ran aground at Tower Island, about a hundred miles below Saint Louis, and broke up, a total loss. This marked the end of Mississippi passenger-boat operations from Saint Louis, ending about 130 years of activity.

ON THE MISSOURI

The wild character of the Missouri River valley, before the middle 1850s, restricted steamboat operations to those primarily engaged in the fur trade. In the summer of 1856 the Pacific Railroad Packet Company, popularly known as the Lightning Line, was established by Captain Barton Able, contracting with the Pacific Railroad to augment rail service to Missouri River points. Able started with three boats in a thrice-weekly trade and began a daily schedule in 1857. The boats connected with trains at Jefferson City, Missouri, a dual mode of transportation that cut hours off travel time. The

In 1859 the Saint Joe and Omaha Packet Company was established when the Hannibal and Saint Joseph Railroad reached Saint Joseph, Missouri. The boat line served as an extension for the railroad until tracks were built to Council Bluffs, Iowa, a few years later. A similar arrangement in 1868 operated farther upstream for the Sioux City-Fort Benton trade, after a railroad reached Sioux City. These boats, which were of extremely light draft because of shallow river conditions, ran until the Northern Pacific Railroad reached Bismarck, North Dakota, and displaced them. This is the champion of all boats in the long run from Saint Louis to Fort Benton, Montana, the Missouri River sternwheeler *Deer Lodge*, completed at Pittsburgh in 1865. The boat, which had dimensions of 165 feet by 35 feet by 5 feet, is pictured at Sioux City, Iowa, in 1867. *Courtesy Montana Historical Society*

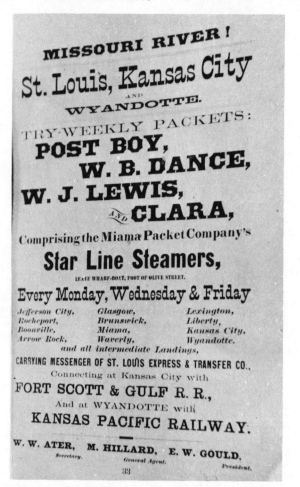

Advertisement for a Missouri River packet line—the Star Line, with railroad connections to the West. *From the Southern and Western Shipping Directory, 1870. Courtesy Ardell Thompson Collection*

1871 the line was reorganized as the Missouri River Packet Company, and was popularly known as the Star Line. Declining business caused a second reorganization in 1878, when the firm was renamed the Kansas City Packet Company. It continued operations until the late 1880s, but in its last years it was forced to operate barges in order to stay in existence. Some boat owners who left the Kansas City line formed the Belle Saint Louis Transportation Company, which ran on the lower end of the river, finally succumbing to railroad competition in 1884.

A prominent operator in the "mountain trade" on the upper Missouri River was Captain William J. Kountz of Pittsburgh, who ran several boats above Bismarck in government contract work. Operations in this area were curtailed with the decline of the fur trade after the Civil War, and were abandoned completely when railroads finally reached the Montana country in the late eighties.

Some boat lines continued on the Missouri in

An advertisement of the Omaha, or "O," Line of packet boats, which operated eight boats on the Missouri River from 1867 until the mid-seventies. A well-managed line, it was abandoned because of the railroads and poor navigation conditions. *From the Shipping Guide and Directory, 1870. Courtesy Ardell Thompson Collection*

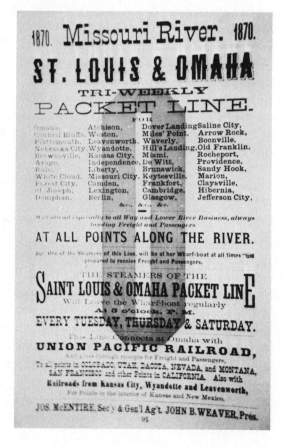

fleet was expanded to six boats in 1858 and carried U.S. mail and much government freight. However, the line had a short life, for when the railroad reached points formerly served by boats alone, the need for river transportation ceased and the steamers were withdrawn.

In 1858 the Saint Louis and Saint Joseph Union Packet Line was formed, with a fleet of twelve boats. This line failed because of the brief navigation season and the dangers inherent in the river over the long distances.

River traffic on the Missouri reached a peak in 1859, when sixty boats were running between Saint Louis and Sioux City, but this had dwindled to only a few small freight boats by 1888.

When river traffic resumed after the Civil War, the Saint Louis and Miami Packet Company was chartered by Illinois in 1866. Originally established to run to Miami, Missouri, the line was later extended to Lexington and Kansas City. Early in

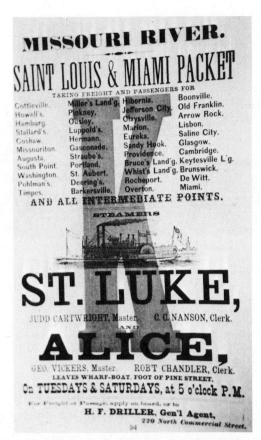

The steamers *Josephine* and *General Terry* transporting Sioux Indians from their camp to the Rock Indian Agency in 1881. *Courtesy Montana Historical Society*

Advertisement of Captain Joseph Kinney's "K" Line. Captain Kinney organized the "K" Line of packets between Saint Louis and Miami, Missouri, in 1870. This line ran in competition with the Missouri River Packet Company, with which line it eventually merged. *From the Shipping Guide and Directory, 1870. Courtesy Ardell Thompson Collection*

The sternwheeler *Helena* made fifty trips to Montana in over ten years. Built in 1878, she measured 194 feet by 33 feet by 4½ feet, and was in the Block "P" Line. She was sunk and lost at Lower Bonhomme Island in 1891. Also covering Montana was the Coulson Line, plying between Saint Louis and Fort Benton, Montana. Founded in 1878, it operated four boats in this long-line trade before disbanding in 1883. *Courtesy Montana Historical Society*

the nineties and after the turn of the century. Among these, running out of Saint Louis, were the Benton Line between 1879 and 1890, the Saint Louis and Rocheport Packet Company between 1891 and 1894, the Kansas City and Missouri River Transportation Company between 1891 and 1909, and the Hermann Packet Company from 1901 to 1909.

ON THE OHIO

The Fulton-Livingston interests organized the Ohio Steamboat Navigation Company, which was chartered in Indiana in 1810. Subscriptions for fifty thousand dollars in capital stock were opened in 1812 for the ultimate purpose of establishing the Fulton combine's claim to sole steamboat rights on the Ohio River from Pittsburgh to New Orleans. Henry M. Shreve and Daniel French founded the Monongahela and Ohio Steamboat Company at Brownsville, Pennsylvania, in 1813 to contest the Fulton claims. Another early line was the Gallatin-Ohio Steamboat Company, which was chartered in Kentucky in 1816, but like the others did not establish a regular service.

The pioneer packet line that ran on scheduled departure times was an outgrowth of the early line

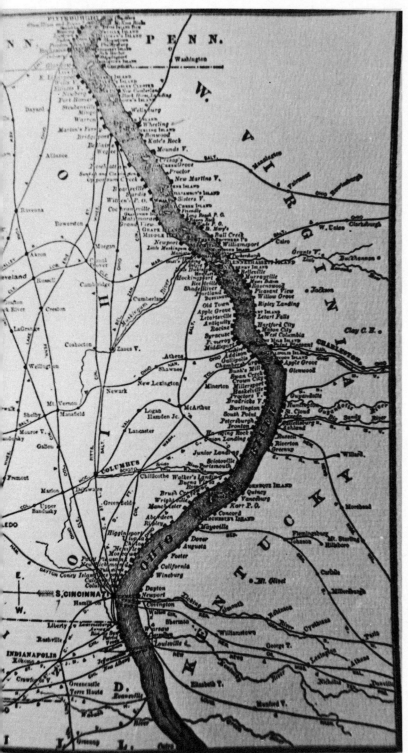

A map of steamboat landings on the Ohio River, showing railroad connections. *Courtesy Waterways Journal*

A record run for the Cincinnati and Louisville U.S. Mail Line: The *General Lytle*, completed at Cincinnati in 1864, set a record of six hours and twenty minutes. This mark stood until the 1890s, when it was broken by the *City of Louisville*. The *Lytle* ran in opposition to the People's Line boat *Saint Charles* and exploded her boilers during a race with her adversary in 1866, opposite Bethlehem, Indiana, with the loss of thirty lives. After she was rebuilt, the *Lytle* was used for experimental arc-light tests in 1875. Damaged by ice in 1881, she sank across the river from Cincinnati and was finally dismantled at Ludlow, Kentucky, in 1882. *Courtesy Boatmen's National Bank of St. Louis*

In the Louisville-Cincinnati trade: The sternwheeler *Mollie McPike*, built at Madison, Indiana, in 1864, measuring 180 feet by 27 feet by 5 feet. She ran later on the upper Mississippi. *Courtesy Boatmen's National Bank of St. Louis*

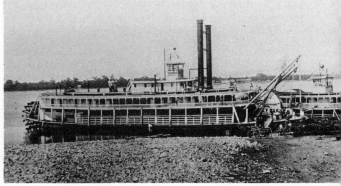

operations on the Ohio by the *General Pike* in 1819. The Cincinnati and Louisville U.S. Mail Line was the oldest and best-known packet line on the western river system. Service between the two terminal cities was begun on a three-times-a-week basis in 1826, and in 1831 daily departures began. By 1850 the Mail Line was operating the largest and finest boats on the Ohio. An opposition line was attempted in 1845 but was soon withdrawn.

The most serious competitor of the Mail Line was the People's Line, which lasted for seventeen months in 1865–1866. The Mail Line's worst disaster occurred in 1868, when two of its finest boats, the *America* and the *United States*, were involved in a fatal head-on collision near Warsaw, Kentucky. It caused a decline in the fortunes of the

The People's Line *Wild Wagoner* built at Cincinnati in 1864 and first operated as a Wheeling-Cincinnati packet. She was sold to the People's Line for service from Cincinnati to Louisville in 1866. On this run she teamed with the *Saint Charles* in opposition to the U.S. Mail Line. Later, in the Wheeling trade again, she finally operated on the lower Mississippi, where she was dismantled in 1876. *Courtesy Boatmen's National Bank of St. Louis*

The Memphis & Cincinnati Packet 632-ton sidewheeler *Alice Dean*, completed at Cincinnati in 1864. She was built short so as to fit in the Louisville Canal locks. She was dismantled in 1872. *Courtesy Boatmen's National Bank of St. Louis*

The sidewheeler *United States II*, constructed on the lengthened hull of the ill-fated first boat of that name, which had a disastrous collision with the *America*. Completed in 1869, this U.S. Mail Line boat was three hundred feet long with a beam of forty feet. She was rebuilt after a collision near Aurora, Indiana, in 1877 and was dismantled at Madison, Indiana, in 1884. *Courtesy Boatmen's National Bank of St. Louis*

Mail Line, and led to its consolidation with the Memphis and Cincinnati Packet Company in 1887.

The first attempt at packet service from Pittsburgh occurred in 1835, when the twelve-boat Pittsburgh and Louisville Line began operations. In 1836 the Good Intent Line and the Ohio Pilot's Line started in the Louisville run, with boats that were well appointed for their time. There was also a line furnishing service from Pittsburgh to Saint Louis, and several others in irregular operations or short trades. This early burst of packet-line activity

Another Memphis boat was the *Pat Clebourne*, originally owned by the Memphis & White River Packet Company, after her completion at Cincinnati in 1870. She later operated in the Evansville-Memphis trade, exploding her boilers opposite Weston, Kentucky, in May, 1876, with the loss of fourteen lives. *Courtesy Boatmen's National Bank of St. Louis*

The Saint Louis levee about 1850. *Courtesy Jefferson National Expansion Memorial, National Park Service*

was terminated by the financial panic of 1837, causing the liquidation of these lines early in 1838.

The next try at regular service from Pittsburgh began in 1842, when the first Cincinnati and Pittsburgh Packet Line was started. This line had its origin in the heavy westward immigrant traffic and started with eight boats in this lucrative trade. The line reached its zenith in the early fifties, when it ran such well-known boats as the *Buckeye State* and the *Keystone State*. After 1854 railroad competition caused serious inroads in packet operations on the Ohio, and by 1856 most of the line's boats, as well as those of the Union Line, had departed for the more affluent waters of the Mississippi.

The Union Line had been organized in 1853 to run between Wheeling and Louisville, in conjunction with the Baltimore and Ohio Railroad, which had reached the Ohio River with Wheeling as a temporary terminus. The railroad arrangement was discontinued after a year because of an insurance dispute. Efforts were then made to merge the Union Line with the Pittsburgh and Cincinnati Packet Company and to extend service to Saint Louis. Disagreements led to disruption of this idea, and by 1856 both lines were dissolved. A packet line from Pittsburgh to Brownsville, Pennsylvania, with four boats operating, was started in the early fifties, as were other lines to Cincinnati and Saint Louis in this prerailroad era.

Packet activity at Louisville began with the organization of the Ohio and Mississippi Mail Line in 1832. This line was designed to furnish service to New Orleans, but failed during its initial season because of a mail contract dispute and attacks by competitors. Louisville interests established the Ohio Line in 1846 for service to Pittsburgh, and a line to Saint Louis was also authorized by its Kentucky charter. Two new boats were built, but difficulty was experienced in raising capital for the second one, and plans to build two others were abandoned. Rates were cut to uneconomic levels to meet competition from other lines, and this caused the line's demise in 1849. The Ohio Line boat *Telegraph No. 2* won a race with the Pittsburgh boat *Brilliant* in 1848, setting a new average speed of twelve miles an hour between Cincinnati and Pittsburgh. Line service from Louisville to New Orleans was resumed in 1851, and by the late fifties several lines provided packet service from Ohio River ports to Memphis and New Orleans.

Two interesting experiments in packet operation occurred in 1853. One was the construction of two boats just for passenger use, built for the Cincinnati and Louisville Packet Company; these were the *Northerner* and the *Southerner*. The other event was the attempt to reintroduce the low-pressure steam engine on the western rivers. This was on the Mail Line boat *Jacob Strader*, which owing to boiler trouble was not a success.

One of the more prominent packet lines on the Ohio after the Civil War was the White Collar Line, founded in 1866. It received its popular name from the white bands painted on the boat's

The Saint Louis levee as seen from Eads Bridge in 1875. Steamboats visible, from right to left, are the *Colossal, Spread Eagle I, Bayard, Rob Roy, Minnesota,* and *Emma C. Elliott. Courtesy Boatmen's National Bank of St. Louis*

Jacob Strader, prominent Cincinnati businessman, after whom the well-known low-pressure U.S. Mail Line steamboat was named. *From* Cincinnati in 1851, *Charles Cist*

The long sidewheeler *Jacob Strader* of the Cincinnati U.S. Mail Line, built in 1853. She measured 347 feet by 38 feet by 8 feet and had a cabin that was 306 feet long. The *Strader* was built with low-pressure engines as a safety effort against boiler explosions. The heavy boilers were replaced in 1860 by conventional equipment. She started in the Cincinnati-Louisville trade in 1853, teamed with the *Telegraph No. 3,* and so continued until the Civil War, when she was used as a troop transport. She was dismantled at Madison, Indiana, in 1866, with her engines going into the low-pressure *Richmond*

chimneys. Officially named the Cincinnati, Portsmouth, Big Sandy and Pomeroy Packet Company, this line was organized by several independents seeking to avoid competition on the upper Ohio. One of the principal factors in its twenty years of successful operation was a contract with the Chesapeake and Ohio Railroad to exchange passengers and freight at its Huntington, West Virginia, terminus after 1872. Since no railroad closely paralleled the river, the steamboat lines enjoyed strong business connections with riverside industries, and they had the advantage of an able management. The White Collar Line absorbed many boats in minor trades on the upper river, and drove off op-

position through rate cutting. The line was involved in consolidations that took place among Ohio River packet lines in the late 1880s. By 1886 the White Collar Line and the Cincinnati and Memphis Packet Company were under the same management, and in the following year, the Mail Line was added to their combine. Commodore Frederick A. Laidley and his associates gained control of the combine in 1890. However, what was left of the White Collar Line was succumbing to the predecessor of the present Greene Line on the upper Ohio.

The Southern Transportation Company, more familiarly known as the Ohio or "O" Line, from

Able management at Cincinnati made for volume business. This wharf scene in 1872 shows, from front to rear, the steamers *R. C. Gray, Argosy No. 3, Ohio No. 4, Andes,* and *Robert Mitchell. Courtesy Waterways Journal*

One of the early boats in the "O" Line, the sternwheeler *Golden Rule II,* built in 1877. It teamed with the *Golden City* in the Cincinnati-New Orleans trade. This boat had its own newspaper published on board. In 1892 she burned at Cincinnati with the loss of six lives. *Courtesy Boatmen's National Bank of St. Louis*

The "O" Line steamer *Guiding Star,* built at Cincinnati in 1878, measuring 300 feet by 41½ feet by 7½ feet. She ran in the trade to New Orleans and featured a cabin that was 265 feet long, with black walnut and maple finish. In 1881 she was sold at a marshal's sale to Captain J. D. Hegler, who purchased Parker's Grove above Cincinnati, two years later, converting it into an amusement park called the Coney Island of the West. The *Guiding Star* and the *Minnie Bay* were the first boats to operate in the local trade to Coney Island. This boat was sunk by ice near New Madrid, Missouri, in 1893. *Courtesy Boatmen's National Bank of St. Louis*

New Orleans levee during the 1880s. *Courtesy Waterways Journal*

the insignia carried between their boats' stacks, was a successful "pool" line. The first boat in this line was the *Golden City,* which entered the Cincinnati-New Orleans trade in 1877. The pooling arrangement among the boat owners in the line's predecessor resulted from similar, earlier attempts on a lesser scale. The line was originally known as the New Orleans Express Line and had a varied mem-

Also in the Cincinnati-New Orleans trade was the sternwheel steamer *John K. Speed,* completed at Madison, Indiana, in 1892. She ran in the fleet of the Cincinnati, Memphis & New Orleans Packet Company. She was destroyed by fire at New Orleans in May, 1902. *From American Steam Vessels, 1895*

The Pittsburgh & Cincinnati Packet Company's sternwheeler *Iron Queen,* built at Harmar, Ohio, in 1892. She ran as the "Friday" boat out of Pittsburgh, along with the *Keystone State* and others, on various days of the week. She burned at Antiquity, Ohio, on April 3, 1895. *From American Steam Vessels, 1895*

The *Charles Morgan* built at Cincinnati in 1873 ran in the "O" Line for several years, and later as an independent. She burned at Cincinnati in December, 1886. *From Captain Fred Bill's Scrap Book. Courtesy Saint Louis Public Library*

The Ohio River sternwheeler *Buckeye State II,* finished at Pittsburgh in 1878 for the Pittsburgh-Cincinnati trade. In 1881 she was in the Pittsburgh-Saint Louis packet run. She sank after striking a canal pier at Louisville in 1882. *From Captain Fred Bill's Scrapbook. Courtesy Saint Louis Public Library*

bership, which by 1876 assessed forty-five percent of each boat's receipts in the line's coffers. This money was divided every sixty days, so that each owner received one share per each one hundred tons capacity. Shares were forfeited if the agreements were not kept. The "O" Line was in a depleted condition by 1893, because of increasing railroad competition, and its two remaining boats were purchased by the Cincinnati and Memphis Packet Company.

The second Pittsburgh and Cincinnati Packet Company, which restored through-service between those two cities, began with the packet *Emma Graham* during the late 1870s. It was joined by the

Hudson, the new *Buckeye State,* and three other boats to provide daily service. A pooling plan was substituted for the original corporate management and since successful operation seemed assured by 1893, the line was chartered, in West Virginia, with a capital of two hundred thousand dollars. Its success was attributed to a freight transshipping arrangement with railroads to southern and western points. Much of the cargo was supplied by iron and steel industries, and low passenger fares between Pittsburgh and Cincinnati, for twelve dollars

The *Keystone State*, built at Harmar, Ohio, in 1890. She survived a fire which destroyed the *Golden Rule*, moored alongside her in 1892, and lost her stacks on a bridge at Cincinnati in 1906. Rebuilt with a new hull in 1909, she was sold into the Illinois River trade in 1910. She was converted into an excursion boat in 1913, renamed *Majestic* and operated on the upper Mississippi. She struck an intake tower at the Saint Louis waterworks at Chain of Rocks in 1914 and sank a total loss

round trip including berth and meals, attracted much business. This line was finally forced into receivership in 1908, along with the Louisville and Evansville Packet Line.

The Colson Line, more familiarly known as the Big Seven, operated through-packet service from Pittsburgh to Saint Louis. In 1880 one of its seven large boats left each terminus daily. The line operated as a freight carrier in conjunction with the C&O Railroad from Huntington westward, and on return trips it handled shipments of agricultural products and raw materials. These times were conducive to good passenger traffic on the well-appointed, low-fare boats. This prosperity did not last for long, however, for by 1882 railroad competition had driven the Colson Line from the river forever.

The Cincinnati and Memphis Packet Company, which consisted of a fleet of six steamers in 1887,

In the Pittsburgh-Louisville trade: The sternwheeler *City of Pittsburgh*, built at Harmar, Ohio, in 1899. She was plagued by bad luck and was unable to reach Pittsburgh in time for a Mardi Gras trip in 1899. She burned at Grand Chain, above Cairo, Illinois, in 1902, with the loss of sixty lives. *Courtesy Saint Louis Public Library*

became the dominant line on the lower Ohio in 1893 when it purchased the depleted Southern Transportation Company. This firm was under the control of Commodore Laidley, who had operated the United States Mail Line in its later years. The name of that line was changed to Louisville and Cincinnati Packet Company, following a government lawsuit concerning unauthorized use of the name "Mail Line."

As steamboat lines continued their decline during the last two decades of the nineteenth century, the long-line runs from Ohio River ports to the lower Mississippi were gradually discontinued. In the nineties Laidley decided to concentrate on the Cincinnati-Louisville trade, and built three new boats for that purpose. These were the *City of Louisville*, *City of Cincinnati* and the *Indiana*. They were well equipped, but were chiefly known for their speed. The *City of Louisville* established the all-time record between the two cities on the 150-mile stretch of river. The boats made money, though on a declining scale for about twenty years, when the *Cincinnati* and the *Louisville* were destroyed in the ice jam on the Cincinnati riverfront in January, 1918. That catastrophe marked the end of the Commodore's river activity.

Passenger traffic on the Ohio was stimulated by improved economic conditions after American entrance into World War I in 1917. During a temporary lapse in Pittsburgh service by existing lines, the Liberty Transit Company was formed. Another

The beautiful sidewheeler *City of Cincinnati* was one of a famous triumvirate of boats of the Louisville & Cincinnati Packet Company built in the 1890s. They maintained a high standard of luxury and speed on this busy run. The *City of Cincinnati* and her sister boat, the *City of Louisville*, were both crushed in the massive ice jam that hit the Cincinnati riverfront in January, 1918. *Courtesy Jefferson National Expansion Memorial, National Park Service*

The *City of Louisville*, built at Jeffersonville, Indiana, measured 301 feet by 42.7 feet by 7 feet. She carried seventy-two staterooms, with a capacity of 160 passengers. The *Louisville* set the all-time speed records between Cincinnati and Louisville: Nine hours and forty-two minutes upstream in 1894, and five hours and fifty-eight-minutes downstream in 1896. The boat is pictured here sunk in the ice jam at Cincinnati in 1918. *Courtesy Jefferson National Expansion Memorial, National Park Service*

The third boat in the Louisville & Cincinnati Packet Company trio was the *Indiana*. Slightly smaller than the other two boats, the *Indiana* had dimensions of 285 feet by 45 feet by 6 feet and was designed especially for low-water operations. She burned at the foot of Main Street in Cincinnati in May, 1916. *Courtesy Jefferson National Expansion Memorial, National Park Service*

newcomer during this period was the Independent Packet Line. When it appeared that a genuine revival of river traffic was possible, the boat lines were knocked out of business by an Interstate Commerce Commission ruling that prohibited railroad-steamboat rating agreements.

Soon after 1900 the Pittsburgh, Wheeling and Parkersburg Packet Line was created by a reorganization of the Wheeling Line. It was one of several short-line packet operations during this period, when tributaries such as the Kanawha, Monongahela, and Muskingum had packet lines running. These lines perished in the general decline that followed during the next few years. Another line involved in short trades in the decade between 1900 and 1910 was the Evansville, Paducah and Cairo Packet Line, which operated two boats in a combined freight and passenger business. On the upper Ohio a short trade of long standing was that between Cincinnati and Maysville, Kentucky, in which packet lines were begun as early as 1848. The Cincinnati, Maysville and Portsmouth Packet Company operated in this run from 1855 to 1859.

The only packet line currently in operation on the western river system is the Greene Line of Cincinnati. It had its beginning in 1890 when Captain Gordon C. Greene spent his savings to buy the steamer *H. K. Bedford,* shortly before his marriage to Mary Becker. His new wife learned the art of navigation at her husband's side, and obtained her pilot's license in 1893. The *Argand* was then purchased and she became its master and pilot. She was so successful that she banked over two thousand dollars at the season's end. The Greene Line attained its success at a time when towboats and railroads forced many packet lines out of existence. In its heyday, the line ran eleven boats on the Ohio and its tributaries. Captain Greene died in 1927, and his wife and two sons continued the business. They purchased the old Mail Line, and business improved so well that more boats were added in the 1930s. In 1931, when the old Louisville and Cincinnati Packet Line was purchased by the Greene Line, it operated only one boat, the *Kentucky.* Among the additional Greene Line boats in the thirties were the *Tom Greene* and *Chris Greene* in 1933 and the *Gordon C. Greene* in 1935.

The Greene Line currently operates the tourist steamer *Delta Queen,* whose survival as the last packet boat on the western rivers was in doubt in 1970 because the boat did not meet Federal marine

Among the short-trade line boats was the *Morning Star I*, built at Howard's yard in 1864 for the Louisville & Henderson Line to Evansville. On the return run of her first round trip she was boarded by guerrillas who robbed the safe and passengers of $2,700. This boat was dismantled in 1886. *Courtesy Boatmen's National Bank of St. Louis*

Morning Star II, in service from the year of her completion in 1901 until 1910, when she entered the Saint Paul-Davenport trade on the upper Mississippi. She was bought by the Coney Island Company of Cincinnati in 1918 and teamed with the *Island Queen I* on excursion runs. She burned in a steamboat fire on the Cincinnati waterfront in November, 1922, along with the *Island Queen, Tacoma,* and *Chris Greene I.* *Courtesy Jefferson National Expansion Memorial, National Park Service*

The steamer *Greenland* was built at Marietta, Ohio, in 1903 for Captain Gordon C. Greene, founder of the Greene Line. She started in the Pittsburgh-Charleston trade in 1903 and made four trips to the Saint Louis World's Fair in 1904. She continued in the Cincinnati-Pomeroy-Charleston trade until she was caught in the great ice jam at Cincinnati in January, 1918. *Courtesy Waterways Journal*

Captain Tom Greene of the Greene Line at the wheel of one of the line's boats. *Courtesy Waterways Journal*

regulations intended to apply to seagoing vessels. However, legislation allowing the *Delta Queen* to remain in service for at least three more years was signed into law by President Nixon in January, 1971.

ON THE ILLINOIS

There were very few steamboats on the Illinois River until 1835, except for infrequent steamers bound for the Ohio or New Orleans in irregular service. The earliest boat known to have operated on the Illinois was the *Criterion* in 1828. As the State of Illinois became more settled, the river traffic grew to such proportions as to merit the organization of regularly scheduled packet service.

The Naples Packet Company was organized in 1848 by E. W. Gould to operate from Saint Louis to Naples, Illinois. It operated in connection with the Sangamon and Morgan Railroad, which ran from Springfield to the river at Naples. The line began with two light-draft sidewheelers making three trips weekly from Saint Louis.

In 1852 the "five-day line," so called for the du-

The *Delta Queen*—on arrival. The tourist steamer of the Greene Line of Cincinnati was built at Stockton, California, in 1926. She operated on the Sacramento River between Sacramento and San Francisco. In World War II she was under U.S. Navy jurisdiction for the duration. Sold to the Greene Line in 1946, the *Queen* was convoyed through the Panama Canal to New Orleans and refurbished at Pittsburgh before beginning her career as the last packet boat on the western rivers. *Courtesy Kentucky Department of Public Information*

Advertisement of packet-line service on the Illinois and Tennessee rivers. *From the Shipping Guide and Directory, 1870. Courtesy Ardell Thompson Collection*

The *Delta Queen*—on departure. By Congressional act she will sail the river at least until November, 1973. *Courtesy Greene Line Steamers, Inc.*

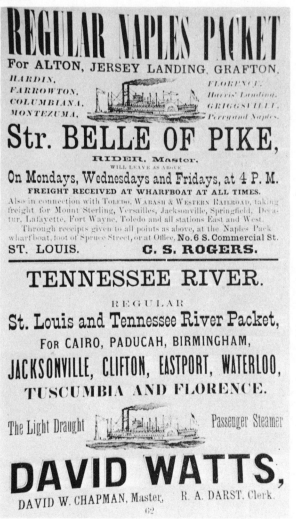

REGULAR NAPLES PACKET

For ALTON, JERSEY LANDING, GRAFTON.
HARDIN,   FLORENCE,
FARROWTON,   Harris' Landing,
COLUMBIANA,   GRIGGSVILLE,
MONTEZUMA,   Perry and Naples.

Str. BELLE OF PIKE,
RIDER, Master.
WILL LEAVE AS ABOVE

On Mondays, Wednesdays and Fridays, at 4 P. M.
FREIGHT RECEIVED AT WHARFBOAT AT ALL TIMES.
Also in connection with TOLEDO, WABASH & WESTERN RAILROAD, taking freight for Mount Sterling, Versailles, Jacksonville, Springfield, Decatur, Lafayette, Fort Wayne, Toledo and all stations East and West.
Through receipts given to all points as above, at the Naples Pack wharfboat, foot of Spruce Street, or at Office, No. 6 S. Commercial St.
ST. LOUIS.   C. S. ROGERS.

TENNESSEE RIVER.
REGULAR
St. Louis and Tennessee River Packet,
FOR CAIRO, PADUCAH, BIRMINGHAM,
JACKSONVILLE, CLIFTON, EASTPORT, WATERLOO,
TUSCUMBIA AND FLORENCE.

The Light Draught   Passenger Steamer

DAVID WATTS,
DAVID W. CHAPMAN, Master,   R. A. DARST, Clerk.
62

ration between trips, was established between Saint Louis and La Salle, Illinois—the terminus of the Illinois and Michigan Canal from Chicago. This proved to be a vital link for travelers on Great Lakes steamers desiring to reach points on the Mississippi River. The operation eventually gave way to railroad competition, but the Naples Line survived because of its own railroad connection. It extended its line farther upstream on the Illinois, and in 1872 was chartered as the Saint Louis, Naples and Peoria Packet Company, to operate to Peoria, Illinois. This line was acquired by the Eagle Packet Company of Saint Louis in 1891.

The Illinois River Packet Company was incorporated in 1858, with several boats. It operated with success for some years, but the inevitable competition from railroads caused the line's failure in 1872, when it was sold to a Saint Louis firm headed by John S. McCune. All operations were abandoned in 1874 because of the lack of navigational improvements on the Illinois.

In February, 1868, the Saint Louis and Peoria Packet Company was formed, with a fleet of three boats. This line ceased operations in 1875.

The Eagle Packet Company continued operations on the Illinois until the 1930s, principally with the steamer *Bald Eagle*.

The Saint Louis and Calhoun Packet Company ran the *Belle of Calhoun* on the lower Illinois up to the late 1920s, particularly in the Calhoun County, Illinois, apple trade.

The *Bald Eagle* of the Eagle Packet Company operated on the Illinois River for many years. She was built in 1898 at Madison, Indiana, and ended her career in the run between Saint Louis and Fort Madison, Iowa, in 1930. She was later used as a quarter boat and sank in 1934. *Courtesy Saint Louis Public Library*

ON THE TENNESSEE

The Tennessee River valley was inadequately served by railroads during Reconstruction, after the Civil War. Consequently, it turned to steamboats to fill its transportation needs. There was only enough business for a few boats in the 1870s, and traffic remained light until the late 1890s. In 1900 at least eighteen boats were in the Chattanooga-Decatur trade, and twice that many were running below Florence, Alabama. Navigation aid by the U.S. government was given through canalization at Muscle Shoals. One of the lines running then was the Evansville and Tennessee River Packet Company, which carried Tennessee Valley products to Ohio River ports. In an effort to secure some of this trade for Saint Louis, interests there organized the Saint Louis and Tennessee River Packet Company in 1887, to run to Florence, Alabama. This line's principal founders were Isaac T. Rhea of Nashville and John E. Massengale of Saint Louis. Their idea was to divert Tennessee Valley lumber to Saint Louis, and they ran several packets and towboats in this trade. They ran in competi-

An advertisement for packet-line service between Saint Louis and Tennessee river points. *From the Saint Louis City Directory, 1866*

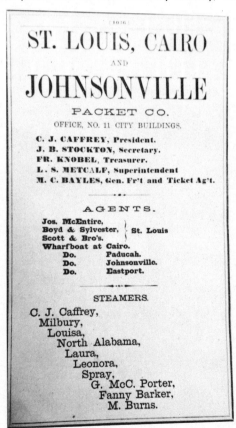

ST. LOUIS, CAIRO AND
JOHNSONVILLE
PACKET CO.
OFFICE, NO. 11 CITY BUILDINGS.
C. J. CAFFREY, President.
J. B. STOCKTON, Secretary.
FR. KNOBEL, Treasurer.
L. S. METCALF, Superintendent
M. C. BAYLES, Gen. Fr't and Ticket Ag't.

AGENTS.
Jos. McEntire,
Boyd & Sylvester,   } St. Louis
Scott & Bro's.
Wharfboat at Cairo.
Do.   Paducah.
Do.   Johnsonville.
Do.   Eastport.

STEAMERS.
C. J. Caffrey,
Milbury,
Louisa,
North Alabama,
Laura,
Leonora,
Spray,
G. McC. Porter,
Fanny Barker,
M. Burns.

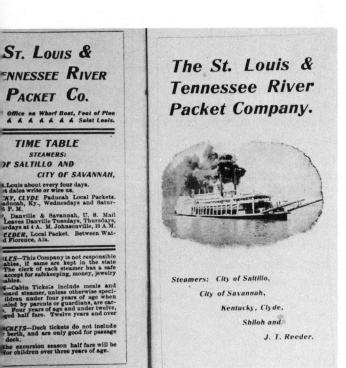

ST. LOUIS & TENNESSEE RIVER PACKET CO.

Office on Wharf Boat, Foot of Pine
▲ ▲ ▲ ▲ ▲ ▲ Saint Louis.

TIME TABLE
STEAMERS:
OF SALTILLO AND
CITY OF SAVANNAH

...Louis about every four days.
...st dates write or wire us.

...KY, CLYDE Paducah Local Packets.
...aducah, Ky., Wednesdays and Satur-
...5 P. M.

...Danville & Savannah, U. S. Mail
Leaves Danville Tuesdays, Thursdays,
...rdays at 4 A. M. Johnsonville, 10 A. M.

...EEDER, Local Packet, Between Wat-
...d Florence, Ala.

...LES—This Company is not responsible
...ables, if same are kept in the state
The clerk of each steamer has a safe
...accept for safekeeping, money, jewelry
...ables.

...S—Cabin Tickets include meals and
...oard steamer, unless otherwise speci-
...ildren under four years of age when
...nied by parents or guardians, are car-
... Four years of age and under twelve,
...ged half fare. Twelve years and over

...CKETS—Deck tickets do not include
...berth, and are only good for passage
...dock.

...the excursion season half fare will be
...for children over three years of age.

The St. Louis & Tennessee River Packet Company.

Steamers: City of Saltillo,
City of Savannah,
Kentucky, Clyde,
Shiloh and
J. T. Reeder.

Advertising folder of the Saint Louis & Tennessee River Packet Company, about 1910. Courtesy Webster Groves Book Shop

The Saint Louis and Tennessee River's steamer City of Florence, built in 1909 for short-trade service on the Tennessee River. Courtesy Jefferson National Expansion Memorial, National Park Service

The Saint Louis & Tennessee River's Tennessee Belle, built at Paducah, Kentucky, in 1923, in a remodeling of the former packet Kentucky. She was sold into the lower Mississippi trade in 1927 and was the last steam packet on the lower river. She burned at Natchez Island, Mississippi, in 1942. Courtesy Jefferson National Expansion Memorial, National Park Service

tion with the Tennessee Navigation Company, which had connections with the Louisville and Nashville Railroad. The Saint Louis-based line eventually emerged triumphant and built up a lucrative trade before finally going out of business in the early 1930s. Its last boats out of Saint Louis were the Alabama and the Tennessee Belle.

ST. LOUIS & TENNESSEE RIVER PACKET COMPANY

LIST of Landings on this Company's Direct Route. Landings on the Mississippi River between St. Louis and Cairo, Ill.

	Miles		Miles
Kimswick.....Mo.	22	Belgique.....Mo.	86
Bushburg	26	Waters	87
Harrisonville....Ill.	28	Anchor	87
Crystal City...Mo.	32	Bishop's	88
Lowry's Ldg....Ill.	36	Hamilton's....Ill.	93
Kemper's Ldg	38	Wagner's	94
Durfee's Pt	39	White's	95
Rush Tower.....Mo.	40	McLean	96
Penitentiary Pt..Ill.	47	Red Rock.....Mo.	97
Cliff's Ldg...Mo.	48	Wilkinson	100
Sycamore Ldg...Ill.	48	'76	107
Ft. Chartres	50	Hager's	107
White Sand.....Mo.	54	Holschen's	108
Ste. Genevieve	60	Lake Ditch....Ill.	114
Ellis Grove....Ill.	70	Brunkhorst	115
Kaskaskia	71	Wittenburg...Mo.	118
Ft. Gage	72	Grand Tower..Ill.	120
Delasus	77	Wolf's	123
St. Mary's....Mo.	72	Hine's.....Mo.	124
Chester....Ill.	80	Lovejoy's	124½
Claryville.....Mo.	80	Neely's	130
Phillips	82	Moccasin Sprs.	135
Crane's Island	84	Willard's	135
Manskers....Ill.	85	Bainbridge	139
Hempsteads....Mo.	140	Goose Island....Ill.	169
Davidson's	141½	Commercial Pt..	173
Brewster's....Ill.	144	Philad'phia Pt.Mo.	173
McClure's	146	Price's	176
Cape Girard'u..Mo.	150	Elkin's	177
Gray's Point	157	Brown's....Ill.	178
Manning's	158	Brook's Point	180
Thebes....Ill.	160	Thompson's...Mo.	185
C. & E. I. R. R.		Bird's Point	200
Wray's....Mo.	162	E. Cairo.....Ky.	200
Commerce	165	Cairo.....Ill.	200

OHIO RIVER LANDINGS—CAIRO TO PADUCAH.

Mound City....Ill.	209	Metropolis....Ill.	239
Cash Island	212	Brooklyn	247
Ogden's.....Ky.	219	I. C. R. R.	
Hilerman's	224	Paducah.....Ky.	250
Joppa....Ill.	229		
C. & E. I. R. R.			

TENNESSEE RIVER—PADUCAH TO WATERLOO, ALABAMA

L'ghton's Blf..Ky.	255	Clear Pond....Ky.	269
McKeys	256	27 Mile Island..Ill.	269
Thompson's	256	Gilbertsville	270
Wilcox	257	Cottonwood	272
Iveletts	258	Pettyways	275
Stanley Brown	258	Moss Ferry	276
Ellis Ldg	260	Jno. Claudet's	276
Birdwells	260	Diamond Lime Wk	277
Had'k's Ferry..	261	Star Lime Wks.	277
Cooper's	262	Eagle Lime Wks	280
Back's Ldg	264	Birmingham	280
Webb's	268	Bridges	284

List of landings of the Saint Louis & Tennessee River Packet Company, 1910. Courtesy Webster Groves Book Shop

ON THE CUMBERLAND

As early as 1819 charters were granted to the Nashville and Columbia Steamboat Companies for operations on the Cumberland River in Tennessee. During the 1880s the Cumberland River Packet Company was organized to control independent competition on the Cumberland. The Ryman Line ran packet boats, on the Cumberland, between Nashville and Evansville, Indiana, early in the twentiety century.

OTHER TRIBUTARIES

These lines were efforts to use surplus boats, idle after the Civil War, to secure Southern trade. They were loosely organized, and boat owners would withdraw from them quite frequently.

The Carter Line, officially known as the Red River Packet Company, was established in 1869. It ran to ports on the Missouri River and to Shreveport and New Orleans from Saint Louis. Its annual receipts were about $650,000, and during its best season it operated a fleet of eight boats. The line lasted only a few years, closing down in 1873. A line from Saint Louis to trades on various southern rivers was organized in 1870. It was the Merchant's Saint Louis and Arkansas River Packet Company. A low-water boat was operated on the upper Arkansas from Little Rock to Fort Smith, while other boats in the line plied in trades on the White, Black, and Current rivers. Merchant's ran successfully for a year or so, but bowed to competition from the Iron Mountain Railroad. A similar fate befell packets running from Saint Louis in the Ouachita River trade by 1873.

EXCURSION BOATS

The first steamboat designed exclusively for excursions was the *J.S.*, built by Commodore John Streckfus in 1901. The Streckfus Line began as a packet operation in 1884 and ran as a joint packet and excursion line between 1901 and 1917. In 1911 Streckfus acquired the four remaining boats of the Diamond Jo Packet Line and eventually converted all of them into excursion boats. The line has been an exclusive excursion operation since 1918, run-

ning trips from many river cities on the Mississippi River system.

Excursion-boat lines grew out of the practice of chartering steamboats for special occasions, usually for short day trips on the river. The earliest boats regularly operated for this purpose began making charter trips during the early 1880s at Saint Louis and other river cities. In later years nightly dance trips became popular.

Some boats were based for an entire season at a major river city, while others would "tramp" up and down the western rivers, playing one-night stands at various smaller river towns during the summer season and on the lower Mississippi in the winter months.

The *J.S.*, built by Commodore Streckfus in 1901, the first steamboat exclusively designed for excursions. *Courtesy Streckfus Line Magazine*

The excursion boat *Corwin H. Spencer* originally the Anchor Liner *Hill City*, built in 1897 and renamed in 1903. She was 327 feet long with a 44-foot beam. She was operated as an excursion boat at Saint Louis during the World's Fair of 1904 and burned near Jefferson Barracks, Missouri, in October, 1905. *Courtesy Jefferson National Expansion Memorial, National Park Service*

The *Louisiana*, operated by the Louisiana Purchase Exposition Excursion Company, moored near the L & N Railroad bridge at Evansville, Indiana, in 1904. *Courtesy Webster Groves Book Shop*

The former Anchor Line boat *City of Providence*, built in 1880, was 273.7 feet by 44.5 feet by 7.8 feet. She was sold to the Columbia Excursion Company of Saint Louis about 1898 and was a popular steamer in the excursion trade at Saint Louis until she was sunk by ice in January, 1910. *Courtesy Saint Louis Public Library*

The upper decks of the *Saint Paul*, about 1930. *Courtesy Streckfus Steamers, Inc.*

The Streckfus Line's steamer *Saint Paul* as she appeared during the 1930s. This boat was built at Dubuque, Iowa, in 1883 as an upper Mississippi packet boat and was bought by Streckfus from the Diamond Jo Line in 1911. She was converted into an excursion boat in 1917 and was based at Saint Louis from 1918 to 1936 and later out of Pittsburgh. Rebuilt and renamed *Senator* in 1939, she ran until retired in 1942 for wartime duty as a Coast Guard training vessel. She was dismantled at Saint Louis in 1953. *Courtesy Waterways Journal*

The *Capitol*, originally built as the *Pittsburgh*, demolished in the Saint Louis tornado of 1896. The hull was rebuilt and outfitted as the *Dubuque* for the Diamond Jo Line. She was sold to the Streckfus Line and was remodeled as the excursion boat *Capitol* in 1919. This boat tramped the Mississippi and ran for some years at New Orleans. She was dismantled at Saint Louis in 1945. *Photo by Phil McPartland. Courtesy Waterways Journal*

The *J. S. DeLuxe*, looking forward from the ballroom on the second deck, 1921. *Courtesy Streckfus Steamers, Inc.*

The *J. S. DeLuxe*, originally the Diamond Jo liner *Quincy*, built in 1896. After her acquisition by Streckfus in 1911, she ran for several seasons as the last sidewheel packet on the Mississippi. She came out in 1919 as an excursion steamer at Saint Louis and scored a big success in her first season. She teamed with the *Saint Paul* in the Saint Louis excursion trade until 1934, when she ran in the upper Ohio trade until 1936. The *J. S. DeLuxe* was dismantled at Saint Louis, along with the excursion boat *Washington*, in 1939. Drawing by the author. *Courtesy Boatmen's National Bank of St. Louis*

The *J. S. DeLuxe* ballroom with bandstand in left center, 1921. *Courtesy Streckfus Steamers, Inc.*

Main lounge of the *J. S. DeLuxe*, 1921, looking toward the stairway to the ballroom deck. *Courtesy Streckfus Steamers, Inc.*

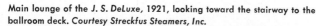

Smoke, cinders, and fun on the top deck. *J. S. DeLuxe* about 1930. *Courtesy Streckfus Steamers, Inc.*

Advertisement featuring the summertime pleasures of an excursion on the river. *Courtesy Streckfus Line Magazine, 1931*

The steamers *J.S.* and *Saint Paul* under the Eads Bridge at Saint Louis about 1925. *Courtesy Waterways Journal*

The excursion boats *J.S.* and *Saint Paul* preparing for departure on a day trip, 1931. The fleet of the Eagle Packet Company is moored in the background. *Courtesy Waterways Journal*

The Cincinnati excursion boat *Island Queen*, built in 1925. This boat was the successor to others of the same name which ran in the excursion trade between Cincinnati and the Coney Island amusement park several miles upstream. The *Island Queen's* fuel tanks exploded while she was moored at the Wood Street wharf in Pittsburgh in September, 1947. The resulting fire completely destroyed the boat, with a loss of nineteen lives. *Courtesy Streckfus Steamers, Inc.*

Passengers disembark from the *Border Star* following a two-hour excursion on the Arkansas River. This weekly excursion provides an excellent view of the expanding river development and activities along the Arkansas River Navigation Project. *Courtesy Arkansas State Parks, Recreation and Travel Commission*

The *Belle of Louisville* is one of the last paddle-wheel steamboats still afloat. Owned by Kentucky's Jefferson County, this romantic relic of a bygone era is in splendid condition and makes excursions up and down the Ohio River from Louisville. She and the bigger *Delta Queen* from Cincinnati highpoint Louisville's Derby Festival by racing up the Ohio to Six Mile Island and back and then engaging in a contest between their ear-splitting calliopes. *Courtesy Kentucky Department of Public Information*

The streamlined excursion boat *Admiral* of the Streckfus Line, leaving her dock at Saint Louis for a day of pleasure on the Mississippi. The *Admiral* was constructed on the hull of the former Vicksburg railroad ferryboat *Albatross*, and was completed at Saint Louis in time to open the 1940 season. The 374-foot *Admiral* has a passenger capacity of 4,400 persons and is said to be the world's largest excursion steamer. Unlike any other boat ever seen on the western rivers, the five-deck vessel is completely air-conditioned by the first installation of its kind on a riverboat. *Walker-Missouri Tourism photo*

FERRIES

While rivers provided a ready means of transport, in pioneer times, however, these same waterways represented a barrier to overland travelers seeking to cross them. This need led to the early establishment of ferry crossings at strategic points. The first ferries were canoes or rowboats, followed by larger craft when the need arose to carry wagons, animals, and heavy goods.

Some of these craft were operated by horse or oxen power on a treadmill, to turn crude paddle wheels. On narrower streams, ropes or wires were used to guide ferries across, propelled by the current acting against the side of the boat. The boat was held at the required angle by the guy wires.

Shown here at Chattanooga on the Tennessee River is a compass-type ferry, which was swung across the river in an arc by the current. Its guide ropes or cables were carried by a series of small barges to maintain the correct alignment. Sketch by Harry Fenn. *From Picturesque America, 1872. Courtesy Saint Louis Mercantile Library Association*

Lithograph by Leon D. Pomarede of an early steam-powered ferry at a landing opposite Saint Louis, 1832. *From* Pictorial Saint Louis, *1875*

The ferryboat *Alonzo C. Church,* East Saint Louis ferry landing, about 1902. *Courtesy Boatmen's National Bank of St. Louis*

The ferryboat *Thomas Pickles,* built in 1892, operated for many years on the lower Mississippi. *From American Steam Vessels, 1895*

The ferryboat *Frederick Hill* approaching a landing, early 1900s. *Courtesy Jefferson National Expansion Memorial, National Park Service*

A double-paddle-wheel ferry on the Missouri River, plying between Niobrara, Nebraska, and Springfield, South Dakota. *Nebraska Game Commission photo*

A ferry advertisement for various services, Saint Louis, 1842. *Courtesy Missouri Historical Society*

Transfer ferry of the Henderson Interurban Line at Evansville, Indiana, in 1915. *Courtesy Saint Louis Public Library*

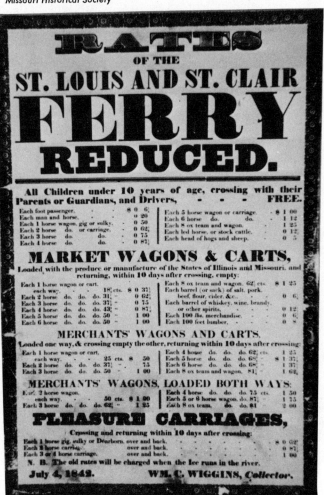

The railroad transfer boat *North Missouri* of the North Missouri (later Wabash) Railroad at Saint Charles, Missouri, in 1869. *Courtesy Saint Louis Public Library*

VI
Life on the River

STEAMBOAT CUSTOMS AND EXISTENCE

The western-river steamboats in the earlier days were crude and ungainly compared with the beautiful "floating palaces" that graced the rivers after 1850. Travelers on some of these early boats during the period 1820 to 1845 were far from enthusiastic in their accounts of accommodations on board. Such boats were variously called floating bathhouses or barracks. Nevertheless, they were vastly superior to any type of overland transport, such as stage or wagon on rough roads.

The steamboat represented the only contact for backwoods settlers with the outside world. A popular comparison for a luxurious home or hotel ashore was that it was "as elegant as a steamboat."

The elaborate jigsaw carpentry ("steamboat Gothic") began to appear on boats in the early 1850s. Steamboat chimneys carried ornamental feathers on their tops and colorful paintings and fancy lettering graced the wheelhouses of sidewheelers. These highly embellished designs reached their zenith after the Civil War, in boats such as the *Grand Republic* and the *J. M. White III*. Some of the decoration served a practical purpose, as with the wooden acorns; as caps for upright posts, they protected the end-grain wood from weathering. The focal point of the bric-a-brac was the pilothouse, which resembled a gazebo topped with lacelike wood finials. Color was applied as a decorative accent to relieve the stark whiteness of the superstructure. Some hulls were painted red or green, and in an extreme case, the chimneys of Captain Tom Leathers' *Natchez* series of boats were red. "Wheelhouse art" paintings were of a boat's namesake, a colorful sunset, or a river scene.

Steamboats were often glamorized, as in the popular Currier and Ives prints of the 1850s. This idealized portrayal is titled *Rounding a Bend on the Mississippi*. Courtesy Saint Louis Public Library

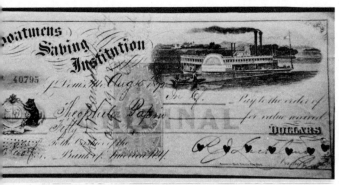

Pictures of steamboats could be found on many letterheads, seals, checks, and other commercial forms in river towns. *Courtesy Boatmen's National Bank of St. Louis*

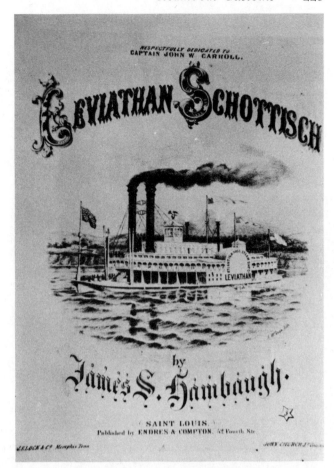

The popularity of steamboats extended to musical pieces, as evidenced by this mid-nineteenth-century dance music dedicated to the steamer *Leviathan*. *Courtesy Jefferson National Expansion Memorial, National Park Service*

Decorated chimney of the *Golden Eagle*. Looking forward on the top deck from amidship. *Photo by Dick Lemen. Courtesy Jefferson National Expansion Memorial, National Park Service*

The ornate *Grand Republic*, one of the most elaborately appointed riverboats of all time. Note the Eads Bridge painted on the wheelhouse. *Courtesy Boatmen's National Bank of St. Louis*

The Saint Louis-owned *Grand Republic* featured a view of Eads Bridge, which was pridefully flaunted before downriver towns still relying on ferries.

The climax of "steamboat Gothic" splendor was achieved in the main cabin or grand saloon. This extended along the center of the boiler deck, through almost its entire length, and, befitting its social function as the centerpiece of steamboat life, was decorated in the most ornamental manner.

Opening into individual cabins on each side of the main cabin were rows of stateroom doors, and overhead were the windows of a clerestory. The ceiling was supported by rows of ornate columns, their connecting arches carved in lacelike patterns. In the stern of the cabin, which was reserved for ladies, a huge mirror created the illusion of doubling the cabin's length. Cabin windows were stained glass, making a colorful interplay of sunlight on the rich Brussels carpeting and fine furniture. Illumination was by crystal chandeliers—equipped with gas or oil lamps—supporting countless pendants.

To avoid the stark-white cabin interiors, some postbellum boats used dark woods—walnut or rosewood—on doors and trim. Fine art—oils of river scenes and symbolic sculptures—decorated some steamboat cabins and handsome upholstered and carved furniture was often complemented by a

The *Grand Republic*'s main cabin, showing the intricately carved detail and fine furnishings of this "floating palace." Courtesy Boatmen's National Bank of St. Louis

Cabin interior on the Anchor Line steamer *Arkansas City* in the early 1890s. Courtesy Jefferson National Expansion Memorial, National Park Service

A typical steamboat cabin chandelier, as reconstructed in a display in the River Room of the Missouri Historical Society at Saint Louis

The palatial sidewheeler *J. M. White III*, as painted by Oscar E. Berninghaus. Courtesy Boatmen's National Bank of St. Louis

Foot of the main stairway leading from the main deck to the second, or cabin deck, of the J. M. White III. Courtesy Jefferson National Expansion Memorial, National Park Service

The head of one branch of the main staircase on the cabin deck of the J. M. White. Courtesy Jefferson National Expansion Memorial, National Park Service

The silver water cooler of the J. M. White. Courtesy Jefferson National Expansion Memorial, National Park Service

grand piano. A large silver water cooler, with drinking cups chained to its sides, was generally located at the forward end of the cabin. A bar was off the starboard side of the cabin, presenting a colorful scene of sparkling glassware, liquor bottles, and mirrors.

The office in the main cabin of the J. M. White. Courtesy Jefferson National Expansion Memorial, National Park Service

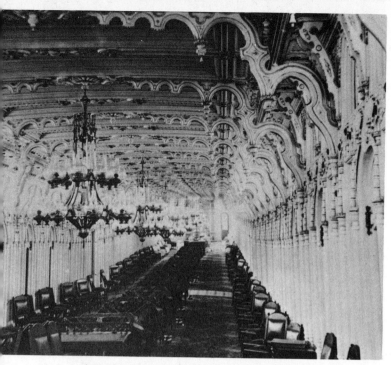

Looking aft in the main cabin of the J. M. White. Courtesy Jefferson National Expansion Memorial, National Park Service

At the after end of the ladies' cabin of the J. M. White. Courtesy Jefferson National Expansion Memorial, National Park Service

Cabin class was for the aristocracy. They always occupied the best quarters on the boats, from earliest times. The ladies' cabin was eventually shifted from a position within the hull to the after-part of the upper deck. The gentlemen's cabin, which was originally located aft of the machinery on the main deck, was finally moved to its traditional place on the forward part of the boiler deck.

Simulated ladies' cabin of a typical western-river steamboat of the 1870s. The authentic furnishings are from several well-known boats, including the J. M. White. They represent the peak period of elaborate Victorian decor. Courtesy Missouri Historical Society

The J. M. White. Main cabin looking forward. Courtesy Jefferson National Expansion Memorial, National Park Service

Simulated steamboat clerk's office of the period 1850–1870. On the right is a wall mail rack, and at the left is a stand-up desk. Note the overhead glass skylight and the stained-glass window on the back wall. *Courtesy Missouri Historical Society*

On the early boats sleeping accommodations consisted of rows of open berths on each side of the main cabin, from which they were separated by curtains or sliding partitions. Enclosed staterooms, with doors on both sides, cabin and deck, came into use during the 1840s. Officers' quarters at first were located at the front of the cabin deck, but occupied the texas deck in later years. The clerk's office and the bar continued to occupy quarters on the forward boiler deck, while the washrooms, kitchens, and service quarters usually were adjacent to the wheelhouses. Staterooms were about six feet square in antebellum years but doubled in size during the 1880s, and beds replaced berths.

The main cabins gradually lengthened until some reached three hundred feet. Stability required that cabins be relatively narrow and that the greatest weight be kept within the confines of the limited hull width.

It was incongruous that amidst ornately decorated cabins and staterooms, amenities such as hot-and-cold running water and water closets did not appear, generally, until after the Civil War. Heating usually was provided by large cast-iron stoves in the cabin and texas, and even in postbellum times steam heating was the exception due to technical difficulties. Illumination by candle or oil lamps in the earlier years lasted until after the war, when gas came into general use. Electricity was introduced in the late seventies, chiefly for searchlights and safety markers. Electric interior lighting did not become common until the end of the century.

Boiler-deck guard of the *J. M. White,* starboard side, looking forward. Note the row of cuspidors along the rail. *Courtesy Jefferson National Expansion Memorial, National Park Service*

The pilothouse of the *J. M. White III* (looking aft) looked like a wedding cake. *Courtesy Jefferson National Expansion Memorial, National Park Service*

227

DINING ACCOMMODATIONS

In accordance with the luxurious furnishings and cabin decor, menus for first-class steamboat dining presented a varied, sumptuous fare. Accommodations were on the hotel-style American Plan, with the cost of board included in the cabin passage price. The quality of the fare depended on the type of boat; "pork and beans" fare could be expected on transient boats on short runs. The traditional eating place for cabin passengers and officers was on long tables set up in the main cabin, while crew members and deck passengers ate wherever they could.

Tables set for dinner in the main cabin on the Anchor Line City of Monroe. *Courtesy Jefferson National Expansion Memorial, National Park Service*

Cabin of the Diamond Jo Line *Dubuque* set for dinner, about 1897. From Captain Fred Bill's Scrap Book. *Courtesy Saint Louis Public Library*

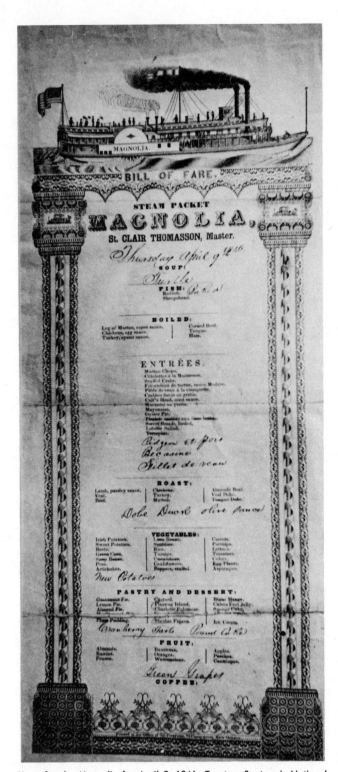

Menu for the *Magnolia* for April 9, 1846. *Courtesy Boatmen's National Bank of St. Louis*

Antebellum menus featured a wide variety of meats, followed by potatoes, corn, and other vegetables. Bread and pastries were available in profusion, but milk and butter either were missing or poor in quality. Wines and spirits were the principal drinks with meals; lack of water clarification made drinking water questionable. Food quality sometimes was poor because of unskilled chefs. In later years steamboat cookery equaled or excelled that of the finest restaurants and hotels.

The best of both worlds is the *Lt. Robert E. Lee,* a modern restaurant-boat replica of an old-time Mississippi River sternwheeler. It has been moored at Saint Louis since 1970. *Courtesy Fred Leyhe*

It was difficult to tell a steamboat menu from a hotel menu—except in the eating. This is the bill of fare of the Planters' House, a Saint Louis hostelry popular with rivermen, August 9, 1857. *Courtesy Boatmen's National Bank of St. Louis*

Lost in a river reverie, watching the slowly passing scenery. Drawing by William T. Smedley. *From Harper's Monthly, 1893*

Passengers relaxing on the deck of a Mississippi River steamboat. Drawing by William T. Smedley. *From Harper's Monthly, 1893*

SOCIAL LIFE

Steamboat passengers had a great deal of time on their hands during the long trips, which could take from a few days to several weeks. People from many backgrounds thrown together in a confined space for a considerable time required different forms of amusement. Watching the scenery was the most common way to pass the time. Reading also became popular, and some boats carried a library.

A few boasted of an on-board newspaper, such as the *Headlight* put out by the *Richmond*. Watching the crew's operations, particularly at landings, interested the travelers. Also, impromptu singing by crew members or skits by talented passengers furnished entertainment, along with dancing and concerts by musicians on the larger boats. Racing rival boats along the way was always favored by the sporting element among the passengers, and card playing helped pass many an hour in relief of boredom. Religious services were held on Sundays, and at other times lectures might be given by informed passengers.

Common acceptance of rules of behavior was general; serious breaches of riverboat decorum were harshly dealt with. In earlier years, steamboat

Unloading cargo. Areas were designated by various colored flags for the crewmen who were unable to read. *From Harper's Weekly, 1867*

justice was administered by a court of passengers, but later the captain was usually called upon to enforce and interpret the rules of conduct. More serious infractions—swindling, theft, illicit sex, murder

Enjoying the passing scenery from the boiler deck of a mid-nineteenth-century steamboat, first class. *From Harper's Weekly. Courtesy Every Saturday Magazine*

A riot aboard the steamer *Dubuque*, just above Davenport, Iowa, on July 29, 1869. About 250 raftsmen and harvesters had taken passage. They drank freely, and at length it became necessary to restrain their movements. The crew of about thirty Negroes tried to repress the tumult and became the victims of the rioters. Six were killed, and on their attempt to escape on their arrival at Hampton Landing, they were pursued ashore. At Clinton, Iowa, a large number of the rioters were arrested. Two of the murderous gang were seriously wounded during the conflict on the boat. Sketch by H. H. Henderson. *From Harper's Weekly, August, 1869.*

Watching the crew's operations. Roustabouts working on the main deck as the boat gets under way from a landing. Sketch by William T. Smedley. *From Harper's Monthly, 1893*

—were handled by turning offenders over to the authorities at the next port or by stranding them at the first landing place, or on a sandbar in midriver. Proselytizing against alcohol occurred on some "temperance boats," as well as a ban on smoking and card playing. While Bibles on board were common, not operating on Sundays was unheard of; captains would not forgo any possible profit.

The highly publicized luxuries of the so-called floating palaces represented only a small percentage of the boats running on the western rivers. Complaints about filth, inadequate accommodations, and poor food were the rule rather than the exception. Rude manners, among crew and passengers, inadequate ventilation, and the rattling vibration from the high-pressure engines were common dissatisfactions. The engine noise and vibrations were distracting to reading, conversation, and sleeping, while boiler heat was a serious discomfort to all. During crowded trips, standards of service deteriorated and meals were served in shifts. Temporary sleeping accommodations were furnished on cots set up in the cabin or on deck. Periods of low water caused protracted delays, sometimes because of grounding on sandbars, and if supplies ran out, passengers and crew had to search the countryside for food—or aid in releasing the boat. But not until the closing decades of the nineteenth century did the speed and accommodations of trains make rail travel preferable to steamboats.

Captain John Brown Rhodes was in command of the *Dubuque* during the riot in July, 1869. Captain Rhodes was a pioneer in upper Mississippi River steamboating in which he made a fortune with the Northern Line Packet Company, and lost it when the railroads put the steamboats out of business. *Courtesy Waterways Journal*

Captain Rhodes's home, the Steamboat House, so called by rivermen because its cupola resembled a riverboat's pilothouse. Located at Savanna, Illinois. *Courtesy Waterways Journal*

On lesser boats, complaints over accommodations were rampant. The steamboat *Peerless* is at a landing on the Gasconade River in Missouri about 1890. Collection of Dr. E. B. Trail. *Courtesy Waterways Journal*

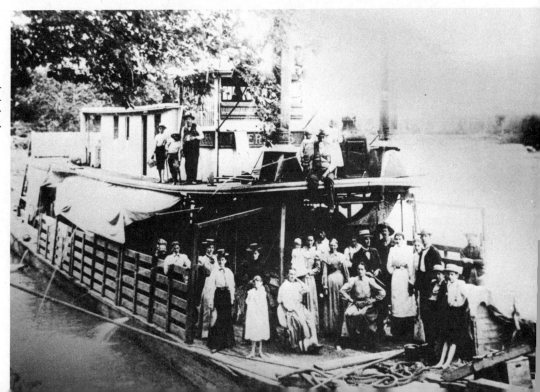

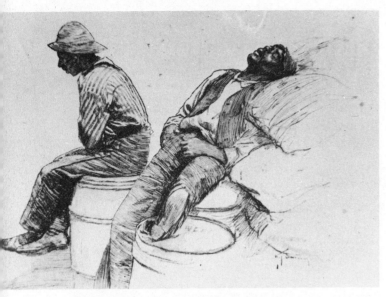

Resting between chores on the lower deck. Sketch by William T. Smedley. *From* Harper's Monthly, *1893*

Hailing a steamboat. Landings were made upon signal from the riverbank in an informal system, to pick up passengers and freight. Drawing by A. R. Waud. *From* Every Saturday Magazine, *October 14, 1871*

Deck fares reached unusual lows during the 1850s, when passage from Saint Louis or Louisville to New Orleans could be made for only three dollars compared with twelve or fifteen dollars or more for cabin fares.

Deck passengers generally exceeded cabin passengers by a ratio of three to two. In antebellum years many of the upstream deck passengers were flatboatmen returning to their upriver destinations. The decline of flatboating after the Civil War and the introduction of low immigrant railroad fares practically eliminated steamboat deck passage by 1880.

Accommodations for deck passengers usually were nonexistent and the deckers found that even soft spots among the cargo were at a premium for sleeping space. If the cargo occupied the entire center deck space, deckers would be forced to find places on the guards, where low bulwarks gave little protection from the weather. An intermediate deck above the main deck at the stern was provided for deck passenger accommodation on some of the larger boats during the late fifties.

The deckers usually brought their own food and utensils to prepare their meals on a stove used for cooking and heating. The food was chosen for durability, as supply sources were scant and prices exorbitant along the river. Filth was ever prevalent and sanitary facilities consisted of washing in muddy river water.

Deck passengers could be found sleeping amid the cargo. Here they are occupying the entire center deck space. This is the *J. H. Johnson,* built at Madison, Indiana, in 1863 (also called the *Harry Johnson* after her captain). She struck the Wabash Railroad bridge above Hannibal, Missouri, in 1874 and sank, but was later raised and dismantled. *Courtesy Boatmen's National Bank of St. Louis*

DECK PASSAGE

Passage for those not able to afford cabin fares meant hardship and deprivation, especially for women and children. Men accustomed to life in the backwoods or river towns could withstand the rigors of deck passage without discomfort. Naturally, the appeal of deck passage was economy.

Drawing by A. R. Waud of deck-passenger quarters on a steamboat. *From Every Saturday Magazine, 1871. Courtesy Saint Louis Mercantile Library Association*

Crew members resented the intrusion of the deckers. This is *Watching the Cargo,* a mid-nineteenth-century river scene painted by George Caleb Bingham (1811–1879), showing crewmen keeping a vigil over the freight from a wrecked steamboat seen in the background. *Courtesy State Historical Society of Missouri*

Deckers could obtain a slight reduction in fare if they agreed to work with the deck crew, principally in wooding operations. Deckers frequently were in the crew's way and relations between them were marked by quarrels and abuse. An added problem was language, as many deck passengers were newly arrived immigrants from European countries.

Disease was especially prevalent among deck passengers because of the crowded and unsanitary living conditions. They were particularly susceptible to cholera, which was introduced at the seaports and spread along the waterways on the steamboats. The dreaded disease reached epidemic proportions in the western river valleys between 1835 and 1870. Newly arrived ships from Europe transmitted the infection annually among the immigrant passengers. The disease rarely affected cabin passengers,

At landings roustabouts would move about unloading freight. Sketch by William T. Smedley. *From Harper's Monthly, 1893.*

233

Sketch of
a roustabout.

who usually had no contact with the deckers or the crew. During the 1850s Saint Louis and Cincinnati established quarantine points where incoming boats were inspected and, if necessary, cleaned in the effort to prevent the spread of cholera and yellow fever. Infected passengers were not permitted to land at the levees.

The close boilers created a constant hazard of fire and explosion amid main-deck passengers. Casualties were always highest among the deckers, who were often trapped, scalded by steam, or drowned after jumping overboard. The main deck was also the most dangerous place on a boat that was sinking, whether from collision, snagging, or otherwise. The deck was the first to submerge, and collisions caused shifts in the cargo, throwing deck passengers overboard, as there were no barriers along the edge of the deck.

Leisure time for the roustabouts between river ports. *From* St. Louis, the Fourth City, 1909

Incoming passengers would be treated to the ever-present levee characters on the riverfront. Sketched by A. R. Waud. *From* Every Saturday Magazine, July 22, 1871

The first regulations to correct unsatisfactory main-deck conditions were contained in the steamboat inspection act of 1852. However, inadequate inspection procedures prevented their enforcement, often with dire results. Better regulations and enforcement prevailed after the passage of a second law in 1871, but the need thereafter lessened considerably. By 1900 only one passenger in ten was a decker.

RIVERBOAT GAMBLERS

The fictionalized professional gambler, in fancy clothes, was a rarity aboard western-river steamboats. They were mostly the kind who might run a shell game in a carnival. The gamblers' victims were usually planters or merchants returning home from a successful business venture. After a few drinks at the bar, they easily fell under the spell of a cardsharp. With so much free time, card playing was a popular diversion, and victims usually were unaware of the unscrupulous practices of the slick gamblers. Some bartenders were hired by the gamblers to make certain that every "new" deck of cards was a marked one. Signs warning against gambling were generally ignored, and many stewards willingly cooperated in providing card tables for games. However, if a victim could prove that he was cheated, the offending gambler was put off the boat as soon as possible. Fabulous amounts of money were said to have changed hands in the big poker games played in the privacy of the texas deck.

Riverboats were favorite locales for the gambler's

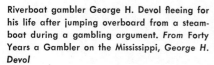

Riverboat gambler George H. Devol fleeing for his life after jumping overboard from a steamboat during a gambling argument. *From Forty Years a Gambler on the Mississippi, George H. Devol*

Games for high stakes always aroused interest among the passengers on a riverboat trip. *From Forty Years a Gambler on the Mississippi, George H. Devol*

operations because they furnished a continuous parade of newly affluent dupes who acquiesced to a friendly game. They would be allowed to win for a time, then, dealt a good hand to foster overconfidence, the shark dealt himself, or his shill, a better one, thus setting the scene for a thorough fleecing.

Top-flight gamblers were equipped with devices for roulette, faro, keno, and poker. One of the simplest games was three-card monte, a sort of shell game played with tickets printed with pictures of a man, a woman, and a child. The object was to pick the baby card after they had been shuffled. Where the hand was quicker than the eye, this was next to impossible; a shill, pretending to be in the game, would mark the baby card.

While gambling was tolerated in many river towns during the early days, the gamblers' rude, insulting practices finally caused a public revulsion. In Vicksburg, in 1835, they were driven out of town by an enraged citizenry.

STEAMBOAT RACING

As with all transport, speed was foremost concerning river steamboats. Records were kept of the best times between principal river cities, and to the fast-

Keno goose and chuck-a-luck cup, with dice, cards, and other gambling paraphernalia from the *Grand Republic. Courtesy Missouri Historical Society*

Another diversion, among the bayous of Louisiana, was shooting at alligators from the deck. *From* Down the Great River, *1887*

Preparing to fleece a potential victim in a game aboard a Mississippi River steamboat. *From* Forty Years a Gambler on the Mississippi, *George H. Devol*

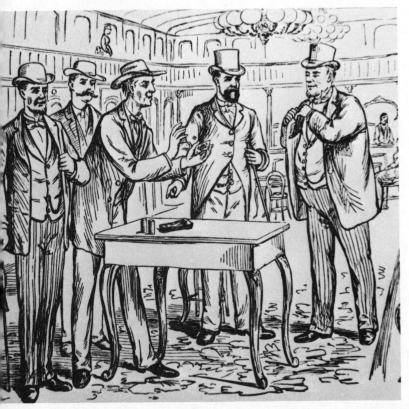

A steamboat race on the Mississippi in the late 1850s. *From Eighty Years of Progress, 1788–1868. Courtesy Saint Louis Public Library*

A Race for the Buckhorns—the Queen of the West *and the* Morning Star. *Currier and Ives print by Fanny E. Palmer. Courtesy Saint Louis Public Library*

est went the honor of "holding the horns." These were a gilded pair of deer antlers, a symbol of the speed king, mounted on the pilothouse. The horns were passed to the fastest boat, and since fast boats attracted business, the holder of the horns was in a unique position to profit from his distinction.

Naturally, there was a prime interest in steamboat racing. Long considered dangerous, the practice could not be stopped by legislation or the raising of insurance rates. The spirit of a contest was shared by passengers and crew alike, whenever two well-matched boats met. Some races were well-planned affairs, with the boats especially groomed for the occasion. All excess weight was removed and the machinery tuned to its best condition. Fuel supplies were prearranged and kept in barges, which could be towed alongside while the transfer

was made. Turpentine, pitch, bacon sides, or pine knots were fed to the boilers to create a hotter fire. Safety valves were ignored or held down by weights to render them inoperable.

Among the better-known races of antebellum times were those between the *Eclipse* and the *A. L. Shotwell,* and the *Baltic* and the *Diana.* The best time for the 1350-mile run from New Orleans to Louisville was four days, nine hours, and thirty minutes set by the *Eclipse* in May, 1853, when she beat the *Shotwell* by only fifty minutes.

The famous steamboat race between the *Robert E. Lee* and the *Natchez* caught the betting public's fancy and generated wide interest, here and abroad. A business rivalry between Captain John W. Cannon of the *Lee* and Captain Thomas P. Leathers of the *Natchez* started it all. Both pub-

Currier and Ives print of *A Midnight Race on the Mississippi*, between the *Memphis* and the *James Howard*. Courtesy Ardell Thompson Collection

Another popular Currier and Ives print of a Mississippi steamboat race, the *Natchez* racing against the *Eclipse*. The *Eclipse* alternated in the Ohio River and lower Mississippi trades until 1860, when she broke loose in a great storm at New Orleans and was severely damaged. Her hull ended its career as a wharfboat at Memphis. Courtesy Saint Louis Public Library

Currier and Ives print of a race on the Mississippi between the *Eagle* and the *Diana*. The *Eagle* operated principally on the Ohio River, while the *Diana* (1857–1866) replaced the *Eclipse* in the Louisville to New Orleans trade and ran a famous race with the *Baltic* on that run in March, 1858. After use as a Civil War transport, the *Diana* was dismantled in 1866. Courtesy Saint Louis Public Library

The famous race between the *Robert E. Lee* and the *Natchez*, depicted by Currier and Ives. Actually, the boats were never as close together during the race as they are shown in so many prints. *Courtesy Saint Louis Public Library*

Captain Thomas P. Leathers, master of the *Natchez*. From The Crescent City Illustrated, *1874. Courtesy Saint Louis Mercantile Library Association*

An advertisement for the famous *Natchez*. From The Crescent City Illustrated, *1874. Courtesy Saint Louis Mercantile Library Association*

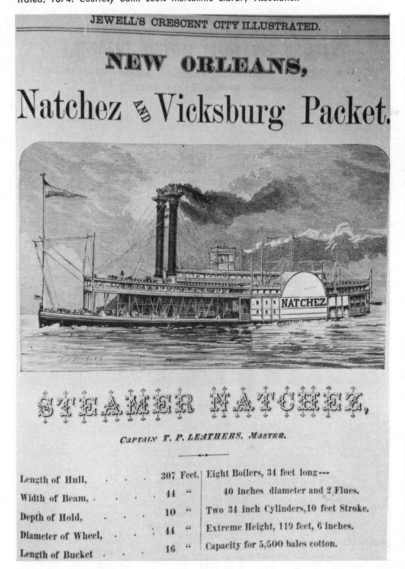

JEWELL'S CRESCENT CITY ILLUSTRATED.

NEW ORLEANS,
Natchez AND Vicksburg Packet.

STEAMER NATCHEZ,
CAPTAIN T. P. LEATHERS, MASTER.

Length of Hull,	307 Feet.	Eight Boilers, 34 feet long---		
Width of Beam,	44 "	40 inches diameter and 2 Flues,		
Depth of Hold,	10 "	Two 34 inch Cylinders,10 feet Stroke.		
Diameter of Wheel,	44 "	Extreme Height, 119 feet, 6 inches,		
Length of Bucket	16 "	Capacity for 5,500 bales cotton.		

licly denied intentions of racing, but they covertly prepared for the inevitable event. Cannon stripped the *Lee* and made provisions for refueling from coal barges en route. A controversial refueling took place above Vicksburg, when the steamer *Frank Pargoud* was lashed to the moving *Lee* to unload a hundred tons of pine knots to the racer. Supporters of the *Natchez* claimed that this unusual refueling gave the *Lee* an unfair advantage. The two racing boats were about evenly matched, although the *Natchez* was slightly larger and had a reputation as a record setter. The race began at 5:00 p.m. on June 30, 1870, from the New Orleans levee, with the *Lee* leaving about four minutes ahead of her rival. As the race proceeded upstream, the *Lee* drew steadily away from the *Natchez*; the boats

239

The *Natchez* of racing fame, the sixth boat in succession to bear that name. She was completed at Cincinnati in 1869 and entered into trades out of New Orleans. After the race, the *Natchez* enjoyed a successful ten-year career and ended her days as a wharfboat at Vicksburg. *Drawing by the author*

The *Robert E. Lee* moored at the Cairo wharfboat in the early 1870s. *Courtesy Missouri Historical Society*

Captain John W. Cannon, who led the *Robert E. Lee* to victory. *Courtesy Missouri Historical Society*

The steamboat *Frank Pargoud*, which participated in the controversial refueling episode during the race between the *Natchez* and the *Robert E. Lee*. The *Pargoud's* career extended from 1868 to 1878. *Courtesy Boatmen's National Bank of St. Louis*

never were as close together as depicted in many pictures of the event. At the halfway point, at Memphis, the *Lee*'s lead had stretched to almost an hour. When the boats encountered fog above Cairo, Illinois, the *Natchez* was slowed further by engine trouble. Even though Captain Cannon ran the *Lee* at reduced speed through the fog, he reached the finish line at Saint Louis on July 4, 1870, at 11:25 a.m., in a record-breaking time. The *Natchez* arrived over six hours later. Later, the racers were treated to a royal welcome at a banquet in the Southern Hotel, at which trophies were awarded. Controversies about the race, especially over the fueling episode, were argued for many years thereafter.

Not all the speed records were set during races. Efforts were always being made for a new mark between certain points. The New Orleans to Cairo run was popular, and varied in distance from 1106 miles in 1844, when the *J. M. White II* made it in three days, six hours, forty-four minutes, to 1030 miles when the *Robert E. Lee* set a new mark of three days and one hour in its 1870 race with the *Natchez*. The 1218-mile distance from New Orleans to Saint Louis was covered by the *J. M. White* in 1844 in three days, twenty-three hours, nine minutes. This record endured until the *Natchez* lowered it to 3:21.58 just before its race with the *Robert E. Lee*. The *Lee* set the final mark of 3:18.14 in winning the famous race.

An interesting comparison between steamboat speeds involves the 268-mile run from New Orleans to Natchez. The *Orleans*, first steamboat to ascend the Mississippi, took six days, six hours, and forty minutes to make the trip in 1814. This was reduced to under twenty hours by the *Sultana* in 1844 and cut still further to seventeen hours and eleven minutes by the *Robert E. Lee* in 1870. The *Lee*'s speed in winning its famous race was slightly over thirteen miles an hour, but it is said that the *J. M. White III* unofficially made much faster time. Captain John W. Tobin of the *White* was a close friend of Captain Cannon of the *Lee*, and he resolved never to take the horns from the *Lee* as long as Cannon lived. The *White* never did, because she burned before Cannon died. The power and speed of the *White* were revealed in an incident with the racer *Natchez*. Tobin was no friend of Captain Leathers and became riled whenever Leathers resorted to his old practice of pulling out from New Orleans slightly after a rival boat and

The *Robert E. Lee* near the finish line as seen from the bluffs at Carondelet, Missouri, south of Saint Louis. *Courtesy Boatmen's National Bank of St. Louis*

The victory bowl trophy presented to the winner. It was accepted by Captain Cannon at a banquet held at the Southern Hotel after the race finished at Saint Louis. *Courtesy Missouri Historical Society*

then passing her. On one occasion, in 1878, Leathers did this to Tobin's boat *Ed Richardson* and then compounded the insult by firing a cannon when passing her. Tobin vowed to get revenge on Leathers and did so with the *J. M. White*. Departing together, Leathers pushed the *Natchez* ahead of the *White*, which had slowed for minor repairs. A short while later the *White* closed the gap and passed the *Natchez* quite handily. The *J. M. White III* reached Baton Rouge in seven hours flat, beating the time of the *Robert E. Lee* by eighty minutes.

A latter-day steamboat race between the *Betsy Ann* (left) and the *Tom Greene* at Cincinnati on July 16, 1929. The sternwheeler *Betsy Ann* was built in 1899 and ran in the Natchez-Bayou Sara trade until 1921, when she came to the upper Ohio. She was purchased by Captains Frederick Way, Sr. and Jr., in 1925 and was operated out of Pittsburgh until 1932 when she was converted into a towboat. The *Tom Greene* was completed in 1923 for the Greene Line of Cincinnati and ran in trades on the Ohio and Kanawha rivers. She won close races with the *Betsy Ann* in 1929–1930 and plied in the Cincinnati-Louisville trade from 1931 until 1947. She was laid up near Louisville in 1950. *Courtesy Waterways Journal*

Entertainment provided by a talented crew member. Drawing by William T. Smedley. *From Harper's Monthly, 1893*

SHOWBOATS

The pioneer settlers not only traveled to their new homes on the western rivers but also depended upon them for the necessities of life. It was natural that they should expect the rivers to bring them some form of entertainment to soften the hardships of their lonely lives. The earliest amusements were provided by itinerant merchants selling patent medicines and whiskey from their flatboats. Music, acrobatics, and comedies were used to attrack crowds of potential buyers. Similar performances were given by talented flatboat crewmen to raise funds for drinks.

The initial attempt to present dramatic presentations was made by Noah Ludlow in 1817. The young actor and a company of professional players set out down the Allegheny River to Pittsburgh in a small boat and then traveled overland to Frankfort, Kentucky, and Nashville, Tennessee. At Nashville the company bought a large keelboat for a downriver trip to New Orleans. It was an eventful voyage, during which they used prop weapons to repel boarding by river pirates. While most of their performances were in impromptu theaters ashore, it is probable that some were held on the boat, which Ludlow named *Noah's Ark*.

The first known boat built especially for theatricals came from Pittsburgh in 1831 and was run by a family of English actors named Chapman. Unable to find work in the East, they decided to bring drama, usually Shakespeare, to the western river valleys. Their boat was actually a one-hundred-foot-long barge on which a barnlike theater was constructed. A makeshift stage with muslin curtains and candles for footlights was at the stern. The audience sat on crude benches on the barge deck. Living quarters occupied the bow. Admissions often were paid in meat, vegetables, or other produce instead of the fifty-cent cash charge for adults. The venture was repeated for several years, and in 1836 the Chapmans purchased a steamboat to expand operations. This was unusual, for a barge pushed by a small steamer was the common style for showboats. The Chapman's success brought many imitators into river drama, with some unsavory results. Showboats were used not only as bases for gamblers but also by quacks selling colored-water patent medicines. Showboats became scandalous and during the 1850s often were met by armed posses at the river ports. Circus performances playing the major river towns became popular during the fifties. Spaulding and Rogers' "Floating Circus Palace" was a huge amphitheater on a barge about two hundred feet long. It had a seating capacity of thirty-four hundred, of which a thousand were in the dress circle and the rest in two galleries. A wax museum was at the stern, as were dressing rooms and stalls for forty horses. The company and crew, more than a hundred persons, lived on the upper decks. The barge was pushed by a steamboat, which contained its own theater for dramatic performances. Both boats were lighted by gas, which was a novelty at the time. The group brought regular circus acts to western-river towns from 1851 until 1862, when the circus barge was confiscated by the Confederates for a hospital boat.

Showboats returned to the rivers after the Civil War, largely through the efforts of Augustus B. French, who made a career of river-borne entertainment. After the war he operated a circus wagon enterprise for some years until a flood ended it. In the late 1870s French built a showboat at Cincinnati, which presented vaudeville acts by French, his wife, Callie, and others. After nine years the show included eighteen acts, but it still faced the problem of gaining acceptance in certain river towns. At one port an all-male audience appeared,

The showboat *Floating Palace* being towed in the Gulf of Mexico on a trip from Mobile about 1853. Lithograph by Sarony and Major, New York. *Courtesy Saint Louis Public Library*

The *Water Queen* showboat, owned by a Mr. Price, towed by the steamer *Argand*, about 1910. *Courtesy Waterways Journal*

which naturally expected a racy performance, much to the chagrin of French. He told them that his wife was in the show and that it merited attendance by all. The men left and later reappeared with their wives, convinced that the show was of high moral character. The episode is credited with breaking down the unfavorable reputation that had been associated with showboats. Morality and refinement were emphasized in showboat advertising, to qualify it as family entertainment. To attract customers, French introduced the calliope on his second "New Sensation" showboat in 1886.

Family ownership and operation became a hallmark of successful showboats on the rivers, creating the right atmosphere of quality to appeal to the rural families. The arrival of the showboat was much like that of a circus, its shrill calliope playing while a band paraded on the town's main street. It practically closed down the town to all but the performance. Vaudeville and melodrama were popularly programmed on showboats. Among the plays presented were *Uncle Tom's Cabin, East Lynne, The Drunkard,* and *Ten Nights in a Bar Room.* Presenting a clear-cut contrast between good and evil, the dramas inevitably ended with virtue triumphant. In later years highly paid performers played some of the bigger boats in large river towns. The trend after 1900 was toward boats up to two hundred feet in length, such as W. R. Markle's electrically air-cooled *Goldenrod,* which could seat fourteen hundred persons. A marked decline in showboat activity began about 1910 with the development of the automobile and motion picture. No longer tied to riverfront entertainment, the playgoing public patronized movies in inland towns wherever their fancy indicated. Interest in showboats revived during the 1920s due to the influence of Edna Ferber's famous novel *Showboat,* which was made into an operetta and a motion picture. Her boat the *Cotton Blossom* actually existed in several showboats, but not as the self-propelled steamboat seen in the movie version.

Burlesque melodrama had its beginning on showboats in 1919, when Billy Bryant's boat was having a poor season on the Cincinnati waterfront. A socialite, whose yacht was moored nearby, offered Bryant twenty-five dollars to present *Ten Nights in a Bar Room* to his guests; at the start, the serious drama got a comic reaction. It continued as

A rendition on the showboat steam calliope was a sure way to attract attention after the boat's arrival. *From Harper's Weekly, 1866. Courtesy St. Louis Mercantile Library Association*

A typical vaudeville troupe. These engaged in variety acts between the regular melodramas aboard the showboats. *Courtesy Waterways Journal*

W. R. Markle's *New Sunny South* showboat at a river landing about 1905. *Courtesy Boatmen's National Bank of St. Louis*

Billy Bryant's new showboat on the Ohio River during the 1920s. *Courtesy Jefferson National Expansion Memorial, National Park Service*

The rebuilt showboat *Golden Rod* with its lights ablaze for a night's performance. *Courtesy Frank Pierson*

An announcement for Ralph W. Emerson's showboat *Golden Rod*, playing out of Cincinnati about 1915. *Courtesy Frank Pierson*

such a burlesque of the play (which was publicized by a reporter in the audience) that a new form of melodrama was born. The longest stand is that of the *Goldenrod*, first moored at Saint Louis in 1937 by Captain Bill Menke and still doing business despite a bad fire in 1962. Beginning as a sternwheel steamboat, it was built at Parkersburg, West Virginia, in 1909 for W. R. Markle. Sold at auction to R. W. Emerson in 1914, the boat came into the possession of Captain Menke in 1922. Monte Blue, Red Skelton, and Kathy Nolan performed aboard her in their early days, and in 1936 she tramped the Ohio River with Major Bowes' Amateur Hour. Extensively remodeled and reopened in 1965 by Frank Pierson, the *Goldenrod* has become a civic attraction on the Saint Louis levee. She was desig-

Captain Bill Menke in front of his showboat *Golden Rod* at the Saint Louis levee about 1939. *Courtesy Frank Pierson*

245

nated a national historic landmark by the National Park Service in 1968. The *Goldenrod* has played before audiences in sixteen states along the Mississippi River system.

UPPER MISSISSIPPI SCENIC ROUTE

The Italian exile and explorer Giacomo Constantine Beltrami was one of the first to describe the scenic wonders of the upper Mississippi River and the Falls of Saint Anthony. In 1823 he was a passenger aboard the steamer *Virginia* which was the first steamboat to reach Fort Snelling, Minnesota, near the present site of Saint Paul. During the 1830s, the allure of the falls began to attract excursionists but it was necessary to make an eight-mile overland journey to reach them. It was not until the 1850s that steamboats were able to brave the treacherous waters below the cataract. During the decade after 1840 trips to the falls were made from towns on the Ohio and lower Mississippi rivers. The impetus generated by these visitors aided in the growth of cities such as Galena, Dubuque, Davenport, Quincy, and Hannibal along the upper Mississippi route.

Closeup of the Falls of Saint Anthony, about 1842. *From Down the Great River, Willard Glazier, 1887. Courtesy Saint Louis Public Library*

Lithograph by Henry Lewis of Fort Snelling and environs, about 1835. *Courtesy Saint Louis Mercantile Library Association*

Through the Bayou by Torchlight, an idealized impression by Currier and Ives of a picturesque night scene on a Louisiana waterway, c. 1850. *Courtesy Saint Louis Public Library*

Lithograph by Henry Lewis of Fort Armstrong, Rock Island, Illinois, overlooking traffic, about 1840. *Courtesy Saint Louis Mercantile Library Association*

Scene at Rock Island today—boat marina. *Courtesy State of Illinois Department of Business and Economic Development*

Western River Scenery, a Currier and Ives print of a typical riverine setting along an unidentified western stream. *Courtesy Saint Louis Public Library*

When the first railroad reached the upper Mississippi at Rock Island in 1854, a new era of prosperity opened up for the upper-river packet lines. Connections with trains brought a tremendous increase in the number of tourists desirous of visiting the falls. The trend began when the contractors for the Chicago and Rock Island Railroad invited many of the nation's leading citizens to participate in a grand rail and steamboat excursion to the Falls of Saint Anthony. President Millard Fillmore, governors, statesmen, and wealthy easterners were among those who came, including the ablest reporters of the nation's press. Seven boats carried the overflow crowds, who were treated to luxurious accommodations and pleasant entertainment. The trip was climaxed by a brilliant reception in the capitol at Saint Paul, following visits to the Falls of Saint Anthony, Minnehaha Falls, Lake Calhoun, and Fort Snelling. Among the boats participating in the fashionable Tour of 1854 were the *Golden Era, Sparhawk, Lady Franklin, Galena, War Eagle, Jenny Lind,* and *Black Hawk.*

George Catlin (1796–1872), who made several trips to the upper Mississippi during his journeys among the Indians in the American West, recorded in many of his paintings the natural beauty of the river scenery.

The Mississippi River in Time of Peace, a Currier and Ives print by Fanny E. Palmer, 1865. *Courtesy Saint Louis Public Library*

Grace van Studdiford (1875–1927), a Saint Louis girl who became famous as an opera and musical comedy star of the early years of the twentieth century. She had a love for steamboats and spent much time on river trips. *Courtesy Waterways Journal*

VII
Disaster on the River

STEAMBOAT ACCIDENTS

Along with the benefits the steamboat bestowed on the western frontier was a series of disasters unprecedented in peacetime. These liabilities visited passengers and crew alike, with a suddenness that limited survival.

The calamities fell into five general groups: boiler explosions and/or steam emissions, snaggings, collisions, fires, and wrecks. Official statistics on steamboat accidents were not compiled until after passage of the steamboat-inspection act of 1852. Private reports before that were generally unreliable and exaggerated. A compilation of 995 accidents up to 1852 is interesting chiefly for its divisions. The list shows a breakdown of 44 accidents from collisions, 166 from fires, 209 from explosions, and 576 from snaggings and obstructions.

SNAGGINGS

Snags presented the most formidable hazard to steamboating, especially in the years before the Civil War. Although they sank numerous boats, snags were not responsible for a great loss of life. The snags would not always penetrate the hull, but could cause damage to extremities such as guards and paddle wheels. The potential damage to a boat can be assessed when it is realized that some snags were large trunks of trees, up to seventy-five feet long and of tremendous weight. These jagged trunks embedded in the river bottom lay poised like spears, ready to impale the hull of any unwary boat. Serious damage resulted when a snag pierced a boat's hull, usually causing the craft to sink. If

Sunk in the Ohio, the White Collar Line steamer *City of Madison*, near Madison, Indiana. *Courtesy Saint Louis Public Library*

Snags and a steamboat wreck on the Missouri River. *From Voyage dans les mauvaises terres du Nebraska, M. E. de Girardin, 1849.* Courtesy State Historical Society of Missouri

the boat went down rapidly, the number of lives lost depended on the water depth. In mid-channel, if the passengers and crew could reach the top deck they usually were saved. If the boat foundered slowly, there might have been time to ground her on an adjacent sandbar. The most serious accidents of this kind occurred at night, on the lower Mississippi, while a boat was bound upstream. Although a large number of these sinkings were attributable to striking sunken rocks and old boat wrecks, snags were a greater risk because such objects abounded from a constant renewal of supply. Snags could usually be seen in daylight and therefore the chances of a snagging greatly increased after nightfall.

Wreckage of the Missouri River sternwheeler *Montana*, Saint Charles, Missouri, 1886. *Courtesy Saint Louis Public Library*

COLLISIONS

At first glance, it would seem almost impossible for two steamboats to collide on a wide river. A closer look would reveal that collisions could be caused by the narrowness of a channel in an apparently broad stream, or by shifting currents and eddies which could lead to a pilot's losing control of his boat. Boats going in opposite directions reacted differently to currents and quite often crossed bows trying to follow their proper courses. Ignorance of passing signals caused some collisions, most of which occurred at night. One of the worst was a nighttime collision in a bend of the lower Mississippi between the *Monmouth* and the *Warren* in

Lithograph by Henry Lewis of the collision of the steamers *Brilliant* and *John Randolph* by the Convent of the Sacred Heart, Louisiana, about 1835. *Courtesy Saint Louis Public Library*

1837. About three hundred Indians perished when the upstream-bound *Monmouth* was struck during a severe rainstorm. She had been engaged in the removal of the Creek tribe to the West from their former southern homeland. Like snaggings, collisions usually caused more damage to the boats than to life. Casualties did occur in collisions in the deep water of mid-channel, principally drownings.

FIRES

Fires and explosions caused about half of the property loss in all steamboat accidents up to 1852, although they involved only one-third of the number of calamities. The wooden construction of western-river steamboats—resinous wood coated with paint laden with turpentine—was especially conducive to combustion. Combustible cargoes such as cotton, hay, and spirits, as well as the piles of cordwood, fueled a fire once it began. The hot boilers were located amidst these flammable materials, and embers fell from open boiler doors and a stream of sparks cascaded from the tops of chimneys. However, the upper decks were sanded against the cinder fall and barrels of water were kept handy for emergencies. Another constant danger was from candles or oil lamps used for lighting.

Fires would spread rapidly once started, particularly if near the boilers, where the draft created by the boat's movement would quickly spread the flames the full length of the open decks. There was a better chance to combat fires that broke out in the hold, where the more solid structure could prevent quick combustion, and fires below deck could be smothered by battening the hatches. Fires in the superstructure were impossible to stop because of the flimsy wooden decks and cabins. In such cases, losses were usually severe, and the casualty list high for passengers trapped in their staterooms by the flames. The hemp tiller ropes, which led from the pilothouse to the rudders, sometimes burned and caused loss of control. This resulted in heavy casualties because of the pilot's inability to steer the boat to shore. Lifeboats and life preservers were nonexistent and very few passengers could swim.

One of the greatest fire tragedies in river history was the burning of the *Ben Sherrod*, in 1837, on the Ohio River near Louisville. The captain was

Lithograph by Henry Lewis of *The Great Fire at Saint Louis in 1849.* This fire started aboard the steamboat *White Cloud* and spread to nearby boats, including the *Edward Bates,* which drifted downstream setting fire to other boats moored along the levee. Twenty-three steamboats were destroyed in this conflagration, which also burned out many blocks of the city's riverfront warehouse district before it was finally stopped by dynamiting buildings in its path. *Courtesy Saint Louis Mercantile Library Association*

Steamboat fire at Saint Louis, January, 1853, in which the steamers *New England, Brunette,* and *New Lucy* were destroyed. *From The Illustrated News, 1853. Courtesy Saint Louis Mercantile Library Association*

Steamboat fire following an explosion on an unidentified boat during the late 1850s. *From Harper's Weekly. Courtesy Saint Louis Mercantile Library Association*

The disastrous steamboat fire at Saint Louis on December 7, 1855, in which the steamers *Twin City*, *Prairie City*, and *Parthenia* were totally destroyed. Nine other boats were seriously damaged. *From Harper's Weekly, 1856. Courtesy Saint Louis Mercantile Library Association*

Another serious fire was the burning of the sidewheeler *Stonewall* on the Mississippi River in October, 1869. *From Leslie's Illustrated Newspaper, November 13, 1869. Courtesy Saint Louis Mercantile Library Association*

Currier and Ives print of the burning of the *Robert E. Lee II* below Vicksburg on September 30, 1882. This boat was known as the *New Lee* because she was the successor of the famous racing steamboat of that name. Twenty-one lives were lost in the fire on this six-year-old boat. *Courtesy Boatmen's National Bank of St. Louis*

racing another boat, and the firemen, who were feeding the boiler with pine knots and resin, were drunk. Fire spread to a pile of cordwood and later burned the tiller ropes. The passengers were not warned until the flames had gained headway and the boat had drifted out of control. The passengers who could escape had no choice but to plunge into the river. Others were trapped by subsequent explosions of barrels of brandy and gunpowder, before the boilers let go. The cries of the victims added to the horror of the lurid, flame-lit scene, which was soon reached by rescue boats. One boat, the *Alton,* reportedly refused aid and ran down victims in the river as she passed. The loss of life was estimated at more than 150, and the disaster led to enactment of the first steamboat act in 1838.

EXPLOSIONS

The most spectacular steamboat disasters were caused by exploding boilers. Their suddenness and force attracted the morbid fancy of the public. The flying wreckage, escaping steam, and scalding water caused more serious injuries than any other steamboat accidents.

The first such disaster occurred on Captain Henry M. Shreve's steamer *Washington* on her maiden voyage in 1816. While the boat was moored at Marietta, Ohio, with steam up, one of the boilers exploded with a terrific blast, blowing the crew overboard. An account states that death and excruciating pain were evident among the victims, some of whom were skinned alive by scalding. A series of steamboat-explosion disasters followed, climaxed in 1838 by the explosions within a week of one another of the *Oronoko* and the *Moselle.* These resulted in a loss of nearly three hundred lives. The frequency of explosions up to the middle of the nineteenth century contributed to the passage of the steamboat-inspection act of 1852, which provided for stringent safety regulations.

Whereas explosions would scatter fiery embers, setting a boat on fire, steam accidents involving pipe breakage or the blowing of a cylinder packing or collapse of a flue were minor in nature and caused few, if any, casualties. The high-pressure steam engine and the methods used in firing its boilers were usually cited in any discussion of the blame for boiler explosions. Excessive pressure buildup and the failure of safety valves were con-

The steamboat *Oronoco* exploded when moored opposite Princeton, Mississippi, on April 21, 1838, with the loss of about a hundred lives. A flue collapsed, spreading scalding steam among the slumbering deck passengers. Many others drowned before rescuers could reach them. *From* Lloyd's Steamboat Directory, *1856*

The tragic explosion of the steamer *Moselle* occurred about a mile downstream from Cincinnati on April 25, 1838. The boat had just picked up some German immigrants on a trip to Saint Louis, when the boilers let go in a terrific blast that claimed eighty-five lives. *From* Lloyd's Steamboat Directory, *1856*

sidered the causes of the explosions, as well as an insufficient amount of water in the boiler which overheated the boiler plates.

Careless and incompetent engineers often were mentioned in complaints about explosions, and this had validity in view of the scarcity of qualified steamboat engineers. However, the entire blame could not always be placed on the engineer, who was responding to orders. Inferior safety equipment or the complete lack of it, which was beyond

The newly arrived *Glencoe*, while landing at the Saint Louis levee on April 5, 1852, blew her boilers, spreading death and destruction in every direction. The entire forward superstructure was demolished, killing many persons assembled on the foredeck. Adjacent boats at the levee were badly damaged, and the blazing *Glencoe* drifted downstream, eventually burning to the waterline. She had been built in 1846 and was 225 feet in length. Records show that about sixty lives were lost in this calamity. *Drawing by the author*

The steam wreck-boat *Submarine No. 7*, built by James B. Eads and William Nelson in 1857. This boat was humorously referred to by rivermen as "the harp of a thousand strings." It was used in salvage work on steamboat wrecks in the riverbed. *From* Sketch Book of Saint Louis, *1857*

REPAIRS AND SALVAGE

the engineer's control, was held equally responsible. Though there were few cases documented, it was frequently charged that some boiler explosions were caused by the high pressures generated during steamboat races. The fact that most explosions occurred in getting underway, rather than while proceeding under a full head of steam, tended to invalidate such charges.

Broken machinery parts were a frequent cause of trouble on steamboats, particularly in isolated locations during the early days. Some boats carried spare parts, as well as carpenters' or blacksmiths' equipment, as a partial solution. Hull damage sustained below the waterline required ingenious methods of repair. During the 1830s floating dry docks were placed in operation at several river towns. A more successful repair technique was the use of marine railways, in which boats, on wheeled cradles supported by cables or chains, were pulled on rails, broadside, up the bank. A sunken boat usually represented a total loss during the first years of steamboating. Underwater salvage operations became feasible through the use of diving bells during the 1840s. This technique was developed by James B. Eads, who became aware of the need for such devices while working as a steamboat clerk. Eads built a series of diving-bell boats, each named *Submarine,* beginning in 1842, which were put to work for insurance companies for a percentage of the value of the salvaged property. Initial salvage attempts were concerned with cargo and machinery removal, but by about 1850 methods for raising entire sunken boats were devised. This was possible through the use of pumps capable of emptying hulls, after bulkheading the damaged area and closing the hatches. Armored diving suits were later used for making repairs. Improved bulkheading techniques and pumps came into use for keeping damaged boats afloat where recovery was possible.

NAVIGATION DIFFICULTIES

Circuitous river routes spread the drop of the river over a greater distance and aided navigation by slowing the current. Steamboat traffic was delayed, however, by the additional mileage. Also, operations were restricted by seasonal patterns. Drought and frost were paralyzing factors for river transportation; boats were frequently laid up during low water in summer and icing in winter.

Water depth governed a boat's draft and cargo weight. Average-sized boats, up to three hundred tons, could not run profitably in less than four feet of water, while any depth greater than six feet was unnecessary. Extremely high water precluded normal landings and was marked by excessive currents, which made navigation difficult. Reduced draft could mean many extra days of steamboating and a pilot's skill in low water could extend the shipping season for a boat owner.

Since navigation depended so closely on weather conditions, the spring freshets and water from melting ice and snow were looked upon as favorable conditions, marking the opening of the steamboating season. Wet seasons meant periods of

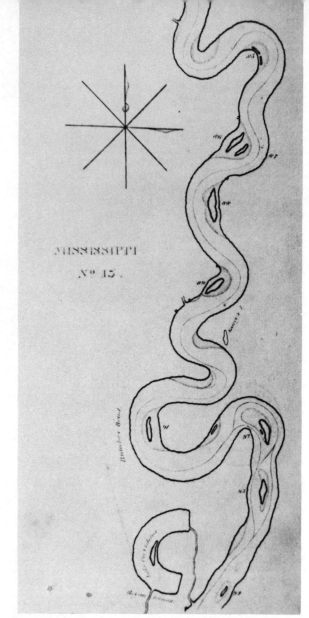

Winding course of the Mississippi River above Lake Providence, Louisiana, 1829. *From* The Western Pilot *by Samuel Cumings. Courtesy Saint Louis Public Library*

Currier and Ives print entitled *Low Water on the Mississippi,* drawn in 1868 by Fanny E. Palmer. Such conditions precluded navigation by all except boats of the shallowest draft. *Courtesy Saint Louis Public Library*

View north from Eads Bridge at Saint Louis during high water in the early nineties. The famous Missouri River sternwheeler *Benton* is in the foreground. *Courtesy Saint Louis Public Library*

Drawing by Harry Fenn of a steamboat on the Tennessee River being warped through the "Suck," a tight, rocky stretch in the mountains. *From Picturesque America, 1872. Courtesy Saint Louis Mercantile Library Association*

unrestricted navigation and were therefore economically favorable; major rivers were marked by a succession of rises that corresponded to the high-water conditions of their principal tributaries. Low-water periods began in June and continued intermittently until the fall season of navigation prevailed. This last included rainy periods and could extend into December, depending upon the advent of winter. Ice and attendant low water could occur from late November until early spring. The Mississippi below Memphis was ice-free all year round, and in mild years uninterrupted navigation for the full year was a distinct possibility.

During the 1820s and 1830s, shipping seasons of under six months were common, but after 1840 improved boats and removal of obstructions lengthened the season to nearly eight months for medium-sized boats. Later improvements enabled even the largest boats to operate on the Ohio below Cincinnati for almost the entire year. The much more limited seasons on the tributaries were due to obstructions and weather. But compared with the Ohio, the upper Mississippi and Missouri rivers had relatively short seasons. Winter conditions closed them down for longer periods, and low water was another dominant factor which caused longer suspensions on the shallow rivers.

NATURAL CONTROLS

During the navigation seasons, three fundamental conditions governed steamboat activity. These were water depth, current speed, and riverbed characteristics. Water depth generally increased from a river's source to its mouth. On the upper Mississippi it varied from two feet at Saint Paul to five feet at Cairo. This ratio could be reversed at times; a swell at the river's upper end could create a depth greater than that much further downstream. Rises could advance downstream at a rate of about fifty miles a day, diminishing in wide places and deepening in narrow confines. Rivers rise and fall almost constantly, due to various controlling factors, so that an even level is seldom maintained.

The current's velocity ceased to be a technical problem with the introduction of more powerful steamboat engines, which could drive a boat against the current without difficulty. The speed of the current was governed by the slope of the riv-

The result of a rising river—Marietta, Ohio, in the late 1850s. Drawing by Henry Howe. *Courtesy Saint Louis Public Library*

At a rapids the gradient and current rose considerably. This is the Falls of Saint Anthony during high water in 1900. *From Historical Towns of the Western States, 1901*

An exposed wreck—the steamboat *Bertrand,* sunk on the Missouri River above Council Bluffs, Iowa, in the late 1860s. *Courtesy Saint Louis Public Library*

erbed and the depth of the water. On most navigable rivers the gradient was less than fourteen inches to the mile, while on the trunk rivers it was about six inches a mile, except at rapids or shoals where the fall was much greater. Normal current speeds ranged from about one mile an hour, in deep pools at low water, up to five miles an hour during flood stages. Over rapids the speed would exceed six miles an hour.

The riverbeds of the Missouri and lower Mississippi Rivers were subject to constant changes in direction, forming new bends and cutoffs. The channel's course for each was irregular, shifting with changes in the water's speed and volume. Erosion of the riverbank occurred as far as two thousand feet inland along some parts of the Missouri River. There were examples where the bank would cut back more than a hundred feet in a half hour, and old wrecks would be successively covered and exposed by river action. New bars and islands were

created, while older ones would be washed away by the vagaries of the capricious river. Questionable channel locations made every trip an adventure even for seasoned pilots in the early steamboat era.

On other parts of the river system the riverbeds were stabilized through rolling country and were not subject to the broad, convulsive actions prevalent through wide alluvial plains, as on the lower Mississippi. Such changes as occurred were confined to beds composed of sand or silt. Rock and gravel bottoms were not subject to extensive erosion. The channel was a smaller version of the larger river, marked by faster current and greater depth, and varying in width with the stage of the river.

ISLANDS

Islands were the most prominent undulations in a river's bed. From a navigation standpoint, islands split the channel and formed sandbars at their head and foot. Islands were quite numerous in all rivers. During the 1820s Zadok Cramer listed 98 islands between Pittsburgh and Cairo and 126 from there down to New Orleans.

BARS

More pertinent to navigation than islands were the low-lying riverbed elevations known as bars. Of many types and sizes, they consisted of sand, gravel, or rock, some permanent, others shifting with rises in the river. Depending on their forms, bars were known as chains, reefs, shoals, ripples, and rapids. They could run parallel to a river's course or angle across it. The higher bars were formidable barriers to pilots; others were problems only during low water.

Sandbars were the commonest, generally most numerous on the lower sections of the rivers. They formed at points where a slowdown in the current caused the water to deposit some of its sand or silt. Gravel bars were more hazardous to navigation because of their less yielding character. Rock bars were evident wherever rocky ledges reached into the riverbed, occurring chiefly on the upper parts of the Ohio and Mississippi and their tributaries. Rock bars were a serious menace to steamboats because a chance encounter with one could mean serious damage to the hull.

A ripple or shoal was a group of sand or gravel bars over which the current descended in a greater than normal slope. A similar series of rock bars was known as a chain. A reef was a lengthy sandbar that rose abruptly on one side.

During low-water periods, bars acted as dams to divide the river into a series of pools. They could be several miles long and quite deep, with a sluggish current. The water ran rapidly over the bars between pools, often in depths of less than a foot. Farther downstream the pools became larger and the rate of fall less at the bars. These pools acted as reservoirs to store and conserve the water supply during these low stages, and concentrated difficult navigation at the bars. Cutting through the bars, to enable boats to cross, tended to lower the level of the upper pool, causing water wastage.

RAPIDS

Probably the most serious river obstructions, because of their extent, were falls and rapids. Rapids were more common on tributaries, and the first to

The rapids at Louisville. *From A Journey in North America—1796, General Victor Collot. Courtesy Saint Louis Mercantile Library Association*

Lithograph by Henry Lewis of the Upper Mississippi Rapids, Moline, Illinois, about 1840. *Courtesy Saint Louis Mercantile Library Association*

be encountered while ascending the river represented the head of navigation. While not so numerous on the trunk rivers, several rapids were especial hindrances to navigation. On the Ohio these included Letart's Rapids, about halfway between Pittsburgh and Cincinnati; the Grand Chain, near Cairo, Illinois; and, the greatest of all, the Falls of the Ohio, at Louisville. Letart's Rapids and the Grand Chain became more passable in later years, but the Ohio falls required construction of a bypass canal at Portland, Kentucky, to circumvent their hazard.

On the Tennessee River there was Muscle Shoals, above Florence, Alabama, actually two distinct waterways, above and below the obstacle. The rapids eventually were remedied by construction of dams, which submerged them. The upper Mississippi was marked by the Des Moines, or Lower Rapids, above Keokuk, and the Upper Rapids, north of Rock Island, Illinois. Although barely discernible, these rapids made it necessary to transship cargoes of all but the smallest steamboats. The rapids finally were eliminated in the river-improvement program in the last years of the steamboat era. The Missouri River, while known for its difficult navigation, did not have any rapids for the first two thousand miles of its length.

WRECKS

Old steamboat wrecks presented a serious hazard to navigation when obscured below the river's surface or shifted by channel changes into the path of boats. A particularly bad area for wrecks was the stretch of the Mississippi between Saint Louis and Cairo. It was called "the Graveyard" for its incidence of about a wreck a mile.

The Eagle Packet steamer *Golden Eagle*, last of the Mississippi River packets out of Saint Louis, sunk below Fort Gage, Illinois, in June, 1941. When such wrecks disappeared below the waterline, they represented a serious hazard to traffic. *Courtesy Jefferson National Expansion Memorial, National Park Service*

SAWYERS

While the most treacherous hazards to steamboating were snags, sawyers—as snagheads lying downstream were called—were more common because a tree trunk had a tendency to swing downstream after its root end became seated in the riverbed. They were called sawyers because of the sawlike action given to them by the current. Sawyers also caused more damage than snags because of the greater speed of downstream-bound steamboats. Snags were prevalent in rivers where erosive action undermined trees along the banks, causing them to fall into the water. They were later removed by specially designed government snag boats. Akin to

An early stream snag boat on the Mississippi River. *From Taylor and Crooks Sketch Book of Saint Louis, 1857*

snags was driftwood, a peril for paddle wheels and hulls in stiff currents.

FLOODS

Variations in the range of water levels between extremes of high and low water on western rivers was extraordinary. During a flood in 1832 the difference on the Ohio ranged from thirty-five feet at Pittsburgh to sixty-three feet at New Albany, Indiana. The lower Mississippi showed extremes varying from thirty-seven feet at Memphis to fifty-one feet at Natchez. Ranges of up to fifty feet were reported on the lower Arkansas and up to thirty-five feet on the Missouri.

In a race with the rushing high water. *From Harper's Weekly, 1859. Courtesy Saint Louis Mercantile Library Association*

Flood in Saint Louis, June 16, 1858, looking north from the foot of Olive Street. *Courtesy U.S. Corps of Engineers, Saint Louis District*

Saint Louis had more than its share of high water. This is the flood of 1892. *Courtesy Jefferson National Expansion Memorial, National Park Service*

Fleeing a Cairo, Illinois, flood in the late 1850s. *From Harper's Weekly. Courtesy Saint Louis Mercantile Library Association*

The force of the water was overwhelming. These men are attempting to repair a crevasse to stem the flow. Drawing by A. R. Waud. *From Picturesque America, 1872. Courtesy Saint Louis Mercantile Library Association*

A break in the levee! A small fissure such as this could easily expand into a major washout. *From Harper's Weekly, 1884. Courtesy Saint Louis Mercantile Library Association*

Floods were among the most dreaded phenomena on the western rivers. Unpredictable and uncontrolled, they could sweep away anything in their path. Boat wrecks and strandings were common occurrences. Economically, floods meant a suspension of business equal to that caused by low water.

WINDSTORMS

Navigation on the western rivers generally was not seriously hampered by the action of high winds. This was due to the relative protection of the many

While less frequent than windstorms, earthquakes and tornadoes sometimes occur on the western rivers. In fact, the entire course of the Mississippi River was changed by the Great Earthquake of 1811–1812, which centered around New Madrid, Missouri, pictured here. The town sank twelve feet below its former level, and only two boats out of thirty escaped destruction. The earth shocks were felt from Canada to the Gulf and from the Rocky Mountains to Pittsburgh for a period of over a year after the initial shock of December 16, 1811. The earth's surface experienced great undulations in the area along the Mississippi from Cairo to the mouth of the Arkansas River, creating new lakes in the river's old course. The largest of these was Reelfoot Lake in Tennessee, which is about sixty-five miles long and twenty miles wide at its widest point. Note the earth fissures, and the log cabins being thrown down. This earthquake is regarded as the most severe ever to hit the North American continent. *From The Great West, Henry Howe*

bends and the closeness of the shorelines. A boat would usually have sufficient warning of an approaching storm to be able to find shelter by tying up at the riverbank. If caught in midstream in a high wind, steamboats were vulnerable to damage, such as the loss of chimneys, pilothouses, or other upper parts of the superstructure. However, on the water surface, the twisting rivers prevented high winds from creating more than a choppiness. The expanse of the river was insufficient for the creation of high waves. In plains areas, such as on the upper Missouri River, the lack of protecting hills or trees could cause trouble from sweeping winds, making it difficult to handle the boat in troublesome places. Tornadoes caused severe damage to shipping, with the Saint Louis tornado of 1896 an outstanding example. Another form of severe windstorm that could cause trouble for river shipping were hurricanes. An unusually bad hurricane hit the lower Mississippi River from the Gulf to above Vicksburg on September 21, 1909. More than three hundred thousand tons of coal on barges were sunk at lower river landings. Many steamboats were sunk at various ports, including the *Belle of the Bends* above Vicksburg. Another casualty was the steamer *Harvester,* which sank at Donaldsonville,

A tornado struck Natchez, Mississippi, on May 7, 1840, resulting in great loss of life and property damage. Several steamboats were destroyed, and many of their passengers drowned. The steamer *Hinds,* seen here, was blown into midstream, and when its wreckage drifted downriver to Baton Rouge, fifty-one bodies were found in the remains. Waves in the river rose ten feet or more, and people found it impossible to stand on shore. Total loss of life was over four hundred. *From Lloyd's Steamboat Directory, 1856*

Louisiana. A new boat, it had lost its cabin in the 1896 tornado at Saint Louis. The 1909 hurricane is generally remembered as "the Big Blow."

The great tornado of May 27, 1896, played havoc with shipping on the Mississippi River at Saint Louis. Rivercraft were lifted bodily out of the water and dashed against the Illinois shore. This picture provides a graphic idea of the magnitude of the storm, which killed 255 persons on both sides of the river, with over $12,000,000 in property damage. The east approach to Eads Bridge was badly damaged, and several ferry boats were completely wrecked. *Courtesy Ardell Thompson Collection*

Wreckage of the Anchor Line packet boat *Arkansas City*, which was blown across the river at Saint Louis by the tornado of May, 1896. *Courtesy Jefferson National Expansion Memorial, National Park Service*

A close-up of the damage sustained by the *Arkansas City* in the 1896 tornado. *Courtesy Saint Louis Public Library*

Steamboats caught in an ice jam at the Saint Louis levee, 1856. *Courtesy Jefferson National Expansion Memorial, National Park Service*

The steamer *Helena* in an ice jam on the Missouri River at Bismarck, North Dakota, 1881. *Courtesy Waterways Journal*

Fog

Fog was a minor problem to steamboat pilots, more of a hindrance than a peril. Since a clear view of the river ahead was imperative, the pilot would tie up to the shore and wait for the fog to lift.

Ice

Ice represented a hazard to steamboating during its formation and breakup. Boats that encountered ice en route usually tried to complete the trip, if possible, rather than lie up at an inconvenient location. In running through thin or drift ice, protective guards were placed at the bow and around the paddle wheels to minimize the danger of damage. When ice broke up in the river, boats moored in exposed positions could have their hulls ripped or crushed by surging ice floes, and sink. Ice could

Scenes during an ice jam at Saint Louis, January, 1888. *Bottom:* wreckage of the U.S. lighthouse tender *Ivy*, crushed against the stern of the *City of Baton Rouge.* *Top:* ferryboat *John Trendley* attempting to relieve the tug *Rescue.* Leslie's Illustrated Newspaper, *February 11, 1888. Courtesy State Historical Society of Missouri*

occur on the northern reaches of the inland waterways from late November until early spring, and navigation was hampered, or suspended, for two or three months. Average suspensions on the upper Mississippi varied from 143 days at Saint Paul, between 1849 and 1866, to 33 days at Saint Louis, between 1866 and 1888.

Ohio River suspensions averaged between eleven and twenty-four days at various times in the nineteenth century. The Ohio below the mouth of the Wabash and the Mississippi below Cairo seldom froze over, although drift ice caused problems in some winters. Severe ice jams, such as at Saint Louis in 1856 and 1866 and at Cincinnati in 1918, were relatively rare. The Mississippi at Saint Louis froze completely across in only several winters during the nineteenth century. Ice and insufficient

water depth still restrict navigation at a few sectors along the Mississippi, but generally only for a short time. Traffic north of Saint Louis is available eight months a year and all year going south. Generally, from March to December, no navigational difficulties are encountered on the Ohio River. In fact, navigation continues throughout the year, except for a few closings.

From 1929 to 1957 at Cincinnati the river was closed only eight times, for an average of three days each time. However, on the Missouri, ice is a problem and compared with the Ohio, Illinois, and Mississippi, the Missouri has played a minor role in the waterways system. The section from its mouth to Kansas City is generally closed to navigation from November 30 to March 15, and the portion above Kansas City is closed a month longer.

The *City of Cincinnati,* crushed by the ice jam at Cincinnati, January, 1918. *Courtesy Waterways Journal*

VIII
Construction and Destruction
on the River

RIVER IMPROVEMENTS

Natural river obstructions were difficult and expensive to remedy and even if an obstruction, such as a sandbar or snag, could be removed at one point, it recurred again elsewhere, in endless succession. Early efforts continued toward eliminating obstacles at specific points, but ultimately the improvement of the entire lengths of some rivers, through canalization, proved necessary. Schemes seeking to eliminate the seasonal limitations imposed by periods of low water usually involved plans for storage reservoirs or for slack-water improvement systems.

General improvements on intrastate rivers obviously could be undertaken only by joint state action or by the Federal government. A four-state survey of the Ohio River was made in 1817–1819,

River-improvement work in progress, 1947—a partially completed timber-piling clump dike at mile 111.9, near Chester, Illinois. *Courtesy U.S. Corps of Engineers, Saint Louis District*

but no action was taken on its recommendations. In 1824 Congress appropriated seventy-five thousand dollars for projects on the Ohio and Mississippi, and approved annual expenditures for the next twenty years. In 1846 President Polk vetoed the river-and-harbor bill as unconstitutional, arousing storms of protest in the Mississippi Valley. Except for the act of 1852, few Federal appropriations for river work were passed until after the Civil War. In 1866 river improvements were authorized in unprecedented form to include even minor tributaries. The largest amounts in history were authorized between 1880 and 1890, but these came too late to be of much benefit in river traffic's losing battle with the railroads. In the twentieth century, the rebirth of river commerce, through barge-line activity, was met by massive government programs of river improvements on all the navigable waterways.

Stone dikes on the Mississippi River north of Cape Girardeau, Missouri, Courtesy U.S. Corps of Engineers, Saint Louis District

ELIMINATING FALLS AND RAPIDS

The worst of the natural barriers, the Falls of Ohio, presented a deceptive appearance, falling only twenty-two feet in two miles. But passage for boats was extremely hazardous, at times impossible, which created a transshipment problem. However, it brought prosperity to the towns located there. In 1825 the Louisville and Portland Canal Company was organized by Kentucky interests and the bypass canal opened in 1830. It was a financial success from the start, but problems of mud and tree trunks left by floods hampered its use. The canal was two miles long and contained three locks, each chamber permitting boats up to 183 feet in length and 49½ feet in beam. Locks almost double in size were completed in 1872, and modern facilities are included in the present Ohio River improvement program.

Muscle Shoals, in northern Alabama, consisted of a series of rapids sixty-five miles long. Its three main falls dropped 134 feet in 29 miles. Except for the Shoals, the Tennessee was navigable for four hundred miles from its mouth to Knoxville. A canal was opened in 1841 but became useless when breaks in its banks were created by a freshet. Nothing more was accomplished until the late 1870s, when the U.S. government took on the job of enlarging the canal. The problem was finally solved

by the construction of the Wilson and Wheeler dams by the T.V.A.

The Mississippi's Lower Rapids, a natural dam of limestone, gave slight evidence of its presence but at low water made passage impossible and difficult at other times. In the late 1830s Army Engineers under Lieutenant Robert E. Lee improved the channel by drilling and blasting. This work continued, though under different supervisors, until after the Civil War, but its limited value led to the river-improvement program in the final steamboat years. A seven-mile-long canal, with three locks, was opened in 1877 on the Iowa side. It was toll-free and could be used at nearly any river level. This was replaced by the present Keokuk lock and dam, completed in 1913. Improvement at the less difficult rapids, the Upper Rapids at Rock Island, consisted in enlarging the natural channel.

SNAG REMOVAL

Snags accounted for more than half of all steamboat accidents up to 1849. Snag removal began shortly after passage of the river act of 1824, when Army Engineers advertised for the best plan to solve the problem. John Bruce, of Kentucky, devised a "machine boat" consisting of two flatboats

U.S. Government Snag Boat No. 2, showing the method used to raise sunken tree trunks, prior to their dismemberment by sawing. *From Harper's Weekly, 1889. Courtesy Saint Louis Mercantile Library Association*

Snag-raising machinery on the double-hulled U.S. Government snag boat *Horatio G. Wright. Courtesy Jefferson National Expansion Memorial, National Park Service*

The *Horatio G. Wright,* about 1910. *Courtesy U.S. Corps of Engineers, Saint Louis District*

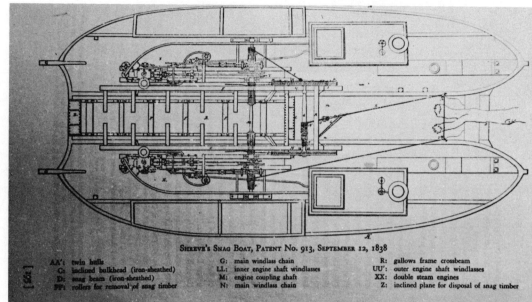

Plan view of Shreve's snag boat, patented in 1838. *From Steamboats on the Western Rivers by Louis C. Hunter, 1949.*

SHREVE'S SNAG BOAT, PATENT No. 913, SEPTEMBER 12, 1838

AA':	twin hulls	G:	main windlass chain	R:	gallows frame crossbeam
C:	inclined bulkhead (iron-sheathed)	LL:	inner engine shaft windlasses	UU':	outer engine shaft windlasses
D:	snag beam (iron-sheathed)	M:	engine coupling shaft	XX:	double steam engines
FF:	rollers for removal of snag timber	N:	main windlass chain	Z:	inclined plane for disposal of snag timber

joined by cross timbers. These supported a wooden lever with an iron claw to seize the snag. The lever was controlled by a long rope attached to a manually operated windlass.

A steam-powered snag boat was designed by Henry M. Shreve when he was in charge of river improvements. Snags weighing up to seventy-five tons could be removed by these boats, which were nicknamed "Uncle Sam's Toothpullers." Snag boats could not operate during periods of high or low water, but were most efficient when snag heads were exposed sufficiently to be engaged by the boat's apparatus.

THE GREAT RAFT OF THE RED RIVER

A tremendous accumulation of snags, logs, and floating trees barred navigation on the Red River below Shreveport, Louisiana. Not a solid mass, but a series of obstructions, it extended for about 150 miles upstream from a point of 25 miles above Natchitoches.

The Raft antedated the nineteenth century and was caused by conditions not present on other rivers. Heavy freshets would sweep across treeless plains to the river and undercut its wooded banks, causing much of this timber to fall into the river. The trees would float downstream to be caught on snags in the slack water of a bend or chute and then begin to build up behind this mass until it extended far up the river. The mass became waterlogged and bound by roots, so as to extend to the

The "Great Raft" on the Red River north of Shreveport, Louisiana, about 1873. From Scribner's Monthly. *Courtesy Saint Louis Mercantile Library Association*

Captain Henry M. Shreve, designer of the first steam-driven snag boat and supervisor in the removal of the Great Raft of the Red River. *From Up the Heights, 1873.*

river bottom, and, acting as a dam, it would cause the river to overflow into a chaos of bayous and swamps. Shreve was given the job of removing the Raft. With snag boats, he set about removing and cutting up the tangled timbers, beginning in the spring of 1833, proceeding about two miles a day. By 1838 the Raft was cleared, and steamboats were able to reach Shreveport. Removal of the obstruction above Shreveport, slowed by natural conditions, was accomplished by 1880. Shreve advocated the prevention of snag formation by the felling of trees along the river before they became undermined.

Snag boats also proved helpful in the removal of boulders and wrecks from river channels. In this work, they were supplemented by diving bells and equipment pioneered by James B. Eads.

REMOVAL OF SANDBARS

Sandbars required much more time and effort in their removal than snags. Since bars, by restricting the current, conserved the water level during dry seasons, their removal could cause stabilization levels too low for navigation. To prevent this, dikes or wing dams of stone and timber were tried. These would concentrate the current in a restricted space,

and the flow would scour a deeper channel across the bar. The scheme was used successfully on the Ohio River before 1830, and a project was built at the mouth of the Cumberland River in 1834. It diverted the channel in the Ohio to Smithland, Kentucky, and removed a bar at the Cumberland's mouth.

Similar work was begun opposite Saint Louis, under Lieutenant Robert E. Lee in 1837, to prevent the channel from retreating from the Missouri side and leaving the city high and dry. Dikes were built to induce the river to flow away from the Illinois side, and to scour away a bar that threatened to preclude steamboat landings at the city's levee. It soon became obvious that while local successes had been made, a general attack upon bars along the entire length of the rivers would be necessary. Unfortunately, only a piecemeal attempt on bars on the Ohio was possible because of the cessation of Federal appropriations after 1846. By the time of the Civil War, most of the early dams had seriously deteriorated through lack of maintenance.

DREDGING

The practice of dredging to clear channels through areas of sand- and gravel bars was not employed ex-

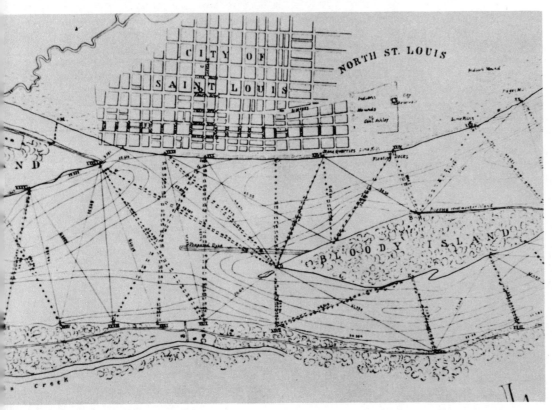

Map of the Saint Louis harbor in 1837, prepared under the direction of Lieutenant Robert E. Lee, showing the location of a proposed dike at the end of Bloody Island. This was planned to direct the river's flow toward the Missouri shore, so as to wash away the sandbar shown below the city. The accumulation of this bar threatened to prevent steamboats from approaching the Saint Louis levee. This was successfully accomplished after the dike work was completed. *Courtesy U.S. Corps of Engineers, Saint Louis District*

U.S. Army Corps of Engineers dredge boat *Thebes*, built in 1898 and used until 1938. This was a dustpan type of dredge, so called because it had a rectangular suction head that was shaped like a common household dustpan. It is equipped with teeth and uses suction in a manner similar to a vacuum cleaner. It moves in a straight line and loosens material on the river bottom with the aid of water jets. The head is connected by a large tube to a rotary pump, which draws a mixture of silt, sand, and water and expels it through a long tube, supported by a series of barges, to a point in the river away from the channel. *Courtesy U.S. Corps of Engineers, Saint Louis District*

tensively until after the Civil War. Started as an effort to combat bars that would not yield to wing dam treatment, the first crude dredges were devised as scrapers drawn across the bars by steamboats. This was intended to loosen the surface of the bar so that the current would wash it away. A twin-hulled, steam-powered "scrape boat," or dredge, was later developed to do the work. The first Federal dredge boat went into operation in 1873.

SURVEYS

Before any general attack upon navigational obstruction on a river-long basis could be launched, a detailed survey was necessary. Such a survey had been started by the Army Engineers in 1836, and had proceeded quite a distance down the Ohio from Pittsburgh before it was discontinued for lack

U.S. Engineers dustpan dredge boat *Fort Gage*, built at Dubuque, Iowa, in 1907 and used until 1946. *Courtesy U.S. Corps of Engineers, Saint Louis District*

U.S. Corps of Engineers dredge boat *Sainte Genevieve*, built in 1932 and still in use. This is a cutterhead type of dredge, which has a semispherical suction head, equipped with knifelike cutters that revolve to cut through harder materials than can be handled by a dustpan dredge. This boat has a capacity of fifteen hundred cubic yards an hour. *Courtesy U.S. Corps of Engineers, Saint Louis District*

Artist's conception of the new *Sainte Genevieve*, now under construction. This five-million-dollar cutterhead replacement is nearing completion. It will be 226 feet long by 58 feet wide and will draw about 6 feet of water. With three thousand horsepower, it will have a dredging capacity of fifty thousand cubic yards a day. *Courtesy U.S. Corps of Engineers, Saint Louis District*

of funds. It was resumed in 1866–1868 to provide fundamental information required for future improvements. Postwar work followed the pattern of wing-dam construction on the Ohio and upper Mississippi. The work was extended to some of the major tributaries as well.

DAMS AND LOCKS

Dams are essential for the maintenance of a fairly even depth of water on navigable rivers to permit year-round operations. Spring floods, summer low-water periods, and winter cold result in considerable variations in the depths of a normal river. These changes can be counteracted by a series of dams. In the process of river canalization, a series of dams control the river flow and store water in slack-water pools above the dams. Adjacent to the dams are the locks, built singly or in pairs, which raise or lower river craft from the level of one pool to another. The locks create a series of watery stair-steps which counteract the changes in elevation of the river's down-slope course. In ascending to the next pool level, a boat will enter the lock at the lower level, and after the lock gates close behind it, the lock chamber is flooded by opening the upper-level gates. When the water in the chamber reaches the elevation of the upper pool, the boat exits through the fully opened upper gates to the higher water level above the dam. The reverse process is used for downstream-bound boats and tows. Dams

An early twentieth-century dam, Dam No. 3 on the Big Sandy River, West Virginia. *Courtesy Waterways Journal*

During low water on the Big Sandy River, Dam No. 1, between West Virginia and Kentucky, built about 1908. *Courtesy Waterways Journal*

Lewis and Clark Lake, created by damming the Missouri River. The lake is thirty-seven miles long. *Nebraska Game Commission photo*

also provide a wide array of such beneficial functions as flood control, irrigation, generation of hydroelectric power, water supply for industry, and water-related recreation on impounded pools.

Lock chambers of adequate size to accommodate the large tows of today are important in the economics of inland waterways barge transportation. Under current Army Corps of Engineers standards, locks up to 110 feet wide by 1200 feet long are being constructed in river improvement work. Locks are designed for the normal passage of boats in twenty or thirty minutes. Oversize tows require double lockage, with a consequent breakup and reassembly of the tow.

The slack-water system of locks and dams was tried with varying degrees of success on several Ohio tributaries, beginning in the 1830s. These streams were too shallow for even the smallest steamboats but were of sufficient commercial importance to justify river improvements. The dams were located to provide a required water stage for navigation, while the locks enabled boats to attain the changing river levels. These projects were delayed because of natural or financial difficulties. The Kentucky River system, begun in 1836, was

suspended in 1842 after completion to Frankfort. A sixty-eight-mile system on the Muskingum was opened between Marietta and Dresden, Ohio, in 1842. Locks and dams on the Green, Barren, and Licking rivers in Kentucky were completed in the early 1840s. The most successful of these early attempts was the system on the lower Monongahela. Plagued by the usual problems and by protests against tolls and navigation impediments by coal boatmen and farmers, it took six years to complete. It was opened in 1844 to Brownsville, Pennsylvania, fifty-five miles above Pittsburgh. The system proved a financial success, first as a connection with the Cumberland Road at Brownsville and later as a transport medium for the local coal trade.

Business losses due to low-water seasons on the Ohio in 1854 and 1856 created a demand for river improvements. The creation of an extensive lock-and-dam system was advocated, but was delayed until after the Civil War. Several methods were proposed: reservoirs, a sluice system, or the diversion of water from Lake Erie. The last proved unfeasible because the lake was lower than the river portion that needed the additional water. The sluice system was considered too experimental,

271

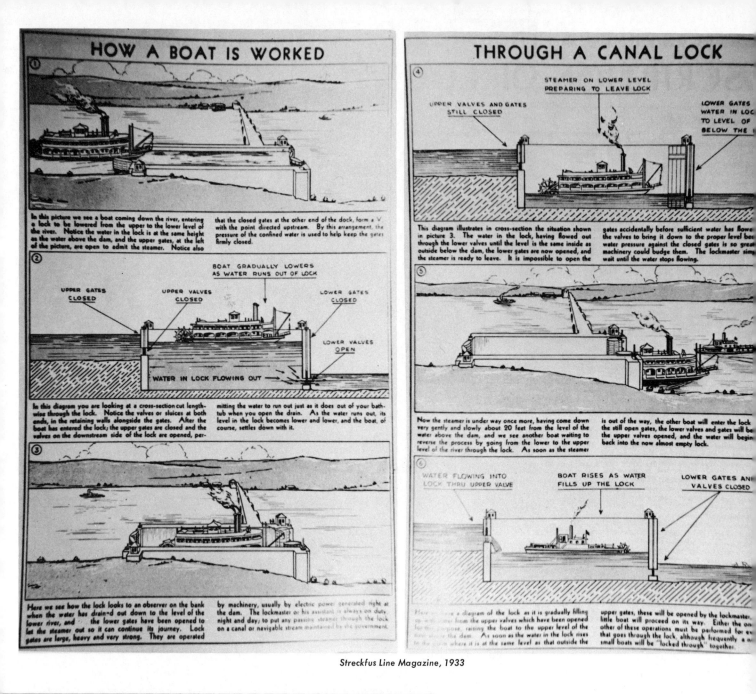

Streckfus Line Magazine, 1933

One of fourteen navigational locks and dams along two hundred miles of the Kentucky River. There is a controlling depth of at least six feet over this entire stretch. *Courtesy Kentucky Department of Public Information*

Modern coal-towboat operators benefit from the early pioneering lock-and-dam solutions. This is a downstream view of the canal that bypasses the difficult Chain of Rocks stretch of the Mississippi River above Saint Louis. *Courtesy U.S. Corps of Engineers, Saint Louis District*

River-channel and levee work was much in demand along such lower Mississippi River areas as this district of Louisiana. The river level is clearly shown to be above the level of the surrounding lowlands. *From Down the Great River, 1887*

while the inundation of valuable land by reservoirs was undesirable, resulting in the ultimate choice of the favored slack-water system.

The transportation picture on the Ohio changed greatly after the Civil War, since railroads had lessened the dependence of shippers upon the river, particularly during low-water stages. The coal trade had been transformed from the use of coal boats riding the flood crests to fleets of barges propelled by sternwheel towboats. The operators of

coal towboats were opposed to any type of dam that would require the breakup of tows for lock passage. The solution chosen by the Army Engineers was a movable wicket type dam of French design. It consisted of a series of heavy, flat timbers, hinged to a riverbed foundation, which could be lowered during high water and raised by a crane boat when the need for a dam arose. In 1875 it was proposed that thirteen such dams be built on the Wheeling-Pittsburgh sector of the Ohio. Despite continued opposition from the coal interests, river-valley opinion realized the need for action. It was shown that coal towing was seasonal and that the more numerous general freight and passenger boats needed year-round navigation. In 1879 Congress authorized the construction of the first Ohio River dam at Davis Island, below Pittsburgh. Its completion in 1885 was marked by a formal celebration inaugurating a new era on the river. This proved to be the beginning of a system of more than fifty dams all the way to Cairo. Beset by many delays, the system was not finally finished until 1929. Currently construction is in progress on a new series of Ohio River locks and dams capable of handling large modern tows.

A Mississippi River Commission was created in 1879 to make surveys and plans relative to channel deepening and bank protection along the Mississippi. Its function was not only navigation improvement, but trade promotion and flood protection as well. Its goal for the upper Mississippi was a maintained channel depth of four and a half to six feet, attained through use of low-water dams to close diversionary channels, construction of dikes or wing dams to concentrate channel flow at wide points, and by dredging and riverbank revetment. This was supplemented by a reservoir plan to store water needed for release during low stages. In the late 1890s passage of the largest boats was possible from Saint Louis to Saint Paul during the low-water periods.

The upper Mississippi runs for 663 miles from Minneapolis to the mouth of the Missouri, and is now dredged to a minimum nine-foot channel by the Army Engineers. Its locks operate for a nine-month season. However, the twenty-six locks in the present system, completed in 1939, are now inadequate for the tows of today. Only the twelve-hundred-foot lock in the Chain of Rocks Bypass

Above the upper entrance to Lock No. 27, at Bi-State harbor, upper Mississippi system. This is on the Chain of Rocks Canal, near Granite City, Illinois. *Courtesy U.S. Corps of Engineers, Saint Louis District*

Entering the Chain of Rocks Canal from the upppr end of Lock No. 27, en route from Saint Louis to Saint Paul with a loaded tow of fifteen barges. *Courtesy U.S. Corps of Engineers, Saint Louis District*

Canal and the lock at Keokuk, Iowa, can handle such tows without double lockage.

The principal achievement on the lower Mississippi after the Civil War was the successful maintenance of New Orleans as a seaport. Larger, oceangoing vessels were unable to cross bars in the Mississippi passes to the Gulf, causing local fears that the city would lose its commercial prominence. The earliest dredging work at the river's mouth was begun following a government survey in 1838. An eighteen-foot depth was attained during the 1850s whenever funds were available. Dredging proved to be unsatisfactory in 1867, and later the construction of jetties at South Pass was proposed by James B. Eads. Begun in 1875, the jetties increased the current in a restricted passage, thus scouring out a deeper channel, which eventually reached a thirty-foot depth.

The Mississippi River Commission decided on a goal of a ten-foot channel upstream to Cairo and an eight-foot one from there to Saint Louis. A

Barge tows about to emerge from the lower end of Lock No. 27, above Saint Louis. *Courtesy U.S. Corps of Engineers, Saint Louis District*

Saint Louis Harbor Model. Model of Mississippi River from just above Chain Rocks Dam to Jefferson Barracks Bridge constructed to a scale of 1:100 vertically and 1:250 horizontally for testing various measures to reduce siltation at the city front at Saint Louis. *Courtesy U.S. Corps of Engineers, Vicksburg District*

Mattress Weaving, part of Mississippi River improvement work in 1884, below Saint Louis, from a series of drawings for *Harper's Weekly*, December 12, 1884, by Charles Graham from photographs by Lieutenant Abbott of the Army Corps of Engineers. *Courtesy State Historical Society of Missouri*

Completed Hurdle Line—view of timber-dike framework. Courtesy State Historical Society of Missouri

Mattress 600 Feet Long Ready to Be Sunk—a mattress of tree branches on a pole framework about to be submerged to help stabilize the riverbed. Courtesy State Historical Society of Missouri

Wattling the Piles—intertwining piles with tree branches as reinforcements in a timber dike. Courtesy State Historical Society of Missouri

Caving Bank at Beard's Island—driving piles to prevent further slippage of the riverbank. Courtesy State Historical Society of Missouri

major objective was to narrow the river at shoal sections in order to stabilize the current, minimize erosion, and create channels across bars. This was to be done with brush-work dikes and stone riprap to set new shorelines, which would be secured by mattress revetments. This program failed in the mid-nineties because of construction delays caused by the unforeseen strength of hydraulic forces.

By this time, the decline in river traffic subordinated the need for navigation measures to flood control which was carried out on the lower Mississippi. This difficult work was characterized by emergencies and disappointments caused by resilting of the channel and the washing out of revetments, as well as breaks in weak levees. Constant research in this work is done by the Army Engineers' River Laboratory at Vicksburg, Mississippi.

The Missouri River has a six-foot channel to Omaha and a four-foot depth beyond there to Sioux City. It is hoped that eventually a nine-foot channel to Yankton, South Dakota, will be maintained on this heavily traveled river. The construction of many earthen dams on the upper Missouri has created vast reservoirs in the Dakotas and Montana, causing disputes between proponents of hydroelectric power and the river interests.

The Illinois River Waterway is canalized and is an important water link between the Mississippi and the Great Lakes. Transshipping at Chicago is hampered by canals with small locks, narrow rivers, low bridges, and close turns at the north end of the Illinois Waterway. Tows that have come up the Illinois and Des Plaines rivers as far as Joliet must be broken up and their barges towed singly for the balance of the distance to Lake Michigan.

The completion in 1971 of the nine-foot channel on the Arkansas River provided adequate locks on the Arkansas and Verdigris rivers.

The Tennessee Valley Act of 1933 led to the nine-foot channel on the Tennessee River from Knoxville to its mouth. This canal includes a series of nine locks and dams, one of which is the spectacular hundred-foot lift at Wilson Dam, above Muscle Shoals. The fifty-two 110-by-600-foot locks in the 1929 Ohio River system are being replaced by 110-by-1200-foot locks now under construction. Besides reducing the necessity for double lockage of large tows, the new lock and dam system will save time and expense by eliminating more than thirty unnecessary lockage operations on the Ohio.

Stone Barges Moving Upstream Over Mattresses—the mattress was weighted with stones to sink it to the riverbed. Courtesy State Historical Society of Missouri

BRIDGES

The bridging of the river at numerous places for railroad crossings was a common cause of complaint by rivermen for a long period. The trouble usually involved low bridge decks, which caused difficulties for boats with high chimneys and masts. Also, they complained about the bridge piers being too close to navigation channels.

Litigation between river interests and bridge builders first occurred in 1849, in a case involving a highway suspension bridge over the Ohio, at Wheeling. A court decision favored the rivermen but it was soon canceled by an act of Congress, which declared the bridge part of a national post road.

The contest between rail and river interests concerning bridges began in the early 1850s over a railroad bridge spanning the Mississippi at Rock Island, Illinois. The first to cross the river, it came to symbolize the steamboatmen's opposition to the railroads. They considered it a threat to river trade —through rail expansion and as a navigational obstruction. It eventually became part of the dispute between Saint Louis and New Orleans against Chicago and the Great Lakes ports.

Following an unsuccessful injunction attempt to stop bridge construction, and a number of minor steamboat accidents, the fight reached its climax in 1856 when the steamboat *Effie Afton* collided with a bridge pier and burned. A damage suit resulted in a hung jury, which was regarded as a victory for the rail interests. The bridge subsequently was declared a hazard to riverboats and was rebuilt between 1868 and 1873. The first railroad bridge across the Ohio River was completed at Steubenville, Ohio, in 1863 and drew protests from steamboat operators. The piers were located so poorly as to create a hazard for towboats and barges. Several later Ohio River bridges caused similar problems. The additional expense of making the spans longer, so that the wide coal tows could pass, was the reason for the offending piers. The problem of low bridge decks was solved by devices lowering steamboat chimneys by telescoping or hinging, a procedure rivermen considered a dangerous nuisance.

The rail network in the upper Mississippi Valley expanded so rapidly that by 1886 the river had been spanned by fifteen railroads. Emotions ran so high in the river–rail bridge controversy that some

The first bridge across the Mississippi, the Rock Island Railroad bridge between Davenport, Iowa, and Rock Island, Illinois, opened in 1855. This was the bridge which drew the ire of rivermen and was the scene of numerous steamboat accidents. *Courtesy Saint Louis Public Library*

To replace the 1855 span, which had been declared a hazard, the Government Bridge between Davenport and Rock Island was completed in 1873. *From* Down the Great River, *1887*

The Hannibal & Saint Joseph Railroad bridge at Quincy, Illinois, built in 1859. This was one of several early spans built across the Mississippi in the late 1850s. *Courtesy Saint Louis Public Library*

The famous Suspension Bridge at Cincinnati, which spans the Ohio River to Covington, Kentucky. It was completed in 1867 and was the first bridge across the river at the Queen City. *From* Cincinnati Illustrated, *1875*

James B. Eads (1820–1887), designer of the great steel-arch bridge at Saint Louis. Eads also invented a diving bell for river-wreck salvage in 1841 and built a fleet of Union iron-clads for use on the Mississippi in the Civil War. He built the Mississippi delta jetties, which helped to maintain New Orleans as an ocean port, during the 1870s. *From History of Saint Louis City and County, J. Thomas Scharf, 1883*

Dedication ceremonies for the opening of the Hannibal Bridge at Kansas City, Missouri, in 1869. This draw span across the Missouri was the first bridge built at Kansas City. *From Harper's Weekly, October 7, 1869. Courtesy Saint Louis Mercantile Library Association*

The Hannibal Bridge with Kansas City in the background. This bridge was supplemented by the Armour-Swift-Burlington Bridge in 1909. *From Harper's Weekly, 1869. Courtesy Saint Louis Mercantile Library Association*

General view of Saint Louis from the Illinois shore, showing the piers erected for the Eads Bridge. Drawing by A. R. Waud. *From Every Saturday Magazine, October 14, 1871. Courtesy Boatmen's National Bank of St. Louis*

Progress on the construction of the Eads Bridge at Saint Louis, about 1873, showing the ribs completed and the roadways begun. *Courtesy U.S. Corps of Engineers, Saint Louis District*

Chicago & Alton Railroad Bridge at Glasgow, Missouri, over the Missouri River, the first all-steel railway bridge in the world. It was constructed in 1878–1879 and was eventually replaced by a new span in 1922. *Courtesy Missouri Historical Society*

The Diamond Jo Line steamer *Dubuque* with its smokestack upper section hinged back for passage under a low bridge. *Courtesy Saint Louis Public Library*

The Huey P. Long Bridge at New Orleans, a modern span. *Courtesy Streckfus Steamers, Inc.*

The John F. Kennedy Bridge over the Ohio River at Louisville, Kentucky. *Courtesy Kentucky Highway Department, Division of Public Affairs*

The West Memphis to Memphis crossing of the Mississippi on U.S. 40-70, the Great River Road. Memphis is shown in the distance. *Courtesy Arkansas Publicity and Parks Commission*

rivermen were charged with contriving boat–bridge accidents to cause removal of the bridges. The railroads' reluctance to build longer and higher bridge spans led to countercharges by river interests that the railroads were trying to block navigation. The dispute was finally solved by government intervention.

NAVIGATION CONTROL INFORMATION

From the earliest years of river navigation, it became obvious that accurate data on river conditions would aid in assuring safe passages. The first serious effort along this line was a river guide called *The Navigator*. Its publication was begun in

1802 by Zadok Cramer, a Pittsburgh printer. The guide contained information about changes in river conditions reported by returning flatboatmen, as well as maps of the river channels. It was the first source to report the many changes in the Mississippi and Ohio river channels wrought by the Great Earthquake of 1811. The *Navigator* had many imitators, but remained preeminent in its field until 1824, when the U.S. government began making river surveys. This was a function of the Army Corps of Engineers. The Corps, once forbidden by law from engaging in flood-control work, was assigned that responsibility following the disas-

The French Grant is opposite Little Sandy in Ohio ; it is a tract of 20,000 acres, extending eight miles on the river, granted by Congress to the French settlers at Galliopolis, as some indemnification for the losses they had sustained ; and 4,000 acres adjoining, granted to Mon. Gervis, for the same purpose. On this last tract Mr. Gervis has laid out a town called BURRSBURGH.

Hale's creek, right side,	12	376
Little Sciota river, 50 yards wide, right side,	2	378

A ledge of rocks puts out here and extends half across the river—the channel at the upper end of the bar is near the left shore ; at the lower end, close a-round the rocks.

Half a mile below Little Sciota is another bar extending also half way across the river ; channel midway between the point of the bar and the left shore.—Just below this last bar on the right bank is *Stony Point* ; and a little above it is every appearance of a body of iron ore.

Tiger's creek, left side,	7	385
Big Sciota river, *(M. D.)*	5	390

This is a large and gentle river of the state of Ohio, bordered with rich flats, meadows, or prairies. It generally overflows in the spring, and then spreads about half a mile, though when confined within its banks it is scarce a furlong wide. Besides having a great extent of most excellent land on both sides of the river, it is furnished with *salt* on an eastern branch, and red bole on Necunsia Skeintat. It is passable for keels, batteaux, &c. a considerable way, and for smaller crafts near 200 miles to a portage of only 4 miles to Sandusky, which empties into lake Erie, and at its mouth is large enough to receive sloops.—The mouth of the Big Sciota river, according to Mr. Hutchins, is in North lat. 38° 43' 28".

CHILICOTHE, at present the seat of government for the state of Ohio, is situated on the west bank of Sciota, 47 miles by land from its mouth. (*See Description, p.* 66)

ALEXANDRIA

Stands immediately below the mouth of Sciota, and

PORTSMOUTH

About half a mile above it. Both these villages are but young, (Portsmouth being the junior,) and they progress but slowly ; but in time may become, from their eligible situation, of considerable consequence.— Goods destined for the upper settlements on the Sciota, are deposited at both these towns, whence they are boated up that river in keels, periogues, &c.

Just above Portsmouth, are high hills topped with pine trees.

Turkey creek right, Conic hills left side,	5	395

Half a mile above this creek, is the residence of Major Belisle.

A page from *The Navigator*, 1808, an indispensable tool for the river pilot. *Courtesy Saint Louis Mercantile Library Association*

The flood that brought in the U.S. Army Corps of Engineers—a crevasse in the Cabin Teel Levee, Louisiana, about fifteen miles above Vicksburg, during the disastrous 1927 flood. *Courtesy U.S. Corps of Engineers, Vicksburg District*

trous Mississippi River flood of 1927. Since then, in response to changing conditions, the Corps has expanded its scope to include water-quality improvement, recreation development, and power generation.

CIVIL WAR IN THE MISSISSIPPI VALLEY

Some of the most active and decisive phases of the Civil War took place in the Mississippi Valley, because possession of its vital resources would strongly influence ultimate victory. The South viewed control of the Mississippi as of the utmost importance in maintaining their flow of supplies west of the river to their armies in the East. The Union considered it essential to gain control of the river to split the Confederacy.

The ironclad *Louisville*, built by James B. Eads for the Union inland waterways navy, completed in 1862. The military necessity for control of the Mississippi River and its navigable tributaries became obvious very early in the Civil War. Attorney-General Edward Bates asked his friend, civil engineer James B. Eads, of Saint Louis, to come to Washington to enforce this theory. Eads had made a fortune in the design and operation of salvage boats to raise steamboat wrecks. He suggested that his *Submarine No. 7* could be converted into an armored gunboat. It later became the ironclad *Benton*. Eads was the low bidder for construction of the newly planned government ironclads, which were designed by Naval Constructor Samuel M. Pook. The resulting boats were humorously called "Pook's Turtles." They had an overall length of 175 feet, a 50-foot beam, and a 7-foot depth in the hold, with a slanting wooden casement to enclose the gun deck, machinery, and paddle wheels. The addition of 122 tons of steel-plate armor resulted from directions of Commander John Rodgers, naval officer in charge. Eads proposed to construct seven gunboats within sixty-four days, four at Carondelet, Missouri, and three at Mound City, Illinois, near Cairo. In September, 1861, Rodgers was relieved by Commodore Andrew H. Foote at Cairo. The construction was delayed by financial difficulties, and the boats were not ready by the contract date of October 10. They were finally commissioned in January, 1862, and saw their first action at Fort Henry early in February. *Courtesy Jefferson National Expansion Memorial, National Park Service*

The ironclad *Cincinnati*, one of seven, built by Eads and named for western-river cities. The four built at Carondelet were the *Saint Louis*, *Carondelet*, *Louisville*, and *Pittsburgh*. The *Cincinnati*, *Cairo*, and *Mound City* were built at Mound City. *Courtesy Jefferson National Expansion Memorial, National Park Service*

The gunboat *Carondelet,* one of the original ironclads, saw her first action at Fort Henry on the Cumberland River. She was the first ironclad to run the batteries at Island No. 10 and suffered damage at Vicksburg in an encounter with the C.S.S. *Arkansas. From American Steam Vessels, 1895*

The *Black Hawk*—Admiral David D. Porter's flagship. When the operation of the Western River Flotilla was transferred from the War Department to the Navy in July, 1862, Commodore, later Admiral, David D. Porter was placed in command. Porter had a large sidewheel steamer converted into a lightly armored "tinclad" for his own use, which became his flagboat *Black Hawk.* Tinclads were designed for speed and light draft to guard Federal communications on the inland waters. *Courtesy Jefferson National Expansion Memorial, National Park Service*

Admiral David D. Porter (1813–1891), foster brother of Admiral Farragut. Porter rendered distinguished service in the Mexican War and the Civil War. During the campaign on the western rivers, he commanded the armored riverboats at New Orleans and during the siege of Vicksburg. Porter was superintendent of the U.S. Naval Academy from 1865 to 1869. *From the Mississippi Valley in the Civil War, 1900.*

The tinclad *Red Rover,* which saw service at Milliken's Bend, above Vicksburg, was converted into the first floating hospital on the western rivers, in 1864. *From Captain Fred Bill's Scrap Book. Courtesy Saint Louis Public Library*

At the onset of hostilities in the valley, Kentucky and Missouri remained neutral, and Union forces were in control of the Ohio River Valley. In Tennessee, Mississippi, and Louisiana, the Southern armies established fortified strongholds along the river. The original Union invasion plan in the Valley called for a gunboat expedition down the Mississippi, from Cairo, to capture and hold strategic positions on the river's banks. These would be used later as bases for sorties into the interior. Difficulties forced revision of the plan to that of using rear-guard operations to force evacuation of Con-

The *Lexington*, a Union wood-clad gunboat that fought in engagements at Columbus-Belmont and Pittsburgh Landing. The *Lexington*, along with the *Tyler* and the *Conestoga*, were the first war vessels converted from river steamers, in May, 1861. From Captain Fred Bill's Scrap Book. *Courtesy Saint Louis Public Library*

Scenes aboard the *Red Rover*, in service from 1862 to 1865. She began her career as a Confederate barracks boat and was captured by the Union navy at Island No. 10 in April, 1862. After conversion, she began her hospital career at Cairo, Illinois. *From Harper's Weekly, May 9, 1863. Courtesy State Historical Society of Missouri*

federate river forts. The Cumberland and Tennessee rivers were cast in prime roles in this plan, along with the railroad network in the southeast. The Confederate lines extended from Columbus, Kentucky, on the Mississippi, through Fort Henry, on the Tennessee, and Fort Donelson, on the Cumberland, to Bowling Green, Kentucky, and thence

The remains of a Civil War gunboat sunk nearly a hundred years ago in the Mississippi River near Kimmswick, Missouri, have been exposed to view by the river's low water level. The wreckage is believed to be that of the *Windsor*, a Union sidewheeler. Her bow was packed solid with railroad ties, then sheathed with iron ribbing so she could ram enemy boats. Before it was ever used, the boat was sunk by an ice jam. *Courtesy U.S. Corps of Engineers, Saint Louis District*

Mortar boats in process of construction. General John C. Frémont was responsible for the construction of a fleet of thirty-eight mortar boats. They were to be rafts of solid timber of sufficient burden to carry a thirteen-inch mortar gun. They were built at Eads shipyard in Carondelet, Missouri. After the addition of false bows and sterns for maneuverability, these mortar boats became operational in March 1862. *From Harper's Pictorial History of the Civil War. Courtesy Saint Louis Mercantile Library Association*

eastward through Tennessee. The Union campaign early in 1862 placed a Federal army opposite the Confederates at Bowling Green, while another, supported by a fleet of gunboats, ascended the Tennessee from Paducah and captured Fort Henry. The boats then returned to the Ohio and ascended the Cumberland to meet the army at Fort Donelson, which capitulated after a fierce struggle. Union armies under Grant and Buell pressed the newly withdrawn Southern lines at Shiloh, Tennessee, early in April, 1862, and turned one of the bloodiest battles of the war into a Confederate disaster.

The Southern forces met additional defeats on the Mississippi at Island Number Ten, above New Madrid, Missouri, and at New Orleans, which surrendered to Admiral Farragut on April 25, 1862. These Union victories gave the North control of the northern and southern reaches of the Mississippi below Cairo, with the Confederates maintaining strongholds at Vicksburg, Mississippi, and Port Hudson, Louisiana. Corinth, Mississippi, and

View of the Mississippi River from Columbus-Belmont Battlefield State Park, Kentucky. Columbus was occupied by Confederate troops in September, 1861, in violation of Kentucky's neutrality. They were ordered out on September 11 when the state rejoined the Union. A Union joint army-navy expeditionary force struck at Belmont, Missouri, opposite Columbus, in November, 1861. The wooden Union gunboats proved to be ineffective against the bluff-top batteries at Columbus. After the fall of Forts Henry and Donelson in February, 1862, the Confederates were forced to evacuate Columbus and surrender to Commodore Foote on March 2, 1862. *Courtesy Kentucky Department of Public Information*

Memphis, Tennessee, fell to the North in June, principally because resistance became futile. The important railway from Memphis to Chattanooga was destroyed. Vicksburg, the last major stronghold, thanks to its batteries, remained impregnable to assaults by Union ironclads under Admiral Porter. Vicksburg's eventual fall was essentially an army campaign. The river fleet served a supporting role to Grant's army, which crossed the river and attacked the fortress from the rear. With the fall of Vicksburg, the Union gained complete control of the Mississippi by capturing Port Hudson in the last river engagement of the war on July 9, 1863. This enabled the river, in the happy expression of President Lincoln, "to run unvexed to the sea."

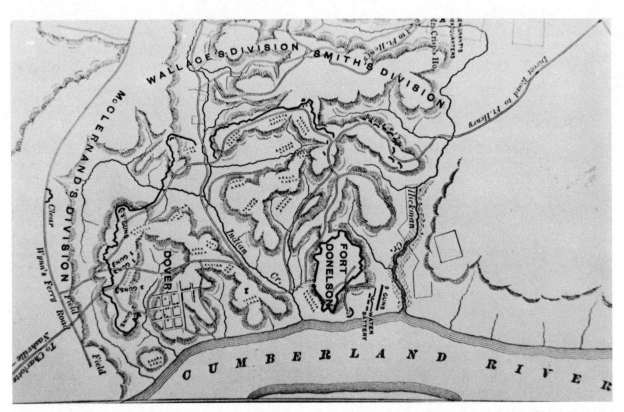

Fort Donelson had three well-placed batteries on bluffs above the Cumberland River. The ironclads sustained damage by moving in too close to the short-range guns and retired downstream. The fort was taken later by Army overland action. *From* The Mississippi Valley in the Civil War, *1900*

Gunboat attack on Fort Donelson. The Confederates achieved victory over the river navy at Fort Donelson with withering fire from batteries near the fort. But the stronghold fell to General Grant's army on February 16, 1862, following a two-day siege. *From* Harper's Pictorial History of the Civil War

Civil War cannon at Fort Donelson National Military Park. *Courtesy State of Tennessee Conservation Department*

Foote's gunboats ascending the Tennessee River to attack Fort Henry. The flotilla of gunboats and ironclads made rendezvous at Paducah with Union troop transports, which they escorted up the river for the attack on Fort Henry in February, 1862. *From Harper's Pictorial History of the Civil War. Courtesy Saint Louis Mercantile Library Association*

General Grant's capture of Forts Henry and Donelson in 1862 was the first real success for the North. After a bloody victory at Shiloh, Grant began the campaign for Vicksburg, which fell after a long siege on July 4, 1863. His armies won a decisive victory at Chattanooga, and, in 1864, President Lincoln made him commander-in-chief of the Union forces. Grant directed the Wilderness Campaign against Lee, culminating in the surrender of the Confederates at Appomattox on April 9, 1865. *From* The Mississippi Valley in the Civil War, *1900*

Bowling Green, Kentucky, was an important Confederate military head-quarters in a defensive line across southern Kentucky. It was evacuated on February 14, 1862, following the fall of Fort Henry. *From Harper's Pictorial History of the Civil War*

Nashville, Tennessee, in Civil War times. When the retreating Southern forces from Bowling Green reached Nashville, they learned that Fort Donelson had also fallen to the North. This made Nashville untenable, so it too was abandoned, on February 23, 1862, two days before the arrival of Union troops under General Buell. *From Harper's Pictorial History of the Civil War*

Nathan Bedford Forrest State Park Monument on the Tennessee River, where the Confederate cavalry sank Union gunboats. *Courtesy State of Tennessee Conservation Department*

Hamburg Landing, a Confederate commissary depot on the Tennessee River, was an important supply point during the Battle of Shiloh. *From Harper's Pictorial History of the Civil War*

The Battle of Shiloh, April 7, 1862. A prime Union objective in early 1862 was the capture of Corinth, Mississippi, which was strategically located at the junction of the principal railroads from Memphis to the East and from Tennessee points toward the Gulf. The Confederates under Generals A. S. Johnston and P. T. Beauregard tried to attack General Grant's army before reinforcements could arrive. The Southerners only succeeded in delaying Grant, in the bloody engagement near Pittsburg Landing and Shiloh, Tennessee, in which twenty-four thousand casualties were sustained. This map shows positions on the morning of the last day of the battle. *From The Mississippi Valley in the Civil War, 1900*

The Tennessee River steamboat *Chickamauga* after conversion for military use. Note boarded-up sides of pilothouse. Photo by E. A. Mueller. *Courtesy Waterways Journal*

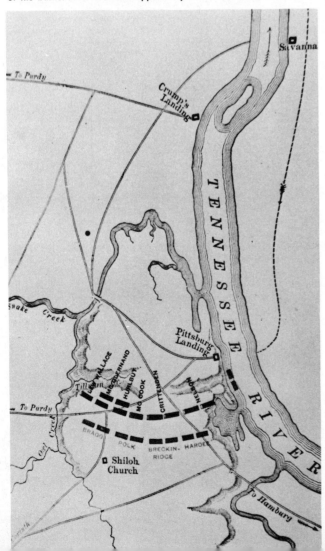

The Union troop transport *W. B. Terry* attempting to bypass Island No. 10 during Mississippi River operations near New Madrid, Missouri, 1862. *Courtesy State Historical Society of Missouri*

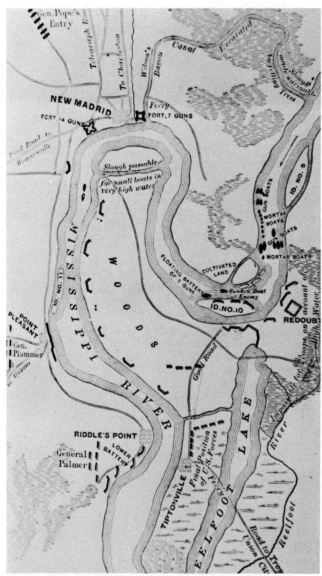

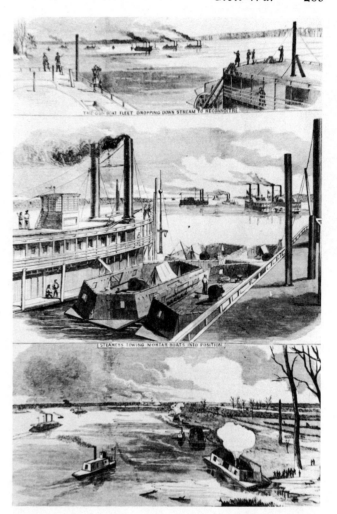

Bombardment from mortar boats against Island No. 10. These boats saw their first action here attacking batteries which effected a blockade above New Madrid. They enabled the shelling of the enemy from a considerable distance upstream, as a preliminary to closer attack by gunboats. *From Harper's Pictorial History of the Civil War*

Following operations on the Tennessee and Cumberland rivers, Commodore Foote's gunboats were dispatched to the Mississippi to aid General Pope in the attack on Island No. 10. This is the plan of New Madrid and Island No. 10, March-April, 1862. The islands in the Mississippi, at the time of the Civil War were numbered downstream from the mouth of the Ohio at Cairo. Island No. 10 was in a bend above New Madrid, Missouri, and was well fortified by the Confederates with more than fifty guns and a floating battery of sixteen more. The batteries were finally silenced by the ironclads *Carondelet* and *Pittsburgh*, which had managed to run past the island on successive nights. The outflanked Southerners then retreated and surrendered. *From* The Mississippi Valley in the Civil War, *1900*

The *Carondelet* running the Confederate batteries at Island No. 10. The Union ironclad ran past the fortified blockade on April 3, 1862, to reach New Madrid, Missouri, and aid General John Pope in crossing the river to the eastern bank. *From Harper's Pictorial History of the Civil War*

A Currier and Ives print of the bombardment of Island No. 10, at the height of the attack. *Courtesy Saint Louis Public Library*

New Orleans, 1862. The South's largest city surrendered to Admiral David G. Farragut on April 29, 1862, following a five-day battle in which the Union fleet fought off an ineffective Confederate navy and silenced Forts Jackson and Saint Philip. *From* Harper's Pictorial History of the Civil War

In the river battle preceding the capture of New Orleans, Admiral Farragut's flagship, the *Hartford,* was grounded on a shoal in a vain attempt to avoid a blazing raft being pushed toward her. The flames caught and danced halfway to her mastheads, but Farragut's calm leadership prevailed and his well-disciplined crew managed to extinguish the fires. *From* Harper's Illustrated History of the Civil War

Admiral David G. Farragut (1801–1870) became a midshipman at the age of nine against Gulf Coast pirates and served in the Mexican War. He was stationed at Norfolk when Virginia seceded, but offered his services to the North. By capturing New Orleans in 1862, and running past Port Hudson, Louisiana, he gained control of the Mississippi to Vicksburg. Farragut captured Mobile, Alabama, in 1864, and following the war, he was made a full admiral in 1866. *From* The Mississippi Valley in the Civil War, *1900*

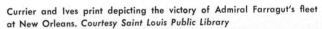

Currier and Ives print depicting the victory of Admiral Farragut's fleet at New Orleans. *Courtesy Saint Louis Public Library*

The Battle of Saint Charles on the White River in Arkansas. In June, 1862, a three-vessel expedition from the Western Flotilla engaged in an abortive sortie up the White River. At the town of Saint Charles, about thirty miles upstream from the Arkansas River, a Confederate shore battery scored a hit on the boiler of the Union ironclad *Mound City*. About 140 casualties from scalding and drowning resulted from the lack of wooden bulwarks to enclose the machinery. The Union gained control of the Arkansas River with the capture of Fort Hindman, at Arkansas Post, in a joint army-navy action in January, 1863. *From Harper's Pictorial History of the Civil War*

Colonel Charles Ellet, Jr., a civil engineer, was the creator of the Union ram fleet, which was made of converted commercial steamboats. It represented the revival of a style of naval warfare that had been unused for several centuries. The introduction of steam navigation made the power-driven ram principle practical as a directed force impossible with sailing vessels. The Confederates used a fleet of rams to advantage against Union ironclads in the Battle of Plum Point Bend on May 10, 1862. Ellet's rams differed from the Confederate version in that their machinery was placed on deck rather than in the hold. This made possible stronger hull structures for more powerful ram thrusts. *From Harper's Pictorial History of the Civil War*

Colonel Ellet's ram approaching Memphis. When the Confederates decided to abandon Forts Pillow and Randolph on the river above Memphis, they fell back on that city for a new defensive position. Since Memphis was not fortified, its defense relied upon their victorious ram boats of the Plum Point Bend battle. On June 6, 1862, this fleet was attacked by five Union ironclads and two of Ellet's rams, the *Queen of the West* and the *Monarch*. The ensuing battle became a rout as the Union navy smashed the Southern rams with deadly gunfire in a running downriver engagement. Memphis fell to the Union in one of the war's most one-sided Northern triumphs. *From Harper's Pictorial History of the Civil War*

Banks landing at Baton Rouge, Louisiana. General Nathaniel P. Banks's army was en route from New Orleans to Vicksburg to aid Porter and Sherman in a second attack there in December, 1862. However, Banks got no further upriver than Baton Rouge on this expedition. *From* Harper's Pictorial History of the Civil War

A wartime view of Baton Rouge in 1862. *From* Harper's Pictorial History of the Civil War

The Union gunboat fleet on the Red River, under Admiral Porter, joined the army of General Banks in the occupation of Alexandria, Louisiana, on May 7, 1863. The Confederate army had just evacuated and was retreating toward Shreveport. *From* Harper's Pictorial History of the Civil War

The *Lancaster* and the *Switzerland* running the Vicksburg batteries. In March, 1862, Admiral Farragut decided to place a new blockade at the mouth of the Red River. When he learned of the absence of Admiral Porter, Farragut suggested to Grant at Vicksburg, that some rams should be sent past the batteries there to join his two vessels in the blockade. General Alfred Ellet took command of the ram fleet at Vicksburg and dispatched the rams *Lancaster* and *Switzerland* to run past the guns to reach Farragut downriver. In the dawn of March 25, the two rams started past Vicksburg, but there was sufficient daylight for them to be observed by Confederate gunners. The *Switzerland* suffered a direct hit on her middle boiler, setting her afire. The *Lancaster*, astern, was penetrated by a shot below the waterline, causing her to sink, a total loss. The *Switzerland*, though damaged, was repaired and later rejoined the fleet in the blockade of the Red River. *From* Harper's Pictorial History of the Civil War

Admiral Porter's "dummy." A temporary break in the period of Confederate control of the Mississippi below Vicksburg was achieved by a dummy vessel improvised by Admiral Porter to resemble an armored sidewheeler. It fooled the Confederate gunners at Vicksburg as it drifted past, as they blasted away with no apparent effect. The dummy also led to the scuttling of the captured Union ironclad *Indianola* by the Confederates in an effort to prevent its seemingly imminent recapture by the approaching presumed powerful vessel. *From* Harper's Pictorial History of the Civil War

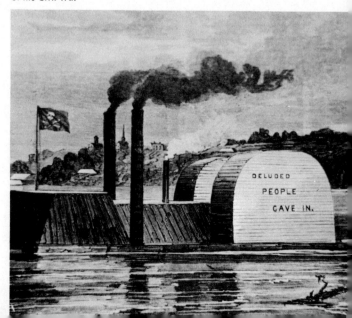

Plan of the defense of Vicksburg. Vicksburg, Mississippi, was the principal strategic stronghold in the Confederacy, providing a vital link as the only cross-river railroad connection between Memphis and New Orleans. The city joined the two parts of the South, which were separated by the Mississippi River. The Confederates developed an invulnerable system of defenses here, which repelled an attack by Farragut in the summer of 1862 and a joint land-river operation by Sherman and Porter in December of that same year. *From* Harper's Pictorial History of the Civil War

The *Arkansas* running through the Union fleet off Vicksburg. The Confederate ram *Arkansas* emerged from the Yazoo in pursuit of units of the Union fleet on July 15, 1862. Seeking the protection of the Vicksburg batteries, the powerful *Arkansas* ran through the entire Union fleet anchored in the Mississippi above the town. Although she was severely damaged, the Confederate ironclad managed to reach safety and resisted later Union attempts to destroy her. *From* Harper's Pictorial History of the Civil War

Admiral Porter's fleet at the mouth of the Yazoo River. Late in November, 1862, Grant's army was moving southward toward Vicksburg from western Tennessee. General Sherman informed Admiral Porter about this expedition, and suggested the possibility of naval support up the Yazoo, in a pincer movement with Grant against the Confederate army of General John C. Pemberton. When Porter's fleet reached the Yazoo, low water prevented his ironclads from ascending the river until December 12, when the fleet engaged in a mine-clearing effort on the lower Yazoo below Drumgould's Bluff. *From* Harper's Pictorial History of the Civil War

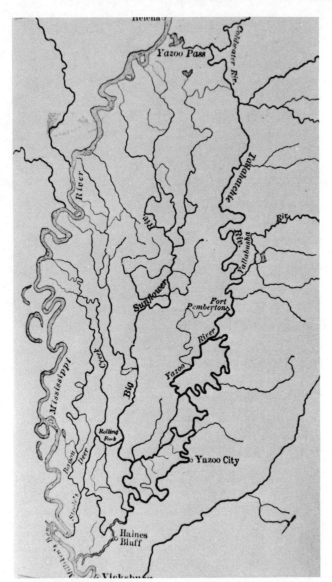

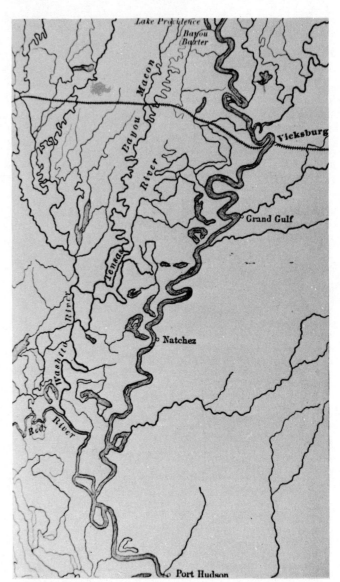

The Yazoo Pass and Big Sunflower experiments of February and March, 1863. Northern ironclads unsuccessfully attempted to get behind the Vicksburg batteries by navigating the Yazoo River and bayous above the city. Access had been obtained through a levee cut, which reopened the Yazoo Pass from the Mississippi below Helena, Arkansas. Progress was impeded by trees felled across the narrow streams by the aforewarned enemy. *From* The Mississippi Valley in the Civil War, *1900*

The Lake Providence experiment of February and March, 1863. As an attempt to outflank Vicksburg by water, the Union forces tried to open a southbound route from Lake Providence through swamps and bayous to the Red River and thence up the Mississippi toward Vicksburg. This idea was abandoned because of difficulties involved in clearing passage through the Bayou Baxter Swamp. *From* The Mississippi Valley in the Civil War, *1900*

The *Queen of the West* and the *Vicksburg*. On February 1, 1863, Colonel Charles R. Ellet was ordered by Admiral Porter to take one of the fast Union rams past Vicksburg to patrol the lower river and to destroy every vessel she met. Ellet prepared the ram *Queen of the West* for this mission by placing layers of cotton bales to protect her most vulnerable sections. Ellet had hoped to leave before daylight, but a late departure found her before the Vicksburg batteries at sunup on February 2. The Confederates opened fire instantly, as Ellet discovered the enemy transport *Vicksburg* moored at the town levee. Ellet found it necessary to approach the *Vicksburg* from across the current, thereby diminishing the effect of a blow by the ram. After striking an ineffective blow on the transport, Ellet fired a combustible "turpentine ball" from his bow gun into the *Vicksburg*, whose crew succeeded in dousing the resulting flames. The bow-gun discharge ignited some of the cotton bales on the *Queen*, causing Ellet to retire downstream under intense enemy fire. After reaching a point beyond the enemy's range, the *Queen* also ran past the fortress at Warrenton, below Vicksburg, and after being repaired was free to cruise in the lower river waters. *From* Harper's Pictorial History of the Civil War

Grant's transports running the batteries at Vicksburg. Grant's plan to attack Vicksburg from the south, necessitated moving downriver from the Yazoo. Most of the fleet ran past the batteries on the night of April 16, 1863, and ten days later Grant's troop transports and supply boats succeeded in running the gauntlet. This placed Grant's army in a strategic position to cross the Mississippi River and led to the eventual fall of Vicksburg. *From* Harper's Pictorial History of the Civil War

The opening of the Mississippi after Vicksburg—the arrival of the steamboat *Imperial* at New Orleans from Saint Louis on July 16, 1863. This was the first steamer to complete the trip in more than two years. *From* Harper's Pictorial History of the Civil War

The *Queen of the West* was lost in an engagement at Gordon's Landing, Louisiana, on the Red River in February, 1863. This was the result of a rash effort by Colonel Ellet to capture three Southern transports by surprise. The enemy learned of the ram's approach and opened fire from a shore battery with devastating effect. The damaged ram had to be abandoned and was captured by a Confederate boarding party. *From* Harper's Pictorial History of the Civil War

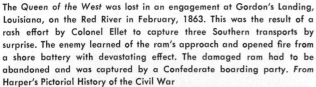

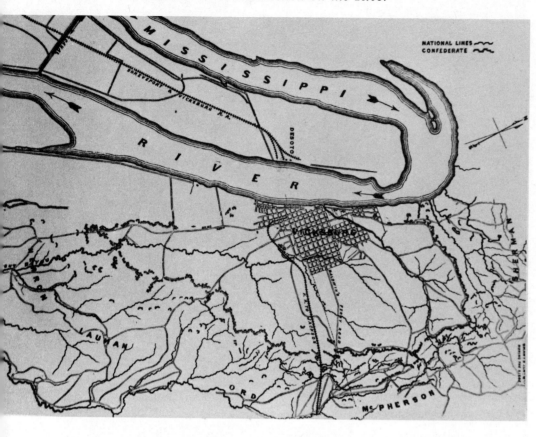

Map of Vicksburg and vicinity during the siege by the Union army from May 18 to July 4, 1863, when it finally capitulated to General Grant. *From Harper's Pictorial History of the Civil War*

Six-ton anchor with chain, which was stretched across the river by the Confederates in an attempt to block river traffic from the north. *Courtesy Kentucky Department of Public Information*

Chain links from a chain that obstructed the passage of boats on the Mississippi during the war. *Courtesy Missouri Historical Society*

IX
Decline of the Steamboat

The decade between 1850 and 1860 is sometimes referred to as the Golden Age of steamboating on the western rivers, a true description in some respects, though this decade also marked the beginning of the final decline of steamboating. Construction of new railroads was making itself felt in reduced traffic on the waterways. The fifties were also significant from the standpoints of serious steamboat disasters and a series of low-water periods, slowing river traffic in several years. Competition from a new form of river transport, the towboat and barge, began to make inroads into the packet lines' freight revenues.

The role of the railroad in the steamboat's decline can be better comprehended by an understanding of the national transportation pattern before 1850. This system was based on natural inland waterways, with the Mississippi and Ohio rivers playing a key part in the circuitous marine route from the industrial East to the Midwest, via sea and river through New Orleans. This was made necessary by the barrier of the Appalachian Moun-

Progress of the Century. Currier and Ives depict the triumph of technology in the nineteenth-century industrial revolution. The newspapers, telegraph lines, steamboats, and railroads are representative of the new order of civilization. *Courtesy Saint Louis Public Library*

Even in the golden age of steamboating, the railroads were beginning to parallel the rivers. View of Saint Louis. *From Thoughts about St. Louis, John Hogan, 1854. Courtesy Saint Louis Mercantile Library Association*

Competition for the western rivers, the building of the Erie Canal at Lockport, New York. This canal, which linked the Great Lakes to the Hudson River and the Atlantic Ocean, was completed in 1825. It helped the lake ports to wrest inland marine commerce from the western rivers, by providing a shorter route to the eastern seaboard. *From The North American Tourist, 1839*

Completion of the Erie Canal in 1825 made New York the dominant seaport in the East and created a vast tributary area in the Great Lakes region. The Erie Canal water route extended its commercial influence into midwestern regions, which formerly relied upon the western rivers. The lake ports expanded their commercial supremacy into the river valleys by means of canals and railroads. Water connections were made between Lakes Erie and Michigan, to the Ohio and Mississippi rivers, through the Ohio Canal—from Cleveland to Portsmouth, Ohio—in 1832, and the Illinois-Michigan Canal in 1848. The latter canal gave Chicago an outlet to the Mississippi. Two-way traffic over these artificial waterways and the Great Lakes followed a

The old Illinois and Mississippi Canal, connecting the Illinois River with the Mississippi River at Rock Island. *Courtesy State of Illinois, Department of Conservation*

A long unused chain-lift bridge on the old Illinois and Mississippi Canal. This canal formerly provided a waterway between northern Illinois and points on the upper Mississippi River. *Courtesy State of Illinois, Department of Conservation*

tains to direct overland transport from New York to the Ohio River Valley, through Pittsburgh. The Appalachian barrier was eventually reduced through the construction of railroads, turnpikes, and canals connecting the eastern seaboard and the Great Lakes with the Ohio and Mississippi Valleys.

much shorter, and less expensive, route to the East than was possible through New Orleans.

Railroad construction proceeded at a rapid pace during the 1850s, so that at the decade's end all of the important river cities were joined by rail. This started a steady diversion of passenger and freight business from the steamboats to the swifter railroads. By 1857 the Ohio and Mississippi Railroad was completed to the east bank of the river opposite Saint Louis, affording a short cut by rail from Ohio River cities to the West. North-south lines paralleling the Mississippi River were soon under construction, principally the Illinois Central route from Chicago to New Orleans. The full effect of

this line on river traffic was delayed by the Civil War, and was not felt seriously until the late 1870s. In the southeast, river commerce on the Tennessee and Cumberland was diverted by completion of the Louisville and Nashville Railroad in 1859. This line provided a short cut to lower Mississippi Valley points from Nashville and the mid-South.

The decline in steamboat traffic, first felt on the Ohio River trunk packet lines, was balanced by the brisk trade on the Missouri and upper Mississippi rivers. However, during the 1850s six railheads were established at points along the Mississippi between Saint Louis and Saint Paul, giving the upper valley direct contact with the Atlantic seaboard.

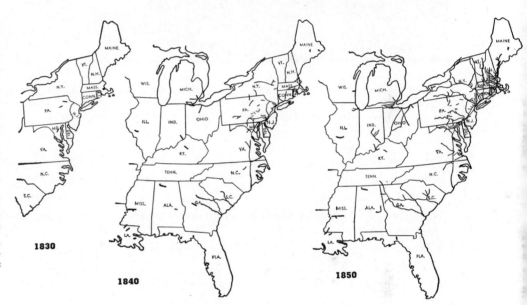

The growth of American railroad lines—1830-1840-1850. The early stages of railway development in America are shown by this set of maps. During the decade 1830–1840, the total length of completed railroad lines increased from 23 to 2,808 miles, and during the next ten years, more than 6,200 miles of railroad were opened, bringing the total network up to 9,021 miles in 1850. The most intensive growth during this period was in the Atlantic seaboard states. In 1850 a trip from Boston or New York to Chicago was made by rail and lake steamers or by stagecoaches, and required several days. One could travel all the way from Boston to Wilmington, North Carolina, by rail, with several changes of cars and a few ferry trips en route. During the first twenty years of railway development, covered by these maps, the population of the United States nearly doubled. *Courtesy of the Association of American Railroads*

1830   1840   1850

The American railroad network in 1860. This map shows the extent of railway development just prior to the Civil War. The decade 1850–1860 was a period of rapid railway expansion, characterized by the extension of many short, disjointed lines into important rail routes. This decade marked the beginning of railway development in the region west of the Mississippi River. By 1860 the iron horse had penetrated westward to the Missouri River and was beginning to make itself felt in Iowa, Arkansas, Texas, and California. *Courtesy of the Association of American Railroads*

Painting by Frank B. Nuderscher depicting the arrival at Saint Louis of the first locomotive for the Pacific Railroad. Shipped by ocean freight from the builders in Taunton, Massachusetts, it arrived via riverboat from New Orleans on August 20, 1852. This is not a factual scene, since the engine arrived "knocked-down" in crates, and cartage cost two hundred dollars to haul it to the rail depot where it was actually assembled, but this is artistic license and does make a more dramatic scene. *Courtesy Missouri Pacific Railroad*

For a few years riverboats made profitable connections for transshipments from the railheads to other river ports. Shipment to Saint Louis in the upper-valley trade above Galena was diverted from river to rail by way of Chicago and Milwaukee. The end of river traffic on the Missouri was foreseen when the railroad was completed to Saint Joseph, Missouri, in 1859. On the eve of the Civil War, dependence of valley commerce upon steamboats was obviously in decline.

In the advancing competition between the steamboat and the railroad, the speed advantage of the rails manifested itself in passenger trade. As railroad accommodations increased in luxury during the postbellum era, even the most elaborate packets began to lose passengers to the trains. Because of the high rail rates for freight, bulk shipments continued to be transported by water, at much lower costs, for some time. Only during periods of low water were the railroads able to draw much heavy freight business from the rivers. The railroads, which had early taken over light freight, eventually gained most of the heavy haulage as well. Aiding this was their independence of such natural conditions as river levels. River shipments of coal from the Pittsburgh area were interrupted by low water during several years in the 1850s,

causing a severe fuel shortage in downriver cities. Shipment by rail became imperative, and these occasions emphasized railroad dependability at the expense of river traffic. A midwestern enthusiasm for railroads greatly increased rail construction, and a consequent slackening in river-borne commerce ensued.

Another competitive disadvantage against the

The speed and efficiency of rail travel quickly outspaced the steamboat. Currier and Ives print, late nineteenth century. *Courtesy Saint Louis Public Library*

Bulk shipments continued to travel the river. Here a large riverside industrial plant of the mid-nineteenth century—the meat-packing firm of Milward & Oldershaw, Covington, Kentucky, in 1850—maintains facilities for loading shipments on steamboats. *From Cincinnati in 1851, Charles Cist*

How the railroads could restrict access to the waterfront in urban areas—the Mississippi riverfront in south Saint Louis, with the Iron Mountain Railroad running along close to the riverbank. *From Pictorical Saint Louis, 1875*

steamboat lines was their inability to expand their commercial areas by branching out. Extension of navigation to tributaries not previously reached by boat either was impossible or economically unfeasible due to the high costs of canalization. The larger the area reached by rail expanded, the greater did the business generated thereby contribute to bigger railroad organizations—capitalized on a scale impossible for packet lines. Flexibility of service was another railroad advantage over river traffic. Tracks could be laid anywhere that business needs

dictated, with spur lines directly up to factory loading platforms, and train sizes could be adjusted to meet differing conditions of traffic volume. The steamboat, conversely, was restricted by a fixed size of displacement and number of staterooms available. Also, the more direct rail routes were far shorter than the lengths of the meandering rivers. For example, by rail Cairo to New Orleans was 560 miles, while by river it was 973 miles. Between Pittsburgh and Cairo, comparable distances were 675 and 979 miles respectively.

Towboats and barges in the postbellum period, though they continued to haul timber and coal into the twentieth century, branched out to include general merchandise. Acres of coal here await high water for passage down the Ohio River, 1908. *Courtesy U.S. Corps of Engineers, Pittsburgh District*

The Saint Louis levee about 1916, showing the preemption of an urban riverfront for railroad use. View is looking north from the Municipal Bridge. *Courtesy City Plan Commission, City of Saint Louis*

Towboat and wooden coal flats, about 1910, on Pittsburgh's south side. *Courtesy U.S. Corps of Engineers, Pittsburgh District*

Tracks could be laid anywhere. *Across the Continent,* a Currier and Ives print of 1870, shows how townsites developed along the new transcontinental railroad, spreading civilization into the American West. *Courtesy Saint Louis Public Library*

BARGE COMPETITION

In the decades after the Civil War, the use of towboats and barges began to branch out from the exclusive haulage of timber and coal in rafts or tows. Carrying cargoes of general merchandise placed tows in direct competition with individual steamboats for freight business. Since barge rates were lower, they became a serious factor in long-distance runs for bulk commodities. A general loss of freight business to the barges failed to materialize because of the barge lines' inability to handle the short-haul trades. Transient steamboats in the distance trades were affected the most by barge competition; short-trade operators continued quite profitably until the turn of the century.

302

RIVER VS RAIL—RIVALRY BETWEEN SAINT LOUIS AND CHICAGO

Illuminating the decline of the steamboat is the struggle for commercial supremacy between the river port of Saint Louis and the railroad center of Chicago, a contest eventually decided in favor of the Windy City. The emergence of the rail lines as the dominant mode of transport in the Mississippi Valley and the West ended it.

Chicago had been a comparatively late arrival among midwestern cities and was not incorporated as a city until 1833. By then Saint Louis was well on its way to becoming the premier river port in the Mississippi Valley. By 1850 Chicago, after surviving the panic of 1837, became the nation's leading grain market and was the railroad capital of the country on the eve of the Civil War. Chicago's most important chapter in railroad history was its becoming the east-west rail link at the completion of the transcontinental railroad in 1869.

From Chicago, the railroad continued in a direct line through Omaha. The decision to build the Union Pacific Railroad westward from Omaha had included a role by Saint Joseph, Missouri, in 1861. In addition to being the eastern terminus for the Overland Stage and the Pony Express, this city, which had grown from a fur-trading post, had become a leading portal to the West through its position as the westernmost railhead upon completion of the Hannibal and Saint Joseph Railroad in 1859.

A singular incident had cost Saint Joseph its chance to become the starting point of the transcontinental railroad: on May 23, 1861, a proslavery mob tore down an American flag at the post office. Saint Joseph was predominantly Southern in its sympathies at the outbreak of the Civil War. On December 2, 1862, President Lincoln made the decision to start the railroad westward from Omaha. This event had been foreshadowed, when the transcontinental telegraph was built up the Missouri River valley from Saint Joseph to Omaha, and thence westward through the Platte Valley.

Because the railroad through Omaha was on a direct line west from Chicago, its completion to California gave a powerful impetus to Chicago's progress, leading to the city's tremendous growth in the last quarter of the nineteenth century.

Currier and Ives print showing a crack express train outpacing a steamboat along a river. *Courtesy Saint Louis Public Library*

Saint Joseph, Missouri, played an important role in the destiny of the West at the time of the building of the transcontinental railroad in the late 1860s. *From Missouri* As It Is in 1867, *Nathan H. Parker*

Saint Louis suffered a commercial setback from the Civil War, which caused a suspension of its river traffic to the South. After the war, Missouri's metropolis continued to place its commercial faith in the steamboat, with a minor reliance on railroads. Saint Louis interests had been unsuccessful in efforts to build a railroad to California via a southern route. As the nation turned increasingly to rail commerce, Saint Louis lost ground in its contest with Chicago. Chicago exceeded Saint

The railroad reaches the Pacific, 1870. Although the American Civil War temporarily halted railway development, many projects were resumed or initiated soon after the close of that conflict. The nation's network increased from 30,626 miles in 1860 to 52,922 miles in 1870. An outstanding development of the decade was the construction of the first railroad to the Pacific Ocean, making it possible for the first time to travel all the way across the country by rail. Railway development in the Mississippi and Missouri valleys was especially notable during this period. *Courtesy Association of American Railroads*

The popularity of the railroads is attested by this urban scene in a Currier and Ives print of the 1870s. *Courtesy Saint Louis Public Library*

Louis considerably in population by 1880, and was never second thereafter. This trend found its parallel wherever competion for trade dominance developed between the railroads and the rivers.

THE RAILROAD IS VICTORIOUS

In the closing decades of the nineteenth century the supremacy of the railroads over the rivers in commercial competition grew increasingly evident.

The railroad network continued to grow at a rapid pace, reaching out to towns and areas far from any navigable rivers. Even along the rivers, the railroads enjoyed the superiorities of greater speed and shorter distance. Where steamboat traffic had survived, it was soon eliminated by railroads built to tap business from towns that had depended upon the rivers. The story was repeated on trunk rivers and tributaries alike as the railroads reached farther up the river valleys. Only on the lower Mississippi did river traffic survive in any degree before

The extent of railway lines in 1880. In the ten-year period prior to 1880, some forty thousand miles of railroad were built, bringing the total network up to 93,267 miles. In 1880 every state and territory was provided with railway transportation. A second line of railroads to the Pacific was nearing completion, and other transcontinental railroads were under construction. Railway development was exerting a powerful influence upon immigration and agricultural and industrial growth throughout the country. *Courtesy Association of American Railroads*

St. Louis Levee *about* 1876

The Saint Louis levee about 1876, during the transitional period when steamboat traffic began to recede before the rising volume of the railroads. Painting by Frank B. Nuderscher. *Courtesy Missouri Pacific Railroad*

the onslaught of the railroad. This was due in part to railroad trackage not being built extensively in the lower valley until the 1880s. Steamboat traffic flourished in hauling huge loads of cotton from the country drained by the lower Mississippi and its tributaries. Large boats such as the *J. M. White*, *Natchez*, and *Robert E. Lee* carried cargoes of thousands of bales on frequent trips. The record load was 9226 bales carried by the steamer *Henry Frank* in 1881. This trade inevitably declined as the railroads moved into the cotton country and covered it by 1886.

The lower valley was the last to hold out against the railroads. *Loading Cotton by Moonlight* is a typical antebellum scene on the lower Mississippi. Currier and Ives print. *Courtesy Saint Louis Public Library*

The plantations had their own steamboat landings for the loading and shipping of the cotton bales. Currier and Ives print. *Courtesy Saint Louis Public Library*

The New Orleans packet boat *Eclipse* loading cotton bales in this Currier and Ives print by an anonymous artist.

Loading cotton bales at Vicksburg, Mississippi. *Courtesy Jefferson National Expansion Memorial, National Park Service*

The sternwheeler *Charles P. Chouteau* with a record load of cotton bales in 1878. This boat had an iron hull which was originally built for the ironclad *Carondelet* in 1863. The *Chouteau* was built on this hull in 1877, and was one of the first steamboats to use electric lights. It burned near Memphis in 1887. *Courtesy Fred Leyhe*

The steamer *Natchez VII* during the heyday of King Cotton on the lower Mississippi, loading up with bales for shipment. *Courtesy Waterways Journal*

Cotton bales on the levee at New Orleans. The first three steamers, *from right to left*, are the *John B. Maud*, *Edward J. Gay*, and *Clinton*. *Courtesy Boatmen's National Bank of St. Louis*

The steamboat *John A. Scudder* with a record load of cotton and other commodities in 1878. After she was dismantled in 1885, her hull was used as a wharfboat at Vicksburg, Mississippi. *Courtesy Boatmen's National Bank of St. Louis*

The cotton packet *America*, built in 1898 for Captain Le Verrier Cooley, who ran her in trades out of New Orleans. She was used in making the movie *Magnolia* in 1924 and foundered at New Orleans in August, 1926. After Captain Cooley died in 1931, the roof bell from the *America* was mounted over his grave. Photo by J. Mack Moore. *Courtesy Boatmen's National Bank of St. Louis*

A busy scene on the levee at New Orleans in the 1870s. Within fifteen years, the scene would change drastically. A Currier and Ives print by W. A. Walker. *Courtesy Saint Louis Public Library*

The steamboat's low-rate advantage dwindled as improved equipment and efficient operations dropped rail charges down to near-competitive levels. Any favorable difference disappeared through extra drayage costs and insurance tariffs. When steamboats were inoperative because of ice or low water, railroads profited by raising their rates by several times. These irregularities were later subject to regulations of the Interstate Commerce Act of 1887.

Railroads, eager to cooperate in joint river-rail shipping arrangements in their early years, later engaged in such cooperative efforts only so long as no all-rail service was available. Rail-river service was hampered by the absence of prorating arrangements between carriers. Compulsory compliance was declared not necessary by the Interstate Commerce Commission, and after 1900 the railroads terminated joint agreements completely, resulting in increased traffic on the railways.

Inadequate terminal facilities plagued the steamboat lines up to the final demise of the packets. Sloping stone-paved or earthen levees for landings, with wharfboats at the larger ports, were the best

Drawing by A. R. Waud of wharfboats at Saint Louis. *From Picturesque America, 1872. Courtesy Saint Louis Mercantile Library Association*

facilities available. Steamboat lines lacked the resources to provide efficient, modern facilities in place of manual loading. Further restriction of urban waterfront facilities to marine interests was achieved by the railroads: they acquired general ownership of the riverbanks. This impaired the ability of barge lines to gain direct access to adjacent warehouses for handling bulk shipments. Also, city growth patterns encouraged industrial development along radiating rail lines, away from riverfront locations.

River transport suffered from deficiencies in river improvements, especially during low-water periods. The several long annual periods of low water during the 1890s caused severe restrictions to an already declining river traffic. The decline was graphically depicted by government figures showing rail-traffic volume at Saint Louis in 1890 at twelve times that of river transport, while the ratio had increased to thirty-two to one by 1900 and to a hundred to one by 1906. Similar disproportionate percentages were compiled at other principal river cities. This data exhibited the steamboat's inability to compete successfully against the railroads for business, particularly in the long-distance trades. Steamboat operations in the twentieth century became increasingly concentrated in short and medium-distance trades.

Railroads were usually cast in the role of the villain after 1900. However, they probably dealt no more harshly with river interests than they did among themselves in that era of cutthroat rail com-

MERCHANTS' WHARF BOAT

VICKSBURG, MISS.

AN INCORPORATED COMPANY—Owned by the principal Business Men of Vicksburg.

Receive and Forward Merchandise

BY ALL

STEAMBOAT LINES.

GEO. A. WILLIAMS,
Cashier.

GEO. W. BAUSMAN,
Superintendent.

Wharfboat advertisement from *The Southern and Western Shipping Directory, 1870. Courtesy Ardell Thompson Collection*

By 1890 this 1850-Saint Louis levee traffic, lined up two and three deep, had all but disappeared to the railroads. *Courtesy U.S. Corps of Engineers, Saint Louis District*

The Saint Louis levee about 1905, with the excursion boat W.W. and an excursion barge in the foreground. *Collection of the author*

"Get a horse!" Three different forms of transportation being used in one unloading operation, c. 1910. *Courtesy Waterways Journal*

petition. River traffic was apparently the victim of progress through changes in the national economic pattern, which placed increasing dependence upon overland transportation at the expense of the inland waterways. Even the few short-line packet companies that remained in operation during the 1920s and 1930s eventually succumbed to the combined competition of the railroads and truck lines.

The steamboat came to be regarded as a nostalgic holdover from a romantic past, and the few that remained assumed the role of antique curiosities. The function of the steamboat as a river carrier passed to modern, diesel-powered towboats, which pushed vast fleets of barges carrying tonnages far beyond the capacity of the old steamboats.

The last of the passenger packets, the steamer *Golden Eagle* of the Eagle Packet Company. She was the last passenger boat to operate in packet service out of Saint Louis, in 1947. She is shown here passing Hannibal, Missouri. *Missouri Tourism Commission photo*

The nearly empty levee at Saint Louis in October, 1928, looking south from Eads Bridge. *Courtesy City Plan Commission, City of Saint Louis*

X
River Traffic Today

Improvements in steamboat-handling techniques led to the evolution of the towing system on the western rivers. It enabled the transport of bulk commodities in quantities that were impossible for individual freight-carrying steamboats. The idea of towing had its first application in the rafts and flatboats of the presteam era.

Towing in the early decades of steamboating consisted generally in taking flatboats along on trips during low-water periods. The idea was to spread the cargo and lighten the draft of the steamboat. This practice did not become too common, owing to navigational deficiencies with the underpowered early steamboats, as well as protests from passengers. The added encumbrances slowed down the steamboats. Numerous accidents, which led to higher insurance rates, tended to discourage this early towing practice with conventional steamboats. The introduction of steamboats especially designed for towing opened broad vistas for the expansion of barge operations and the creation of new navigational techniques.

Rafts were assembled so as to take advantage of high water during the annual spring rises. Timber and coal were the principal cargoes. Timber rafting was prominent on the upper Mississippi until the late nineteenth century, when the timber reserves in the northern states were exhausted. Coal rafting on the Monongahela and Ohio rivers had an early beginning, and had reached a significant degree of development during the 1830s. It was carried on in crude flatboats built for floating downstream. Steamboats came into use as towboats for coalrafts during the 1840s. Pittsburgh became the distribution point for vast quantities of coal from the Monongahela Valley to river towns on the Ohio and Mississippi. These cargoes were carried in large, boxlike, flat-bottomed boats with square ends, holding up to twenty thousand bushels of coal. They were floated downstream in pairs during flood periods, while being guided by long oars, and were sold for kindling after being unloaded at lower river ports.

A few years after the use of steamboats for mov-

Towing coal on the Ohio. The sternwheel towboat *John W. Hubbard* of the Campbell Line of Pittsburgh. *Courtesy Jefferson National Expansion Memorial, National Park Service*

These coal rafts are being towed on the Monongahela River at Pittsburgh in the late 1890s. *Courtesy Jefferson National Expansion Memorial, National Park Service*

Towing by pushing made for greater maneuverability. Underway with a tow of barges, in the 1930s. Photo by Bill Reed. *Courtesy Waterways Journal*

One development in towboat design resulted in the sternwheeler W. M. Rees, with its four smokestacks. *Courtesy Saint Louis Public Library*

An early steam towboat Gouverneur belonging to the Army Corps of Engineers. *Courtesy U.S. Corps of Engineers, Saint Louis District*

ing coal rafts was begun, the practice of towing by pushing was evolved, permitting improved maneuverability. Improvements in the design of barges and towboats brought a great impetus to the coal-towing trade during the 1850s. This low-cost haulage of coal by barge was not challenged by the railroads, nor did it greatly concern the steamboat owners, who did not carry such bulk commodities. Tows increased in size, and coal shipments rose in volume, to pass the million-ton mark annually by 1857.

After the Civil War, towboat operations began to make inroads into the general commodity traffic in competition with packet lines. Transport of grain by barge developed from an attempt by Saint Louis interests to divert such shipments from rail and lake routes. From down the Mississippi to New Orleans, they continued by sea to east-coast ports.

The Mississippi Valley Transportation Company of Saint Louis, popularly called "the Barge Line," was organized in 1866. It used towboats that pushed special barges, and it constructed grain elevators at important ports. This business proved quite profitable, and by 1881 the line's barges had an estimated monthly cargo capacity of three million bushels. On return trips upriver, lesser volumes of low-value products were transported. A considerable trade in grain towing developed on the upper Mississippi and some of its larger tributaries, such as the Minnesota and the Illinois.

Towboats and barges were not as expensive to construct or operate as the steam packets, being functional in design and free from luxuries and the problems of carrying passengers. The only cargo carried on towboats was fuel used in the transfer of barges, which could easily be picked up or detached. This flexibility permitted preloaded barges to be attached to tows, eliminating costly delays in loading and unloading. The typical towboat of this period was a sternwheeler with multiple rudders for emphasis on control. The boat had a squared bow adapted for pushing the integrated tow of barges.

The navigational technique of "flanking" was evolved for handling large tows around difficult river bends. Reversing the engines, as the tow entered the bend, slowed down forward movement and increased turning power. With the paddle wheel in reverse, the water, driving against the

Preloaded barges were assembled for the tows. Here the towboat *Aliquippa* is departing from Pittsburgh with a five-thousand-ton tow of steel products, April 3, 1922. *Courtesy U.S. Corps of Engineers, Pittsburgh District*

Squared bows were adapted to aid pushing. This is the towboat *I. Lamont Hughes* of Pittsburgh with six coal flats on the Monongahela River Pool No. 2, 1940. *Courtesy U.S. Corps of Engineers, Pittsburgh District*

Difficult bends in the river evolved new navigational techniques for towboats. The *Monongahela* with a 22-barge tow of steel and coal, on the Ohio River, March 1939, has just completed its turn. *Courtesy U.S. Corps of Engineers, Pittsburgh District*

rudders, created a stronger stream for additional turning pressure. This procedure kept the barges in mid-channel and permitted them to drift with the current until the center of the bend was rounded.

The towing trade was generally divided into two principal parts, the downstream movement of great quantities of coal and timber, and the general freight shipments, both upstream and down. Requirements for protection of valuable cargoes in the freight business led to the design of improved barges, with hulls shaped like those of steamboats. For some purposes the barges were roofed over and enclosed. These tows usually did not include more than six barges. The size of coal tows increased in later years, with the all-time record set by the huge

Closeup of the sternwheel towboat *Missouri,* the type in use in the 1940s. *Courtesy Jefferson National Expansion Memorial, National Park Service*

The sternwheeler *Sprague,* affectionately known among rivermen as "Big Mama," was the largest steam towboat in the world. She was built at Dubuque, Iowa, in 1901 and completed at Saint Louis in June, 1902. Her dimensions were 276 feet by 61 feet by 7.4 feet. After a career of almost half a century of service she was taken out of operation in 1948. She was later donated by the Standard Oil Company to Vicksburg, Mississippi. The *Sprague* is now maintained by the city and contains a theater for melodrama and the River Hall of Fame Museum. She is moored at the Vicksburg levee on the Yazoo Canal. *Courtesy Harbor and Port Commission, City of Vicksburg*

towboat *Sprague,* with a tow covering about seven acres, carrying sixty-seven thousand tons of coal. After 1900 full-sized tows carried from thirty to fifty thousand tons on each trip.

Since timber towing in the large rafts on the upper Mississippi was all downstream, the rafts relied to a large extent on the current for motive power. These rafts ranged from six hundred to

more than a thousand feet in length, and were quite unwieldy in difficult waters. Unlike coal tows, where the towboat was an integral part of the tow, the stern of a timber raft towboat was swung from one side to the other by means of lines attached to the stern corners of the raft. This action was performed by a special winding engine on the boat and helped steer the raft as the exigencies of navigation required. Increased control was possible for extremely large rafts by the use of an auxiliary bow-boat at the raft's lower end.

In the contest with packet boats for the general freight business, the barge lines' advantage of lower rates did not apply in short-haul trades. The barge shipments were superior only for trunk-line runs with quantity shipments. By the end of the nineteenth century it was apparent that the movement of most freight, except bulk commodities, was primarily a function of the railroads and that river traffic would consist chiefly of the towing of massive shipments.

A prominent feature of the towing business during the late nineteenth century was the trend toward consolidation into virtual monopolies. The coal interests owned fleets of barges and towboats in mergers, which eventually resulted in organization of the Monongahela River Consolidated Coal and Coke Company, generally known as the Combine. This vast fleet represented sixty-three percent of the total marine tonnage on the Mississippi River system after 1900. Other fleets were devoted to the exclusive haulage of various bulk items, such as iron ore transport by the Gray's Iron Line of Pittsburgh. Grain movements on the Mississippi were consolidated in 1881 by the merger of the three principal grain haulers into the Saint Louis and Mississippi Valley Transportation Company.

The barge lines became victims of the same low-water periods that plagued the packet lines in the nineties. River shipments to and from Saint Louis dropped from over 1,250,000 tons in 1890 to less than 400,000 tons in 1905. During this same period, railroad shipments at Saint Louis rose from sixteen million tons in 1890 to almost forty million tons in 1905. One result of this trend was the abandonment in 1903 of bulk grain movements by barge to New Orleans. Only the coal towing operations on the Ohio River and its tributaries managed to continue running during the period between the turn of the century and the start of

The advent of the railroad left river traffic to consist of the towing of massive shipments. *Early Railroad Building in Missouri* shows the construction of the Pacific Railroad westward along the Missouri River. Painting by Oscar E. Berninghaus. *Courtesy Boatmen's National Bank of St. Louis*

World War I. Even the long-haul coal trade began to disappear with the conversion of some southern industry to oil fuel.

The railroads proved to be unequal to the task of national transportation demands during World War I, which caused a group of Midwestern industrialists to propose government operation of a barge fleet to supplement the rail network. This suggestion led to the organization of the Federal Barge Line operated by the U.S. Railroad Administration in 1918. Its small fleet of five towboats and twenty-five barges soon proved what rivermen had always contended, that bulk freight could be transported much less expensively by water than by rail. Convinced, Congress appropriated forty-two million dollars in 1922 for river improvements and raised this amount to fifty-six million dollars in the following year. The Army Corps of Engineers began work on the canalization of the Ohio River, under authority of a 1910 act of Congress which authorized a system of locks and dams to create a nine-foot channel. The impetus started by the Federal Barge Line and government river-improvement work resulted in the organization of several private barge lines by 1925. The Ohio River work was completed in 1929, when the river became a flight of water steps, through locks and dams, from Pittsburgh to Cairo. The opening of the Illinois River Waterway to Chicago in 1933, and of a nine-foot channel on the upper Mississippi in 1939, with the completion of the last of twenty-six locks and dams between Saint Louis and Saint Paul, set the stage for the renaissance of river commerce on the western rivers. Improvement work on the lower Missouri River was also underway at that time.

New Orleans in 1893. About this time railroad shipments rose while those of the steamboat steadily declined. Sketch by William T. Smedley. *From Harper's Monthly*

One of the earliest riverside docks built for barge-line activity, the Saint Louis Municipal Dock, during the 1920s. *Courtesy City Plan Commission, City of Saint Louis*

In 1958 the president of the Federal Barge Lines, Captain A. C. Ingersoll, Jr., described the revival this way: "As the work of developing the network of channels progressed, commerce and industry came again to the rivers, slowly and hesitantly at first, then with increasing enthusiasm as the efficiency and dependability of the new barge transport was demonstrated. This rush of industry to the inland waterways has been particularly pronounced since World War II."

The modern towboat had its inception during the early 1930s with the introduction of the diesel engine and replacement of the sternwheel by the screw propeller. The only operational features these pioneer diesel towboats took from their steamboat predecessors were flanking rudders and tow-knees. The rudders were repositioned in front of the propellers for improved maneuverability. Another step toward safer and more efficient towboats and barges, during the thirties, was the supplanting of riveting by welding in construction. During World War II, the full use of the year-round operational capabilities of the canalized rivers was utilized to accomplish a tremendous task of emergency transportation of vital materials. This culminated in the movement in 1944 of more than thirty-billion ton-miles of oil, sulfur, coal, steel, wheat, and many other bulk commodities on the inland waterways. An important gain in towboat efficiency was the wartime development of depend-

The modern towboat can be traced to the 1930s. This is the model of the motor vessel. *A. G. Haynes II* of the Mississippi Valley Barge Line. *Courtesy Missouri Historical Society*

The engine-control panel attested to the maze of new techniques. This is the *Sohioan,* 1943. *Courtesy Jefferson National Expansion Memorial, National Park Service*

Towboats and barges on the Mississippi River near Thebes, Illinois, in the early 1950s. *Courtesy U.S. Corps of Engineers, Saint Louis District*

The diesel-powered towboats revitalized the industry. This is the 3600-horsepower towboat *James R. Hines,* completed in 1960. *Courtesy Saint Louis Ship, Inc.*

The Wisconsin Barge Lines twin-screw motor vessel *Kathryn Eckstein,* five-thousand horsepower, built in 1967. *Courtesy Saint Louis Ship, Inc.*

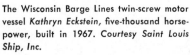

The 6300-horsepower *F. R. Bigelow,* of the Ingram Barge Line, measuring 166 feet by 45 feet by 11 feet, was completed in 1968. *Courtesy Saint Louis Ship, Inc.*

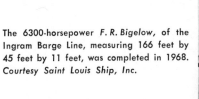

able reversing-reduction gears capable of transmitting high horsepower, permitting engine operation at the most efficient rpm.

The diesel-powered towboat is responsible for bringing the towing industry to its place of national prominence today. Its development has produced the most efficient application of maximum usable power in the job of moving freight. An important factor in this improved power application was solving the problem of space limitations of shallow-draft towboat hulls. An aspect of the problem is the design of the tunnel stern. The propeller is placed above water level in a recess in the hull bottom, which fills with water by the vacuum ac-

One of many ingenious improvements, for placement under the propeller, are these Kort nozzles of the quadruple-screw motor vessel *United States*. They add thrust to the propeller's drive. *Courtesy Saint Louis Ship, Inc.*

Universal Marine's towboat *Universal Trader*, with its telescoping pilothouse in raised position. *Courtesy Saint Louis Ship, Inc.*

Pilothouse lowered for passage under an approaching low bridge. *Courtesy Saint Louis Ship, Inc.*

The Federal Barge Lines motor vessel *United States* under construction. *Courtesy Saint Louis Ship, Inc.*

The Federal Barge Lines motor vessel *America*, which with its twin ship, the *United States*, are the largest towboats on the western rivers. *Courtesy Saint Louis Ship, Inc.*

tion of the revolving propeller. Another ingenious device is the Kort nozzle, a funnel-shaped housing around the propeller that concentrates the flow of water through its blades, thereby adding considerable thrust to the propeller's drive.

The telescoping pilothouse—for clearance under low bridges—further attests to the ingenuity of towboat designers in improving operational efficiency. The modern towboats' increase in size has culminated in the Federal Barge Line's twin boats, the *America* and the *United States*. Each craft develops nine thousand horsepower from its four engines. These craft can move tows covering six acres and carrying nearly fifty thousand tons, the capacity of fifteen freight trains. Consisting of about forty fully loaded barges, each 35 by 195 feet, this tow could be pushed by these powerful towboats at speeds exceeding fifteen miles an hour.

The upper engine room of the *United States*. Courtesy Saint Louis Ship, Inc.

The Delco generators of the *United States*. Courtesy Saint Louis Ship, Inc.

The guest lounge aboard the *United States*. Courtesy Saint Louis Ship, Inc.

Pilothouse control stand of the *United States*. Courtesy Saint Louis Ship, Inc.

River craft today employ every modern device for safe operation, including radio and radar systems, which enable day and night navigation through most weather. While radio provides inter-boat communications, radar tracks navigation obstacles during periods of low visibility. Steering is by fingertip control of levers actuating large hydraulic rams, which align a double set of rudders. One lever for each engine instantly provides the desired speed, power, and rotational direction required by the pilot. For night navigation, convenient electrical controls operate a three-mile beam from each of two or three searchlights. Instructions to crewmen working on the barges are through a directional bullhorn on the roof of the pilothouse. Communication within the towboat is through an intercom system, and walkie-talkie radio is widely used for ship-to-shore messages. Dispatches and instructions from the barge line's home office reach

One of about sixty vessels being built in Japan for international shipping is the Greek-owned three-thousand-ton mini-freighter *Mini Lily* here shown docked at Saint Louis in October, 1970. This innovative diesel-powered vessel can operate in less than five feet of water, as well as on the high seas. She can make inland river towns the point of origin for direct shipments to overseas ports. *Photo by the author*

The mini-freighter from the stern. She has her own crane for hoisting at ports where no regular docks are available. Another innovation in marine freight handling is the "lighter aboard ship," or LASH, barge system. These are smaller-than-conventional (61-feet long) river barges and are carried aboard special large oceanic freighters and then unloaded to proceed up-river in a tow. Seventy-three of these LASH barges are carried at a time. This eliminates the expense and time of cargo transfer between ships and river barges. *Photo by the author*

The first mini-ship entering the harbor at Greenville, Mississippi, September, 1969, the inland waterways base of operations for the little freighters. *Courtesy Waterways Journal*

the pilot through long-range radio. Automatic-pilot devices provide accurate steering when vision is restricted and also more efficient guidance, with less rudder angle, in clear weather.

Barges propelled by towboats or tugs and shallow-draft freighting vessels carry nearly ten percent of the nation's domestic commerce at the low average cost of three mills per ton-mile. This is about five times less than the nearest competition. These barges are unimpressive except for their size, but they can carry five times their weight. They are secured to the towboat by lashing to the dual tow-knee uprights on the bow, which also act as pusher plates against the barge tow. Towboat and barges are so securely joined by lashing that the integrated tow navigates like a single vessel.

TYPES OF BARGES

Many types of barges are in use, including open-hopper barges for various all-weather cargoes, covered barges for dry cargo, tank barges for transport of liquids, and deck types which serve a variety of purposes.

Covered barge tow on the Missouri River as seen from the pilothouse of a towboat. *Nebraska Game Commission photo*

The simplest type is the open-hopper barge, an open box used for weatherproof bulk cargoes. Closed-hopper barges (covered barges) have weathertight sliding hatch covers, and are used for cargoes such as bags of cement or rolls of paper. The deck barges are open to the weather and carry wheeled cargoes lashed to their decks. They can carry loaded truck trailers or railroad cars in a sort

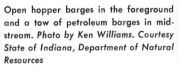

Launching a box-type hopper barge. *Courtesy Saint Louis Ship, Inc.*

Open hopper barges in the foreground and a tow of petroleum barges in midstream. *Photo by Ken Williams. Courtesy State of Indiana, Department of Natural Resources*

Tank barges taking on gasoline at Arkansas City, Arkansas, on the Mississippi River. *Courtesy Arkansas Publicity and Parks Commission*

of marine version of the piggyback system used on railroads. Tank barges includes gases as well as liquids in their cargoes. Barges carrying petroleum are hollow and carry their cargo inside their metal walls. Another type has a special inner plating to separate its liquid cargo from the hull plating. These inside tanks are often lined with erosion-proof coatings. Still another type of tank barge carries its tanks on deck or in open hopper hatches. Some tanks are heated, others cooled or pressurized

depending upon the requirements of the liquid cargo. Experiments with such materials as aluminum or plastic to lessen barge weight are conducted in an endless search for additional economy and efficiency.

The basic principle in barge design is to enable them to glide through water with a minimum of resistance. This is accomplished by raking or sloping the bow ends of the lead barges and the stern ends of the rear barges. Since the inner ends of these barges are squared off, a correct assembly of such barges would present a virtually unbroken underwater hull surface, which would create very little turbulence. A tow made up in this manner is known as an integrated tow. They are generally used when the entire cargo is carried continuously from one point to another. Changes at intermediate points could require shunting of the interior barges, which have double-squared ends, a clumsy, difficult arrangement since they lack the raking at one end. Because most tows comprise a variety of barge types, destined for different points, most of these tows include all single-raked barges in a semi-integrated assembly. A tow made up entirely of double-raked barges is said to be unintegrated.

Tows are handled by experienced officers and crewmen familiar with all phases of the intricate job of controlling such a vast floating assemblage. They have compiled an outstanding record of safety. Personnel are provided with clean, quiet liv-

The *United States* pushing a large tow of loaded barges upriver on the Mississippi. Sloping of bow and rear makes for a gliding ride. *Courtesy Saint Louis Ship, Inc.*

ing quarters, hearty meals, and labor-saving equipment.

Barge transportation, which has become a prime stimulator of business growth, has returned to the nation its water resources—in quite measurable value. The Mississippi Valley's cities and towns, and vast hinterlands, which owe their origin and existence to the western rivers, still depend upon these inland waterways for their continued prosperity.

A covered semi-integrated closed hopper barge. *Courtesy Saint Louis Ship, Inc.*

Making for an unbroken underwater surface is this well-integrated series of barges, loaded with grain, pipe, and petrochemical products heading up the Mississippi. *Courtesy U.S. Corps of Engineers, New Orleans District*

Antlers. Deer antlers were the symbol of speed supremacy in steamboats. A speed contest was commonly referred to as a race for the "horns."

Bars. Low-lying riverbed elevations of sand, gravel, or rock as obstacles to navigation.

Bayou. A secondary waterway or an intermittent water course, chiefly in the lower Mississippi basin.

Beacons. Lights set at dangerous points along the river shore to act as guides for night navigation.

Bight. A bend in the shoreline.

Bits. Anchor posts on the forecastle for head lines.

Boiler deck. The deck above the boilers, which supports the cabin and staterooms.

Boom. The pole carried at about a forty-five degree angle between the deck and the derrick from which the stage is suspended.

Bow. The front part of the boat.

Bridge. The raised platform above the topmost deck on the front part of the boat. Extending from one side of the boat to the other, the bridge is the station of the captain during landings and departures.

Buckets. The blades of the paddle wheels.

Bulkhead. Partitions dividing the hull to give added strength.

Cabin. The interior portion of the boat on the boiler deck. It contains the staterooms and the main saloon.

Capstan. A large power-operated cylinder on the foredeck, used for pulling in lines.

Cavels. Anchor posts on the guards for tying lines to shore.

Chain. A series of rock bars in or across a channel.

Compartments. Watertight rooms which divide steel hulls.

Cross chains. Chains used to support guards extending on each side of the hull.

Cutoff. A short new channel formed when a river cuts through the neck of an oxbow bend.

Doctor engine. An auxiliary engine used for running pumps. Its use makes it possible to shut down the main engines at landings or whenever needed.

Escape pipes. Exhaust stacks for expelling steam.

Forecastle. The front part of the first or main deck that extends forward of the other decks.

Freeboard. The distance between the waterline and the guards.

Galley. The boat's kitchen.

Guards. The portion of the main deck extending over the sides of the hull.

Hatches. Openings in the deck.

Hawser. A rope or cable used in mooring or towing a boat.

Hog chains. Iron rods or chains fastened to hull timbers at the bow and stern and carried over a series of struts rising from keelsons. These could be adjusted for rigidity to prevent arching or sagging of the hull.

Hogging. Arching of the hull due to distortion from weight or shock.

Hull. The frame or body of a boat or ship.

Hurricane deck. The upper deck of the steamboat.

Jackstaff. The pole on the bow of the boat. The pilot sights along it in steering the boat's course.

Keelson. The main bulkhead in the center of the hull, running fore and aft.

Leadline. A long cord marked at intervals which is used to sound water depths greater than nine feet. A six-pound weight is attached to the cord's end.

Main deck. The first deck, which is used to support the boat's machinery and boilers and also used for cargo stowage.

Mark twain. A twelve-foot (two fathoms) depth sounding.

Midship. The center of the boat, between bow and stern.

Monkey rudders. Auxiliary rudders on each side of the main rudder used for quicker response in steering.

Mud clerk. The assistant clerk on steamboats was

called the "mud clerk" because in doing his job of checking freight at landings, he often returned aboard from the riverbank with muddy feet.

Nighthawk. A bulbous device on the jackstaff which was used by pilots at night to ascertain indistinct shorelines.

Oxbow. A U-shaped river bend where only a narrow neck of land remains between two parts of the stream.

Packet boat. A river steamboat providing accommodations for overnight trips.

Paddle box. The semicircular housing for paddle wheels on sidewheel steamboats.

Pilothouse. The uppermost part of the superstructure, which houses the pilot wheel and controls for operating the boat. It affords a sweeping view in all directions.

Pitman. Connecting rod between engines and paddle-wheel cranks.

Planter. A snag which has one end firmly fixed in the riverbed and stands in a nearly vertical position.

Port side. The left side of the boat looking forward toward the bow.

Purser. Boat's officer in charge of tickets and finances.

Quarter twain. A thirteen-and-half-foot depth of water.

Reach. A straight stretch of river.

Reef. A long sandbar which rises abruptly on one side.

Revetment. A facing of stone or concrete to sustain an embankment.

Ripple, or *shoal.* A group of bars over which the current descends on a slope greater than normal.

Riprap. A sustaining wall of stones thrown together at random.

Rudder. The boat's steering device, consisting of a broad piece which is hinged at the boat's stern and controlled by the pilot wheel or steering mechanism.

Sawyer. A tree fastened in the riverbed, with its branches projecting to the surface and bobbing up and down with a sawing motion in the current.

Sheer. A deviating course of a boat.

Skylight. A low deck with windows on each side designed to admit light into the cabin below.

Slough. A side channel or inlet from a river.

Snag. A tree or branch embedded in the river bottom and not visible on the surface, forming a hazard to navigation.

Sounding pole. A pole marked with one-foot intervals which is used in determining water depths of less than nine feet.

Soundings. In depths greater than nine feet the soundings are marked as follows:

Quarter less twain . . .	9½ feet
Mark twain	12 feet
Quarter twain	13½ feet
Half twain	15 feet
Quarter less three . . .	16½ feet
Mark three	18 feet
Deep four	24 feet

During the steamboat, era, the soundings were relayed by the mate to the pilot by shouting or through a megaphone.

Stage. A long platform or gangplank suspended from a derrick on the forecastle. In a landing it is dropped to act as a bridge from boat to shore.

Starboard. The right side of the boat looking forward toward the bow. This side carries a green light at night, while the port side carries a red light.

Stern. The rear end of the boat.

Striker. An apprentice steamboat engineer.

Texas deck. The topmost deck containing cabins, it is just below the pilothouse.

Torch baskets. Metal containers on long poles to hold torches for illumination at night on steamboats, before the days of searchlights.

Whistle signals. One blast means to pass on the right. Two blasts means to pass on the left. Three bells are sounded to signal departures.

Yawls. Lifeboats which are lifted and lowered by large arms known as davits.

BIBLIOGRAPHY

Alsberg, Henry G., ed. *The American Guide.* New York: Hastings House, 1949.

Babcock, Mrs. Bernie. *Arkansas, Yesterday and Today.* Little Rock: Jordan & Foster Printing Co., 1917.

Barkhau, Roy. *A History of the Eagle Packet Company.* Cincinnati: Young & Klein, Inc., 1951.

Beck, Lewis C. *Gazetteer of Missouri and Illinois.* Albany, N.Y.: C.R. & G. Webster, 1823.

Belcher, Wyatt W. *The Economic Rivalry Between Saint Louis and Chicago—1850–1880.* New York: Columbia Union Press, 1947.

Bennitt, Mark, ed. *History of the Louisiana Purchase Exposition.* Saint Louis: Universal Exposition Publishing Co., 1904.

Bill, Fred A. *Album of Upper Mississippi River Boats.* Scrapbook in the Art Room, Saint Louis Public Library, n.d.

Casseday, Benjamin. *The History of Louisville.* Louisville: Hull & Brother, 1852.

Cist, Charles. *Cincinnati in 1841.* Cincinnati: 1841.

——. *Sketches and Statistics of Cincinnati in 1851.* Cincinnati: 1851.

Collot, Victor, *A Journey in North America—1796.* Paris: Published for Arthur Bertrand, 1826.

Comettant, Oscar. *Voyage pittoresque et anecdotique dans le nord et sud des Etats-Unis Amérique.* Paris: 1866.

Compton, Richard J., and Dry, Camille. *Pictorial Saint Louis.* Saint Louis: Compton & Co., 1876.

Crockett's Almanac for 1838. Nashville, Tenn.: Published by the heirs of Col. Crockett, 1838.

Cumings, Samuel. *The Western Pilot.* Cincinnati: Morgan, Lodge and Fisher, 1825.

Dana, Charles B., ed. *The United States Illustrated.* New York: Hermann J. Meyer, 1855.

Devol, George. *Forty Years a Gambler on the Mississippi.* Cincinnati: Devol & Haines, 1887.

Dorsey, Florence. *Road to the Sea.* New York: Rinehart & Co., 1947.

Drake, Charles. *Natural and Statistical View of Cincinnati.* Cincinnati, 1815.

Edwards, Richard, and Hopewell, Mena. *Edwards's Great West.* Saint Louis: Edwards Printing Co., 1860.

Fiske, John. *The Mississippi Valley in the Civil War.* Boston: Houghton Mifflin Co., 1900.

Fowke, Gerard. *Archaeological History of Ohio.* Columbus: Ohio State Archaeological and Historical Society, 1902.

Glazier, Willard. *Down the Great River.* Philadelphia: Hubbard Bros., 1887.

Gould, Emerson W. *Fifty Years on the Mississippi.* Saint Louis: Nixon-Jones Printing Co., 1889.

Graham, Philip. *Showboats, the History of an American Institution.* Austin: University of Texas Press, 1951.

Guernsey, Alfred H., and Alden, Henry M. *Harper's Pictorial History of the Civil War.* Chicago: McDonnell Bros., 1868.

Habermehl, John. *Life on the Western Rivers.* Pittsburgh: McNary & Simpson, 1901.

Hall, Basil. *Forty Etchings from Sketches Made with the Camera Lucida in North America in 1827–28.* Edinburgh: Cadell & Co., 1829.

"Historical Pictures Relating to the Louisiana Purchase." *Saint Louis Globe-Democrat.* Saint Louis: 1902.

Hogan, John. *Thoughts about Saint Louis.* Saint Louis: Chambers & Knapp, 1855.

Howe, Henry. *The Great West.* Cincinnati: 1873.

Hunter, Louis C. *Steamboats on the Western Rivers.* Cambridge, Mass.: Harvard University Press, 1949.

Incidents and Sketches of the West. Cincinnati: 1851.

Jewel, Edwin L., ed. *Cresent City Illustrated.* New Orleans: 1875.

Kenney, Daniel J. *Illustrated Cincinnati.* Cincinnati: R. Clarke & Co., 1875.

King, Moses, ed. *King's Handbook of the United*

States. Buffalo: Moses King & Co., 1893.

Lewis, Henry. *Das Illustrirte Mississippithal*. Dusseldorf: Arnz & Co., 1858.

Lloyd, James T., *Steamboat Directory and Disasters on the Western Waters*. Cincinnati: J. T. Lloyd & Co., 1856.

Lorant, Stefan, ed. *Pittsburgh, the Story of an American City*. New York: Doubleday & Co., 1964.

Merrick, George B. *Genesis of Steamboating on the Western Rivers*. Cleveland: A. H. Clark & Co., 1909.

Missouri Geological Survey. First and Second Annual Report—1853–54. Jefferson City: 1855.

Parker, Nathan H. *Iowa As It Is in 1855*. Chicago: 1856.

———. *Missouri As It Is in 1867*. Philadelphia: 1867.

Petersen, William J. *Steamboating on the Upper Mississippi*. Iowa City: Iowa Historical Society, 1937.

Piercy, Frederick. *Route from Liverpool to the Great Salt Lake Valley*. Liverpool: F. D. Richards, 1855.

Powell, Lyman E. *Historic Towns of the Southern States*. New York: J. Putnam & Co., 1901.

———. *Historic Towns of the Western States*. New York: J. Putnam & Co., 1901.

Read, Frederick B. *Up the Heights*. Cincinnati: William H. Moore & Co., 1873.

Rosskam, Edwin and Louise. *Towboat River*. New York: Duell, Sloan & Pearce, Inc., 1948.

Samuel, Ray; Huber, Leonard V; and Ogden, Warren C. *Tales of the Mississippi*. New York: Hastings House, 1955.

Saxon, Lyle. *Father Mississippi*. New York: The Century Co., 1927.

Scharf, J. Thomas. *History of Saint Louis City and County*. Philadelphia: Louis H. Everts Co., 1883.

Siler, Jacob. *Siler's Historic Photographs*. Saint Louis: 1904.

Southern and Western Shipping Guide and Directory. Saint Louis: 1870.

Spears, John R. *A History of the Mississippi Valley*. Cleveland: A. H. Clark & Co., 1903.

Stanton, Samuel W. *American Steam Vessels*. New York: 1895.

Stebbins, L. C. *Eighty Years of Progress*. Hartford: 1868.

Stevens, George E. *The Queen City in 1869*. Cincinnati: G. S. Blanchard & Co., 1869.

Streckfus Steamers, Inc. *Streckfus Line Magazine*. Saint Louis, 1934.

Sunder, John E. *The Fur Trade on the Upper Missouri 1840–1865*. Norman: University of Oklahoma Press, 1965.

Taylor, J. N., and Crooks, M. O. *Sketch Book of Saint Louis*. Saint Louis: George Knapp & Co., 1858.

Twain, Mark. *Life on the Mississippi*. Boston: Osgood & Co., 1883.

Wade, Richard C. *The Urban Frontier—Rise of Western Cities 1790–1830*. Cambridge, Mass: Harvard University Press, 1959.

Walker, C. D. *The Mississippi Valley in Prehistoric Times*. Burlington, Iowa: R. T. Root Co., 1880.

Way, Frederick C., Jr. *Way's Directory of Western River Packets*. Sewickley, Pa.: Steamboat Photo Co., 1950.

Wayman, Norbury L. *A Pictorial History of Saint Louis*. Saint Louis: Norbury L. Wayman, 1968.

Wells, William. *Western Scenery on Land and River, Hill and Dale in the Mississippi Valley*. Cincinnati: O. O. Onken, 1851.

Wied-Neu-Weid, Prince Maximilian, and Bodmer, Carl. *Travels in the Interior of North America—1832–34*. London: Ackermann & Co., 1843.

Wild, John Casper, and Thomas, Lewis F. *The Valley of the Mississippi Illustrated*. Saint Louis: Republican Printing Office, 1841.

INDEX

Italic figures refer to illustrations